LIVING IN PARADISE

MOHAMMAD L. RAJA

authorHOUSE®

AuthorHouse™ UK
1663 Liberty Drive
Bloomington, IN 47403 USA
www.authorhouse.co.uk
Phone: UK TFN: 0800 0148641 (Toll Free inside the UK)
*   UK Local: (02) 0369 56322 (+44 20 3695 6322 from outside the UK)*

Published by AuthorHouse 09/25/2024

ISBN: 978-1-6655-8684-9 (sc)
ISBN: 978-1-6655-8683-2 (hc)
ISBN: 978-1-6655-8685-6 (e)

Print information available on the last page.

WE THE HUMANS ARE RESIDENTS OF PARADISE BECAUSE WE ARE DESCENDANTS OF ADAM, AND OUR FATHER ADAM HAD A HOUSE IN PARADISE, AND THEREFORE THE ULTIMATE SUCCESS FOR US IS TO GET INTO PARADISE.

INTRODUCTION

Seerah

THE LIFE OF THE PROPHET (PHUB) IN MAKKAH

The life of the Prophet Muhammad (pbuh), who is the final Messenger of Allah (swt) and the greatest human being to have set foot on the face of the earth. We ask Allah (swt), to bless this narration and to benefit us with what we learn. We ask ALLAH (swt), to make us of those who follow the Prophet Muhammad (pbuh), to love him and to be close to him. We ask ALLAH (swt) to make us of those who will be with him in Paradise.

First of all, we start with the definition of Seerah. What does Seerah mean? The word Seerah has linguistic meaning; it is the path and walking is called 'seer'. When one walks from one place to another it is called 'Seerah of land'. It is the path that the person takes during his lifetime. The dictionary gives the meaning as conduct, 'demean'; attitude, behavior, way of life, position, manners, actions, way of actions and biography. All these are the meanings of the word Seerah and it could be the biography of any person, not necessarily the Prophet Muhammad (pbuh). However, we have denoted the word so much with the Prophet Muhammad (pbuh), that when we say Seerah, we are referring to the life of the Prophet

Muhammad (pbuh). One can say Seerah of Abu Bakr and Seerah of Umar.

It is the biography of any person and their life. In this narration we are studying the life of the greatest Prophet Mohammad (pbuh).

WHAT IS THE IMPORTANCE OF STUDYING SEERAH?

The history of Islam starts with the life of the Prophet Muhammad (pbuh). Studying the life of the Prophet (pbuh) is studying the history of Islam. In the Prophet's Biography, the Seerah, we shall find situations and incidences that will help us in everything we need to know in our life of invitation. We must note that we are not studying the life of an ordinary person, but we are studying the life of the greatest person.

Saad bin Waqas who was given news of Paradise during his life, glad tidings of Paradise, his son Muhammad (Abpwh) said that our father would teach us the battles of the Prophet, he would teach us the Seerah and he would tell us that these are the traditions of your father, study them.

Megasies means battles; the last part of Prophet's (PBUH) life was spent in Megasies, which is the whole life of the Prophet (PBUH). Imam Hussain, the grandson of the Prophet (pbuh) and the grandson Abu Talib, would say we were taught the Seerah like the Holy Quran, and that is how important the Seerah was for them. This makes sense because if we want to study the life of other Prophets today, for example, we go to the Holy Quran. However, if we want to study the life of the Prophet (pbuh) only bits and pieces are mentioned in the Holy Quran, but we do not have intricate details, as we do have for the other Prophets. For the life of the Holy Prophet (pbuh), we go to the Seerah his biography. Many Prophets are mentioned in the Holy Quran, with the exception of the Prophet (pbuh). There are some references in the Quran to the life of the Prophet (pbuh) and we shall talk about those references to understand the Quran through the Seerah.

TO DEVELOP PROPER LOVE OF THE PROPHET MUHAMMAD (PBUH) IN OUR HEARTS

It is part of our religion to love the Prophet (Pbuh). The Prophet (Pbuh) said that you do not attain full faith unless you love me more than yourself, your parents and your children. We do not become true believers unless we love the Prophet more than anything else. So, it is part of Islam to love the Prophet, Mohammad (Pbuh).

UMAR BIN KHATTAB came to the Prophet (Pbuh). Umar was a very honest and straight forward person. He went to the Prophet (Pbuh) and said "O' Messenger of Allah I love you more than anything except myself".

The Prophet (Pbuh) told him until you love me more than yourself, you will not attain complete faith. Umar came back and said "O' Messenger of Allah now I love you more than anything, including myself". The Prophet (Pbuh) said only now you have attained complete faith. The Ummah today loves the Prophet (Pbuh). If you ask any Muslim, do you love the Prophet (Pbuh), the answer will be yes. But love cannot be deep and sincere unless you know the person. If you have shallow information about someone you cannot love them a lot. To love a person, you need to know them more. This is true with the Prophet (Pbuh), the more you know, you will be impressed with his personality and you will love him even more. Even with the shallow information the masses love the

Messenger of Allah. But we cannot have the deep love for the Prophet (Pbuh) unless we know him.

The companions of the Prophet (Pbuh), they knew more about the Prophet and were close to the Prophet; they loved him. For example, AMER BIN AUSS, he was an enemy of the Prophet. He was one of the top plotters against Islam. Later he became a Muslim. On his death bed he started crying. His son Abdullah bin Amar, told his father, reminding him that, the Prophet gave you glad tidings so many times (Hadith). The Prophet said Amer bin Auss has attained full faith and this was witnessed by the Holy Prophet (Pbuh) himself, that Amar bin Auss is a momin. Higher level of momin, is a true believer. "Now why are you crying" Amar bin Auss turned around and said "I went through 3 stages in my life, first the most despised person was Mohammad (Pbuh) to me. Amar bin Auss said, "My desire was if I got hold of him, my desire was to kill him. That was my aspiration and wish to kill the Prophet (Pbuh)". He says that if I had died at that time I would be in the hell fire. Then Allah put the love of Islam in my heart. I went to the Prophet (Pbuh) and said "O' Muhammad I want to become a Muslim, extend your hand so that I can pledge allegiance to you". Amar bin Auss says the Prophet (Pbuh) extended his hand forward and I pulled my hand away when the Prophet (Pbuh) was ready to put his hand in my hand. The Prophet (Pbuh) said, what is the matter? Amar bin Auss said, I have a condition. "What is the condition? he said, "my condition is that you pardon me." Amar bin Auss knew that the crimes he had committed against Muslims were enough for his execution. He wanted to make sure that the Prophet (Pbuh) will not hold anything against him. The Prophet (Pbuh) smiled and said "ya Amar, don't you know that Islam erases everything before and Hijra erases everything before and Hajj erases everything before?" Amar bin Auss said, "I became a

Muslim at that stage and the Prophet (Pbuh) who was my enemy, then became the most beloved person to me. He said, "I love him so much and respected him so much; I couldn't even get a full glimpse of his face". "Whenever I would see him I would look downwards. If you ask me to describe him to you, I cannot". He said "if I had died then I could have hoped for Paradise. Then he said later on things came and we don't know where we stand".

There are other parts to this Hadith. But when Amar knew the Prophet (Pbuh) they became friends. Sohail bin Amar was sent by the Quraish to negotiate before Sulah Hudaibia. Sohail bin Amar was an international negotiator. He had been to the courts of the Persian Emperor, the Roman Emperor and the Emperor of Abyssinia. He was a well-connected man. Quraish sent him to negotiate with the Prophet (Pbuh). He went to Madinah and when he came in, he had firsthand experience of how the Sahaba treat the Prophet. Sohail bin Amar went back to report to Quraish. He said I visited the Roman Emperor, Persian Emperor and I visited Najashi of Abyssinia, but I have never in my life seen a leader that is loved and respected so much by his followers like I have for Muhammad (Pbuh). I have seen nothing like it in the world, even though they have powers and Empires. He said I saw amazing things, Muhammad (PBUH) would make Wudhu and the Sahaba would be rushing to grab the water dripping from his body. So he told them, do whatever you like, but these people will never give up their leader. The Sahaba would give their own lives first. So, if you want to love the Prophet (Pbuh) we need to know more about him. Even though we don't know enough about him, he is the most loved person, his name is the most common name in the world. How many people are named after Muhammad? There is no other person who has ever lived in history that has had so many people named after him. (The story of the Nigerian man, Al Asher). Also, Mohammad is a common name for the people of Pakistan.

WHAT IF WE STUDY SEERAH?

His name is the most frequently mentioned name. Around the clock, people are mentioning the name Muhammad (Pbuh) and there are Muslims worldwide. By the way the name Muhammad (Pbuh) means the praised one; there is no one else who is praised like the Prophet Muhammad (Pbuh). His name fulfils its meanings. He is the most praised one, whenever we hear his name, all Muslims say after his name "Peace be upon him (Pbuh)". If we want to develop love for the Prophet (Pbuh) we can do this by studying his life.

Allah says, if it be your fathers, your sons, your brothers your mates or your kindred, the wealth you have gained the commerce which you fear of decline or the dwelling in which you delight are dear to you more than Allah or his Messenger then wait about Allah who brings his decision and Allah does not guide who are rebellious. And striving in the cause of Allah should be paramount to everything else. Allah and his Messenger and Islam should be the dearest thing to every one of us.

WHY DO WE STUDY THE SEERAH?

We study the seerah, to follow the way of the Prophet Muhammad (Pbuh). Whoever seeks Al-Akhira and embodiment, let him follow the Prophet (Pbuh). He is the embodiment of Khaliq. By studying his seerah we shall be able to follow his way.

Understanding the Holy Quran, there are some Ayat, (verses), which are independent of the circumstances of revelation. Like the Ayat, about Al-Akhira. There are some Ayat, which happened during the life of the Prophet. Some Ayat were revealed prior to an event and some Ayat were revealed after an event. Some Ayat were revealed concurrent with an event.

The Seerah gives us the explanation of these Ayat. For example, Surah Al-Ahzab, many Ayat were revealed regarding the battle of Aza. There are many Ayat in Surah Al-Imran, relating to an event that happened during time of the Prophet (PBUH). A major part of Surah Al-Imran was a dialogue between Muslims and Christians based on the Christian delegation that came from Najran to visit the Messenger of Allah. These Ayat came to support the holy Prophet (Pbuh) in dialogue with the Christians. Then the later part of Surah Al-Imran is dealing with Ghuzva Al-Audh. The details are not given in the Surah but how can we explain this? We can explain this by going to Seerah.

The life of the Prophet (Pbuh) explains the methodological steps of Islamic movement. The messenger went through stages, he went through steps starting by the secret invitation, Dawah. And then became public and then later on Jihad. So, it went through stages, these stages are important to learn a Devine study. Allah has guided for all these steps. And it was not a reaction to emerging circumstances; they were planned by Allah and guidance for us to establish Islam. It is important to look through these stages. What the Prophet (Pbuh) went through and the progression of his invitation.

The Seerah taught us how to be guided by Quran and to be moderate. Quran and Sunnah are verbal teachings, but how do we apply these teachings? By looking at the life of the Prophet (Pbuh) and the Sahaba (companions of the

Prophet (Pbuh). They took these verbal teachings into actions. Followers of another Prophet have lost their seerah.

We know how the Quran was being practiced then. There is a story, during fasting, the Sunnah states, 'white string and black string'. Eating and drinking during Ramadan, one Sahaba had a string under his pillow and he continued eating until he could see the 'white' and came and told the Prophet (Pbuh). The Prophet (Pbuh) laughed at this. The meaning of the white string is the light of the morning.

STUDYING SEERAH IS IBADAT (WORSHIP)

Studying seerah is considered part of Islam. This is not to entertain ourselves, there is a reward in studying this. We are practicing Islam by studying the seerah. We hope that through this study, the gatherings will be surrounded by Angels. Allah will show us his mercy and tranquility in such studies. Allah says if you love me, follow the Prophet (Pbuh). Allah will love you and forgive your sins, Allah is most forgiving.

Developing a Muslim, I.D there is a global culture. That culture does not give choice. To destroy people, you must sever their roots.

THE LIFE OF THE PROPHET (PBUH) IS TESTIMONY TO HIS PROPHETHOOD

The greatest miracle of the Prophet (Pbuh) is The Quran. There are so many miracles other than that but just studying his life is an evidence of his Prophethood. Here we have a man who for 40 years was leading a normal life the outstanding in the life of the Prophet (Pbuh) is that his first 40 years, his morality and character did not show any aspiration to power, nothing at all.

After 40 the Prophet (Pbuh) brings the greatest change the world has ever seen; that is a miracle. The Prophet (Pbuh) was illiterate (couldn't read or write) and then presents the greatest Book that was ever produced and we can go on and on that things, could only be explained, that Mohammad (Pbuh) is a messenger from Allah, who has Devine help. Otherwise, it is impossible, there is no way to explain seerah that he was a messenger from Allah. It is impossible to achieve what the Prophet (Pbuh) achieved through revelation. So, it is a testimony to his Prophethood. After 40 years he suddenly becomes a political leader, military leader, and religious leader. Head of a large household, law maker, teacher, imam and we can go on and on, that things Prophet (Pbuh) used to do all of that was done in 23 years which leads to the next point that we are studying the life of the greatest man that ever-set foot on this earth.

Mohammad (Pbuh) is the greatest whatever benchmark one uses. He will still become the greatest. Michael Hart, an American, a book the '100 Most Influential People Who Lived in History'. After studying the history, it became clear to him that Mohammad (Pbuh) is the greatest man that ever lived. We are studying the life of 'Al-Mustafa', 'the chosen one'. He is chosen out of all the creation of Allah. There may be other reasons also, which are not revealed.

When Mohammad L Raja writes 'Allah says' he is referring direct from the Qura0n, Taura or Bible. When he writes Allah, he is referring to God.

THE SETTLEMENT OF MAKKAH: THE BIRTHPLACE OF THE PROPHET (PBUH)

We start with the Prophet Ibrahim, when he travelled a long distance with his wife and newborn son about 3,000 years before the birth of Prophet Muhammad (Pbuh). When we talk about Mohammad (PBUH), we have to talk about his ancestors. Starting by Ibraham (PBUH). The emphasis is on the story of Hagar and Ibraham rather than the story of Sara and Ibraham because that is the lineage of the Prophet. We will start by talking about Ibraham, Hagar and Ismail when they travelled to Land of Ejaz. Ibraham, his wife and newborn son came to Land of Ejaz, Ibraham (Pbuh) took them to present day Makkah. At that time there was nothing there. Nobody lived there, there was no cultivation, it was a dead valley, but the place where the house of Allah (Kaba) was sacred, since the earth was created. In fact, there is a difference of opinion on who was the first one to build the Kaba. The majority opinion is that Ibraham (Pbuh) is the one that built the Kaba, but there are other schools of thought, that say that Adam (Pbuh) was the one. Regardless of who built it first, the place itself, with the building, or without the building, the place is holy and sacred from day one. Ibraham, his wife and son arrived in that valley and the place where there is zam zam, at present, obviously there was no zam zam at that time. Ibraham (PBUH) left his wife and child, his son Ismail. He left with them some water and a leather bag of dates and he walked away. He just turned away and left. Hagar (Abpwh) knew that Ibraham was going to leave them but didn't expect to be left in such a place in the middle of the desert. She followed him and she said "Ibraham are you going to leave us in this place, where there is no cultivation and no one is living". Abraham (PBUH) did not respond. She asked him again, but no response. She asked him the third time and he didn't respond again. Then Hagar (ABPWH), said "did Allah tell you to do so?" Ibraham (PBUH) said "yes". "Then Allah will take care of us. If this is the command from Allah than I have trust in Allah that he will take care of us". Look at the faith of this woman? "In the middle of nowhere, but if this is the command from Allah, have trust in Allah, he will take care of us. Allah will not waste us and Allah will not neglect us".

Ibraham (Pbuh) left and when he reached the place where they couldn't see him anymore, Ibraham (PBUH) turned around and faced the Kaba or the place of the Kaba and prayed to Allah. He said, "O' Allah, I am leaving my offspring in infertile land, no cultivation, next to your sacred house, this was known as a sacred place. Even though the Kaba wasn't built, Ibraham (PBUH) made prayer. Everybody knows what a pyramid is, what is a foundation, what is the first human need to be satisfied. First thing is physiological need that is the foundation of the pyramid, the most important need for humans. What is the next need, social and the third one is spiritual. (1) Food and shelter (2) social (3) religious and then the peek is actualization. First need food and shelter social life. Then spiritual need once one has realized first two. Then religious need according to Muslims, finally the self-actualization. According to Ibraham the first thing he asked for is not food and drink or shelter, but the first thing he asked for "O' Allah may they establish prayer". First spiritual need salah and then second, make people love them. Asking Allah to draw people to his family, bring people and make them love his family, this is the social need.

Finally, he said then provide them with fruits. Ibraham started with Salah, then social needs and then physiological needs. Even when he asked Allah for fruits he also connected it with, so they may be grateful. "Give them fruits so they may be thankful to you". That is true when Allah determines everything for you. When you are eating, drinking and sleeping you are doing everything for Allah. That is the true tranquility that is self- actualization. Then the Prophet Abraham (Pbuh) left Hagar made use of the small amount of food and water that he left with them. After a short while they ran out of food and water, and Hijra breast fed Ismail. But her milk was drying up. They were thirsty and hungry. Now Ismail began to cry, he was hungry. Haggar couldn't bear to see her son agonizing in pain. There was nowhere to go, but she left him and started climbing a hill, later this hill is called 'Al-Safa'. She climbed on top to see anybody or any help in horizon. She looked left and right but saw no one, she climbed down and reached in the valley, she would tuck up her clothes and run, then she would climb another hill which was later called Al-Marwa. She reached the top and looked in the horizon to see if there was anybody. Her son was twisting and turning in pain. Haggar was running up and down these hills and she did it 7 times. At the seventh time, when she reached the top of the hill, she heard a 'sound'. She stared around to see where that sound was coming from. To her amazement she saw that the sound was coming from underneath the feet of Ismail (Pbuh). The Angel Gabriel descended. The water was coming out from underneath Ismael's (Pbuh) feet. Haggar rushed in happiness to the source of the water, and because it was a dry desert and would soak up all the water, she made a pool around the water to contain it.

The Prophet (Pbuh) when narrating this story said "Rehm Allah". May Allah have mercy on the mother of Ismail (Pbuh), if she had left it alone it would have been a flowing river, but because of her interference it was a well. If she had left the miracle alone it would have been a flowing stream, the Prophet (Pbuh) smiled and said, "May Allah have mercy on her". Think of Hagar, what were her feelings, when she was running up and down those hills. Her heart was broken, she might have been crying because of the pain and suffering and seeing her son suffering in front of her eyes. She had trust in that Allah would not abandon them.

Hagar was a believing woman; a righteous woman and Allah was testing her and Allah was hiding from her something in the future that she didn't know. So, at that time naturally as a mother she must have been in extreme pain. Seeing her son crying and the fact that she was in the middle of nowhere, running up and down these hills.

Now just imagine if Hagar is resurrected at the time of Hajj, then she would have a chance to see what Muslims from all over the world are doing. The Prophet (Pbuh) said that is why we go to Safa and Marwa. So, we are following the footsteps of Hagar. If Hagar knew that time will come, when people will come from four corners of the world, to follow her footsteps and millions will do what she did, she would have gone through Safa and Marwa with a big smile on her face.

Brothers, when we are going through trial, we don't know what Allah is hiding on the other side. This is a gift Allah has given to Hagar in this world, just think what Allah will give her in Al-Akhirah. For example, Moses (Pbuh), lost his direction, when he was with his family, he got lost in the desert. It was a cold, windy and dark night and Moses lost his direction. He didn't know which direction Egypt was. He saw a fire in the distance and he told his wife, 'I shall go to that fire to bring some light and some guidance'. He wanted light because it was a dark, dreadful night and some warmth for the cold weather and he wanted some guidance. He expected that since there is fire, there will be people around it. I shall ask them for direction, and that is all that Moses (Pbuh) wanted. Some light and some guidance toward Egypt. But Allah was hiding something better for him. Allah tells us a story in the holy Quran, that when Moses (Pbuh) went there, he met Allah and Allah spoke to him. Rather than Moses going back with light for that dark night and guidance towards Egypt, he went back with light towards humanity and he went back with guidance not to Egypt but to Paradise. When he went there that was the announcement of his Prophet Hood then and there.

Moses was lost and he went there and Allah said "I am Allah, and there is no God beside me or other than me. Worship me and establish prayer to remember me in my name". Moses wanted something, but he got something better. Sahaba go through difficulty, but Allah reserves for them top levels of Paradise.

Let us think about ourselves when we go through moments of difficulty. Now in the desert when there is water it will immediately attract form of life. Now birds are flying over water, which was previously a dead valley.

There was a tribe called Jurm, who were nomads in that area. Jurm was a tribe moved out of Yemen. Yemen was the birthplace of Arabs and Arabic language and that is where the Arab tribes emigrated from. There is a whole chapter in the Holy Quran called 'Saba'. Allah tells us that these are the first people who built a dam, because of that they had year-round source of water, and a massive network of irrigation, that went on for 100's of miles. Holding huge populations, because of the water (there are stories fruits).

It is in the Holy Quran that because of wealth they didn't feel any pain in traveling, these people asked for difficulty like the rest of the world and Allah made it difficult for them. They rejected the message of Allah and Allah destroyed the dam. It flooded the area and agriculture collapsed. People immigrated into Arabia. I am giving you this history because Jurm was one of these tribes.

Jurm were familiar with that area and knew that there was no water in that area. When they saw birds hovering in the sky, they wondered what was going on. They sent two men to investigate. These men came back and reported that there is a well (water) in that area. Now Jurm had come to the place where zam zam is located and asked Hagar a strange question and they got a stranger answer. They asked Hagar 'can we settle in this place?' The reason why this question is strange is because this is a tribe of warriors and fighters and here, they are asking permission from a lonely woman with a child. If they wanted, they simply could have pushed her away, but they were kind to ask her permission to stay there. Even though that was an empty place and no one was living there, her answer was even more amazing, because she bargained, she had no power, but said if you want to stay, and the water belongs to us. The Prophet (Pbuh) says, deep in her heart she wanted them to stay because she wanted to have some company, but she was negotiating to get a better deal and she did. They agreed and settled there, which later became known as Makkah.

Ismail (Pbuh) grew up with them and adopted their language that was the Arabic language. Ibrahim was from

Iraq and his language was different. Ismail grew up and married from the Jurm. This is the beginning of the lineage of the Prophet (Pbuh). Ismail, Makkah and Jurm had political leadership in Makkah. Later, Ismail grew up and his father Ibraham came and built the Kaba. The Religious leadership remained with Ismail and continued down to his descendants. Jurm never had religious authority over the Kaaba, it always remained in the hands of the descendants of Ismail and political leadership was in the hands of the Jurm. They stayed there for a long time, 2000 years. They became corrupt and tyrannical. Allah then sent on them a new tribe, Khaza and they kicked them out of Makkah. This was another tribe from Yemen. They came to Makkah and kicked Jurm out of Makkah.

Jurm, before they left, they did two things (1) they dumped the well of zam zam and erased all its marks. (2) They stole the treasures which were inside Kaba. Khaza became the new leaders of Makkah. In the meanwhile, the descendants of Ismail increased in numbers and spread out in Arabia, but there was one branch that remained in Makkah, Quraish. Quraish was one of the tribes of many who descended from Ismail, they are called the descendants of Adnan. Quraish were still living in Makkah but Makkah was ruled by Khaza.

The leader of Khaza ruled Makkah. The Head of Quraish was Osuy bin Kalab. He was able to unify Quraish and to lead a revolt against Khaza. He was able to drive them out completely from Makkah. Now descendants of Ismail unified both political and religious leadership. Osuy bin Kaleb unified all powers under him. He controlled guardianship of the Kaba, which is a Nobel thing. He controlled the supply of the food and water to pilgrims. He was providing for the guests of Allah and this a big honor. They used to fight for this right.

All the pilgrims of Arabia will be hosted by Quraish in the season of Hajj.

Quraish also had hold on the parliament, (Nadwa). He held control over all that and control over war. When Osuy bin Kaleb died the different departments and powers were split amongst his children. The grandson of Osuy, Amar, ended up inheriting from his father the provisions of Al-hajj, providing them with food and drink. Amar did something new in feeding hajjis. Rather than providing soup he started crushing bread into soup. In Arabia this is called Hashim. He was nicknamed Hashim, which was the great grandfather of the Prophet (Pbuh).

Hashim married from Medina, went to Palestine for business and died in Ghazwa. His wife become pregnant and she gave birth to a child whose name was Sheeba. Sheeba means old man. The reason is that he was born with some grey hair. Because his father died his mother stayed with her parents in Medina. He was brought up by his family in Medina.

One day a man came to Medina, his name is Mutlab. He is the brother of Hashim. He claimed his nephew Sheeba was about eight years old. He wanted to take his nephew back to Makkah. The mother's family refused to give him up, but he was able to convince them that he belongs to the most noble family in Quraish, in Makkah. Mutlab brought this child with him. Nobody had seen this child in Makkah before. In those days' slavery was in use, people thought he was Mutlab's slave. They called him Abdul Mutlab. This is the grandfather of the Prophet (Pbuh) Abdul Mutlab (two stories linked to them).

Now the well of zam zam was unknown for 300 years. Jurm had erased all its marks. Khaza ruled for 300 years or more. Abdul Mutlab saw a dream. Someone comes to him and tells him dig tayba, tayba means pure. Abdul Mutlab in his dream questions, what is Tayba? He doesn't hear anything back and that was the end of the dream. The following night the same voice comes to him and says, 'dig the precious'. Abdul Mutlab says, what is the precious? He doesn't hear an answer back. The third night the same voice comes and says dig zam zam. Abdul Mutlab asks what is zam zam? The voice tells him 'it will never fail or dry up (water).

The grand pilgrim lies between blood and dong, near the nest of the crow with white legs, next to the colony of ants. These are the sign'. But Abdul Mutlab is unable to decode these signs. 'Zam zam, it never runs out of water and it will provide for grand pilgrims. Every year it is enough, then it says, it is between dong and blood'. Next day Abdul Mutlab going around the Kaba sees dong and blood, a camel was slaughtered in that place, the insides of the camel on one side and blood on the other side. Then he saw a crow with white legs in the same area and there was a colony of ants. Abdul Mutlab realizes that this is the place where the well of his grandfather is. He calls his son Harris and start digging. Since it is not far from the Kaba, people didn't like digging next to Kaba.

People kept protesting, but he continued digging. At the time Abdul Mutlab had only one son. Suddenly people heard Abdul Mutlab shout, praising Allah. People came rushing and to their amazement they saw that Abdul Mutlab had uncovered the rim of zam zam. Now all the leaders came and claimed that this was the well of their grandfathers. 'This belongs to all of us, let us share'. Abdul Mutlab said 'wait, I am the one who saw the dream, I uncovered it, and it belongs to me alone. There was a Dispute (Bini Saad's' witch). If there is a dispute in tribal society, the strength lies with how many men one has. One can only count on relatives. Abdul Mutlab felt weak because he had only one son Harris. He promised to Allah, if you give me 10 sons, I shall sacrifice one in your name. Allah blessed him with 10 sons and 6 daughters. Now was the time to fulfill his promise to Allah, that he will sacrifice one son in the name of Allah.

During these times, they had idols, which they worshiped, Hubble was the large one. They cast lots and left the decision in that random way. It came on Abdullah the first, second and third time. Abdul Mutlab took his son next to Kaba and was ready with the knife to slaughter him. Abu Talib went to his father and said we cannot allow you to kill your son. Other relatives of Abdullah also came and said we cannot allow you to kill him. People were telling him, that if you do this then it will become a Sunna for other people, because Abdul Mutlab was their leader. They were already killing their daughters, now they would start killing their sons, so they stopped him. Abdul Mutlab said that this was a pledge he made to Allah and cannot stop it. There was a dispute on how to resolve this. 'Let us go to the witch'.

They went to the witch and she said come back tomorrow, 'I shall consult my Jinn'. Next day they went and she had an answer for them. She asked them, 'what is the retribution you pay for a man (blood money)'? The answer was 10 camels. She said put 10 camels on one side and Abdullah on the other side and cast lots. If the arrow points towards Abdullah, then add another 10 camels. They agreed, and spined the dice, the arrow pointed towards Abdullah, they added another 10 camels and like this went up to 100 camels. Finally, the arrow pointed towards the camels, to make sure, they cast the lots again, the second and third time and every time the arrow pointed towards the 100 camels. Abdul Mutlab slaughtered 100 camels and had to pay for them all. Abdul Mutlab was a generous man, he refused to take any meat. He gave it out and there was so much meat, enough to feed the birds and beasts. Later, he became famous that he fed humans, beasts and the birds in sky. Now the blood money changed from 10 camels to 100 camels and it is still the same today.

Now Abdullah and Aminah are the parents of the Prophet (Pbuh). Later, they would tell Mohammad (Pbuh) that you are the son of two sacrificed ones. They are Ismail (Pbuh) and Abdullah. Abdullah married Aminah bin Toha. Here we are done with the ancestry of the Prophet (Pbuh).

THE RELIGIOUS BACKGROUND OF ARABIA

They started with Toheed, the 'oneness of Allah'. This was the invitation of Ismail (Pbuh). Ismail was their Prophet and Arabians followed him and believed in the 'oneness of ALLAH'. What went wrong, that they reached at this level, when the Prophet Mohammad (Pbuh) was sent to them, there were 3 religious Idolism, Christians and Jews.

Ibra and the son of Mr. Kabana (the true King) they agreed to resolve the dispute with a one-to-one fight, but Ibra made a secret agreement with some of his security guards that if you see me loosing then jump in and help, but if I am winning then leave me alone. People were watching. Ibra and Aryat were in the middle. Aryat was a tall and thin man. Ibra was a short and chubby man. Aryat was able to strike from the top and he chopped off Ibra's nose. Ibra was called 'Ibra AL ashram' that his nose was chopped off. When that happened the body, guards jumped in and killed Aryat. It was against the rules, but the issue was over with Aryat's death.

Ibra now took over and was ruling over Yemen. Ibra wanted to change the religion of the people and force them to become Christian. Since the Arab's were attached to the Kaba. He built a Cathedral church, to counter the Kaba. The Cathedral was called 'Oclace'. It was a wonderful piece of art.

One man did not like this idea, what he did next was a bit crude. He went to Oclace and he desiccated there and he spread it over the walls. Ibra was furious and angry at this. He was so angry that he decided that he must get rid of Kaba. He mobilized an army and marched towards Makkah. There was some resistance on the way by one of the chiefs of a tribe, his name was Nafail. He put up some resistance but was defeated. Ibra had a powerful army and captured Nafail.

In Twaif people assisted Ibra and one man offered himself to be a guide for the rest of the journey. This man's name was Argery and he went with the army, but when they came out of Twaif he died. Ibra made it to the outskirts of Makkah. Here there were some Sheppards with camels grazing. He took possession of them. Two hundred of these camels belonged to Abdul Mutlab, the grandfather of the Prophet (Pbuh). Abdul Mutlab then came out to meet with Ibra. Abdul Mutlab had to arrange the meeting using some connections. Abdul Mutlab happened to be friends with Nafail, who was captured as a prisoner of war. Nafail was carried with the army and he was friendly with a man called Anace. Anace was an important person in the army. He was a pilot of an elephant and that was important equipment. Abdul Mutlab came to Nafail and he in turn arranged a meeting though Anace. And Ibra welcomed Abdul Mutlab.

Abdul Mutlab walked in and he is described with an extraordinarily strong presence and personality. When one sees him, one becomes impressed? Ibra held him in high esteem. The rules were that Ibra sits on a high throw and people sit on the ground. When Ibra saw Abdul Mutlab, he did not feel comfortable having Abdul Mutlab sit under him. Also, he would not allow anybody to sit with him on the throne, what he did was, he came down and sat with Abdul Mutlab on the ground. Through an interpreter he asked, Abdul Mutlab, what does he want? Abdul Mutlab straight away said that he has taken possession of his 200 camels and he wants them back. Ibra said 'when I saw you I had so much respect for you, but I have lost it all now. I am coming to destroy your honor and the honor of your fathers. I am coming to destroy the Kaba. And you are asking me about camel'? Abdul Mutlab responded and said, 'I am the owner of the camels, so I am responsible for them and this house belongs to Allah and Allah will protect it'. Ibra gave the camels back. Abdul Mutlab went back to Makkah and told his people, 'Do not fight and leave Makkah', these were clear instructions, and 'we are not going to fight Ibra. We are going to leave'. They all went to the mountains. Abdul Mutlab was the last one to leave and before he left, he was hanging on the door of the Kaba and prayed to Allah to protect his house and then he left. Makkah was evacuated.

Ibra issued his instructions to his army to March forward, but the elephants refused to move. In all other directions the elephants would stand up and run, but towards Kaba they would not move. This was a miracle, but it is said that the man Nafail freed himself from the chains, jumped on an elephant and said in the ears of the elephant that, this is the House of Allah do not destroy it. Eventually they left the elephants and marched forward towards the Kaba. Allah sent on them an army of birds. No one knows the 'soldiers of Allah' anything can be a soldier of Allah. Water is a source of life and water killed the 'tyrant Pharaoh'. Wind is a soldier of Allah and Allah says, 'no one knows his soldiers but he himself'. Allah sent an army of birds carrying missiles (stones). Birds were sent on the army of Ibra and all were killed. This event is recorded in 'Surah Feel' in the Holy Quran. The Prophet (Pbuh) was born in this year.

BIRTH OF THE PROPHET (PBUH)

The Prophet Mohammad (Pbuh) was born in the year of 'Feel'. The mother Aminah (Abpwh) was pregnant and the father Abdullah was on a journey in Sham. He died close to Medina and was buried there. He died before the birth of the Prophet (Pbuh). The Prophet Muhammad (Pbuh) was born and his mother saw a light coming out of her and this light was reaching towards Sham. This was interpreted as Muhammad (Pbuh) 'a light reaching to the world'.

There are some Hadith, the first; 'Allah says; Allah knows best, where to place the Prophethood. Allah chose the best to be his messenger, Muhammad (Pbuh). Imam Ahmed says that, people say different things about Muhammad (Pbuh), like 'Muhammad (Pbuh) was a green tree grown in a desert', trying to say that, he was the only 'good person amongst his clan'. Abbas says certain things reached to Mohammad (Pbuh) and he stood on the pole pit and asked, 'who am I'? They, the people said, 'you are the messenger of Allah'. He replied 'I am Muhammad bin Abdullah bin Abdul Mutlab. Allah devises the creatures and made me part of the best. Placing me in the better group. I am the best, but also from amongst the best, my clan and tribe are noble'.

Another hadith; that Muhammad (Pbuh) is from true marriages, from Adam to his parents (no fornication) Allah granted purity. The name Muhammad was given by his grandfather Abdul Mutlab. Muhammad means 'to be praised'. Allah has fulfilled the name Mohammad, there is no one in the history who is praised liked the Prophet Muhammad (Pbuh).

Ahmed, 'the one who praises', is another name and there are other names besides this. Another name is Al-Hashim that means 'gatherer on the day of judgment'. He, the Prophet (Pbuh) will be the first one to be raised, then we shall all be raised, every one of us. Al-Maqfi means 'he is the last one to succeed as a Prophet and there will be no Prophet to succeed after him'. There are many other names besides these.

The Prophet (Pbuh) was nursed first by his mother, then by Uma Barka, then Uma Amin. It was a tradition in Arabia that, the newborn was sent into the desert for the first few years, as they believed the desert is a clean, pure environment and healthier. This happened to the Prophet (Pbuh), he was brought up in the land of Banu Saad.

Halima Sadia narrates the story; she says that she came with her friends to Makkah, so they could take the children with them, to nurse, and for this they were paid. Halima says that year there was famine, they were very poor. She and her friends went around Makkah, searching for children who need to be nursed. She says, Muhammad (Pbuh) was offered to everyone, but they decline to accept him. They refused him because he was an orphan. 'Who will pay us'? There was no fixed price, but they nursed the child and parents would give a reward as a gift. Halima says that, at the end of the day all my friends were going back to camp with children except myself. She told her husband that, she shall take Muhammad (Pbuh) instead of going back empty handed. She says that her husband agreed. The next morning, she went to Muhammad's mother Amina bin Tawa and accepted the child. Halima says, 'the night before we couldn't get any sleep, because our camel was not providing any milk and because of famine and hunger I was not providing enough milk for my child, so he cried throughout the night and kept us awake, a poor situation'.

Halima says as soon as I picked up Muhammad (Pbuh), I took him back to the camp and my breast welcomed him and provided as much milk as he needed. He was satisfied and there was also enough milk for my son. That was the first night we were able to sleep. The Burka of Mohammad (Pbuh) was immediately apparent. Then my husband milked the camel and there was so much milk that my husband said, "O' Halima you have brought us a blessed soul, there is something going on". Now they were ready to go back to the desert. Halima said, when we were coming to Makkah, I was riding a donkey that was old and weak, and it was slowing down the whole group. So annoying, this donkey, so old and weak, sometimes instead of going straight, the donkey would go sideways, very tired and disoriented. On our way back, my donkey was the fastest among the group. Friends were asking is it the same donkey. Halima said yes.

Halima said "we send out our goats to graze and they would come back full. And we would milk them, whenever we want, but in our tribe the other animals would be hungry, without any milk."

People started to complain to their Sheppards', 'why don't you graze in the same place as Halima's'. They would follow us to the same grazing place, but ours would come back full and theirs would come back empty.

The child was growing up and we had the blessing of Allah and we recognized blessings of Allah. Then he reached two years of age, now Muhammad (Pbuh) was growing up, a sturdy fine boy. Not like other children, at the age of two he was a sturdy boy. We took him to this mother. They went to Makkah and told the mother of the Prophet Aminah, we want to keep the boy with us. They made excuses like Makkah may

16

not be a good place, dangerous and unhealthy. They kept on trying until Aminah agreed and they took the child back with them.

One day, Muhammad (Pbuh) was playing with his foster brother. His foster brother came in rushing and said, me brother from Quraish? Asked what happened to him he said, "two men dressed in white, came and knocked him to the ground, and then they opened up his (Abdomen) Halima said, we went rushing, we came to see Mohammad (Pbuh). His color was pale and we asked him what happened? He said that two men came, opened my chest and they took out something from it.

Halima, she loved Muhammad so much, she didn't want anything to harm him. She rushed back to Makkah and she went back to Aminah and said, "here is Muhammad and now you can have him." We have fulfilled our responsibility. Aminah said "how? You are bringing him back, when you were so interested to keep him." Halima wouldn't say anything but Aminah bin Toha, the mother of the Prophet, would insist, to find out what happened? Halima eventually told her that incident. Aminah responded and said that, are you afraid for him that Satan might hurt him? "By Allah that will not happen, when I was pregnant with him that was a very light pregnancy and when I delivered him his birth was not like any other child's. When he came out, I saw a light reaching to Sham. The protection of Allah is with him and I am sure he will have a great future."

Now Muhammad (Pbuh) was back with his mother and his mother passed away at the age of six. Now at the age of six, he lost both his parents, his father and mother. His grandfather took responsibility for him, but then died when Mohammad (Pbuh) was eight years old. Now Uncle Abu Talib took responsibility for Mohammad (Pbuh), who protected, helped and supported him for the next 40 years. These are the early years of the life of the Prophet Muhammad (Pbuh).

Muhammad (Pbuh) was protected by Allah, he would not commit sins, (usual or normal) amongst his people, and Allah was keeping him away. Muhammad (Pbuh) says that I was a Sheppard, one day I told another Sheppard, and 'tonight I want to go to Makkah to attend the parties. The Prophet was a young man; all others would attend parties except him. He joined the party, but then fell asleep. By the time he woke up, the party was over. The next day the same. Muhammad (Pbuh) realized this was a sign from ALLAH.

Zaid bin Harsa, said that there was a 'brass' (a brass Status) and people would touch this before tawaf, for barakah. The Prophet told, 'not to touch (Idols)'. These are instructions from Allah. The Prophet never saluted, touched an Idol. Also, Ali bin Abu Talib never worshiped idols, because he was raised in the house of the Prophet. Quraish would participate in Hajj, but would not go to Arafat, as it is out of boundaries. All other Arabs would go to Arafat but the Quraish. Mutumum bin Jabore lost his camel and went to look for it, he went to Arafat. He saw Muhammad (Pbuh) there and Allah was guiding Muhammad (Pbuh) on fitter (natural) to go to Arafat during Hajj.

THE PROPHET'S FIRST PROFESSION

The Prophet's first profession was a Sheppard, all Prophets are Sheppards, also Muhammad (Pbuh), with compensation from the people of Makkah.

THE MARRIAGE OF THE PROPHET MUHAMMAD (PBUH) TO KHADIJA

Khadija was a well-known and prosperous woman in Makkah, she wasn't married. She was old in age (may be a widow). She used to hire men to travel for her business. Traders used to travel to Syria and Yemen, (Surah Quraish), a journey in the winter and a journey in the summer.

Khadija happened to hire Muhammad (Pbuh), she had heard about his honesty and she wanted to hire someone trustworthy. She had her servant to accompany Muhammad (Pbuh) and her servant's name is Maysa. Muhammad (Pbuh) went to Sham to do business for her and came back. Maysa reported back to his Master (Khadija) and told her, that this man's honesty is amazing and he praised Muhammad (Pbuh). Khadija became interested in Muhammad (Pbuh); his character was admirable. Khadija, who was a wealthy woman, who was sought after by the noble men of Quraish. She said, "I want to marry you" and Muhammad (Pbuh) agreed. Muhammad (Pbuh) was 25 years old and she was 40 years old. The difference was 15 years and Mohammad (PBUH) never married again during her lifetime. All of the surviving children were from Khadija. Fatima (Abpwh) was the daughter of Khadija and Muhammad (Pbuh). Khadija had six children, Zainab, Rukhya, Kalsoom, Fatima, Qasim, and Ibrahim. None of them had any descendants except Fatima. The lineage of Muhammad (Pbuh) continues through Fatima and Ali (Abpwh). The Prophet loved Khadija so much and continued his loyalty even after her death. The Prophet would always remember her and always mentioned her name. This sometimes-caused jealousy amongst other wives of the Prophet.

Khadija always stood up and supported the Prophet when others betrayed him. Aysha was the most beloved after Khadija. Aysha said, "she was only jealous of Khadija, nobody else". The Prophet sometimes would slaughter sheep and say, "send it to the friends of Khadija". Once the Prophet said, "God gave me her love". In another Hadith, in Tirmzi, it is said that the Prophet would not leave home without praising Khadija. One day Aysha said "she was old and Allah replaces with better", but the Prophet (Pbuh) said, "No, Allah has not replaced with better, because she believed in me when everybody betrayed. She made me comfortable with what she had when people denied me. Allah has blessed me with children from her.

Before the death of the Prophet (Pbuh) he visited the graveyard of the people, about 70 of these died in the battle of Uhud. He made prayer for them, saying that soon we will meet. Khadija was a special person. When she was alive, the angel Gabriel descended and said that Khadija is approaching and she is carrying some food. When she arrives tell her that 'Allah send her Salaam' and tell her 'I am (Gabriel) giving her Salaam'. And then Gabriel says give her glad tidings, that she will have a palace in Paradise (Jannah).

Khadija is one of the four greatest women who have ever lived; first is Marriam bin Imran, the mother of Isa, and there is no dispute that she is the first and this is mentioned in the Qur'an; second is Khadija bint Khoyal, the wife of the Prophet

(Pbuh); third is Fatima bint Muhammad, the daughter of the Prophet (Pbuh); Forth is Acia bint Umrad, she brought up Moses (Pbuh) and is also the wife of the Pharaoh. These are the greatest four women who have ever lived.

Muhammad (Pbuh) at the age of 25 was chaste in an environment which was corrupt. After the death of his wife Khadija, Muhammad (Pbuh), remained unmarried for two or three years, after then he married.

Sauda, another widow, her husband died and there was no body to provide for her and she was in old age. In the last 10 years of the Prophet's (Pbuh) life, he married several times. When the Prophet (Pbuh) left this world, there were nine widows. The reasons for the marriages were firstly to forge alliances with different tribes. He is the messenger of Allah, he devoted all his efforts to promote Islam, and even to get married would be to strengthen Islam, for stronger relationship and family ties.

The Prophet married the daughter of Abu Bakr and married the daughter of Umar bin Khattab and then married his own daughters to Usman and Ali. These relations strengthened the family relationships and conveyed the religion. Who will convey family life? If there was only one wife, she could be discredited (Sunnah).

There are two controversial marriages; first marriage to Ayesha and second marriage to Zainab bint Josh. The marriage of Ayesha is controversial because she was of an incredibly young age. The marriage to Zainab bint Josh was controversial because she was married to his adopted son. These two marriages were Divine instructions, instructed by Allah.

The Prophet's (Pbuh) marriage to Zainab was instructed in the Holy Quran, in Surah Al-Hza; when Zaid, her husband left her, "we command you to marry her". The marriage to

Aysha was instructed through a dream, and this dream is in Bukhari Sharif. The Prophet says, 'Gabriel came to me and I saw you Ayesha covered in a silk curtain, you were wearing a silk dress. In the dream when I uncovered you Gabriel told me this is your wife'. Then the Prophet looked at her, and that was Ayesha and Gabriel told him this is your wife in this world and in Al-Akhirah. The Prophet Muhammad (Pbuh) saw this dream twice and we know that the dreams of Prophets are revelations.

When people of weak faith attack at this, the answer is that Muhammad (Pbuh) did this because Allah commanded him, it was Divine. It is not part of Sunnah; in Sunnah we are only allowed four wives. The situation of Ayesha is not allowed. It was an exception and that was for the Prophet (Pbuh).

These were Divine marriages and therefore we have no right to question. These were not initiated by the Prophet (Pbuh).

The question raised by non-believers is less about the marriage to Ayesha, but more about the belief that Muhammad (Pbuh) is the messenger of Allah. You do not believe that he is receiving revelations and that God commanded him. If one believes that he is a Prophet of Allah, then we have no right to question. Allah guides him. Allah owes nothing to us, but we owe everything to Allah. If Allah has instructed someone, we do not have to understand it, we must just obey it. Allah says to Muhammad (Pbuh), 'The Quraish are not disbelieving you but they disbelieve the message. You are only a messenger'.

The marriage of the Prophet with Ayesha is one of greatest blessings of Allah on us Muslims. Ayesha had a mind of Scholar; she would ask questions. Amongst the top seven Hadith narrators, she is number four. She has narrated two thousand two hundred Hadiths.

AN IMPORTANT EVENT

An important event, a flood damaged the structure of Kaba and the people felt that the Kabba should be rebuilt. The Kaba has been rebuilt four or five times, depending on who build it first. There is a difference of opinion whether Ibrahim was the first to build the Kabba. Some scholars refer to Adam. Quran says Ibraham was raising the foundation of Kabba. That means that the foundation was laid by Adam (Pbuh). But the common belief is that Ibraham first built it. However, there is no dispute of the holiness of the place, since the day the earth was created.

The second time when Makkah was flooded, they had to tear down the Kabba to rebuild it, but no one wanted to make a move. Then one person with his sons started, by praying O'Allah we only want well. It just so happened that, a Roman ship crashed near the port, they brought the wood and there was a Roman builder who helped. This was the first time they made the roof of Kabba from wood. Quraish decided that only Halal money will be used to rebuild the Kabba. They were short of funds, therefore, before the Kabba was rectangle in shape, rather than square. Because of the shortage of funds, they ended up shortening from one side. They made it square to save money. The area they left out is what we refer to today as Al-Hajir. There is a circle which was once part of the Kabba. Kabba also had two gates, which is now one and they raised the doorstep. Now to get access to the door, you must climb (issue of power).

After the conquest of Makkah (Hadith); The Prophet Muhammad (Pbuh) is saying to Ayesha, that the people were short of funds and they left some of the Kabba out. Now there are new Muslims or nonbelievers, otherwise I would have put two gates one on each side and would include the area of Al- Hajir. A statement was made when Makkah was opened, the Prophet (Pbuh) wanted to build on the original foundations. But Islam is soft on new Muslims, it may be a fitnah for them, if the Kabba is reconstructed.

At the age of thirty-five Muhammad (Pbuh) participated in rebuilding the Kabba. They reached the holy place to place the black stone. The dispute was who will have the honor to place the black stone back in its place, because every tribe took responsibility to build one side. One tribe BANU-DADAR, came with force and a pot of blood, they placed it there in front of the Kabba, and they then put their hands in it and pulled out. They did this as a warning to others that this will happen if we are not allowed to place the black stone. Pledge to fight and to die. That was drastic but still not enough to deter the others. Another tribe brought their own pot of blood and they did the same. Then all of the tribes did the same.

Four to five days passed and war was about to be erupted amongst them. Then the oldest man Omea, he then suggested let us agree that the first man who comes towards the Kabba, he will be given complete authority to decide between us. So, they all gathered and waited for the first person to come and the first person to walk in was Muhammad (Pbuh). They all said truthfully and trustworthy we all agree. Muhammad (Pbuh) asked them to bring a cloth. He picked up the black stone and placed it on the cloth. Then asked a representative from each clan to hold it and raise it together. Therefore, everybody participated in lifting the black stone. When they all lifted it then he himself, with his blessed hands, placed it in its rightful place. That was the second time Al-Kabba was rebuilt. Years later, Abdullah bin Zubair became the Ameer of Makkah. He knew of this Hadith, because Ayesha was his aunt. His mother is sister of Ayesha. He decided to rebuild the Kabba on the original foundations. Now people have been

Muslim for a long time. Also, the Kabba was burnt down because of Hijaj bin Yousaf who laid siege on Makkah. At that time there was a war between Abdullah bin Zubair and Banu -Omiya in Syria.

Abdullah bin Zubair, built as described in the Hadith, two doors and area of Hijr included gates that were lowered this was the third time Al-Kabba was rebuilt. Abdullah bin Zubair lost the war and was killed then Hijaj bin Yousuf took over. The Khalifa Amar bin Marwan was not familiar with this Hadith. He commanded to build Kabba as it was before Abdullah bin Zubair. So, the Kabba was shortened again as Quraish had made it.

After the Khalifa of Banu Omiya, Banu Al-Abbas was the family of Khalifa. The Khalifa of Banu Al-Abbas was thinking to rebuild the Kabba again on the original foundations and he consulted Imam Malik. Imam Malik told Khalifa, he said we do not want Kabba, as a toy in the hands of the kings as they keep changing its size every now and then. Let us keep it, as people have known the stones. We know the Prophet (Pbuh) prayed inside the Kabba. Now over the time the height has been increased but size is the same. Some of the stones are original, used by Ibraham (Pbuh) but not all of them.

The Black stone was originally used by Ibrahim. There are stories related to the black stone. It is blessed and the only part of Kabba which is kissed.

THE PROPHET MUHAMMAD (PBUH) NOW SPENDS TIME IN THE MOUNTAIN OF GHAR-E-HIRA

Now, the Prophet Muhammad (Pbuh) would leave Makkah and spend time in a cave (Ghar-e-Hira), this is a mountain, a few kilometers from Makkah.

The Prophet (Pbuh) would take provisions, would go and stay in this cave, worshiping Allah. In those days the Kabba could be seen from the cave that was before Muhammad's (Pbuh) Prophethood. This was the time of darkness.

Zayed bin Nofail; Vraka bin Nofal is a Christian also Salman Farsi; they were all looking for the truth. It is a long story.

Read in the name of your lord who created man from clot, read in the name of your lord who teaches a pen who knew nothing.

GLAD TIDINGS; THIS HADITH, BY IBN ISHAQUE

A book is delivered to The Prophet (Pbuh) was told to read, and he responded, "I cannot read". A book is not learned. These are the exact words given to Muhammad (Pbuh) by the Angel Gabriel.

Read in the name of your lord who created man from clot.

Read in the name of your lord who teaches a pen who knew nothing (Bible Prophesize).

THE PROPHETHOOD

The Prophet used to spend a long time in the cave Hira. One day he was visited by Angel Gabriel in his original form. Muhammad (Pbuh) saw Gabriel in Angelic form and not as a man. Angel Gabriel came in a form of a man later.

Hadith by Umar bin Khattab (Allah be pleased with him): "A man with very dark hair, bright white clothes and we don't see any traces of travel on him. He appeared in the form of a man.

In the cave the angel came in original form. That happened twice. Angel came to Muhammad (Pbuh) and said," Iqra", this word Iqra has two meanings one is to read and the other is to recite. In this situation, the meaning is recite. Muhammad (Pbuh) responded I cannot read. Angel Gabriel grabbed Muhammad (Pbuh), squeezed him and crushed him and then released and said, "Iqra". Muhammad (Pbuh) responded a second time and said, "I cannot read". Gabriel held him second time and pressed him hard, and then released him again and said, "Iqra", this happened three times and then Gabriel recited the first verses of The Holy Quran. Recite in the name of your lord. The one who created man from clot. Recite in the name of your noble lord who taught a pen what he did not know. This was the first encounter between the Prophet (Pbuh) and Angel Gabriel.

The messenger of Allah was terrified by this incident. He went home and went to his wife Khadija. "Wrap me in a garment, wrap me in a garment". The Prophet (Pbuh) was shivering. He was feeling cold. The Prophet (Pbuh) was terrified because of this incident, plus the Prophet (Pbuh) had disliking for Jinn, this is another agenda, spirits and sorcery. He thought what happened to him perhaps happens to sources. The Prophet (Pbuh) explained the incident to his wife Khadija. She responded and said, "No, Allah will never for sake you because of your generosity, you help the poor". You are generous towards guests. She knew the prior conduct she knew Allah will protect the Prophet (Pbuh). Do not worry. What happened to you cannot be from Satan. Then she offered to take him to her uncle or cousin Varka Bin Nofal. He was a Christian, learned (educated) and had some scrolls from which he studied. Khadija (Abpwh) took Muhammad (Pbuh) to Varka bin Nofal. Varka bin Nofal asked to describe what happened exactly. After knowing the story, he said, "This is

Angel Gabriel", who came to Moses (Pbuh), who descended on Moses. Varka bin Nofal knew immediately that this is Angel Gabriel and is revealing to Muhammad (Pbuh) as he did to Moses (Pbuh). This was like what was given to Moses (Pbuh) and then Varka bin Nofal said something interesting. He said, "I wish I was young when your people will drive you out of your land".

This was a surprise to Muhammad (Pbuh). Muhammad (Pbuh) questioned Varka bin Nofal, they would drive me out of my land? How, could that happen? Muhammad (Pbuh) had every right to question, Muhammad (Pbuh) was the most loved and admired man in Makkah. Muhammad (Pbuh) belonged to a noble family in Makkah. He had no quarrel with his people. Plus, they were living in a tribal society where it is not acceptable to drive somebody out. Extreme loyalty to tribe. Family relationship is strong. Varka Bin Nofal said "anybody says like this people throw him out". He was a wise man and had studied history and knew the difference between truth and falsehood. Amazingly, what Varka Bin Nofal said became word to word true. It happened as he stated. The words of Varka Bin Nofal were an early warning as to what was coming. Iqra, these words had powerful effect on the illiterate nation. Soon after the Muslim Ummah was the most educated nation on the face of the earth.

Muhammad (Pbuh) did not learn how to read and write, with him the word meant recite and repeat. Allah wanted him to be illiterate. Allah says "if you had known the scripture before this or were able to write. Then this would cause doubts. The Prophet (Pbuh) was receiving the knowledge from Allah through Angel Gabriel. Allah makes an oath in Surah Qulim. It was in the battle of Badr, prisoners were freed if they taught ten people how to read and write. This is the importance Islam gave to knowledge. But not any knowledge, but relevant material. In early years in Madinah, the Prophet (Pbuh) saw Umar (Abpwh) reading Tora. The Prophet (Pbuh) didn't like that. But that was not permanent, only until Muslims were on solid foundations.

But the Prophet (Pbuh) said, "Any Israeli stories, don't believe nor disbelieve". We know this, in Surah Baqarah, two angels came to teach people magic, Haroot and Maroot. They were teaching people knowledge that was evil and told people this is not good for you.

THE TYPES OF REVELATIONS

For 6 months before receiving the revelation the Prophet (Pbuh) used to see dreams frequently. He would see a dream at night and fulfillment during the day. This continued for 6 months. The Prophet (Pbuh) says true dreams are 1/46 of Prophethood with the prophet's dream this is a form of revelation. For us there are three kinds of dreams (i) true dream (ii) a dream from Satan, he wants to inflict harm, if so, seek refuge from Allah and do not tell anyone. Because that is what Satan wants, he wants the person to be miserable and tell everybody how bad it was. (iii) The Prophet (Pbuh) says, the thought during the day and dream at night. This is meaningless.

The second type of revelation is where the angel inspires but does not appear. (Inspirations).

The third type of revelation is where the angel appears in the physical form of human being.

The fourth type of revelation is when the angel sounds like a bell, and weight. Once Zaid bin Harsa said the words of the of the holy Quran are heavy.

The fifth type of revelation is when the Prophet saw Gabriel twice in original form and that is in Sura Najam. Gabriel in original form has (huge) wings that will cover the horizon. The Prophet (pbuh) says wherever he would look he would see the wings of Gabriel. The sixth type of revelation is when Allah spoke to the Prophet (Pbuh) directly without any intermediary and this occurred in Al-Miraj. Allah spoke directly also to Moses (Pbuh).

The Prophet (Pbuh) was initially instructed to keep the message private not to make it public but to the ones very close to him. The first person to believe both from men and women was Khadija. She was the first to accept Islam, the leader of the pack as it was.

Fatima was daughter of the Prophet (Pbuh) and wife of Ali bin Abu Talib. Ali heard that the Prophet (Pbuh) had received some slaves, they wanted a helper in the house, because Fatima had a lot more work than she could manage. They went to the house of the Prophet (Pbuh) and he wasn't there, but they spoke to Ayesha. They told her they wanted a servant because of the hardship Fatima was going through. She was suffering from hard work and serving in her house. The Prophet (pbuh) was told by Ayesha and he went to the house of Ali and Fatima. Ali bin Abu Talib tells the Hadith. When Prophet (pbuh) came we were ready to go to bed. As soon as we saw the Messenger we stood up. The Prophet (Pbuh) said, remain there and came and sat between me and Fatima. He was touching both of us. The Prophet Muhammad (pbuh) loves his daughter and once said Fatima is part of me. What hurts her, hurts me and what pleases her pleases me. Fatima was the only surviving child. The Prophet (Pbuh) wanted to do what is best for his daughter. The Prophet (pbuh) had the ability to give them a servant. The Prophet (pbuh) said, I have something better for you. Before you go to bed say Subhan Allah 33 times, Alhamdulillah 33 times and Allahu Akbar 34 times that is better for you than a servant.

Ali bin Abu Talib said Fatima was using stone mill, until her hands became harsh. She was drawing water out of the well until that left a mark on her neck, cleaning and cooking. First slave who became Muslim was Zaid bin Harsa. First child who became Muslim was Ali bin Abu Talib. And the first free man who became Muslim was Abu Bakr. Old Discussion about who was the first man who accepted Islam, if it is solved like this that is Abu Bakr, because Ali bin Abu Talib was never a non-Muslim. Ali never worshiped idols and never embraced the religion of the people of Makkah. He was brought up in the household of the Prophet (pbuh). The acceptance of Islam by Abu Bakr was more beneficial because he was highly respected, wealthy and a leader of Quraish. He admired spending his wealth for Allah, his messenger and Islam. Everyone hesitated in accepting Islam except Abu Bakr. He is first in accepting Islam. He was the first to believe Isra Wal-Miraj and accompanied the Prophet (PBUH) at Hijra.

Abu Derja narrates this Hadith. There was a dispute between Abu Bakr and Umar. These were two advisers to the Prophet (pbuh) and they were awfully close to him. Ali bin Abu Talib said he saw the Prophet (pbuh) leaving with Abu Bakar and Umar and coming with them. He would sit with them, both on each side. Still the messenger had the loyalty to the ones who were with him from early days. This dispute between Abu Bakr and Umar the Prophet (pbuh) said "Allah sent me to you, and all of you said, you're a liar."

Except Abu Bakr who said, he spoke the truth, and he dedicated himself and his fortune to me. Will you leave that friend of mine to me and he said it twice, leave him alone.

The early secret stage of invitation (Dava) was over, when Surah Ishara. It was revealed to the Prophet (PBUH) and the Prophet (PBUH) stood on top of Safa. Mountain of Safa and he called Wasbha like sounding the Alarm. Everyone who heard came to the source of the emergency Alarm and the ones who could not go sent someone to report back to them. When people gathered, the Prophet (PBUH) asked them. "If I tell you that there is an army behind this hill which is about to ambush you, would you believe me?" They said we have never heard you lie. The messenger of Allah said, I am here to warn you of a severe punishment. Allah has sent me as Warner to you, and I am warning you of a severe punishment if you don't believe. These were the words the Prophet (pbuh) chose to give first warning to the people of Makkah (Quraish). It was direct and straightforward because the Prophets of Allah, Allah guides them that your duty is to give the message plainly. The message should not be confusing.

Abu Laub responded and said, "May evil fall on you for the rest of your days". This is why, you called us? Abu Laub was upset, angry because the call was during business hours. He said, "Wasting my time. I could have made money in that time".

Abu Laub was not alone, Allah revealed a Surah. The hands of Abu Laub will perish and his wealth will not do him any good. This Surah is a miracle in the Holy Quran. It says Abu Laub and his wife are in hell fire and this Surah was revealed while Abu Laub and his wife were still alive. If Abu Laub and his wife wanted to prove the Holy Quran wrong, they could have said we are Muslims. But they died disbelievers. This is a miracle of the Quran, speaking about an event which had not happened yet.

The first verses revealed were Surah Alk. After that, the revelation stopped for a while. That was to make the Prophet (pbuh) love the revelation and miss it, which he did. After that Surah Muzamal and Surah Mudassar. There is a difference of opinion which was the second i.e. First between the two, but there is an agreement that is a set of second and third. These Ayat form the manual for invitation (Dava). We can Summarize Iqra, Qum Qum. Iqra means learn and recite. Qum means stand up and practice at night and then Qum means Stand up and warn, preach and teach. To practice that was mandatory on early Muslims, but after few years this was abrogated, but for the Prophet (pbuh) remained throughout his life.

WHAT WAS THE RESPONSE OF QURAISH TO THE INVITATION (DAVA) OF THE PROPHET (PBUH)?

They responded in various different ways, (i) Mockery, (ii) Insult and harm (iii) character assassination (iv) Deforming the message (v) Bargaining (vi) Temptation luring (vii) setting challenges (viii) Pressure (ix) Jealousy and Hatred (x) Persecution (xi) and finally, assassination attempt.

1. Mockery; Allah says when they see you, they ridicule you and say is this the one whom Allah has sent as a messenger. There was no one better than you to send as a Prophet (pbuh). They would make fun of the Prophet (pbuh) and mock at him. Even though the Prophet (pbuh) was from the noble family but he was not the wealthiest or powerful, they made fun of him. People are attracted to the wealthy and powerful. In Surah Baqarah, Bani Israel went to their Prophet and said point a king over us and we shall fight. Taloot was appointed King, they refused to accept him because he was not wealthy or rich, and there are people among us who are more prominent to be King.

When the Prophet Muhammad (pbuh) went to Tawaf one of the men said, "Didn't Allah find anybody better than you to send as a Prophet?" (That is a separate story).

2. Insulting and harming; Abu Herrera narrates Hadith; Abu Jehail, he came to some Quraish leaders sitting next to the Kabba and told them. Are you allowing Muhammad to rub his face in the dirt? That was his evil way of saying about Sajood. If I see him do that I shall trample on his neck. And I shall rub his face in the dirt. The messenger of Allah came and started to pray. He would pray publicly in front of people, Muhammad (pbuh) was praying in front of the Kabba, Abu Jehail and his friends saw this. He went to fulfill his threat. He walked up to Muhammad (pbuh), he was in Sajood, suddenly they saw Abu Jehail falling back and he was waving his hands as if he was repulsing a danger falling upon him. Abu Jehail came back they asked him, what happened? What was wrong? He said, "What do you mean? What happened didn't you see?". They said we didn't see anything there was nothing. All we saw was you falling on your back and waving your hands. Abu Jehail said there was a trench in front of me fire, wind and terror. The Prophet Muhammad (pbuh) said those were angels, and if he had come any closer to me, they would have torn him to pieces. Abu Jehail saw that but nobody else saw. Attaba bin Abu Mooen, came to Muhammad (pbuh) one day next to the Kabba. Most of these events occurred near the Kabba because that is where Muhammad (pbuh) prayed publicly and they always would try to stop him from doing that. Attaba bin Moeen put a cloth around the neck of the Prophet (pbuh) and squeezed the cloth to choke the Prophet

(pbuh). Until Abu Bakr stepped in and pushed Attaba bin Moeen away and said do you want to kill a man just because he says my lord is Allah.

For some people they don't mind, being cursed and humiliated. But Umbia of Allah are very sensitive and have dignity and they all have respectable personalities. These insults were hurting the Prophet (pbuh) but he would continue his invitations (Dava) and carry on and he would follow the instructions from Allah to ignore them. The Prophet (Pbuh) would not respond to them and would not fight with them but would get on with his work.

Another incident in the Hadith narrated in the Bukhari Sharif. The Prophet (pbuh) was praying next to the Kabba and Abu Jehail came to the leaders of Quraish, they would always meet and sit next to the Kabba and he told them someone has slaughtered a camel who would go and pick up the contents of inside of a camel and dump them on the Prophet (pbuh) while praying, the most evil amongst them being Attaba bin Abu Moeen. He picked up the challenge and brought the inside of the camel and waited until the Prophet (pbuh) was in the position of Sajood and dumped them on the back of the Prophet (pbuh). The Prophet (pbuh) continued with his Sajood as nothing happened and then his daughter Fatima (Abpwh) saw what happened to her father and removed that. It is very hurting to children to see their parents being insulted and abused. The Prophet Muhammad (pbuh), after he finished his prayers, he made Dua against seven people and did this publicly in front of the people. O' Allah punish 1. Abu Jehail, 2.Attaba bin Moeen, 3.Otaba bin Rabia, 4.Sheeba bin Rabia, 5.Waleed bin Magira, 6.Omea bin Khalaf and7. Nazar bin Harris.

Abdullah bin Masood, He is a narrator of Hadith. This was very rare that the Prophet (pbuh) would make Dua against some people. The Prophet (pbuh) was hurt and made Dua in front of the Kabba. Abdullah bin Masood said, "I have seen with my own eyes all of these men were killed in the battle of Badr that was the fulfillment of Dua". They all died kafir (non-believers). And there are many other examples one can go through.

CHARACTER ASSASSINATION

Accusing the Prophet (pbuh), character assassination, they would attack the character of the Prophet (pbuh) to destroy the message, they would accuse the Prophet (pbuh) as being a magician. O' you are receiving the revelation you are insane, a magician and a liar. He is a sauth-sear. They would use any slandering term. Allah says they do not disbelieve you but they are rejecting the signs of Allah. Deep in their heart they know you are truthful and honest because they reject the message and they are attacking you. All the attacks are not because of your character but they are because of religion. Varka bin Nofal gave these words warning that you will be driven out of your land.

The Prophet Muhammad (pbuh) would go to the marketplace where people have competition in poetry and competition in speeches. Market place was a cultural center. And the best poems used to hang on the walls of the Kabba. Muhammad (PBUH) would also speak to the public, in this hadith, narrated by Imam Ahmed. Rabia bin Habab says I saw the Prophet in the market, he was saying, O' people say there is no God but Allah and you will be successful. He would repeat the message again and again, he would walk and meet different people. Rabia said, "there was a man following him, this man would go to the person the Prophet (pbuh) had spoken to and would say do not believe him. He is a liar".

Abu Laub, Rabia, asked people who that man was. People replied that was his uncle. We feel encouraged after seeing the fruits of our efforts for motivation these are the rewards. Before the Hajj season, Waleed bin Al-Magira addressed a meeting. He told them the season of Hajj is approaching and Arab delegations are coming. Let us unify our opinion and not contradict each other. What he was suggesting was that Muhammad (pbuh) will be visiting them and speaking to them. Let us have a unified opinion in order to go to people and warn them about this man people said sauth-sear. He said "No, people wouldn't believe he is not crazy, not a poet and not a sorcerer. Waleed bin Al-Mugair, after all they agreed on sorcery. But he said afterwards he is like a palm tree whose branches give a lot of fruit. The closest thing is to say he is a sorcerer who comes between a man and his religion, a man and his father, a man and his wife., A man and his brother and a man and his tribe. Allah revealed ayah: Surah Al-Mudassar.

CHANGING THE MESSAGE

A man went to Persia to learn stories. He came back and whenever he saw the Prophet (Pbuh) with people or speaking to people, he would call people and say come to me I have better stories to tell you. These are past stories who knows what happened to Moses and Jesus (EISA Pbuh).

Allah says, they claim these are tales or stories of the past, fabricated untrue. Who knows what happened to Moses and Jesus (Eisa Pbuh).

BARGAINING

Bargaining; the people of Quraish came to Muhammad (pbuh) and said, let us make a deal, we will agree to worship Allah one day and you worship our Gods another day, the messenger of Allah told them I shall never agree to do such a thing. They came back another time and said we have a better offer to make we shall worship Allah for one week and you worship our Gods for one day. The Prophet (pbuh) said no. They came back and offered we worship Allah for a month and you worship for one day.

The Prophet said no; Allah revealed Ayat; they wish to compromise with you. Their religion is manmade there is no control. But the Prophet is receiving messages from Allah, he cannot change. He cannot compromise on the message, O' disbelievers I am not going to worship what you do, nor you are going to worship what I do, you do what you do, I shall do what I do, I cannot worship your Gods for one minute in my life. You have your way and I have mine. They tried all different ways. But it would never work with Muhammad (pbuh). The Prophet (pbuh) said, I am only a conveyer of the message, the message is from Allah.

TEMPTATIONS - SETTING THE CHALLENGES

This narration is by Ibn Ishaque. Ibn Ishaque says leaders from Quraish met. They were next to the Kabba and send for Muhammad (pbuh). They wanted to try everything. Ibn

Abbas says Muhammad (pbuh) came. He was eager because he thought they have changed, maybe they are willing to listen. He came in a hurry, when he arrived, Ottaba started to speak to Muhammad (pbuh). Many other leaders were there, they said, O' Muhammad (pbuh) we want to reconcile with you started with a nice statement. By God we do not know anybody who has caused as much trouble as you have, you have criticized the religion and ridiculed the values. Cursed the Gods, divided our community. Every unpleasant thing possible you have done to make a rift between you and us, we have not seen another person who has brought so much evil as you have.

Now they are trying to throw temptations to Muhammad (pbuh). O' Muhammad (pbuh) if you are presenting us with this message because you need money, we will collect money until we make you the wealthiest among us. If you want power, we will appoint you king over us. If you desire women, we will choose the best 10 women and marry all of them to you. If there is a Demon, we will spend wealth to cure you. Tell us what you want. The Prophet (Pbuh) responded and said that what you have said doesn't apply to me, I have not brought the message to seek money or honor among you. I have been sent as a messenger to warn you. I have brought you the message from my lord and have given you the council. If you accept the message that is good for you in this world and in the hereafter, if not then I shall wait until Allah decides between you and me. These are the approximate words of the Prophet Muhammad (pbuh).

Then they said, "if you are turning down our offers, then you know how narrow our land is", For those of you, who have seen Makkah. Makkah is surrounded by mountains, It is a very rough environment, how poor we are and how difficult our life is. Ask your Allah to remove these mountains away, just level them, give us more space, land and ask your Lord to flow some rivers in Makkah like the rivers of Syria and Iraq. Also ask your Lord to bring back some of our forefathers, and bring back O'sai bin Kalab, who was a true Sheikh. We want to ask him what you are saying is true or not. O' Muhammad (pbuh), if you do that and our forefathers agree then we shall follow you. Muhammad (pbuh), responded and said this is not why I have been sent. I have only brought from God, what he has sent me with. A message if you accept it is good for you in this world and other, if not, I shall wait for Allah's decree to decide between us, they continued and said how about, if you ask your Allah to send down angels to witness and ask your Allah to give cattle treasures Gold and silver.

Why don't you ask Allah to fulfill your needs ask him to give you wealth, so we know how close you are with him. That is if you are claiming to be a messenger.

The Prophet (pbuh) replied this is not for me. I am not for that; God has sent me with a message.

Then they said, ask your God to bring down the punishment. Bring the sky over our head and show us if you can. The Prophet (pbuh) said that is up to Allah, they said O' Muhammad (pbuh) doesn't your lord know that we are about to ask you these questions and he is not helping you answer them. We know who is teaching you. You are being taught the Holy Quran by a man his name is Rakhman. We are never going to believe that man. Man from Yamama called Rakhman. Something they made up and fabricated.

They left and one of them came back to Muhammad (pbuh), Abdullah bin Omea felt sorry for what had happened. One might think, perhaps he wanted to become Muslim. His mother is the aunt of the Prophet (pbuh). He came and said O' Muhammad these people have offered you the best, but you turned them down, and they asked you to perform miracles for them and you refused. They asked to bring down punishment on them and you didn't. Now, bring down a ladder and go to Allah, while I am watching ask Allah to write a letter stating that you are his Prophet. Have him sign it and then we want that document to come down with four angels to witness that you are a messenger from God. Even then I am not going to believe you. Dead End; nothing will work with these people (If they see every sign they would not believe) The Messenger of Allah went back home disappointed.

Pressure: Akeel the son of Abu Talib. He says Quraish came to Abu Talib and told him, your nephew is disturbing us, tell him to stay away from us, Abu Talib send Akeel to call Muhammad (pbuh). Akeel says he found Muhammad (pbuh) in a small room or tent. It was very hot. Muhammad (pbuh) came, Uncle Abu Talib told him people are complaining, and people say you are disrupting them, meaning disturbing them in their meetings so why don't you stop. Abu Talib was not giving an order but advising that it is better in a way. The Prophet (pbuh) looked up in the sky and said "O' my uncle you see that sun", uncle said yes. The Prophet said," I am no more capable of stopping it than you are able to get me a flame from the sun". This is part of me I cannot stop. Invitation (Dava) in my life spreading Islam is my mission, I cannot give it up. Also, you must have heard that the Prophet (pbuh) said, if they put sun on my right hand and moon on my left hand I shall not give it up until Allah decides or I lose my life.

Uncle told the Prophet (pbuh), I know you are telling the truth, I believe you and go and continue. When Muslims fled and went to Abyssinia, Quraish would not give up and sent some delegation to persuade Najashi to turn these people out. Muslims were no threat to Quraish in Abyssinia. Quraish wanted to stop this message by all means possible.

JEALOUSY AND HATRED

Al Waleed bin Mugharia said, If Allah wanted to choose a Prophet (pbuh) why didn't he choose me. I am wealthy, wise and older than Muhammad and there was a similar claim made in Tahaif. Two prominent towns were Makkah and Tahaif.

Allah revealed an Ayat, explaining why this Holy Quran was not revealed on a great man. From one of the two towns referring to Makkah and Tahaif. Al Mugharia bin Shaba was from Tahaif visiting Makkah, he said (Hadith), my first contact with Muhammad (pbuh) happened one day when I was walking with Abu Jehail in Makkah and we met Muhammad (pbuh). He walked up to us and spoke to Abu Jehail and gave him invitation (Dava), believe in Allah, Abu Jehail responded and said, O' Muhammad when are you going to stop cursing our Gods. If you want us to testify that you have fulfilled your mission, we all testify for you. If I knew you were telling the truth, I would have already followed you. Muhammad (pbuh) left, because the Prophet (pbuh) was saying again and again my role is to convey the message. It is up to Allah to convert you.

Al-Mugharia said, Abu Jehail looked at me and said I know he is telling the truth. But there is something holding me back. The descendants of Kasai bin Kalab wanted to have Hajaba- Honor, the power and authority. We gave the authority of Hajaba and Nadwa. Now we are competing with them and they say we have a Prophet among us. How can we compete with that, by God we are never going to accept this power struggle. Element of jealousy and power. The messenger will change the status. If we accept i.e. Quraish we would not be able to take advantage of others and to enslave others. This religion will free others to worship Allah.

PERSECUTION

Although the Prophet (Pbuh) wasn't harmed and insulted but false accusations directed against him. He was not persecuted. This is the part of protection from Allah. Allah has protected the Prophet (pbuh) in his early years through his uncle Abu Talib. Later on, they would try to assassinate him, Allah will protect even though Uncle Abu Talib has passed away.

But his followers were persecuted. This is the opinion of Ibn Ishaque. That used to hurt the Prophet, because he cared about them so much. Nearly all of the followers were persecuted one way or the other. They would wrap them up in the sheets of iron and leave them in the sun to burn. The strongest inciter was Bilal. The more they punish him the stronger he would become. He was asked how you could say Allah is one when being punished. He said I found out when I say Aud, Allah is one that would make them angry. He sold himself to Allah, Gave himself to Allah. He would say Aud and Omea bin Khalf would become angry. He would add the punishment and Bilal would say Aud loudly. There were different forms of torture. And the torture was not limited to slaves and servants but to some noble people, Usman bin O'Fan belonged to Banu Amia, one of the noble families of Quraish, he was wrapped in a carpet and they would jump over him and crush him inside the carpet. You are familiar what happened to slaves like Somia, her husband and her son. Somia and her husband both were killed under severe torture of Abu Jehail. In one narration Abu Jehail struck Somia in her private parts with a spear until he killed her.

All of that sociological and physical pain, the son saw his mother and father were killed. Omara (son of Somia and her husband) Buckled under this pressure and spoke some words

45

against Muhammad (pbuh). When he woke up from pain, he went to Muhammad (pbuh), he was sad and sorry, and also told what had happened. Allah revealed a Surah dealing with that particular situation. Saying one is excused to speak, some words with the tongue under this torture. If the heart is confident with the faith. Allah doesn't over burden a person. This presentation continued with all except few, who had strong family background, Abu Jehail was at the forefront. Ibn Ishaque says Abu Jehail incited the Quraish men. When he would hear some one of a status has accepted Islam he would upgrade his insults by saying you have abandoned the religion of forefathers. A man better than you, we will depreciate your value, your opinion and we would boycott doing business with you. We will ruin you. If Muslim was defenseless he would incite the others, May Allah destroy Abu Jehail. Abu Jehail was a spear head of the efforts of Quraish against the Muslims in Makkah. Umar bin Khattab would torture a slave girl. Sometimes he would stop, but say no sympathy words, but taking a rest, only because he was tired. But Allah guides whoever he wills.

ASSASSINATION ATTEMPT

When everything else failed they tried to eliminate the messenger of Allah. These attempts occurred after Abu Talib passed away. They knew, they could not do that during his life. Allah says, they attempted to drive you out of your land to imprison you and to kill you.

How the Prophet (Pbuh) responded to all that. In Bukhari Sharif. Khabab bin Ark went to the Prophet when he was leaning with the wall of the Kabba. And said "O' messenger of Allah why don't you make Dua for us?" The message implies we are going through a lot. Why don't you ask Allah to ease the pain. Later on, when Umar was Khalifa, Umar was asking around to talk about their experiences in Makkah. When the turn of Khabab bin Ark came, he didn't speak but lifted his shirt and exposed his back. Umar bin Khattab says, "I have never seen anything like this". What happened to you?

Khabab bin Ark had deep black holes in his back. He said, when I was in Makkah, Quraish would bring some rocks and burn them on fire until they turn red, then they lay them on the hot sand of Makkah and threw me on top of it. These rocks would burn through my flesh. And I would hear the burning of my flesh. And smell my fat. Khabab bin Ark had something to complain about. All he asked was, why don't you ask Allah to give us victory, what was the response of the Prophet? The Prophet (pbuh) sat straight and his face turned red, that would happen when the Prophet (pbuh) was angry. And then he said, a believer among those, before you, used to be combed with iron combs that would separate flesh, nerves from bones. But they will never desert their religion e.g. Moses and magicians, and they would bring one of them and put a saw on top of their heads, they would be cut in 2 halves. And yet they would never give up their religion in the name of Allah.

Allah will give his religion victory between Hazra Moat and Sanna, they will fear no one but Allah. Be patient. Allah has some laws you have to go through, what the nations before you went through with no short cuts. The Prophet wanted his Ummah to be the best. Hadith: Get married and multiply. Second hadith: I saw a huge nation, I asked the angels accompanying me, and these angels replied this is the Uma of Moses (pbuh). Bani Israel is the second largest Ummah after the Ummah of the Prophet Muhammad (pbuh). Then the angel told me to look on your right side. I saw people filling the horizon. Angels asked to look on the left side, I saw people filling the horizon. The Angel told me this is your Ummah. Allah will give you 70,000 who will enter paradise without reckoning. The Prophet said in another hadith, I was impressed and proud. Because he saw signs of Wudhu and Sajood.

Allah will complete his religion until, a traveler will leave Sanna and Hazra Moat, fearing no one but Allah. Yemen used to be and still is tribal society. At the time of the Prophet all that area was covered by arm tribes and insecure area, when Islam came to Yemen the whole area was peaceful and today it is again and insecure area. Because the people have left Islam. Quraish gathered and wanted to find expertise in poetry and magic to go to Muhammad and ask him how to deal with him. They decided to send Attaba bin Rabia who was an expert in these areas. He went to the Prophet and said, "O' Muhammad tell me, who is better you or Abdul Mutlab?" These questions are set up. In Arabian society, they have respect and glory for the ancestors. The family of the Prophet was held in very high esteem. Osuy bin Kalab, Hashim and Abdul Mutlab, these were glorified people. One cannot just speak against any one of them. Attaba who is not from the family of Banu Hashim is asking the opinion of the Prophet (pbuh) about them. The Messenger of Allah didn't answer but remained silent. Attaba said, "If you feel they are better than you, they have worshiped the Gods you dislike". If you claim that you are better than them, then speak we can hear what you say. By God we have never seen any fool more harmful than you.

Arabs say, there is a magician or a sorcerer amongst Quraish. Attaba is putting blame on the Prophet. But the rumors were started by Quraish and Attaba was among them. As a result, we are waiting for a cry of a pregnant woman meaning Quraish will be fighting each other, then he made the offers again. The Prophet allowed him (Attaba) to carry on with this nonsense without interrupting him. The Prophet was a good listener. When Attaba finished. The Messenger of Allah asked him, O' Attaba are you done. He said yes. The Prophet (pbuh) did not respond to his words. But he started reciting from Surah Bismillah (Ameen). A revelation from most merciful and beneficent. A book whose verses are in Arabic for people who are aware. He went on and on about a page. Quite a few Ayat, He went on until he reached I warn you about a terrible punishment like it destroyed Audh and Sa- mood. Nations of Hud and Saleha, in one narration it is said when the Prophet recited these Ayat. Attaba placed his hands on the mouth of the Prophet (pbuh) and urged him to stop. Because this Ayat warns, about punishment. Attaba knew in his heart, Muhammad (pbuh) is truthful. He never said anything, which did not come to happen, and he is threatening us with punishment. He said, I ask you in the name of relationship between us to stop. In another narration, Attaba went back to his people they asked him what happened? He said, the Prophet (pbuh) recited Holy Quran, I didn't understand anything except he threatened with punishment like Audh and Sa- mood, they said, woe to you, he was speaking to you in Arabic and you didn't understand him. He said in the name of Allah, I did not understand what he was saying. In the same Ayat, the Holy Quran says some people have a seal over their heart, so they will not understand. The Messenger of Allah dealt with different situations in different ways, and many times he would use Holy Quran.

The story of Womadh Al Azadi from Southern Arabia. He heard from people in Makkah someone who is obsessed by jinn, they were referring to Muhammed (pbuh). He used to heal people who were obsessed by jinn with right intentions

Womadh Al Azadi went to the Prophet (pbuh) to offer his help. It was insulting but Prophet (pbuh) was very patient, that this man might have heard wrong information. The Messenger of Allah started with the words Khutbah Till-Hajj. Praise be to Allah we praise him and seek his help whomever Allah leads right, no one can lead astray, and whomever Allah leads astray no one can lead him right. I bear testimony that there is no God but Allah alone, who has no associates, words in Arabic are beautiful. But translation is not the same. Womadh interrupted the Prophet, he said O' Muhammed can you repeat these words again please. The Messenger repeated words again like this. Womadh said I have never heard these words, which are so wonderful they will reach the bottom of the ocean. The Messenger of Allah said, "then pledge your allegiance to me and become Muslim." He immediately extended his hand and read Kalma Shahadat (second Kalma) The Messenger asked how about your tribe? He said, "I shall pledge for my people". He left after a short meeting as a Muslim that was the personality of the Prophet.

Years later the Muslim army was sent in the area where his village was. The leader of the army asked, "Have you taken anything from these people? "One soldier said yes, I have taken a strong camel. The leader said, give it back because there are the people of Womadh. The Messenger of Allah has given them protection.

Another story, A man called Amer bin Afsha, a man from Arabia, Amer bin Afsha says, in the time Jahiliya in the time of ignorance, I had belief in my heart that the religion of my people is false. I had no trust in worshipping Idols, one day I came to know that there is a man in Makkah preaching a new religion. I went on my camel to meet him. But a person from outside Makkah, couldn't meet the Prophet publicly. He had to meet secretly. He asked who you are! The Prophet replied I am a Prophet. He said what does that mean, the Prophet said, I was sent by Allah. What did he send you with? One can notice the simplicity of this Badoo, they sent me with a message worshipping him alone. Associating no Gods with him. And to destroy Idols. He said can I follow you? The Prophet said, you cannot follow me now, you know my situation, but go back to your people. When you hear that I prevailed then come and see me. The Messenger of Allah knew that he will prevail one day. Amer bin Afsha said, I left, and I would ask for any news about the Prophet. Until one day I heard that the Prophet has migrated to Madinah, and has been victorious, so I went to meet him there. He says, I approached the Prophet and asked him, do you know me? This was years later and I had met for a short time. The Messenger of Allah said yes. You are the man who came and met me in Makkah. This is another leadership quality. You know your followers (Amer bin Afsha). The Prophet Suleyman (pbuh) was inspecting his Army, made of human, Jinn and Birds. He noticed the absence of one bird hudhud (Hoopy). One soldier was absent, and only Allah knows the number of his army.

The prophet (pbuh) taught Amer Bin Afsha, Salah and Wudhu. Another story of Abu Zr Ghaffari but it is a long story. Amar bin Ass, He was a diplomat and a highly intelligent man. He had wide connections. He was friendly with many kings of the world. He was a mastermind in plotting and planning. He was a leader against Islam. That was Amer bin Auss before Islam. Amer bin Ass went to Najashi. He met top officials first and gave them gifts. He wanted to say that in your land, there are some fools who ran away from Makkah they do not believe in our religion nor do they believe in your religion.

HIJRA TO AL-HABSHA, THERE ARE TWO MIGRATIONS THAT TOOK PLACE.

The first migration happened in the fifth year of Prophethood, after revelations. That was a small group of twelve men and four women. The second Hijra that was a larger group of eighty-three men and eighteen or nineteen women.

When the first group went they heard rumors that the people of Quraish have become Muslim. The Messenger of Allah received Ayat of Surah Najam. He recited those Ayat. Those Ayat were so powerful that they influenced Quraish, when they heard the lost Ayat which is the Ayat of Sajood.

The Prophet and Muslims made Sajida and Kufr made Sajood with them. And that was the origin of the false rumors. The Quraish have become Muslim, the first group came back, but it was false. Then the second Hijra was a larger group. The Messenger of Allah saw this pain and suffering, he said, why you don't go to Habsha, because there is a king who doesn't oppress anyone. The king is just, so they went. The first ones to leave were Usman and his wife, the daughter of the Prophet Muhammed (pbuh). There is a saying, Usman bin O'Fan made Hijrah for the sake of Allah, they went to Habsha and the second group came in. But Quraish wouldn't leave them alone, the people of Quraish assembled a delegation to ask Najashi to turn over these Muslims. Delegation brought some gifts.

They chose Amer bin Auss and Abdullah bin Rabia. Amer bin Auss went to Najashi and told him to give back the fools who came to your country. Najashi said, no until I hear their side of story. Najashi called the Muslims to come and meet him. Muslims had Shura, had advised Jaffar bin Abu Talib to be their spokesman, and they will speak the truth.

Najashi asked, you have left your religion, and did not join mine. Who are you? Hadith narrated by Uma Salma. Jaffar said, He is also the cousin of the Prophet Muhammed (pbuh). (These are the exact words) OK we were people of Idolism, we worship idols. We ate the meat of dead animals, offended rules of hospitality and permitted forbidden, we shed the blood of each other (killing each other). We completely ignored rules of right and wrong. So, God sent us a Prophet who is trustworthy and honest, we knew him well. He gave the history background and established integrity of the Prophet. He summoned us to pray to God alone without associates, told us the rights of kinship and honor rights of hospitality. Pray to God who is glorious, fast for him and worship none other than him. Tawheed and morals of Islam. He called us to God, to affirm his oneness and teardown other idols, whom our forefathers worshipped. He ordered us to be truthful in our speech. To our trust and to respect kinship ties. And to abandon forbidden things and shedding of blood. He stopped us from immoral things, lies to misuse the funds for orphans and to make false accusations against women of virtue. He ordered us to worship Allah and associate no one with him and told us, to pray and keep fasts. It was a brief and to the point speech. He didn't turn it in to an argument or debate. Remember he is dealing with a king. And so, we believed in him and trusted him. But our people were aggressive and harmed us. We chose your country and your hospitality and we hope we shall not be harmed in your domain. The king said, have you brought anything with you i.e. (the Holy Quran). Jaffar bin Abu Talib recited some Ayat from the Holy Quran which one did he choose? (Surah Marriam).

Amma Salma says, I swear the Najashi wept, his beard was soaked, and all their bishops cried, they wet their bibles. King Najashi refused to hand over the Muslims to the Quraish delegation, as soon as the Muslims and the Quraish delegation left, Amer bin Auss threatened to come back, and I shall bring an end to Muslims. Abdullah bin Rabia, his assistant said, do not do that, they are our relatives. But Amer bin Auss said, I am going to tell the king that Muslims say Jesus is a slave. He came back the next day and told Najashi, that Muslims say Jesus is a slave and he is not a Son of God. 'Amer bin Auss doesn't believe but to cause fittana'.

Najashi was concerned. He is a religious person. He recalled the Muslims again Amma Salma says, that worried us. But we decided to speak the truth. Najashi asked what you say about Jesus. Jaffar said, we say he is a messenger of Allah he is servant of Allah; He is the word of Allah casted on Mary (the chosen one and virgin). The king said there is no difference what you say and what I say. But bishops didn't like that response from Najashi. How he can approve such a thing Najashi said, say what you like but these people are going to be free in my land. Amer bin Auss and partners were forced to leave and even their gifts were returned, they were disgraced. Because Najashi had asked Amer bin Auss what did you bring. He replied leather goods, reasons (I) fled persecution (ii) to save religion. (Once a man came to the Prophet) and brought pure gold, the size of an egg and said this is all I have. The Prophet didn't want people to give up all their money and then ask for help. Keep some for yourself.

ABU BAKR'S STORY

Different reasons, some well-of people fled (Uma Habiba). (Nagas became Muslim, he didn't practice but he believed). But his Islam was not made public, on his death the Prophet said, let us pray on him. People when meeting Nagas would make Sajood. Amer bin Auss told him that Muslims will not, when Muslims came they did not make Sajood. Najashi was angry why don't you make Sajood. Muslims said we only make Sajood to Allah, Muslims were organized as they had an Ameer Jaffar bin Abu Talib.

HAMZA BIN ABDUL MUTLAB AND HIS ACCEPTANCE OF ISLAM

He was a hunter. He would go out hunting and on his return, tell the stories of what happened during those days. One day while Hamza was out hunting Abu Jehail approached the Prophet (pbuh) and started cursing him. The Messenger of Allah stayed silent. The Prophet (pbuh) would not respond to ignorant words. Muslim should not involve invitation (Dava) into personal things. If a person is calling to Islam and insults are directed at him, he shouldn't take it personally. Allah says they are not rejecting you but the message you are presenting. Abu Jehail threw a rock at the Prophet (pbuh) that hit him in his head. The Prophet was bleeding, a slave girl saw that and when Hamza came back from hunting she told him the whole story. Hamza was very upset. When he found out that, this had happened to his nephew. Although Hamza was Mushriq (non-Muslim) at the time. Because of the relationship he felt that attack on Muhammed (pbuh) was an attack on him. He walked up to Abu Jehail who was sitting with other leaders of Quraish in front of the Kabba.

Hamza had just come back from hunting and was carrying his bow with him. He walked up to Abu Jehail and hit him on his head with his bow. He said, take it and I am now following the religion of Muhammed (pbuh), when Hamza said that he did not say it out of conviction. He said it out of pride and anger to Abu Jehail. Blood was flowing (Banu Mukhzoom), the relatives of Abu Jehail stood up to fight Hamza but then Banu Hashim stood up to protect Hamza. They were about to fight until Abu Jehail said leave Hamza alone, because I did attack his nephew, Muhammed (pbuh) shamelessly. Abu Jehail calmed things down. When Hamza went home he was surprised at the action he himself took. Later on, he started to assess things, was it right or wrong? He thought he was in trouble because he did not think it properly. He asked a question to himself should I become Muslim or not. If I withdraw, I have already told Abu Jehail this will be dishonoring on my part. In their culture it is not right, one day say, I am Muslim and next day no I am not a Muslim.

It was difficult for him to back out but also difficult to commit, because he never really thought about it. Hamza says, he prayed to Allah at night to guide me to the truth. O' Allah if it is the right decision then put the love of Islam in my heart and if it is wrong then show me the way out of this. Early in the morning Hamza bin Abdul Mutlab says when I woke up. I had my heart filled with the love of Islam. I went to the messenger of Allah and told him; I am a Muslim. That was one of the greatest moments for the Prophet to have his uncle on his side that is how Hazrat Hamza bin Abdul Mutlab became Muslim. It would have caused sorrow for Abu Jehail.

UMER BIN KHATAB AND HIS ACCEPTANCE OF ISLAM

Umar bin Khattab was an enemy of Islam and was very ruthless. One day, Layla the wife of Rubia, met Umar bin Khattab, Umar asked Uma-Abdullah where are you heading. She said you have maltreated us. So, I am going to leave to go to one of God's countries to worship my Lord. She was going to Abyssinia. Umar told her May peace be with you, may you have a safe journey, that was a strange statement coming from Umar. Umar bin Khattab showed no sympathy towards any Muslim male or female. When her husband came she told him. Her husband laughed and said are you expecting Umar to become a Muslim. She said maybe, the husband said Umar will not become Muslim until the donkey of his father becomes Muslim. It is impossible.

Umar bin Khattab narrates his own story and says I use to love drinking. I had some friends we would meet every night. We are to meet in a place called (Hazara). One evening I was late and didn't find anyone. I decided to go to a wine dealer, but I found his shop closed. Umar says I went looking for other options, I did not find any. He thought why not make tawaf around Kabba. I (Umar) went there and found Muhammed (pbuh) there. There he saw the Prophet (pbuh) was praying late, there was no one else and the Prophet (pbuh) did not sense my presence. Umar says, I wanted to sneak and attack him i.e. (the Prophet), Secondly, I wanted to listen to what he was reciting. Muhammed (pbuh) would pray, with Kabba in front of him also towards Jerusalem, the Emily corner with the black stone. Umar says I went from behind and I was between cloth and the wall of the Kabba (sneaked inside the cloth).

Back towards the wall, and cloth covered him one can't see him. Umar says I was sneaking around the wall of the Kabba until I came right in front of Muhammed (pbuh). There was nothing between us other than the cloth of the Kabba. Umer says, then I was able to hear his (the Prophet's) recitation. He was reciting from Surah Al- Haqq, Umer says I just froze in my tracks. Listening to the wonderful words of The Holy Quran. Then I told myself these must be the words of a poet. The next Ayat was these are not words of a poet little you believe. Umer says, I was shocked, how did he know what was in my heart must be words of a sorcerer. The next Ayat was that there are not the words of a sorcerer little do you remember. Umer says that was the first step bringing me near to Islam. Now the Kufr in the Heart of Umer is cracked. But his heart is still filled with hatred towards Muhammed (pbuh) and Muslims.

One day Umer decides, he will end the misery amongst the Quraish once and for all. He is going to kill the Prophet. Anyone who becomes Muslim they will call him Sabaean. Umer found out Muhammad (pbuh) was in Darul-Arkm with his followers. Umer knew he could be killed but he was determined to do that. He picked up a sword and he was walking alone down the streets of Makkah. He met one of his relatives who was Muslim in secret. His name is Naheem. Naheem saw Umer, saw evil in his eyes, he asked Umer where are you heading? He said, I am going to Muhammed (pbuh) to kill him. Naheem had to think on the spot. Naheem said, why you don't take care of your household first. Umer said, what is wrong with my household? Naheem said your sister has become Muslim. By saying that Naheem has put Umar's sister and her husband in danger (Fatima bin Khattab) Fatima was the wife of Saeed bin Zahid bin Amr bin Nofail Saeed is one of the ten (10) people who has been given glad tidings of paradise (Jannah). Umer bin Khattab changed course and was heading towards his sister's house. Khabab bin Ark was teaching Fatima and her husband Holy Quran. He had his scrolls with him and was reciting Surah Taha, when they heard the footsteps of Umer, Khabab bin Ark went in to hiding and Fatima put the scrolls under her thigh then Umer came in. He asked what that sound that I heard, they said we didn't hear anything but Umer said I did hear you, tell me what it was? Then he said I have heard you have become Muslim and immediately attacked Saeed bin Zahid. Umer started punching him and Fatima interfered, and stood up to defend her husband, Umer hit her in the face. When Umer saw blood on his sister's face he became very sorry, and he apologized, she said I am Muslim and my husband is Muslim and do whatever you want.

Umer asked for scrolls, she said no Umer swore in the names of his Gods that I shall return it back to you. She said you are polytheize and impure. Umer went and washed himself and came back (Fatima). She gave him the scrolls and he recited the first verses of Surah Taha. Bismillah we have not sent down the Quran that you be distress, but only as a reminder for those who fear Allah. A revelation from the one who has created the earth and the highest heaven the most merciful, to him belongs what is in the heavens and what is on the earth and what is in between and what is under the soil. If you speak loudly he knows what is secret and what is even more hidden. Allah, there is no deity except him, to him belongs the best names. When Umer finished, he said these are wonderful words. When Khabab bin Ark heard that he came out of hiding and said O' Umer, I hope that God will choose you. Because I heard yesterday, the messenger of Allah made Dua. O' Allah guide one of the two Umars. Umer bin Khattab or Umer bin Sham. And I hope you are the one Allah will select. Umer bin Khattab told Khabab bin Ark, I want to become Muslim. Where can I meet Mohammed (pbuh)? Khabab bin Ark told him in Dar -ul -Arkm. Umer bin Khattab went to Dar -ul -Arkm. He knocked on the door that was a secret meeting place. One of the companions peaked through the door, he saw Umer bin Khattab. He told the Prophet (pbuh). The Sahabi were frightened and told Umer bin Khattab, is outside and he is carrying his sword too. Who in that gathering offered to open the door? Who can stand up and face Umer bin Khattab?

Hamza bin Abdul Mutlab. He said O' messenger of Allah if Umer came with good reason we will reciprocate but if he came with bad intention then I shall kill him with his own sword, the messenger of Allah said, No I shall open the door for him. The Prophet (pbuh) went and opened the door. Umer bin Khattab was one of the tallest men of Quraish. When Umer bin Khattab was Khalifa, they received some pieces of cloth from one of the Islamic states. Umer bin Khattab distributed evenly, one piece to each one. When Umer bin Khattab stood up to give Khutbah. He had two pieces on him. He said, listen and obey, Suleyman Pharsi stood up and said we shall not listen and not obey. Umer said, why? Suleyman Pharsi said you have given us one pieces and you have two pieces of cloth. Umer bin Khattab did not respond but told his son Abdullah to respond. Abdullah bin Umer stood up and said, my father is a tall man, very well built and one piece of cloth wouldn't be enough for him therefore I gave him mine. Suleyman pharsi said, now we shall hear and obey, that was the standard of justice they had. Even the Khalifa could not have preference over masses. The messenger of Allah opened the door for Umer and Muhammed (pbuh) was medium height and medium built. The Prophet (pbuh), hold Umer by his clothes and dragged him in and brought him down on his knees and said O' Umer when you are going to stop. Are you waiting for Allah to strike you with the thunderbolt? Umer bin

Khattab said, O' messenger of Allah, I have come to become Muslim.

This happened between the Prophet and Umer, near the gate other Sahaba did not see what was happening as they were in another room. When Umer said that the Prophet (pbuh) said Allah Hu Akbar, other Sahaba realized Umer has become Muslim, they were so happy with the news. They made loud Takbir and immediately dispersed. The Takbir was heard by the people of Makkah. Islam of Umer was a turning point, in the history of Islam in Makkah. Abdullah bin Masood says Islam of Umer was a victory. His immigration to Madinah, helped Islam and his Reign as Khalifa was mercy. Abdullah bin Masood says we were not able to pray in front of the Kabba publicly until Umer became Muslim. Islam of one person changed the Muslim community that is how valuable assert Umer was. Abdullah bin Masood says after Umer became Muslim we would proudly proclaim Islam.

It is in Seerah history, when Umer became Muslim the Prophet (pbuh) lined up Muslims in two Ranks. One Rank headed by Hamza bin Abdul Mutlab and the other by Umer bin Khattab, they went down the streets of Makkah marching publicly, proclaiming their religion while the Prophet (pbuh) walking between the two Ranks. When Umer became Muslim he asked who is the biggest mouth in Makkah, who can publicize this news. that was Jamil. He announced to the people Umer has become Muslim. After People heard the news, they wanted to kill Umer bin Khattab. But a relative of Amer bin Auss gave protection to Umer bin Khattab.

When Quraish saw that Muslims were living in Abyssinia, Land of King Nagas. And Umer has accepted Islam along with Hamza bin Abdul Mutlab, Islam was catching up rapidly. Now the only solution was to kill the Prophet. That led them to sign embargo against the Prophet (pbuh). Now Quraish asked

Banu Hashim to handover Muhammed (pbuh). Well, Banu Hashim refused. As a result, was between various tribes of Quraish to boycott Banu Hashim. The message started, in the 7th year in the month of Mahram, then embargo started. Embargo: It was no one will deal with them, no trade will be conducted, and no one will marry them or until they get rid of Prophet Muhammed (pbuh). It was commercial blockade. The Quraish wanted no food to he supplied to Banu Hashim and Banu Mutlab. The Quraish signed the document and posted inside the Kabba, things became very harsh. Banu Hashim and Banu Mutlab were suffering hunger. Two to three years passed and Hashim bin Harris was helping secretly. He found four other likeminded people next day in Nadwa. They spoke against the document, when they went to tear it down, the termite had eaten, the document but two words. Bismillah. Embargo was ended. This was the first miracle.

THE SECOND MIRACLE, AN INCIDENT

Rukhana was the strongest wrestler in Makkah. Rukhana never lost a wrestling match. He was a Mushriq (non-Muslim). He came to Muhammed (pbuh) and said would you challenge me? The Prophet (pbuh) amazingly accepted the challenge, Rukhana had an evil intention. He wanted to humiliate the Prophet. He wanted to lay his hands on the Prophet but he did not know the surprise waiting for him, they started to fight, the Prophet of Allah was able to turn him upside down and throw him on the ground. Rukhana could not believe what had happened, he stood up again and wanted to fight second time, the Prophet did it a second time, then Rukhana tried a third time and he lost for three times in a row. Rukhana said, no one had put my back on the ground except you and no one was more hateful in my eyes than you. But now I testify that there is no God but Allah and that you are the messenger of Allah. By the way, the agreement was that whoever wins will get one hundred sheep. After that betting was made Haram. The Prophet gave Rukhana back the one hundred sheep. But that shows us the strength the Prophet had. The Prophet had the strength of 30 men.

THE THIRD MIRACLE

The people of Quraish asked for a sign, (the Holy Quran is the greatest miracle). But Allah revealed it through Angel Gabriel. If they are asking for a sign, we shall split the moon. The time was set, the Prophet called the non- believers and said, the moon will be split. The non-believers gathered and right in front of them, the moon was split in two halves, and then it came back together. This is a unique miracle and it is firmly established in the books of Hadith, in Bukhari Sharif and Muslim, and in the Holy Quran. In Bukhari Sharif, the splitting of moon came between Hijrah to Hubisha and Umer accepting Islam. In Muslim, Hadith: by Abdullah bin Masood, He says, "we were with the Prophet in Minha, the moon was split up in to two halves. One part was behind the mountain and other part on this side of the mountain". The messenger of Allah said, bear witness to this. Allah says when they saw the sign of Allah what did they say? They said he threw or cast magic on our eyes. Allah says the hour of judgment is near, they accused the Prophet of performing magic. We say that the moon did split up. Another sign there was continuous rivalry between the Roman and Persian Empires, they were the two superpowers of the world. Persia had Iran, part of Iraq, Afghanistan may be part of India and went up north.

Roman Empire included Turkey, parts of Eastern Europe. Armenia and Azerbaijan. These were the two superpowers of the world. In one critical battle the Persian defeated the Romans. The pagans of Makkah were incredibly happy. And Muslims were sad at this outcome. Because Persians were worshippers of fire, and pagans were closer to them therefore non-Muslims of Makkah were happy when pagans won. While Christians were on the side of Romans, people of the book, closer to Muslims. Mushriqeen of Makkah went around telling Muslims, just like that we are going to defeat Muslims.

Allah revealed the verse, Allah says Romans have been defeated but they will be victorious within 10 years. Abu Bakr learned these verses and went to Abu Jehail. He said, I tell you that Romans will win in less than 10 years there was a bet of one hundred camels. Abu Jehail saw, that Persians were rolling on and nothing will stop them. But Abu Bakr believed the verses of the Holy Quran. Allah says when Romans win the believers will be joyful, due to the victory of Allah. Allah is the one who gives victory to whom he will. Romans will win and believers will be happy. Eight years passed, and the Romans won. The news reached to Muslims. They did really care about it. The reason was that the day they received the news that day they won, the battle of Badr, that overshadowed everything. That was the true rejoiceful for the believers. Earlier, Muslims were only watching, they were not the major players of history. Now Muslims were fighting the kufr and were major players. But the miracles do not end there, there is another miracle, which falls under the scientific miracle of Quran. The word use in the Ayat means (i) the nearest and (ii) the lowest. Nearest, because Shaam was the nearest land to Arabs, new understanding, scientific where the battle occurred next to the Dead Sea in the lowest point on the face of the Earth. It is over 400 feet below sea level that is another miracle mentioned in this Ayat.

About 6 months after the end of Embargo the man who supported the messenger of Allah was now on his deathbed, leaving this world. Abu Talib was dying and Muhammed (pbuh) was on his side, the messenger of Allah told his uncle, say La Ilaha Ilala, there is no God but Allah, give me this word so that I can witness for you on the Day of Judgment. Give me something in my hand so that I can argue on your behalf on the Day of Judgment. All I want from you is to say La Ilaha Ilala, sitting on the other side was Abu Jehail. In Seerah, Abu Jehail is always in front. He was relentless in his efforts to fight the Prophet. He didn't give up until the last moment. Abu Jehail and Abdullah bin Abu Omiya were sitting on the other side. He said are you going to die on the religion other than Abdul Mutlab? The Prophet repeated O' my uncle says La Ilaha Ilala and Abu Jehail continued interrupting that went on until Abu Talib pronounced his last words. He said, I am dying on the religion of my father Abdul Mutlab. Those were his last words. This narration is in Bukhari Sharif there is another narration in Muslim Sharif. Abu Talib passed away the Prophet (pbuh) said, "I shall continue to ask Allah to forgive him", that was an exceedingly difficult moment for the Prophet (pbuh). Remember, Abu Talib took care of Muhammed (pbuh) at the age of eight. Abu Talib was defending, protecting and helping for forty-two years. Muhammed (pbuh) continued to ask Allah for forgiveness for his uncle, until the verse revealed. It is not fitting for a Prophet and those who believe that they should invoke Allah to forgive pagans even though they be a relative (kinship), after it becomes clear to them that they are companions of the fire. It is not for you to ask for forgiveness for one who died on disbelief the Prophet was forbidden from doing that.

In Muslim Sharif the Prophet (pbuh) was asking his uncle to say, La Ilaha Ilala, the uncle said, if it was not, that the Quraish would say I said it out of fear of death, I would do so and please you. Abu Talib knew it would please the Prophet (pbuh). It was a matter of honor. Allah says you cannot give guidance to the ones you love that is up to Allah, to guide whoever he pleases. The mission of the Prophet (pbuh) is to convey the message and not to convert. Converting the heart of a person is in the hands of Allah. Therefore, in Islam coercion is not allowed in religion, this is beyond our ability, it should be a matter of choice. The messenger of Allah was sad, and two months later Hazrat Khadija dies. The Prophet is dealing with the death of his dear uncle, now his dear wife dies. Both of his most beloved people passed away. This year was called Amal-Hazel (the year of sorrow), and this was the tenth year after the revelation. This was a tragic year for the Prophet (pbuh). He lost two of his most influential people in his life. Hazrat Khadija would offer encouragement, financial support and comfort. Abu Talib would offer physical support, suddenly these two pillars collapsed. It was a set back to the preaching of the message, the Prophet (pbuh) had freedom to go around because of his uncle, but now he was being watched. The Prophet remained two to three years unmarried. It was a difficult time.

Some scholars say, there is wisdom in this that Muslims would depend more on Allah. Allah revealed a Surah called Al-Ashura with difficulty comes easiness. This tragic time was followed with the best blessings given to him by Allah. Because of the size of the calamity the bounty that followed was even greater.

AL-ISRA WAL MI' RAJ

In Bukhari Sharif, the Prophet (pbuh) says while I was in the Kabba at night, I received a visitor, an Angel, who came and opened my Abdomen (Chest) and pulled out my heart, then my heart was placed in a Golden Basin filled with faith (Iman) my heart was placed in it and washed then stuffed and replaced. And then I was presented an animal smaller than horse and larger than a donkey. Anse bin Malik was narrating this hadith. A student asked a question, is this animal Al-Barak and he said yes. The Prophet (pbuh) said this animal will take a stride as for as it can see. The messenger of Allah is trying to describe the speed of this animal with one gallop, it would satisfy the whole distance as for as you can see, that was a very fast animal. Angel Gabriel told me to mount up this animal and then he would guide me (the Prophet). Muhammed (pbuh) says in another hadith in Muslim Sharif, (not Bukhari Sharif). The Prophet says that Angel Gabriel took me to Jerusalem and I tied my mount at the gate of the masjid (Al-Aqsa). Then I entered and prayed two Rakat. The messenger of Allah was an Imam and the people who were following him were the Prophets. Then the Prophet (pbuh) says I was led by Angel Gabriel up in the heavens, we made it all the way to the gates of the nearest heaven. Angel Gabriel knocked on the gates, the gate keeper said, who is it? Angel Gabriel said, it is Gabriel and the gatekeeper said who is with you, Muhammad was given permission Gabriel said yes. They responded by saying he is welcome and his arrival is a pleasure and they opened the gates. No one can enter without permission. Angel Gabriel was going up and down with Wahi (messages). The Prophet (pbuh) says I went in and I found in there my father Adam (pbuh). The Prophet (pbuh) said Gabriel introduced me to Adam (pbuh) and said this is your father Adam, and I said Assalaamu Alaykum.

Adam saluted me in return, and said Walaikum Salaam, then Adam said welcome to my pure son. Welcome to the pure Prophet, just imagine the pleasure and happiness the Prophet had. Adam is meeting his brightest son for the first time. After thousands of years. Imagine greeting to each other, it was a pleasure, they perhaps wanted to sit down and have a discussion but the schedule of the Prophet Muhammed (pbuh) was tight. Gabriel took Muhammad (pbuh) and they went to gates of the second Heaven. Gabriel knocked; the question came who are you? Answered; Gabriel, who is with you? Muhammad, permission, yes the Prophet (pbuh) says we went in. I met Isa (Jesus) (pbuh) and Yaya (John the cousin). As John the Baptist. The Prophet (pbuh) said, I exchanged the greetings with them Assalaamu Alaykum. Then we moved ahead to the third Heaven, knocked on the gates went through, there I met with Yusuf (Joseph) (pbuh), the Prophet says he has been given half of the beauty. We made it to the fourth heaven went through I met with Idris (pbuh). Allah says we have elevated him in the high fourth Heaven. We went to fifth Heaven, I met, Haroon (pbuh). Then to sixth Heaven there I met Musa (Moses) (pbuh).

It was an eventful meeting. Moses is always surrounded with important events. In the Quran one of the scholars says the Quran was going to be the story of Moses. Moses is mentioned frequently in Quran, one hundred and twenty-four times. When Muhammed (pbuh) passed him Moses started to weep, they greeted each other and Moses welcomed Muhammed (pbuh); Moses started to weep, when asked why are you weeping?, he said a young man given Prophethood. After me, but he will have more followers entering paradise (Jannah) than me. Up until that moment Moses had the largest following than any other Prophet the children of Israel are the largest believing nation. The Prophet says that I moved up to the seventh Heaven. I went in and met my father Ibraham (pbuh). In one narration, Ibraham was sitting leaning his back with Bait Ul-Mamoor is mentioned in the Holy Quran. Allah is making an oath in an established House. Bait Ul-Mamoor is equal to the Kabba to us. Just as we tawaf around Kabba and this is the first House established for worshiping to Allah on earth. The same is said about Bait Ul-Mamoor. As Muslims visit Kabba angels visit Bait Ul-Mamoor.

The Prophet (pbuh) says Bait Al-Mamoor is visited by 70,000 angels every day and they never come back to it again. How many angels are there and for how long? Then the Prophet says I went to Sidra Tul Mantha. It is a tree but it is at the end of the Heavens, beyond that the other life, paradise, thrown of Allah, Sidra Tul Mantha, the end of the universe created by Allah, beyond that is a different world. The Prophet (pbuh) saw four rivers emanating from it. The Prophet (pbuh) asked Gabriel what are these four rivers? He was told two of them are apparent and two of them are hidden, the apparent ones are the River Nile and River Ufratas and hidden ones are two rivers of paradise. River Nile and River Ufratus are two rivers blessed on earth and there are two equivalents. The tree is where two rivers are passing under it, seven Heavens, Bait ul Mamoor, Sidra Tul Mantha, and then another world. Comparatively the lower Heaven compared to the one above in a ring in the desert, likewise second to third and fourth and so on. And then the seventh Heaven compared to the throne of Allah is like a ring in a desert. All the universe is within the lowest Heaven. Allah says we have downed the lowest Heaven with stars. All the stars are located in the lowest Heaven. We have not been able to reach the creation of lowest stars. Every now and then we are discovering new galaxies, new clusters and new stars. It is a vast creation. The Prophet (pbuh) had the chance to go through all of it on that amazing journey. After passing the tree Sidra Tul Mantha. His trip went further up all the way until the Prophet (pbuh) met Allah. That was the combination of the trip. He reaches to the height and speaks to Allah directly, Allah prescribed on Muhammed (pbuh) 50 daily prayers. The Prophet (pbuh) says I descended on my way back I passed by Moses and Moses asked, what did Allah tell you? The Prophet said Allah has prescribed 50 daily prayers on my nation, Moses said your people will not be able to handle that, I have tested people before you and I have experienced children of Israel for a long time, go back to your lord to ask him to reduce it. Tell him to give you relief, Muhammed (pbuh), followed this advice and went back to Allah, and told him relieve me of some of the prayers. Allah reduced them by ten. Muhammed (pbuh)

Muhammed (pbuh) went down, Moses asked, what happened? Muhammed (pbuh) told him reduction often. Moses said, go back and ask for further reduction, Muhammad (pbuh) went back again and ten were reduced again Moses said go back the third time, Muhammed (pbuh) goes back another time Allah reduced from 30 to 20. Moses tells Muhammed (pbuh) to go back again they were reduced from 20 to 10. Moses said go back another time Muhammed (pbuh), goes back reduced to 5. Goes down reports to Moses, Moses (pbuh) says I know I have experience your nation will not be able to handle it. Go back and ask Allah to reduce them further Muhammed (pbuh), said I am ashamed to go back to Allah and ask for further reduction, I cannot. This is the difference between the personalities of Moses and Muhammed (pbuh). Moses would argue with Allah. Moses is the one who said O' Allah I want to see you. Allah has given the favor to Moses to speak to him. Moses wanted more. We know what happened, he collapsed. Moses (pbuh) is the one who punched the angel of death and knocked his eye out. Moses was strong, all Prophets are strong but have different personalities. Muhammed (pbuh) did not go back, but heard a voice saying, this is the prescription five daily prayers but you will receive the reward of fifty. The Prophet Muhammed (pbuh) made it back to this world on the same night. The Prophet went to Uma Amin and told her what had happened. He said I went to Jerusalem and back in this night. She said O' messenger of Allah do not tell anybody about this because no one will believe this. It is impossible, but Uma Amin believed herself, the journey towards Jerusalem use to take one month. The Prophet Muhammed (pbuh) said, "I will tell people". I shall convey the message regardless of what people will say. It is part of my mission I shall tell them what happened, my responsibility is to convey, the Prophet (pbuh) realized the weight of this news and how difficult it will be.

He went out, was quiet and sober (Clearheaded). He started to speak to some people, the news reached to Abu Jehail. The Prophet (pbuh) was sitting in the mosque, quiet and worried about the consequences of this news. Abu Jehail came to Muhammed (pbuh) and said, "O' Muhammed anything new?" Muhammed (pbuh) said, "Yes". Muhammed (pbuh) said this night I visited Jerusalem and came back. Abu Jehail said, "Jerusalem" Muhammed (pbuh) said yes. Abu Jehail said O' Muhammed if I call your people now, would you tell them the same thing what you have told me?" Muhammed (pbuh) said yes I would. Abu Jehail was happy and pleased, went running calling the people of Quraish. O' people of Quraish come forward. When they were all present and said O' Muhammed, can you please tell your people what you have told me a moment ago; Muhammed (pbuh) without any hesitation said, I have been to Jerusalem and back the previous night.

The narrator of the hadith says people started clapping, whistling and laughing. They made a big joke out of it. Some of the seasonal travelers who have been to Jerusalem asked Muhammed (pbuh), to describe the Mosque. Describe Jerusalem to us. The Prophet did not spend that much time there to remember every single detail of the place. But then Muhammed (pbuh) says Allah showed me the mosque, in front of my eyes and I described it stone by stone and brick by brick. They, the people said it is an exact and accurate description. In another narration by Ibn Ishaque: when Muhammed (pbuh) was coming back from Jerusalem to Makkah, he passed by a caravan belonging to the people of Quraish, they had lost a camel and because Muhammed (pbuh) was up in the air, he was able to see it. Muhammed (pbuh) called them and told them where the camel was, they didn't know where the voice was coming from, and then the Prophet (pbuh) drank some of their water and remembered the description of their caravan.

The Prophet (pbuh) told the people about this and they could confirm it. Also described the camel in front and its load. Quraish, immediately sent some people before the caravan reaches Makkah. It was still some distance away, the person found out the description to be accurate. They lost a camel, heard the voice from above and also missed some of their water. Even then all that was not sufficient for them to believe. The story of Al Isra Wal Miraj is so difficult for some people to handle. It caused some weak Muslims to apostate to change religion. But this is the case with amazing miracles of Umbia.

(i)   Opening the chest, twice
(ii) Isra, traveling at night
(iii) Miraj means ascending. Isra, journey from Makkah to Jerusalem, Miraj, Journey to Heavens
(iv) second conversation with Moses

When Moses went to meet Allah, the journey of 40 days, Allah told Moses in your absence your people have worshiped the calf. People deviated due to Sammary he made a calf out of gold. Allah told Moses everything that happened. Moses received from Allah ten tablets, (commandments). When Moses went back, he saw his people worshiping the calf. He threw tablets from his hand. Moses knew before, but his response was different when he saw. Because seeing is not like listening. When prayers came down to five, Moses wanted Muhammed (pbuh) to ask for a further reduction. He was right, we know now. May Allah, reward Moses (pbuh) that the prayers were reduced to five. The importance of Salah, there is no other command prescribed on us in heavens except Salah. Every other Ibadat was prescribed on earth. It was given special, during a one-to-one meeting between Allah and Muhammed (pbuh). Salah was given direct from Allah to Muhammad there was no one in between. Also, Moses received Salah in a direct meeting between Allah and Moses at Kohinoor. Surah Taha; I am Allah, there is no God beside me so establish prayers in my remembrance, and that was the moment when Moses (pbuh) became a Prophet. He was given the command when he became a Prophet. First La Ilaha Ilala and Second to pray. The Prophet (pbuh) says if Muslims do not pray, they have left Islam, prayer is the most important ritual in Islam.

THE IMPORTANCE OF HOLY LAND

Exalted is he who took his servant from Masjid Al-Haram to Masjid Al-Aqsa. Allah says, that is a blessed land, to show him our signs. Jerusalem was promised to the believers. Ibrahim (pbuh) was given that promise the believers will be the guardians of the holy land and that promise was fulfilled through Prophets of children of Israel. Allah also promised Jerusalem to Moses (pbuh). He did not see but it occurred in the lifetime of his successors, the Prophet Joshua (pbuh), the children of Israel remained in that land as long as they were the bearers of the truth.

A JOURNEY TO TAWIF

Abu Bakr was not present; he was coming to Makkah. Someone told him that Muhammad (pbuh) says he went to Jerusalem and back in one night. Abu Bakr replied, if the Prophet (pbuh) said it then it is true. Now the Prophet (pbuh) had lost the protection of Abu Talib. His effects of invitation (Dava) are being blocked. He tried to search for other alternatives. The messenger of Allah made a journey to Twaif. Zaid bin Harsa accompanied him. They went to Twaif, and the Prophet (pbuh) went to leaders of Twaif, the Prophet (pbuh) entered through the gate. The Tribe of Saqeef and there were three brothers, the Prophet (pbuh) presented the message to them and then asked them for help and support. These three men responded in a miserable way. The first one said I am going to tear apart the clothing of the Kabba if Allah has sent you as a Prophet. The clothing of the Kabba was sacred to them. The second among them said, his statement was that God could not find anybody else to send as a Prophet meaning isn't there anybody better than you? And the third one said, I cannot speak to you. Because if you are a messenger from Allah as you claim then you are such an important person, I don't think that I am qualified to speak to you, and if Allah has not sent you and you are lying then it is not appropriate for me to speak to a liar. When the messenger of Allah heard their response, he said, if you do not accept my message, keep this meeting secret. The Prophet (pbuh) did not want this news reach to Makkah, that the people of Saqeef have turned the Prophet down. Because it will only add to persecution by the people of Quraish. But they were such evil men, rude. What they did, they gathered fools among themselves, slaves and servants they told them to go and make noise, scream at the Prophet, crowds came pelting the Prophet (pbuh) and Zaid bin Harsa with rocks. Screaming at them, yelling and chasing them away the Prophet (pbuh) and Zaid bin Harsa had to run out of Tawif. Zahid bin Harsa was protecting the Prophet (pbuh) from the rocks people were throwing at them and took refuge in a farm owned by two men from Quraish Ibn Rabia. They finally ran away from the fools of Saqeef. The Prophet (pbuh) was exhausted, his feet were bleeding and he was hurt because the way he was treated by the people of Saqeef. Allah sent his help. He was hungry at the time, the two owners of the farm belonged to Makkah, they told their servant Adus, who was Christian, to take some grapes and give them to the Prophet (pbuh). They felt sympathy, even though they were stanch enemies. But now, they are in a foreign land in different territory.

They felt sympathy and thought that they should stand up for their tribe's man. At least they sent a plate of a grapes for the Prophet (pbuh). Adus carried the grapes and presented them to the Prophet (pbuh). The Prophet (pbuh) said, in the name of Allah and said it loudly. Adus was surprised, he asked the Prophet (pbuh) these words are not spoken or said in these lands. Arabia people in this area don't speak these words. The messenger of Allah thought he is a foreigner and he might be following a different religion. The Prophet (pbuh) asked Adus where are you from. And what is your religion? Adus said, I am a Christian man from Nineveh in Iraq. The Prophet (pbuh) said you are from the village of a pious man, Younis bin Amati, a Prophet of Allah. Adus said, how do you know about Jonna son of Amati. Muhammed (pbuh) said, he is my brother, he was a Prophet and I am a Prophet, when Adus heard that he immediately bent down and started kissing the feet of the Prophet (pbuh) then hands and head. Now the two owners of the farm from Quraish, when they saw that, they looked at each other and said look: He has already corrupted our slave. When Adus came back, they asked him what is wrong with you, you were kissing his feet, hands and head, he said, on the earth there is no man better than him. He told me something, only a Prophet would know, they told him Adus, do not allow this man to make you leave your religion and your religion is better than his. Question, the two sons of Rabia what do they know about Christianity? But it is the kufr in their heart to say whatever to people.

The Prophet Muhammed (pbuh) was reciting the holy Quran in a desert where there were some Jinn, they were attracted, and they listened. They came to the Prophet (pbuh) learned some verses and became Muslim. Jinn are intelligent creatures; they live on earth with similar life structure. They have tribes, clans and nations. They have their own language and follow different religions. They are like humans the difference is they are created from fire. We are created from clay. They can see us but we cannot see them. Surah_Jinn and Surah Haqq, mentions O' Muhammed (pbuh), when we directed some Jinn, listening to the holy Quran, when they attended they said listen quietly when it was concluded they went back to their people as warner's they said O' our people indeed we have heard a reciting of a Book after Moses (pbuh) confirming what was before it, guide the truth and straight path, these Jinn were Jewish named Moses and not Jesus, they were following the message of Moses. When they heard the Quran, they said this is a revelation, which came after Moses. Perhaps these Jinn were from Yemen, where there were Jews. O' people, ask Allah for forgiveness. But he who doesn't respond to the caller of Allah. The Prophet had to enter Makkah again, it was easy to leave but not easy to enter Makkah again. Especially after the news that Muhammed (pbuh) went to tawaf and preached his message. The Prophet had to seek the protection of someone in order to go back to his own town.

The Prophet (pbuh) was camping outside of Makkah to find someone who would give him protection. He sent a message with a man named Orefa to go to Al-Akhnas who was a Quraish but was living in Makkah, when Al-Akhnas received the message from the Prophet, he said, since I am an alliance with Quraish, I cannot give protection to a Quraish. He turned down the request. The Prophet (pbuh) sent the same message to Sohail bin Amer. He refused that I cannot give protection to another clan, third time request to Mathan bin Audhay. He did accept and gave protection, the Prophet (pbuh) went and spent the night at his house. Early in the morning Mathan asked his six or even seven sons to take up the swords and put on some special clothes and escort the Prophet (pbuh) to the Kabba. When they went there they had a seat, watching Muhammed (pbuh), making Tawaf. Abu Sufyan came to Mathan and asked him are you giving him protection, or are you following him? Al-Mathan said, I am only giving him protection. Abu Sufyan said if that is the case we will accept your protection. Now, Muhammed (pbuh) is giving invitations (Dava) in Makkah, under the protection of Al-Mathan bin Zubair, after the death of Abu Talib and Khadija it become a stalemate, even some people were coming in, but overall, this was stopped, many avenues were being blocked. Therefore, the Prophet was meeting delegates from Arab at the time of Hajj. Hijra Allah says O' my servant fear Allah and do not worship idols. Allah revealed in Makkah in the Holy Quran, my servant fear your lord, earth is spacious meaning if suffering in Makkah can move and fight in the path of Allah. Allah says who moved for Allah will be settled in a good place and benefits far greater in the other world, Hijra has a high status. Nisar helped Islam.

HIJRA

Before the Prophet (pbuh) decided to leave Makkah, the people of Makkah plotted against him and started to discuss about how to deal with the Islamic problem. Some suggested to throw Muhammed (pbuh) in jail. Response was no don't do that because his followers will come and take him out. Secondly some suggested to exile him, the answer was no because his talk is very sweet. He will deceive other people and he will come back. Abu Jehail said kill him and suggested how to do that. Appoint a strong man from every clan, give them swords and all should strike Muhammed at once. His blood will disperse among different clans of Makkah the family of the Prophet (pbuh) will not be able to seek revenge and we shall pay blood money gladly. Allah says remember O' Muhammed (pbuh) those who plotted against you, to prison to restrained you, evict you or to kill you, they planned and Allah plans. Allah's plan is the best. Surah Al-Asra. Allah told the Prophet to recite Dua, say, my Lord cause me to enter a sound entrance and sound exit and grant me from yourself a supporting authority. Cause me a sound entrance to Madinah and cause me a sound exit from Makkah. Allah is teaching Muhammed (pbuh) that this religion is supported by a supporting authority. The Prophet says Allah sometimes supports this religion in such a way that the Holy Quran cannot support. That is a reason that Khalifa was an especially important concept for Muslims. In fact, the Sahaba sorted out Khalifa even before they buried the Prophet after the death of the Prophet "Allah revealed in Makkah".

The Prophet Muhammed (pbuh) set out to prepare for Hijra. Ayesha says one day at mid-noon in the house of Abu Bakr, we saw a man approaching us and he was masked. Abu Bakr saw, that was Muhammed (pbuh), he said Muhammed (pbuh) would not come at this time unless there is something important, people usually sleep at noon. The Prophet (pbuh) came in and said O' Abu Bakr have everyone in your house leave. Abu Bakr said, that is only my family, consider it as your family. You can trust speaking in front of them. The Prophet (pbuh) said, "I was given permission to leave and make Hijra to Madinah". Abu Bakr said O' Messenger of Allah can I be your companion? The Prophet said, yes. Abu Bakr started to weep with joy. Ayesha says, I have never seen anybody weeping because of joy, like my father that day; this was not an entertaining journey, Abu Bakr knew he was risking his life. Ladies and Gentlemen, this shows Abu Bakr's love for the Prophet (pbuh) and he was ready to sacrifice his life. The Prophet (pbuh) appointed Hazrat Ali to sleep in his bed. That was very risky, that is a level of sacrifice. Second person, they were the Sahaba that shows how far they can go. Two people shared the secret. The Prophet (pbuh) left Makkah with Abu Bakr from the back door. The Prophet (pbuh) loved Makkah so much. He, the Prophet (pbuh) looked back, from little distance and said, "I in the name of Allah". Makkah is the most beloved land to Allah and if it wasn't that I was driven out, I wouldn't leave. I would not leave Makkah if I had a choice.

The journey started, Abu Bakr sometimes walked in front and sometimes at the back of the Prophet (pbuh). The Prophet of Allah noticed and asked Abu Bakr, sometimes you walk in front and sometimes you walk behind, why? Abu Bakr said when I remember somebody can ambush from front I walk in front when I remember one can attack from behind I walk behind. Then the Prophet (pbuh) asked O' Abu Bakr what do you think if harm happened to me or to you? Abu Bakr said, O' messenger of Allah I want that any harm should happened to me, then they reached the cave. Abu Bakr went in to check the cave and then asked the Prophet (pbuh) to come in. when they were in the cave Kufr reached there following their tracks they reached to the mouth of the cave. Abu Bakr told the Prophet (pbuh) if one of them would stare right under his (their) feet, they would see us. The Prophet (pbuh) with all confidence said, "O' Abu Bakr, there are two men and Allah is the third". Abu Bakr, how would you regard the safety of two people as Allah is their third companion? What stopped them from entering the cave? That was a web of a spider, Allah says about the web, the feeblest house is the house of a spider with one finger one can tear down the whole web. This feeble, weak web was a soldier of Allah that stopped the disbelievers from entering the cave. This shows that Allah can choose sometimes the weakest of his creatures to be his soldier. Allah revealed an Ayat (verse) later in Surah Toba. Allah telling the Sahaba. If you do not aid him Allah has already aided him. Where on that day only Abu Bakr was a companion and kufr were surrounding the cave. Allah did not need anybody's help, Allah aided him. When those disbelievers had driven him out as one of two, (Allah calls Abu Bakr as a companion) do not grieve. Allah is with us, Allah sent down his tranquility upon him. And supported him with soldiers he did not see, one of the soldiers is a spider, and made the word of those the lowest while the word of Allah is the highest unseen soldiers were angels, but a spider was seen as a soldier.

They stayed in the cave for 3 days. During those three days, Abdullah the son of Abu Bakr would spend a day in

Makkah, listening to conversations and spying what they say about Muhammed (pbuh), he would go to the cave at night and spend time with the Prophet(pbuh) and Abu Bakr. Amr bin Farah would follow him with his sheep. Double purpose, sheep will provide milk to the Prophet (pbuh) and also sheep will cover the tracks of Abdullah and Amr. No one will know where they went. On the third day then the guide showed up. Abdullah bin Aratan. He was a Mushriq disbeliever, but because he had an alliance with Quraish, Prophet (pbuh) hired him. He would take them through a different root. They started the journey to Madinah; they went on the coastline. The Quraish set a bounty, one hundred camels for each, dead or alive. They were sending out their messenger to the badoos of the desert. The experts of the roots of the desert talking about price, bounty one hundred camels for each. Saraka bin Malik, he was the head of one the Badoo tribe.

He says, I was sitting in a gathering of my people when a man showed up and said I saw two men in the horizon, and I think, these are the two men Quraish are looking for, Saraka said, no these men were here, they just left, Saraka says I told him to deceive him. I knew that those men were Muhammed (pbuh) and Abu Bakr. Because I wanted to have the bounty (camels) for myself. Saraka says, I stayed for a while, so they would not be suspicious, then I left and went home and told my servant to prepare my horse and hide the horse behind the hill. Then I left from the back door. Also, I was carrying my spear, dragging it on the ground because my spear was long and I did not want anyone to see it. Then he says I mounted my horse and went in the direction where that man had seen two men. And as I thought two men were Muhammed (pbuh) and Abu Bakr. Now he was thinking to become rich with one hundred camels for each (bounty). Saraka says, Abu Bakr was looking back while the Prophet (pbuh) was reciting the Holy Quran and never looked back, the Prophet (pbuh) was confident but Abu Bakr was concerned for the safety of the Prophet (pbuh). Abu Bakr told the Prophet (pbuh) that somebody is pursuing us. Prophet (pbuh) made Dua and the horse of Saraka sank in the sand and Saraka fell off its back. Saraka says I cast lots should I follow them or not? The lots told me that I should not follow them. But his greed, insisted to follow them. He followed them another time and the same thing happened. He fell off. He says this never happened to me, I never fell off my horse, the third time a cloud of dust exploded in my face, from in front of my horse, so I knew. Allah is supporting this man. So, I rushed towards him asking him to grant me peace. Saraka who was pursuing the Prophet, now became pursued. Saraka who wanted to kill the Prophet now worried for his own life asking for peace. Prophet (pbuh) granted him peace, Saraka wanted to write on paper. Prophet asked Amr bin Farah to write down Muhammed (pbuh), granted peace to Saraka. Saraka kept that document and years passed by and after 8-9 years. Saraka was arrested while Muslims were laying siege to Twaif. When he was about to be killed. He pulls out that document, that Prophet (pbuh) granting me peace, that document saved his life. When Saraka went back he told Quraish you are not going to find the Prophet, forget about it, because the Prophet told him, to discourage anyone who is pursuing us. Saraka who wanted to arrest them, now he was their guard.

THE PROPHET (PBUH) AND ABU BAKR VISITED A TENT IN THE DESERT

The Prophet (pbuh) and Abu Bakr visited a tent, there was an old woman in front. Her name is Ama Mabat. She was a very generous woman, she would provide food or drink to any traveler passerby; when the Prophet and Abu Bakar arrived, she didn't provide them with anything. The Prophet (pbuh) asked her, if she had anything to spare? She said, if I had anything you would not have to ask. The Prophet saw in the corner of the tent a very weak goat. The Prophet asked her, what is the problem with this goat? She said that goat is too weak to go out with rest of the flock to feed, Prophet asked is there any milk in her? She said, she (the goat) is weaker than that, Prophet said, would you allow me to milk her, she said go ahead. Prophet asked for a big container, then he touches the goat and starts milking, milk is flowing out, filled the container and all that foam on top of it. Then milk is given to Ama Mabat first, she drinks then to Abu Bakr, Amr and Abdullah bin Rabia and the Prophet is the last to drink and said, servant of the people is last to drink. Then they left and there was lot of milk left in the container. Then the husband comes home with the flock. He asked where this milk came from. She said, a blessed man visited us. And he is the one who milked the goat.

The husband asked her to describe this man. Ama Mabat gives a description, and that is the best description until today. Even though she only met him once. I saw him; a man, evidence of splendor, fine in figure, face handsome, slim in form, head not too small, elegant and good looking. Eyes were large and black eye lid long, voice deep, highly intelligent. Eyebrows high and Arch, his hair in place, his neck long and beard thick. He gave an impression of dignity when silent and highly intelligent when he spoke. His words were impressive, and he was decisive not trivial not trait. His ideas like pearls moving on string. He seemed splendid, fine looking man from a distance and best of all from close by. He is medium in height. Eye finding him not too tall not too short, a tree branch as it was, finest looking from three. The best proportion, center of attention of his companion when he spoke they listened well and if he ordered they hurried to obey. A man well helped, well served never silent and never refused.

Husband said, that must be Muhammed (pbuh) whom Quraish are pursuing. If I meet him, I shall pledge allegiance to him and become Muslim. Ama Mabat did pledge allegiance and became Muslim. Hadith: Figurative Hijra to leave what Allah dislikes. Allah says in the Quran stay away from impurities, from idol worshiping, from evil. This type of Hijra is mandatory. Literal Hijra to leave the land of evil to the land of good. The whole story of Hijra was preserved and narrated by Hazrat Ayesha. It was a hot summer day; the guide took them to the Kabba. Monday twelfth Rabi ul Awal, the heat was at its extreme, the sun almost reached its zenith. It was in the middle of summer extremely hot. The Prophet and Abu Bakr made Hijra. The Ansar would go out of Madinah every day in the morning in anticipation of meeting the Prophet and greeting him. But when the heat became too extreme they would go indoors. One day Ansar went waiting for the Prophet, he did not show up, they went indoors. There was a Jew who was on a high building and he saw the Prophet and Abu Bakar approaching, they were dressed in white. The reason they were dressed in brand new white clothes, they had met with Zubair bin Awa, who was coming back from a business trip from Syria he had some new clothes. He gave to the Prophet and Abu Bakr gifts of clothes and then these clothes they put on when they went to Madinah. This Jew saw the Prophet approaching, he called with the top of his voice, O' Arabs here is your man, and he has arrived.

The Ansar rushed to get their weapons and marched out to greet the messenger of Allah. It was their tradition to meet someone to have their weapons on. The other reason could be for protection. The Prophet (pbuh) and Abu Bakr arrived, people started greeting them, they arrived on the out skirts of Madinah, which is Kuba, and Prophet stayed in Kuba for fourteen days that is when the first mosque was built in Islam. This mosque is special, if a Muslim make wudhu at home and go to mosque Kuba, pray two Rakat, it counts as if you have made Umrah. The Prophet stayed in the house of bachelors, while he was there the Prophet sent messengers to Madinah asking permission to come in. They sent a large delegation, said, come in you will be safe and you will be obeyed. The Prophet is not coming to Medina as a guest. He is coming to lead the people of Madinah. Allah says, every messenger we have sent, we have sent him to be obeyed. Now, the Prophet (pbuh) goes into Madinah. It was an amazing day, huge celebration, people came out to greet him. The people of Abyssinia were dancing with their spears, women were standing on roof tops, children were in streets, and everybody wanted to see the Prophet. Anees bin Malik says we never saw such a day. People were happy.

Anees bin Malik says I witnessed the day the Prophet arrived, and I witnessed the day he the Prophet (pbuh) died. And I never saw two days as those two days in my life. One day was the happy, bright when they arrived and the other day was the darkest day in my life and I witnessed both days. The Prophet (pbuh) was offered to stay in every house in Madinah. But the Prophet (pbuh) wanted to stay with Banu Najjar, because Banu Najjar are the relatives of the Prophet (pbuh). Hashim married from Banu Najjar and Banu Najjar are from Al- Khazrj therefore the maternal uncles of Abu Mutlab are from Banu Najjar and asked which house of Banu Najjar is closest to me, Abu Ayube Ansari said my house, and the Prophet (pbuh) stayed in Abu Ayube Ansari's house.

The Prophet (pbuh) wanted to stay in the lower portion that was two-story house. The reason was that there were visitors coming to meet the prophet (pbuh). Lower level was more suitable. He remained there for seven months, people loved the Prophet (pbuh), young girls sang songs, we are the girls from Banu Najjar, how wonderful if Muhammed (pbuh) was our neighbor. The Prophet (pbuh) said, Allah knows my heart loves you all. Allah has chosen the people of Ansar, towards the end of his life the Prophet said, if it was not for Hijra I would consider myself from Ansar.

There were five tribes living in Madinah, three of them were Jewish and two of the tribes were Arabs. The Jewish tribes were Banu Kaneka, Banu Nadeer and Banu Kirova. Banu Kaneka lived in the center of Madinah. Near the marketplace they were in the business of jewelry. The Jews had forty-nine fortresses, their fighting force was around two thousand, Arabs tribes were Al-Ouse and Al-Khazrj their fighting force was about four thousand, they lived in Madinah, south and north, Madinah was a collection of small villages, livelihood was agriculture and palm growers. Jewish tribes would lend money to Arabs and charge interest, point of conflict between Arabs and Jews of Madinah. Now when Islam came Muslims, pagans and Jews. It was a complicated society.

One day the Prophet (pbuh) was riding a donkey and went towards a gathering, of mixed races and belief including Jews, when the donkey arrived, there was some dust. Abdullah bin Abbey later became the head of the Munafiqeen, he said, keep this dust away from us. The Prophet did not respond to him and started preaching Islam to them. Gave talks about Islam when the Prophet (pbuh) finished. Abdullah bin Abbey said, do not come and bother us in our meetings with your talk, stay at home whoever comes to visit you tell them your stories. Abdullah bin Roha, a Muslim said, we want him to come to meetings and talk to us. Then people started shouting and a war was about to breakout. The Prophet (pbuh) calmed them down, when they came home, told Saeed, didn't you see what Abdullah bin Abbey did? Saeed asked what happened. The Prophet told him, then Saeed said O' Prophet Abdullah bin Abbey was about to be appointed king. When you arrived, he thinks you stripped his kingship. It is understandable that he is against you.

THERE WERE FIRST FOUR PROJECTS

(i) mosque
(ii) brotherhood
(iii) covenant to govern different people in Madinah and
(iv) army.

THE FIRST PROJECT WAS MOSQUE IN MADINAH

In Kuba, Masjid Nabvi in Madinah is the center for learning. How they chose the place for the Masjid. The Prophet was riding a camel, everybody wanted to pull the camel in their direction. Prophet said leave it because it is being commanded by Allah. The Camel was going and then stopped at this particular location, which was a field for drying dates. This field belonged to two orphans in Madinah. The Prophet (pbuh) said this is our place. The location for a mosque and for living quarters. The Prophet (pbuh) wanted to purchase this area, from orphans but they said O' Prophet (pbuh). We are going to give it to you. There were some graves, the Prophet (pbuh) uncovered the graves and changed the location, and they started building Masjid Nabvi. Mud, bricks and roof was palm leaves. Floor was sand, the Prophet helped in building the mosque. The Prophet says, one Salah in Masjid Nabvi is better than one thousand (1000) Salah in other mosques. Except Masjid Al-Haram that is in the Kabba one is equal to eighty-three years. Also, only travel to three mosques, the Kaaba, Masjid Nabvi and Bait ul Muqaddas in Jerusalem.

HOW TO INVITE PEOPLE FOR PRAYER?

Abdullah bin Zahid saw a dream; someone was selling a bell. He wanted to buy it. The man suggested Adhan, and "Qaima". He told the Prophet (pbuh). He said teach it to Bilal, also Umer bin Khattab saw the same dream, the Prophet said the two dreams mean it is a true dream. Qibla was towards Bait ul Muqaddas. Few months after Hijra the Qibla changed from north to south towards the Kabba. Abu Huraira, the narrator of most of the Hadiths.

THE SECOND PROJECT WAS
ESTABLISHING BROTHERHOOD

Migrates and An-sar, third covenant (4) establishment of Muslim army. Second Project: Brotherhood is especially important in Islam. Allah says hold firmly to the rope of Allah together and do not become divided and remember the favor of Allah upon you. When you were enemies we brought your hearts together. You were on the edge of fire, and he saved you. Allah made his verses clear so that you may be guided. Allah has brought their hearts together. All praises to Allah, no amount of wealth could have brought their hearts together. That is only Allah. Allah is telling Muhammed (pbuh), you cannot buy hearts of men. Allah brought migrates and An-sar together and made them brothers. Allah says about An-sar.

An-sar will give preference to migrates. This brotherhood was just like blood brothers. The rules of inheritance will apply as they were blood brothers. Example; Brotherhood between Saeed bin Rabia and Abdul Rahman. Abdul Rahman Bin Auf was a mahajir from Makkah. He is one of ten people who was given the glad tidying of paradise (Jannah). He stayed at the house of Saeed bin Rabia. Saeed bin Rabia told him O' my brother, I am one of wealthiest men in Madinah. I shall split my wealth in half and give it to you, and I am married to two women. You can take a look at both of them and choose who is the one you want. I shall divorce her and after she completes her Iddat. You can marry her. This is the level of sacrifice they were willing to go to. Abdul Rahman said, may Allah bless your wealth and bless your family. Show me the way to the market.

He said thank you, Saeed bin Rabia did show him the way to the market of Banu Kanuka. Allah blessed Abdul Rahman from an early stage he established himself and he became a very wealthy man. He went to the market, worked and made some money. One day the Prophet (pbuh) saw on him some yellow color. This was a type of powder as women would use for make up in Madinah. That was on his face. The Prophet (pbuh) asked him what is this. Did you get married Abdul Rahman bin Auf said, yes. The Prophet asked what did you give her as Asma (Haq-Mehr) and where did you get the money from? Abdul Rahman bin Auf said I gave her gold the size of a date seed as Huq Mehr. The Prophet then told him, make a walima even if you slaughter one sheep or goat. These brothers would advise each other for example Solomon Pharsi and Abu Darja. Abu Darja was an abide (knowledge), worshipper of Allah, and he was Zahid. Solomon Pharsi saw his wife was not taking care of herself. Solomon asked her what is the matter. This was the wife of Abu Darja. She said your brother

Abu Darja is not interested in this world, therefore there is no need for her to look good in front of her husband Solomon Pharsi. When Abu Darja came, he brought some food and told Solomon Pharsi to eat. But Abu Darja himself, said that he is fasting. Solomon pharsi said that I am not going to eat unless you eat with me. He forced Abu Darja to break his fast, and when night came, Abu Darja stood up for his Ibadat. Solomon told him 'go and sleep', so he slept. Then he woke up and was told by Solomon Pharsi to go to sleep again, and then towards the end of the night Solomon told Abu Darja, 'now you can pray'. The Next day, Abu Darja went to the Prophet (pbuh) and told him that Solomon Pharsi had told me to break the fast and made him sleep. The Prophet (pbuh) said, Solomon was right. Solomon said, you have obligations towards Allah, you have obligation to yourself, and you have obligations towards your family. So, fulfill the obligations of everyone, Solomon Farsi is giving advice to Abu Darja, because Solomon Pharsi is more knowledgeable. An-sar asked Prophet to split their land, but the Prophet said no, migrates will work in farms and they split the harvest, that was agreed. Even then An-sar, ended up doing most of the work. Mahajreens came to Prophet (pbuh) and said we have never seen people like this, they comfort us when poor, they are generous when well off. They work in the fields and split the harvest with us. We think they will take all the rewards and leave us with nothing. The Prophet (pbuh) said no, as long as you are grateful and make Dua for them, this relationship carried on for some time, when migrates improved then it was dissolved. But general brotherhood of Uma remains.

THE THIRD PROJECT WAS COVENANT

Covenant, a document to govern different communities in Madinah. The terms of the document were narrated by Ibn Ishaque. The messenger of Allah made a contract between immigrants and helpers in which he expressed reconciliation terms. In the name of Allah, the merciful, the beneficent, this is a document from Muhammad (Pbuh) the unlitted father, between believers and Muslims of the Quraish and their followers, allies, and supporters establishing that they are a one nation apart from all others. The immigrants from Quraish will maintain their current practice and will honor blood money contracts between themselves and will treat their weaker members with kindness and justice. The Bani Auf shall, maintain their current practice and honor, their former blood money contracts. Each party treating their weaker members with kindness and justice amongst all believers, the believer shall not leave someone with the burden of debts, paying for him any ransom and blood money he owes. A believer shall not be an ally with the second believer. Believers will unite against any wrong doer. Even if he was one of their own sons. Any matter (controversial) should be referred to Allah and his messenger. The Jews will pay expenses along with Muslims so long as they are allies in warfare. The Jews will have their own religion and Muslims their own. The Mahajreen were homesick as well as Bilal, people used to get fever in Madinah, the Prophet (Pbuh) made Dua and the Mahajreen loved Madinah.

The most knowledgeable person was Abdullah bin Salam, when he heard of the Prophet (Pbuh) he came to meet him. Abdullah bin Salam wanted to test the Prophet (Pbuh). The Jews had signs, for the upcoming Prophet. He said, I shall ask three things, three questions, and only a Prophet shall know the answers;

(i) what is the first sign of the Day of Judgment?
(ii) What is the finest food that the people of paradise will eat?
(iii) What causes a child to resemble his father or Mother?

The Prophet (Pbuh) said the angel Gabriel told me the answers to these questions a short while ago. Abdullah bin Salam said that Gabriel is our enemy amongst the angels. The Prophet (Pbuh) recited the Ayat Surah Al-Baqarah, 'Allah says whoever takes his angels as enemies then Allah dislikes those disbelievers. All the angels are created by Allah, they should not be considered as enemies. Then the Prophet (Pbuh) answered the questions. The Prophet (Pbuh) said; (i) there will be a fire, which drives the people from east and leaves them in the west. (ii) the food in paradise, will be whale's liver (iii) if the male liquid precedes the child, the appearance will be like the father and if the female liquid precedes, then that child will resemble like the mother, whoever's genes are dominating ones. Abdullah bin Salam said, I testify, there is no God but Allah, and that you are the messenger of Allah. These were the correct answers, so he became a Muslim and then he said, (Reference Bukhari Sharif), 'but Jews are liars, if you ask them about me (Abdullah bin Salam), before telling them about me accepting Islam, they will tell you lies'. Abdullah bin Salam went into hiding and the Prophet (Pbuh) invited other leaders of the Jews. The Prophet (Pbuh) asked them about Abdullah bin Salam they said he is our leader and the son of our leader. He is the most learned man amongst us. Prophet (Pbuh) asked Abdullah bin Salam to come out, he came and said, 'O' Jews fear Allah, you know, he is the messenger of Allah and brings you the truth'. Then the Jews said you are the worst one and the son of the worst one amongst us. He Abdullah bin Salam knew this, that is the reason he requested to ask the Jews before telling them that I am a Muslim.

Surah Al-Imran, Allah says, the people of the book, they are not all the same, and Allah knows the righteous ones. An important event occurred after 14 months of Hijra that was the change of the Qibla. In Makkah, the Prophet (Pbuh) used to pray towards Jerusalem, (Bait-ul-Maqdas), but the Kaaba was in between, now in Madinah the Kabba is in the other direction. Allah (swt) then revealed an Ayat in which Muslims were told to change the Qibla to face Kabba. One of the Sahaba went out of Madinah and saw people facing towards Jerusalem. He told them that the Prophet (Pbuh) was facing the Kabba, when he was praying, so then they all turned towards the Kabba. This shows the trust. But this event caused controversy. Allah (swt) revealed over 40 Ayat in Surah Al-Baqarah dealing with this incident alone. This was a test from Allah (swt). It was a test for the Mushriqeen they said that he has reverted back to 'our' Qibla, the Kabba. And also said that he will revert back to our religion as well. Ibn-Kayum says it was a test for the hypocrites. Who said Muhammed (Pbuh) does not know what to do and he changes his mind. It was a test from Allah for the Jews who said he has left the Qibla of Ambia who came before him and that shows that Muhammed (Pbuh) is not a Prophet of Allah. They considered Jerusalem was the Qibla of Ambia and it was a test for the believers to whether they will stand firm with the Prophet (Pbuh) and change the Qibla. The foolish amongst the people will say, what has turned them away from the Qibla, which they used to face. Say, 'to Allah belongs east and west', Allah guides to whom he wills to the straight path. It is up to

Allah to choose. Jews would say, Allah does not change his mind.

The Question is first Qibla or second Qibla, which is right. If the first Qibla is right, then the new prayers will not be accepted, and if second Qibla is right then the old prayers are not accepted. Allah says I did not make the Qibla, but to see who will follow the Prophet (Pbuh), we have seen the turning of your faces towards the heavens. The Prophet (Pbuh) wanted to change the Qibla, and I will turn you to a Qibla for which you will be pleased. So turn your face towards Masjid Al-Haram and wherever you are, turn your face towards it. Those who have been given the scriptures will know this is the truth from your lord. Allah is not unaware of what they do. Allah is over all things competent.

Fasting

The second year of Hijra, Surah Baqarah, O' you who have believed the decree upon you is fasting as it was decreed upon those before you, so you become righteous the purpose behind fasting is Taqwa, so you become righteous.

Jihad

Jihad means struggle. Islam gave special meaning, and while in Madinah the Prophet (pbuh) took part in nineteen Ghuzva and sent fifty-five expeditions to us. Ghazwa, Suraya in total seventy-four battles that is an average seven every year, time to prepare and to finance. Jehad's meaning in Islam is to fight for the sake of Allah. Every war is unjust with the exception of fighting in the path of Allah. Surah Al-Nisa verse 76, Allah says only war in the path of Allah is just others are evil wars. In the first place, Muslims were not allowed to fight and therefore they were wronged and persecuted in Makkah. They used all various forms of aggression against the Muslims, the Arabs were difficult to restrain, there were no peace movements at that time. They were asked to be patient, "it was on the cards that we shall have to fight back to restrain them", said Abu Bakr. Permission to fight back was given in the early times of Madinah. Some say permission to fight was granted before hijra but actual practice was in Madinah. Now to fight against the enemies of Allah, demanded preparation. The prophet (pbuh) was preparing the Muslim community and training them. This training was in two forms; (i) physical training and (ii) spiritual. This will lead us to the fourth project, establishment of the army.

THE MUSLIM ARMY

This was not a professional army; it was more of a militia (a citizen's army). There were no professional soldiers, anyone who fulfilled the five requirements, was expected to participate in the army. The five requirements were, (i) must be a Muslim, (ii) must be at least the age of puberty, (iii) sanity (must have a sound mind), (iv) must be free of defects (no disabilities) and (v) must be financially stable. Any male who passed the five requirements was fit for military service. The holy Prophet (pbuh) was preparing the army spiritually, Allah says in Surah Toba (Verses 111 and 112), "Indeed Allah has purchased from believers, their lives and their property in exchange for Paradise, so they (the army) fight in the cause of Allah. They are killed, and they kill, this is the true promise binding on Allah." In the Torah and in Gospel (Bible) and in the holy Quran, this is the true covenant of Allah, and who is better than Allah? Allah is teaching them to be patient, if a wound should touch you, that has already touched an opposing person. One day you win, and one day you lose, Allah may make this evident for those who believe. Allah may take matters from you, and Allah does not like wrong doers. And Allah may purify the believers. Or do you think Allah will enter you into Paradise without evidence? Now you have wished for martyrdom. Before you were looking on, Allah was preparing the Muslims and this is in Bukhari Sharif, narrated by Abu Huraira. A man came to the Prophet (pbuh) and asked, tell me something as virtuous as Jihad. The Prophet (pbuh) said, "I cannot find any", the prophet told the man when Mujahid goes out in the path of Allah, can you enter your mosque and pray continuously without any rest and fast without breaking it? The man said, "Who could do that?" The Prophet (pbuh) means when someone does Jihad he gets more reward than someone who prays continuously without rest and someone who fasts without breaking it.

When they were coming back from the Ghazwa of Tabuk, the holy Prophet (pbuh) told Moaz bin Jabal, if you want, I shall tell you it's head and its peak. The head of the affair is Islam and its pillar is Salah and its peak is Jihad fi-sabeelALLAHA. The Prophet (pbuh) says in Bukhari Sharif and Muslim Sharif, "The paradise is under the shade of the sword", the holy Prophet (pbuh) says "who even finances in the path of Allah, he is considered as he has fought. And whoever takes care of a family of a fighter has fought. In Muslim Sharif, hadith, one day of fighting in the path of Allah is better than one month praying and fasting. The Prophet (pbuh) says "Just standing in the ranks, is better than 60 years of prayers", all these hadiths were to prepare the Muslims spiritually. They were facing enemies from every direction, the physical training, that is military training, the Sahabah were physically fit, they had active lifestyles. Wherever there were deficiencies, for example swimming, target shooting, marksmanship, it was worship to Allah (i) walk between the targets (ii) training your horse, (iii) playing with your wife, and (iv) learning how to swim and teaching others. These 4 types of worship are Ibadat.

Any other form of entertainment is a waste of time. The holy Prophet (pbuh) says fight with non-believers with your wealth, arms and tongue. This was to defend the newly formed Muslim community. We have to look in context of that time. It was a difficult time for Muslims, the Quraish were threatening them, for example Quraish sent a letter to Abdullah soon after Hijra, telling him you have given sanctuary to Muslims, hand them over to us or we shall kill you and leave your women widows and children orphans.

Another example, when Saad bin Moaz went to visit Makkah he was a friend with Omiya bin Khalf, he told Omiya, I want to make Tawaf around the Kaaba, tell me when it is less crowded. They waited until later and went to make Tawaf. Abu Jehail saw them, and came and asked Omiya, who is this man? Omiya said, this is Saad bin Moaz. He was well known, he was the head of Al-Auss, one of the two tribes in Madinah. Abu Jehail said to Omiya, I do not want to see you making Tawaf with this man, when they have given sanctuary to Muhammad (pbuh) and his followers. Saad bin Moaz responded and said, "If you prevent me from making Tawaf, I am going to prevent your caravan from reaching Shaam (in Syria)". The caravans of Quraish pass next to Madinah. The prophet (pbuh) after getting permissions, started sending out Surya and Ghazwa, the difference is when the Prophet (pbuh) participates specifically that is Ghazwa. And when the army is sent by the Prophet with a leader appointed, and not participating specifically, that is Surya The first Ghazwa, the

Prophet (pbuh) participated but there was no fighting. First Surya was Obada bin Harsa, shots were fired but there was no killing. The first one to shoot was Saad bin Abu Waqas. Saad bin Abu Waqas said, he is the first one to shoot an arrow in the path of Allah, then Surya of Hamza bin Abdul Mutlab. 30 Muhajir, this time they were riding, they met a caravan with large numbers of guards, no fighting occurred. After this Abu Jehail warned Quraish that Muhammad (pbuh) is there be careful. He was telling his people that he was like an angry lion, parties were at war because we have driven them out like the insects from back of a camel. War had started when Quraish forced them out of Makkah. There were quite a few Surya and Ghuzva. Some successful, some unsuccessful, all these occurred within 2 years of Hijra before the battle of Badr.

One important Surya happened; it is important because of the consequences of it. This is called the Surya of Abdullah bin Josh. This was a small group of Sahabah who were sent out to pursue a caravan belonging to Quraish. Abdullah bin Josh, the leader of Surya was handed a letter by the prophet, the letter was sealed and Abdullah bin Josh was told to open it after two days, the Prophet (pbuh) told him to go to such and such place and after two days read the letter. Abdullah bin Josh opens the letter after two days and the letter states, I instruct you to a place which was between Makkah and Tawaf but ask your team members to follow you but make it a voluntary event. This was a voluntary Surya. Ask whether they want to join you or not. The reason was because it was a risky operation. These men were going deep into the territory of Pagans, between Makkah and Twaif. This caravan was not near Madinah. That used to be the route for Quraish to Syria. Abdullah bin Josh tells the party that this is what the Prophet (pbuh) says. I shall go and if you want to follow me that is up to you. They all said we will go with you; they were all willing to die for the sake of Allah. We have said Allah says all wars are evil except for the sake of Allah.

They did spot the caravan belonging to Quraish, which was lightly guarded, only four guards. They were within the striking distance, but the dilemma was that this was a sacred month. There are four months in a year, where Arabs do not fight. This was their agreement and held in high esteem. They took these months seriously. They would not violate these months and would not fight. They were on the last day of Rajab, one of the sacred months. They were not supposed to fight, the question is why not wait for another day, and then it will be Shaban (the month after Rajab) and they can attack. But the problem was that if they wait for a day the caravan will reach within the limits of the sacred place around Makkah. There they are not supposed to fight either, but in either case they will be violating the sanctuary of the four months or the sanctuary of Makkah. They held Shura and decided to attack in the month of Rajab, the holy month.

They shot their arrows, one of the four guards was killed, one ran away, and the other two were taken prisoners. The guard who died was Amer bin Hisramy and the whole caravan fell into the hands of the Muslims. They brought them to Madinah, and that was a breaking news. Everybody was talking about it and the Quraish made a big deal out of this. They took this opportunity and milked it to the limits. They went around saying Muhammad (pbuh) and his followers violated the sacred months. They are shedding blood. They have taken prisoners. They have stolen our wealth, all in the holy month. When the men came back in Madinah, the Prophet (pbuh) said I did not tell you to fight in the holy month. Muslims were reapproaching Abdullah bin Josh asking him, who told you to fight in the holy month. These men were in a difficult situation. They were worried, what have we done. How will Allah judge this? The Prophet (pbuh) refused to take the prisoners and refused to take the caravan. The Ayat in the holy Quran were revealed, (verse 217) from Surah Al-Baqarah. "They ask you about fighting in a sacred month, fighting in the holy month is a great sin, what the Sahaba have done in the holy month was wrong". But then Allah lists four more sins. (i) awarting people from the path of Allah, Quraish were standing to prevent people from becoming Muslims, (ii) disbelief in Allah is a great sin (iii) preventing Muslims from Masjid Al-Haram (iv) expulsion of the people from it, as migrates were driven out of Makkah. Those sins were greater than what Abdullah bin Josh did. Allah is putting those prospectuses.

Then Allah says, "seducing people away from Islam is a greater sin then killing in a holy month". Allah says about disbelievers, "Although what Abdullah bin Josh did was wrong, what Quraish have being doing for the past 30 years are worse". After these Ayat Abdullah, bin Josh and his companions in that Surya were happy, they also wanted to take credit for what they did. Allah reveals Ayat 218. Allah says "indeed, those who believe and immigrated and fought in the cause of Allah, those expect the mercy of Allah, and Allah is merciful and forgiving". Allah is telling them, expect the mercy of Allah, and credit for it. And the reward of Mujahidin. They were the first when these Ayat where revealed. The Prophet (pbuh) took the caravan and took the two men as prisoners.

When the Quraish came to ransom them, what had happened. A camel was lost and two men from the Surya went looking for it. They had not come back yet. The holy Prophet (pbuh) told Quraish, I am not going to hand back their two men, until our two men have returned, we fear that you might kill them. This shows the care the Prophet (pbuh) had for his followers. When those two people came back, the holy Prophet (pbuh) returned their two men but Quraish had to pay ransom. And one of those two prisoners became Muslim and didn't go back. Later on he was martyred, while the other went back and died as a disbeliever.

When migrates were kicked out of Makkah, parties were at war with each other, and these attacks were to make them recognize the Muslim army, as the fighting force. That was to inform other parties that Muslims' state is strong and do not attempt to attack it. Because if other tribes feel that this is a weak state, they will try to take advantage and attack.

These Suryias were deterrent because Badoo tribes had respect for Quraish. Because they were the custodians of the Kabba. The Prophet (pbuh) wanted to break this belief and let people know that there is Muslim power against the Quraish. Secondly, the holy Prophet was winning over tribes and establishing alliances, this was the time when non-Muslims could be allied partners. These raids were the economic reasons. In Islam, if Muslims' state is in war with an enemy, that makes their killing and wealth halal. This was a serious threat to Quraish, and that lead to the battle of Badr. It started as we shall see because the biggest caravan lead by Abu Sufyan was led to be taken over. This was a training for the army. Also, the method was successful for the Muslims' state but the Quraish didn't have this. The Prophet (pbuh) in Madinah was not properly secured as it was not very big and the Muslim numbers were small.

The Prophet (pbuh) was unable to sleep one night, and he wished there were some guards to guard him. Suddenly the Prophet (pbuh) heard a sound and asked, who is it? It was the Sahabi, Saad bin Abu Waqas who came to guard the prophet. This is a lesson for the Ummah to be careful and alert. Allah revealed to Muhammad (pbuh), "Allah will guard you, you do not need guards. Allah will protect you. And then the holy Prophet said to Saad bin Abu Waqas go back, Allah has given me his protection. The total number of Muslim men of fighting age was 1500.

THE BATTLE OF BADR

A major caravan headed by Abu Sufyan himself, he is a Quraish leader. Muhammed (pbuh) heard about this and sent out spies to bring him news about this caravan. News came to the prophet Muhammed (pbuh) that a caravan has been spotted at such and such place. The Prophet (pbuh) came out and said, whoever has his camel ready shall join us. We are ready to leave now, the total fighting force was one thousand five hundred but not enough time was given and a small number were able to join. Just over three hundred. Some say three hundred and seventeen. And some say three hundred and nineteen. The purpose of this army was to take over the caravan led by Abu Sufyan. Some of the Sahaba said to the prophet (pbuh) our rides are out of Madinah. But the Prophet (pbuh) said no, we are leaving now. Therefore, not everybody had time to prepare themselves. The prophet (pbuh) said that this caravan belongs to the Quraish and has much wealth. May Allah present this to you? Abu Sufyan was very careful, Also Abu Jehail had given the warning to the people to be careful. Your financial lines are being attacked. Abu Sufyan was alerted and was sending his own spies to find out the whereabouts of Muhammed (pbuh) and his people. Abu Sufyan reached to the place of Badr. This is 150 kilometers from Madinah. He passed the wells of Badr and he asked the people who were drawing water from the wells. Have they seen any strangers in that area? They said yes, we saw two men. Abu Sufyan went to that place where their camels were resting. And then he held some Camel manure in his hand and crushed it. He said, this manure has animal feed of Madinah in it. That is the crushed date seeds, People used that to feed camels in Madinah. He realized the owners of these camels were from Madinah and they were the followers of Muhammed (pbuh) and were pursuing him.

Abu Sufyan sent a very urgent message to Quraish in Makkah, your caravan is being threatened, you need to come and protect it. The messenger was Amer bin Omea Gommary. At the same time, he changes his course and went towards the coast and successfully avoided the Muslims. Now there are three parties, we have to consider each separately. (i) the party of the prophet Muhammed (pbuh), (ii) the people in Makkah (iii) the caravan itself. Firstly, we go to Makkah. Atika bint Abdul Mutlab, she is the aunty of the Prophet Muhammed (pbuh). Atika bint Abdul Mutlab saw a dream; she saw a man riding his camel and he rushes into Makkah. He screams to gather the people of Makkah around him. And then his camel stands on top of the Kabba. After that it stands on a mountain in Makkah and warns the people of Quraish. 'In three days, you will perish.' And throws a rock. It lands in the valley of Makkah and explodes and every house in Makkah is hit that was the dream of Atika bint Abdul Mutlab. She tells this dream to her brother Al-Abbas and says this dream worries me. But I do not want to tell this to anybody else. Al-Abbas listens to the dream and says that was some vision but keep quiet about this, do not tell anyone. But the next day Al-Abbas tells the dream which Atika saw to his friend Al-Waleed bin Ottaba. And says do not tell anybody. But Al-Waleed bin Ottaba tells the dream to his father. Then the news is all over Makkah.

(A lesson, if you want to keep a secret do not tell anybody. If you cannot protect the secret yourself, do not expect others to keep a secret) Al-Abbas says I got up early the next day to make Tawaf of Kabba. I saw Abu Jehail sitting with the other Quraish leaders, they were discussing the vision of Atika. They asked Al-Abbas to come and join them. Al-Abbas says, when I finish tawaf I will come and sit with you. Now Abu Jehail spoke and said to Al-Abbas how long has your family of Abdul Mutlab had this female Prophet? Al-Abbas pretended, that he does not know what he is talking about. Abu Jehail said, we are talking about the vision Atika saw. Abu Jehail said your family of Abdul Mutlab are not satisfied that your men are becoming prophets. Has it got to be your women now? Atika says, the man said come in three days you will perish. We are going to watch you closely for three days. If what she says, it happens, so be it. But if it doesn't happen in three days, we shall judge you as the biggest liars in Arabia. Abu Jehail has insulted the men and women of Abdul Mutlab. Al-Abbas went home, and says, that night every woman of Abdul Mutlab's family came to see me and said "have you agreed to let that dirty old reprobate attack first your men and then your women? Didn't anything he said offend you?" Al-Abbas says, I would have answered him but I did not have any problem with him before. I shall confront him if he says anything. I shall take care of him for you. Al-Abbas was charged up now. After three days Al-Abbas goes back and close to Abu Jehail to argue with him and avenge him, to take revenge. Al-Abbas says he was extremely angry that he let him get away with something he should have put a stop to. Al-Abbas went to the Mosque. Al-Abbas says, I swear, I was walking or making towards him to make him retract what he had said. Abu Jehail was a sharp man with a sharp gaze. He hurried off towards the door of the mosque. Al-Abbas said I asked myself, what could be the matter with the fellow? Whether he was fearful of me and was running away. But he had heard something which I had not. He had heard the voice of Bum-Bum Ghaffari who was out in the center of the valley standing by his camel. This was the messenger sent by Abu Sufyan. He arrived three days after the dream of Atika. Bum-Bum Ghaffari, by looking at him sends fear in the hearts of the people. He came in and cut the nose of his camel, the saddle is upside down, tears his shirt, screaming, Quraish your caravan has been raided by Muhammed (pbuh) and his men. I do not think you can save it. HELP, HELP.

Al-Abbas says this diverted all of us now everybody was trying to get ready for an emergency. Quraish wanted to go and save the caravan. They mobilized. Now we shall go back to the Muslim army, the prophet (pbuh) had conference, asked the Sahaba to give me council. Abu Bakr spoke and then Umer bin Khattab spoke. But the prophet (pbuh) wanted someone from Ansar to speak and give their opinion. Saad bin Moaz said O' messenger of Allah we shall fight. Go towards what Allah has instructed you to do. That made the messenger of Allah happy and satisfied. Because that pledge was to protect him. Saad bin Maze led us to occasions. The prophet (pbuh) returned some youngsters back,(Abdullah bin Umer and Al-Bra). Because they were young. One, a non-Muslim came to join. The prophet (pbuh) refused because he did not want any help from non – Muslims. Non – Muslim came back again and was refused but a third time he became a Muslim and was allowed to join. Financially, Muslims were going through hard times, the Muslim army had two horses and Seventy Camels. Every three men were sharing a camel. Muhammed (pbuh) was also sharing like the rest of the Sahaba. When their turn came they said O' messenger of Allah you ride, and we shall walk. But the prophet (pbuh) said, you are not stronger than me, nor can I dispense with the reward more than you can. Allah be praised. This was the leader of the Muslims and their teacher that is why they all loved him so much. Never, in the history, we have seen anybody loving their leader as the Sahaba loved the prophet (pbuh). They carried on towards Badr to pursue the caravan. Now the third-party Abu Sufyan, he passed the wells of Badr, he found crushed date seeds in the camel food by crushing the camel manure. He changed his course and escaped he had gone via the course route. He sent a letter saying to Quraish, you came out to defend the caravan. Allah has saved the caravan, now go back. Now we go back to Quraish. Abu Jehail said, by Allah, we will not turn back until we reach Badr. Badr was the place where Arabs would hold market fare each year.

Abu Jehail said, we will stay there for three days, slaughter some camels, eat well, drink wine, and entertainers will play music for us. The Badoo, people will know this and will respect us for that. Let us proceed ahead. Abu Jehail was flexing his muscles. Arabs will see us as powerful. Allah says, "Quraish came to show their power", and Allah says, "do not be like them". Now we go back to the party of Muhammad (pbuh). The Prophet (pbuh) thought that the caravan had gone, and instead of forty men, the guards of the caravan because they wanted to take over the caravan. That is the reason they came out. But now they will be facing an army of one thousand strong. Muhammad (pbuh) had a Shura asking what do you think? Abu Bakr and Umer bin Khattab spoke. Then Abdullah bin Maqdad spoke and then Abdullah bin Masood says, "I shall sacrifice the world for those words". Maqdad said "Messenger of Allah, go far to what Allah has commanded you to do, we are not going to tell like the children of Israel told the Prophet Moses (pbuh). The Israelis said to Moses (pbuh) go and fight with your lord, we are going to wait here. But the story of Moses (pbuh) we will leave there. Maqdad said, "we shall fight in front of you, behind you, to your right and to your left. And we say go and fight with the help of your lord, and we will fight with you". The face of the holy Prophet (pbuh) lit up in happiness. This hadith is in Bukhari Sharif. Some Sahaba were reluctant. Allah says in the holy Quran and tells us, "whatever is in the hearts' of the people, Allah knows." It is just as your lord, who brought you out of your homes for the battle of Badr. We would not have known otherwise, what some of the believers had in their hearts and minds. Some were unwilling, they disliked fighting.

Allah says, "fighting was prescribed on you and you dislike it". Then Allah says, "you might dislike something when it is good for you." Allah says, "remember all believers, when Allah promised you one of the two groups will be yours". Some wanted to raid the caravan for wealth. But Allah had a plan, that was fighting between good and evil. That was to abolish the falsehood. For that, it would be the day of Furkan – meaning it separates good and bad, as we shall see later on. Muhammad (pbuh) was gathering intelligence about the army of Quraish and also about the caravan. The messenger of Allah and Abu Bakr met an old Badoo man. Muhammad (pbuh) asked him the whereabouts of the Muslim army and about the army of Quraish. The man said, "I won't tell you until you tell me who you are." The messenger of Allah told him, if you tell us, then we shall tell you. The man said, "Muhammad (pbuh) and his men are in such and such place. If the one who told me has told the truth, and he gave the right place." Then he said "the Quraish army are in such and such place, if the one who told me told the truth, then Quraish will be in such and such place." This was valuable information. Now it is the turn of Badoo, he asked, "who are you", they answer "we are from water", meaning created from water. But

Badoo still asked "which water, water of Iraq or what?". But the Prophet (pbuh) walked away so that Badoo will not be able to ask more investigative questions.

Ali bin Abu Talib and Zubair, they were also gathering information and found a servant of Quraish, they brought him back and the holy Prophet (pbuh) was praying at that time. They asked the servant some questions, "who are you", and "who do you belong to?" He said "I belong to the Quraish army" but the Sahaba wanted to know the whereabouts of the caravan. He said, "I do not know." The Sahaba beat him to get a better answer out of him. Then the servant gave in and agreed to answer their questions. The Sahaba asked again "where is Abu Sufyan?". And he said, "I do not know." They would beat him again. When the holy Prophet (pbuh) finished his salah, he said, "leave him, when he tells you the truth, beat him and when he lies, leave him." The Prophet (pbuh) wanted to ask him some valuable questions. Muhammad (pbuh) asked him about the number of soldiers in the Quraish army. He said, "I do not know, but it is a very large army." The next question was, "how many camels do they slaughter every day?". He said, "one day nine, and the next day ten." Now the estimate was that the Quraish army was between 900 and 1000. There was 200 cavalry slave girls and 600 coat nails.

In the Muslim army there was 86 Muhajirs, 170 Al-Khurazj and 61 Al-Auss. Over 300 warriors. It is in Bukhari Sharif, Al-Bra says, "the number in Badr is equal to the number in Taloot, 310." At that time believers were 310 Israeli who passed the test. Also, in Badr, the best of the best. Muslims had banners, flags, slogans, and battle cries. The banner was white; it was given to Msaiba bin Amer. He was carrying the flag. There was a black flag named Al-Aqab, this flag was for migrates, and Ali bin Abu Talib (Abpwh) was carrying it and there was a black flag for Ansar. Battle cries for encouragement, the Muslim army had two horses they belonged to Zubair and Maqdad. And 70 camels, three Sahaba would share a camel and the Prophet (pbuh) was taking turns like anyone else. Muhammad (pbuh) was loved for this action. The holy Prophet (pbuh) was sharing with Hazrat Ali and Al-Habab who was ansar. The Muslim leader was sharing rides, praise be to Allah. Now, what about the choice of the location? The holy Prophet (pbuh) chose a place for camping, Habab bin Mugheera, he came to the holy Prophet (pbuh) and said, "is this the place Allah has told you or is it a question of tactics?" The Prophet (pbuh) responded, "this is for warfare and tactics. This was my opinion."

Al-Mandir said, "Messenger of Allah, we should go ahead and stop near the well, the well should be behind us and we should have water to drink and they will have no water. And we shall not allow them access to water." The holy Prophet (pbuh) said "that is a good idea. Build a sustenance pool and stock up water."

A DREAM OF THE PROPHET (PBUH)

The night before the war, the Prophet (pbuh) saw a dream, where the Quraish army is fewer than what they were in real life. Why? Allah wants to strengthen the hearts of the believers, the Quraish army is three times bigger than the Muslim army. The Muslims should have hope for victory. Allah is showing the enemy army as small. Allah says, "remember Muhammad (pbuh), when Allah showed them to you as a dream as few, and if he showed them to you as many, your followers would have lost courage and disputed whether or not to fight. Allah saved you from that, and Allah knows what is in the hearts, this was to strengthen them as it happened the night before. The following day, in the morning, they had rain. It was not a rainy season.

Ibn Ishaque says, the valley has soft ground, and the water from the sky dampened the earth for the messenger of Allah and his force but did not impede their problems. For the Quraish, they had so much rain upon them, that they could barely move. This is rain showered upon both the Muslims and non-Muslims, for Muslims it became firm but for Quraish it became muddy and sticky. The same rain had a different effect on both sides, and this is a miracle of Allah. Also, the rain washed the Muslims, this was a spiritual cleansing for them, Allah says "remember, the sound sleep and water to clean disregards evil suggestions, and made their hearts firm, and placed their feet firmly. This rain served all those purposes.

Ali bin Abu Talib says, the night before the battle, all of us fell asleep. The people should be anxious, worried, afraid, overthinking, but they were sleeping soundly. Allah be praised. The scholars say that sleeping before the battle is a sign of Eman (faith). And sleeping in salah is a hypocrisy. Sleeping or drowsiness shows confidence of the heart. Sleeping in salah, Allah says about Munafiqeen, that when they go to pray, they go in laziness. They do not mention the name of Allah frequently. Ali bin Abu Talib says, "the only person who was awake was the holy Prophet (pbuh)."

Allah describes the scene, "remember when you were in the near side of the valley and they were on the further side of the valley, and the caravan was on the further side of the valley. If you had made the appointment to meet, you would have missed. Allah says the meeting of the armies was not via the appointment, it was unplanned. You wanted the caravan, but Allah wanted to meet the armies. If you had planned, you would have missed it the appointment. The Muslims did not want to meet the army of Quraish, nor Quraish wanted to meet the army of Muslims.

Abu Sufyan and some other members of the Quraish army, were telling them to go back, some of them were afraid, because they were fighting the messenger of Allah. Not all non-Muslims honestly believed that Muhammad (pbuh) was a false prophet or a liar. Many of them knew he was a true prophet of Allah. But they were arrogant, which kept them away from Islam. Disbelieve because of arrogance. They knew he is a messenger of Allah; they knew he was speaking the truth, and that made them fearful of facing him in the battle. Also, many Muslims were reluctant to fight because they were not prepared to fight. They came out lightly armed. But Allah might accomplish a matter already destined. Those who perish were perished on evidence. And those who lived on fate, lived upon evidence. Indeed, Allah is knowing and hearing, the battle ground is the ultimate test of Eman (faith).

Saad bin Moaz suggested to the prophet a tent to be built and some Guards and a camel should be ready. If we win, that is what we want. But if we lose, then you should go back to Madinah and there are people in Madinah, they love you as we do and they will help you continue the mission. Because the people in Madinah, they did not have time to join as they were not ready. What Saad bin Moaz suggested is that you go back and those people will fight side by side with you and help you continue your mission. The Prophet (pbuh) liked this idea and stayed in that tent and Abu Bakr was his guard.

When the army of Quraish first appeared, Ibn Ishaque says, when the messenger of Allah saw them coming forward into the valley, from their position from behind the sand hill, he said, "O'Allah, these men advancing are the Quraish, in all their vanity and pride. They are antagonistic to you, they do not believe in you, and they call your prophet a liar. O'Allah, give us your victory. O'Allah destroy them this morning." This is what the Prophet (pbuh) said when he first saw the army of Quraish. One was riding on a red camel, the Prophet (pbuh) said "whatever good in them may be, that is in the man riding the red camel."

"If they were to obey him, they will be well guided." He was referring to Ottba bin Rabia, why did the holy Prophet (pbuh) say that?

The Quraish sent Amer bin Wahab to scout and gather intelligence about the Muslim army, how large it is for example. Amer bin Wahab went and came back, and said "O'Quraish, what I saw was camels bearing death. They are people, their only aid and refuge is their swords. I swear, I do not foresee any of them being killed before they kill one of you. The army was not large, a small force, but when you look at their faces, these men were willing to die." Another kufr saw them stuck like snakes, stealth movement, twisting like snakes at the back of the camels.

Carrying their weapons with them, one can imagine sun baked skin, still holding their weapons, it was a dreadful scene. Hakim goes to Ottba bin Rabia, one of the prominent leaders of Quraish, he says "O'Ottba, shall I suggest something to you, if you do this you will carry the honor until the end of time". Ottba bin Rabia said "what is it?". Hakim bin Hazam said "you will draw this force back to Makkah, and you pay the blood money of your ally, Amer bin Hazrami". Who is Amer bin Hazrami? We remember the Suryia of Abdullah bin Josh, when they killed this man in the sacred month. That was the man Hazrami, and he was the ally with Ottba bin Rabia. Although Quraish came to defend the caravan, they also came to avenge the death of Amer bin Hazrami. The man responsible for that was Ottba bin Rabia. Hakim bin Hazam said "let us withdraw this army, you pay the blood money, and spare ourselves from this war. We are fighting with our own relatives. Ottba liked the idea. He said, "consider it done.

However, you go and convince Abu Jehail, he is the one I am afraid of. He might spoil this idea, go and convince him." Then Ottba bin Rabia stands up and says, "O'Quraish, by fighting Muhammad (pbuh) and his followers you will accomplish nothing. If you attack him, everyone will be looking at you, and you will be known to have killed their cousin or member of their tribe. Go home and leave Muhammad (pbuh) to other Arabs. If they kill him, that will accomplish your aim, otherwise you will not be exposed to the risk you plan. We shall be killing our own sons, brothers, and fathers. These are the people we are facing, leave this to other Arabs. If they kill him, that is fine, but if Muhammad (pbuh) wins he will not take revenge on the people who fought him."

Ottba bin Rabia was talking to Quraish, and Hakim bin Hazam went to Abu Jehail. He finds Abu Jehail in a gathering and gives him the message from Ottba. Abu Jehail tells him, "Ottba didn't find anybody else but you?" Hakim bin Hazam said "he could have sent someone else, but I could not be a messenger for anyone else." Abu Jehail says "I swear I saw his lungs filled with fear and terror when he saw Muhammad (pbuh) and his men. Ottba is not sincere in what he says, he sees Muhammad (pbuh) and his men as fodder for his camels, waiting to be slaughtered. And his own son is there amongst the Muslims, he is scaring you for his own sake. What he means, is that we will slaughter them, we will win, and Ottba is afraid that his own son is Muslim and does not want him to be killed. That is why he is asking us to withdraw."

Then Abu Jehail, a devil, goes to the brother of Amer bin Hazrami and says, "you are an ally of Ottba, and he wants us to withdraw. He wants to withdraw the army back." Now he says to him, "go and inspire the army to not withdraw."

He is talking to the brother of Amer bin Hazrami. And Amer's brother goes and screams, "WOE TO AMER, WOE TO AMER!" And marches in front of the army, inspiring them to fight and not withdraw. Ibn Ishaque says, so the mood of warfare becomes heated, and the attitude of the Quraish hardened, and Ottba's advice is ignored. Ottba says "that fellow with a filthy yellow backside will find out whether it is he or me, who's lungs were filled with terror."

Not only did he incite the army, but also cornered Ottba, so he asked first for duel. He was the first with the Muslims, this shows how effective this devil Abu Jehail was. Let us take a stop, the holy Prophet (pbuh) was saying, whatever good there maybe, that was in the man of the red camel. If they listen to him they will be well guided. Now brothers and sisters there are men of reason, there are people who are moderate, however when it becomes a battle against Islam, when it is a religious war, with intention to find the truth, these voices of reason are swept aside. The voices of fanatism and extremism gain the upper hand.

Abu Sufyan asked them to go back. Now there is another tribe called Banu Zara, they withdrew. They refused to fight. Now Ottba tried, Hakim tried, but the disbelievers have different standards. Abu Sufyan's son was taken a prisoner of war by the Muslims. Abu Sufyan said "they have killed one of my sons and let the other one stay with them. There was a member of a Muslim tribe who went to Makkah for Umrah. Now Quraish would honor any pilgrim, they would never violate him, any pilgrim would be respected, honored and hosted by Quraish. The honor of Quraish was to be generous to pilgrims. Now, this Muslim was taken as a prisoner, Ibn Ishaque says "this was the first time, they violated this law, Abu Sufyan took him as a prisoner, the pilgrim went to the Prophet (pbuh) and told him their son has been taken prisoner. The Prophet (pbuh) freed Abu Sufyan's son, and Abu Sufyan freed the pilgrim he took prisoner. The reason for this story is to show that kufr, when dealing with Muslims, they have different standards. And this is the truth. Although Ottba tried, Abu Jehail won the argument. Muslims slept the night, the Earth was firm, and the Muslims were active and ready to fight.

Allah blessed them with something else, the Prophet (pbuh) saw a dream where the Quraish army were less than they actually were. When the Muslims saw the Quraish army, they also saw them less than they actually were. Allah says, "remember, when he showed them to you as fewer than they were, so that Allah might accomplish a battle already destined, and to Allah all matters return. Allah gives us the explanation, when the enemies saw the Muslims, they also saw them as less. And that would make them more eager to fight. It also made them careless, overconfident.

But when they met the Muslims, their moral went down. For Muslims to see the enemies less, would also give them confidence, and strength to fight. The strategy of the Prophet Muhammad (pbuh), they used the tactics, which were not used by Arabs before, perhaps used by other armies, but not by Arabs. The Arab method was Al-Cur Wal Fur, attack and withdraw. This was a disorganized attack. The Prophet (pbuh) was applying the method of ranks. 1st rank, armed with lances, the ranks in the back were archers armed with bows and arrows. The archers will fire from behind and lances will fight in front to stop the advance of the opponents. This was a new tactic, applied by the Prophet (pbuh). In Surah Suf, Allah says "Allah loves those who fight in his cause in rows. This method gives the leader greater control over his army. It is called Suf. The Prophet (pbuh) was also encouraging the army, and that is the instruction from Allah. O'Prophet, urge the believers to battle, inspire them. If there are 20 Muslims who are steadfast, they will overcome 200. And if among you, there are 100 steadfast Muslims, they will overcome 1000 disbelievers, because they are people who do not understand." The holy Prophet (pbuh) stands up in front of the army and says, "any free man who fights without retreating, Allah will give him paradise."

This is in Muslim Sharif, the Prophet (pbuh) stands up in front of the army and says, "go forth towards the gardens of the Paradise, the size of the earth." One of the Sahaba, his name is Amer bin Khmam says "O messenger of Allah, could the gardens be the size of the Heavens and the earth combined?" The Prophet (pbuh) said "yes." Then Amer bin Khmam says "fine, fine." The holy Prophet asks him "what makes you say that?" Then Amer says "O'messenger of Allah it is my hope to be one of those people. I want to be in Jannah (Paradise)". The holy Prophet (pbuh) said "you certainly will be." Amer bin Khmam stands up, draws his sword. He got some dates out of his pocket and started to eat those dates and said, "if I live long enough to finish these dates, that will be a long life." He was so inspired by the words of the Prophet (pbuh), he was in hurry to die in the path of Allah. And he rushed in fray of battle. That is how much the Sahaba were inspired by the Prophet (pbuh).

WHAT HAPPENED TO OMIYA BIN KHALF

Saad bin Moaz said "I was a friend with Omiya Bin Khalf, when he visited Madinah, he would stay with me, and when I visited Makkah, I would stay with him." He visited Makkah and stayed with Omiya bin Khalf. Saad bin Moaz told Omiya bin Khalf he wanted to perform Umrah. When they were performing Umrah, Abu Jehail saw them. He came and said to Omiya, "who is this man?", Omiya said "he is Saad bin Moaz." Abu Jehail said to Saad bin Moaz, "you have given sanctuary to Muhammad (pbuh) and you say that you will help him to be a victor. If you were not with Omiya, I would have killed you." Saad bin Moaz said, "if you do that, I shall do worse to you, we shall prevent your caravans from passing through Madinah." Madinah controls the lifeline of Quraish. Omiya bin Khalf then told Saad bin Moaz, "do not speak like that to Abu Al-Hakam, because he is the chief of this valley." Saad bin Moaz said "let us not talk about this anymore," he also said, "I also heard that the Prophet (pbuh) has said, that they will kill you." Omiya bin Khalf said, "did he say that?", and Saad replied "yes." Then, Omiya bin Khalf asked a question, "did he say he will kill me inside Makkah or outside of Makkah?" Saad bin Moaz said, "I do not know." Omiya told his wife that my friend from Madinah told me that Muhammad (pbuh) promised his followers that he is going to kill me. Then his wife asked if he told him where Muhammad (pbuh) was going to kill him. He told her, that he asked whether it was outside Makkah or inside Makkah, and Saad bin Moaz said he does not know. But I am never going to leave Makkah. Allah be praised, they would accuse the Prophet (pbuh) of lying but would believe everything he said. Deep in their hearts, they knew that he is the messenger of Allah, they are rejecting the messages, even though they know that they are true.

When the call came to respond to the battle of Badr, Omiya did not want to leave. Abu Jehail brought him a box, that is a joker's dress. They burn inside of the box. He gave it to Omiya and said, "use it like an old woman." Abu Jehail was insulting Omiya, that he will stay behind like an old woman. Abu Jehail kept on trying, until he was able to convince Omiya to come with him. Omiya went home to prepare, his wife asked him if he remembers what his friend from Madinah told him. He said, "yes I do. But I am going to go so far with them, and then I shall come back." Ibn-e Kathir (Katheer) says "whenever they would stop, he would make the intention that the next stop will be his last, until he ended up entering the battle." Now Abdurrahman bin Auf tells the story. Abdurrahman was also a friend of Omiya. He had some coat nails he picked up from the battlefield, and they are expensive. He had collected them as booty. One by one, then Omiya bin Khalf sees him and said "Abdurrahman", there was no reply.

Abdurrahman and Omiya were friends in Makkah. The name of Abdurrahman was Abid Amir, when he became Muslim, he changed his name to Abdurrahman. Omiya bin Khalf said, "when I called Abid Amir, he did not respond, and I cannot call you Abdurrahman. So, choose a name just for me and you. And he chose the name Abdullah, meaning servant of Allah. They agreed because non-Muslims would recognize Rahman. The other narration is (in Bukhari Sharif), Abdurrahman told Omiya, that he will look after his business, interest in Madinah, and he will take interest in his business in Makkah. Abdurrahman says, "when he called Abdullah, I responded," Omiya said, "do you want something better than those coat nails you are carrying? Abdurrahman asked, "what is it?" Omiya said, "me and my son". Omiya is rich, his ransom will fetch a lot of money. Same with his son Ali. Abdurrahman says, "I threw the armors away, and held Omiya and his son in each of his hands". Now they are his prisoners of war (P.O.W.). Now officially, he should get the ransom for them, and that was a better deal for Abdurrahman. But someone spots Omiya, that was Bilal bin Raba. Bilal bin Raba, the old slave of Omiya, the one who was tortured by Omiya. And the story of the torcher of Bilal is incredibly famous. Bilal said after having seen Omiya, "he is the head of the disbelievers," Abdurrahman said, "hey Bilal, this is my prisoner (Omiya)." And Bilal says, "I shall not live if he does." Bilal goes to some of the Ansar's and tells them that man is Omiya bin Khalf, the head of the disbelievers. He tells them he will not live if Omiya does. Abdurrahman says, "they attacked, when I realized I cannot defend Omiya and his son, I released Ali (Omiya's son). So that they get busy with him, and I told Omiya to run with me. They attacked Ali and killed him, cut him in pieces. He was telling Omiya to run, but he was a heavy man, and they ended up catching up with them. He told Omiya to lie down, and then I jumped over him to protect him with my own body. The swords of Ansar were digging deep under me, tearing Omiya apart. In fact, one of them injured my foot. The narrator of this story says, "Abdurrahman would show us the scar that was left, and he would say may the mercy of Allah be on Bilal, he made me lose my armors, and lose my prisoners. I lost both. This is what happened to Omiya bin Khalf, whom Bilal said was the Imam of the disbelievers. When they were walking through the site of Badr, Omiya asked who that man was who had Oster's feathers across his chest. And Abdurrahman said, "that was Hamza bin Abdul Mutlab." Omiya said, "this is the man who ruined us," Hamza bin Abdul Mutlab was truly the lion of Allah.

MUBARAZA – DUELING

Ottba, his brother Sheba and his son Waleed, they came in front of the army for one-to-one dueling. And three young men from Ansar jumped forward. When they approached, Ottba said, "who are you, introduce yourselves." They introduced themselves as the opponents. Ottba said, "we have no quarrel with you, we want men of Quraish. Send people equal to our status." The messenger of Allah wanted his own family to go out, when they came back, the messenger of Allah sent Hamza, Ali and Obeda. Then the Prophet (pbuh) says, "O'Hamza, stand up, O'Ali, stand up, and O'Obeda, stand up." Obeda bin Harris, is the cousin of the Prophet (pbuh). This was the first-time face to face, this fight is not for wealth, but for the lord. They came, Ottba against Obeda. They were old and they went against each other. Ali went against Waleed, and Hamza went against Sheba. Ali and Hamza both killed their opponents, but Ottba and Obeda both exchanged multiple blows. Both of them fell down, they could not fight any longer, but were still alive. Ali and Hamza both attacked Ottba and killed him. The Prophet (pbuh) did not say anything, which means what they did was acceptable. They then carried Obeda back, he was injured. The Prophet (pbuh) honored him by putting his head on his lap. Long time ago, Abu Talib said, "we shall serve the Prophet (pbuh) with our wives and children. We shall lay before him, our sons, our wives, and our lives." Obeda said, "O'messenger of Allah, if Abu Talib could see me, he said those words for me," and then he sadly died in the cause of Allah. The Prophet (pbuh) said, "I testify that you are a martyr," at that the Quraish were enraged and started advancing towards the Muslims. The Prophet (pbuh) had given instructions, stay calm and shoot when they are in range. Preserve your arrows. Allah be praised. When the battle started, the, Mushriqeen (non-Muslims) saw that the Muslims have double the amount of people as before (in Quran, there is a sign for two armies who met, one fighting in the cause of Allah, and the other one of disbelievers.

The Muslims had battle cries, 'AUD, AUD' (one, one). Harsa, one Ansar was shot by a stray arrow. He was killed by friendly fire. After the battle, Harsha's mother came to the Prophet (pbuh) to find out whether he was a martyr or not. The Prophet (pbuh) said, "there are plenty of gardens in Paradise, and your son has earned one of the highest. Allah has given you victory when you were fewer in numbers. Fear Allah, you may be grateful. The number of angels could be 3000 or more, victory is from Allah. I saw Angel Gabriel taking his horse by reigns, all of the angels were wearing white turbans, except Angel Gabriel, he was wearing a yellow one. He was the leader of the angels on that day." There is a hadith in Muslim Sharif, 'when one of the Muslims were pursuing a Mushriq, he heard above him, noise of a whip, and the rider's voice was saying "giddy up, Hazam Aik dum, when Muslims saw the Mushriq in front of him, he found him prostrated on the ground. Seeing him closely, the man's nose was split, and his face smashed, by a whip, and all turned black.' This was a whip of fire. The fighter went to the Prophet (pbuh) and the Prophet (pbuh) said, "you speak the truth, this was the angel named Hazam."

Two young men, non-Muslims, they were there to watch on the day of Badr. They say, "we were up on a mountain, waiting for the battle to start, to see who would win the battle. Then near the mountain, we heard a voice saying, 'Hazam, giddy up Hazam.'" One of them suffered from a heart attack and died on the spot. While the other one fell unconscious, but later recovered. One Muslim says that he was pursuing the Mushriq, his head fell off. Then the Muslim thought he was killed by somebody else, but in reality he was killed by an angel. The qualities could be distinguished, who were killed by angels, Anice bin Malik says, "not only did the angels kill, but they also captured enemies. Al-Abbas, the uncle of the Prophet (pbuh), was captured. One Ansar said he captured him, but Al-Abbas said it was someone else on a horse. But the Ansar said it was him. The Prophet (pbuh) said "Allah helped you." The only battle the angels actually fought in was the battle of Badr, others they supported, but never actually fought. The death toll, 70 Mushriqeen (non-Muslims) were killed. And 70 were taken prisoners. Among the Muslims, no one was captured but there were 14 martyrs. Six from among Mahajreen, six from Al-Khazrj and two from Al-Auss.

DEATH OF ABU JAHL

Abdurrahman bin Auf says he was flanked by two young men on each side, normally soldiers want to have good soldiers right and left. Abdurrahman was not happy that he had two young men with him. Then the one on his right side said "O'uncle, show me which one is Abu Jahl". Abdurrahman responded, "Why do you want to know about Abu Jahl?" The young man said, "I swore to Allah, if I see him either I shall kill him or die in front of him". Now Abdurrahman is changing his mind about who is flanking him, then he points out Abu Jahl to him, and the man on the left whispers and asks the same question, they were whispering because they were competing with each other. Abdurrahman says, "When I pointed Abu Jahl to them, there was a crowd around Abu Jahl, they flew at him like a falcon". Also in Bukhari Sharif, it is added that two young men from Ansar, Amaz ibn Amer bin Jamoor and Alf bin Afua struck Abu Jahl down. In another narration they were two brothers, and in another narration, when they reached with Abu Jahl one of them struck the foot of Abu Jahl and the foot flew off like the kernel of a nut by a nutcracker. Then Akrama, son of Abu Jahl saw and he cut off the shoulder of Amaz, but the arms stayed with the body. Amaz said, "I carried on fighting, dragging my arm behind me until it started bothering me. I stepped over it and tore it off. Abu Jahl was disabled and was laying on the ground in his last moments."

The Prophet pbuh asked the Sohaba who will find out what happened to Abu Jahl, Abdullah bin Masood said, I went there, when I realized the man lying there is Abu Jahl I stepped over his neck. He once held me captive in Makkah and hurt me. Kicked me, then he asked him, so Allah has put you to shame, you enemy of Allah." Abu Jahl said, "how has he shamed me, am I not the most Noble man you have ever killed? Tell me which side won the day." Even in his last moments he wanted to know the result of this battle. Abdullah bin Masood said, "it went to Allah and his messenger," another narration, Abdullah bin Masood says "when I saw Abu Jahl, he was laying but holding a fine sword protecting him, while I had a poor sword, I struck his arm, his sword fell of and then I picked up that sword and I sat on his chest to sever his head. He said you have climbed extremely high for having been just a Hurds man.

Abu Jahl was even arrogant when dying, Abdullah bin Masood said I then severed his head and took it to Prophet pbuh. Abdullah bin Masood says "he was like walking on air, speeding off, happy to go and deliver the head of Abu Jahl to Prophet. He said O' Prophet this is the head of Allah's enemy. Is it really by Allah, no other or by non-other than him, and Abdullah bin Masood said yes. Then he threw the head down in front of Prophet, then praised Allah. Allah has disgraced you, you enemy of Allah. Abu Jahl was the Pharaoh of his people. Every nation has a Pharaoh and the Pharaoh of our nation was Abu Jahl. Ibn Kathir says "the death of Abu Jahl came on the hands of the youth of Ansar." There, after Abdullah bin Masood was placed over him. Look, whom Allah chose to kill Abu Jahl, two young men from Ansar and Abdullah bin Masood. Abdullah bin Masood was belittled by Abu Jahl.

Abdullah bin Masood was thin and slim, one day he was climbing a palm tree, wind was blowing, wind shock Abdullah bin Masood. He was a lightweight, the Sohaba laughed after having seen the thin legs of Abdullah bin Masood, the Prophet (pbuh) said "are you laughing because of his skinny legs they are heavier on the Day of Judgment than the mountain of Uhud." Allah will give you victory over them and satisfy the breast of believing people and remove the fury in their hearts.

THE STORY OF AL-QLEEB

Anis bin Malik says, "the messenger of Allah ordered that twenty-four bodies of the Quraish leaders should be thrown in the dirty well at Badr, (Al-Qleeb). The twenty-four bodies of the Quraish leaders were dragged into this grave. It was dirty because rubbish were dumped there." Anis bin Malik describes this, "when the body of Ottba bin Rabia was thrown, his son Adehefa was watching it. The Prophet (pbuh) looked at his face and saw that he was distressed and sad." The Prophet (pbuh) said, "O'Abu Adehefa, are you very upset at your father's fate?" Abu Adehefa responds, "I swear on the messenger of Allah, I have no problem with my father's fate, but I once knew him as a man of goodness, good judgement and reason. And I hoped that those qualities would lead him to Islam. When I saw what his fate was, how he died, in disbelief, despite my hopes for him, I was saddened." The Prophet (pbuh) prayed for him. Dear brothers and sisters, the issue of guidance is something in the hands of Allah. Here Abu Adehefa is saying that his father was wise, he was a man of reason, and he was a man of good judgement. He hoped that these qualities would guide him to Islam. But things did not turn out as he would have liked them to. And that is the case with Hazrat Abu Talib also. Abu Talib, the uncle of the Prophet (Pbuh) carried the same qualities, in fact he protected the messenger of Allah for an entire period in Makkah, until he passed away. Abu Talib never became Muslim. When it turns to the issue of guidance, one cannot tell who will be guided, and who would not be guided. Umer bin Khattab, he was on the forefront of the torcher of the Muslims, he became Muslim, and we have talked about his story. And we know, when one of the Sahobiat told her husband that Umer bin Khattab spoke softly, her husband told her, if you think he will become Muslim, he will never until his father's donkey becomes Muslim.

Meaning, get this idea out of your mind. Such a person will never become Muslim, but he did become Muslim. And he became an exceptionally good Muslim. He became one of the best Muslims. Only Allah knows who will be guided to Islam and who would not be, do not make a judgement on who's heart will be turned to Allah. At the end, Abu Talib dies as a Kufr, and Abu Sufyan died as a Muslim. Abu Talib supported all his life, but he will go to Hell fire. And Abu Sufyan, who fought against Muhammad (pbuh) most of his life, ends up becoming Muslim. Some issues should be left on Allah's will. Allah says to the messenger of Allah, "you do not guide the ones you want, or you love, but it is Allah, he guides who he wants. This is a matter of the Qadr of Allah. It is for Allah. Here Abu Adehefa was upset because his father did not become Muslim. It also shows that our loyalty should go to Allah entirely. Even though Abu Adehefa was sad that his father died a disbeliever, that did not make him forsake his religion, or blame someone. He accepted it, and said, "O'messenger of Allah, I have no problem with my father's fate, I accept it. I accept that it is from Allah." The Prophet (pbuh) tried extremely hard for his uncle, but it did not work.

While people came from far, far away, and accepted Islam. For example, Suleyman Pharsi and Abu Zar Ghaffari. The messenger of Allah, it was his habit to stay at the site of the battle for three days, before he would leave. When he was about to leave the site of Badr, he visited the Al-Qleeb, the well where twenty-four leaders of Quraish were buried. And he was speaking to them. The Prophet (pbuh) said, "would you now be pleased to have obeyed Allah and his messenger? We have found that Allah's promises are true. Have you found that what your lord promised you is true?" Umer bin Khattab said, "O'messenger of Allah, why do you speak to bodies who have no spirit in them?" The messenger of Allah said, "by him who holds the soul of Muhammad in his hand, you do not hear what I say, any better than them." And this is in Bukhari Sharif, Allah made them hear what the messenger of Allah was telling them, and this is to add to their punishment.

THE NEWS AFTER THE BATTLE

The Prophet pbuh, sent Abdullah bin Roha and Zaid bin Harsa, to Madinah to deliver the news. Zaid bin Harsa was riding the camel of the prophet pbuh. Abdullah bin Roha went to the upper part of Madinah. He delivered the news to each house of Ansar and Zaid bin Harsa went to the center of Madinah. He was riding on the camel of the prophet pbuh, when he came delivering the news that Autba bin Rubbia, Sheeba, were killed, Ibne Hijaj was killed, Abu Jahal was killed. He was mentioning the famous names of Quraish who were killed. The munafiq and the Jews said, this man does not know, what he is talking about, he is confused. He has run away from the battlefield. Muhammad himself was killed and the evidence is that Zaid is riding his camel. They went around spreading this news. Osama says, he went to his father and said, O' father, is this news true? That you are delivering, his father said, yes my son this is true. Osama was left behind to care for Rukiya (the daughter of the prophet pbuh) and Hazrat Usman. People were going to Abdullah bin Roha, asking him, Is this news true ? He responded yes, the news is true and the prophet pbuh is bringing the captives tomorrow. It was difficult for people to believe, what had happened. A force little over 300 defeated 1,000. Also famous Quraish were killed Ibne Hijaj, Abu Jahal al-Waleed, Sheeba,

Autba they were all killed on that day. Sohail bin Ahmar was captured, he was taken as prisoner. It was too good to be true.

Next day the prophet pbuh came in with prisoners and with victory from Allah. Prisoners were placed in a certain location. Umma Sauda, the wife of the prophet pbuh, when she saw Sohail bin Ahmar with his hands tied to his neck, he was one of the noble men of Quraish. She said, "Why you did not die as a noble man ? Why did you allow yourself to be humiliated?" The prophet pbuh said, are you asking him to fight Allah and his messenger. In fact she was asking why you did not fight. But to fight, he had to fight against the messenger of Allah. She apologized and said O' Messenger of Allah when I saw him in this state, I couldn't but say such a statement. That shows us that leaders of Quraish were humiliated because of their disbelief.

The Prophet pbuh stopped at Rooah to receive congratulations from people. One of the Ansar said, what is that you are congratulating us for, we only met old bold men like camels waiting slaughter, and we slaughtered them. The prophet pbuh said, hay, my cousin, do not say that. These are the chiefs. This Ansari was saying it was so easy, the people we faced were old men who did not know how to fight. That was Allah who helped you otherwise they were strong opponents. But Allah helped us. The news was delivered to Makkah. A man called Al-Hashem bin Qusai, he went to Makkah and says Abu ul Hukum was killed, Ottaba was killed Sheeba was killed, Waleed was killed. He is going down the list Omea was killed Safwan bin Omea was listening and said, this man has lost his mind. Ask him about me, to make sure that he is not crazy. They asked him, what happened to Safwan ? He said Safwan is sitting right there, but I have seen death of his father and his brother with my own eyes. This was a very bad news for people of Makkah. How could Abu

Jahal be killed, Omea and Ottaba be killed. It was impossible for them to believe. But surely the news was sinking in.

ABU LAHAB

Abu Lahab stayed behind but he sent someone else to fight. Raffah says, he was a servant of Al Abbas and our household was muslim. Raffah himself, Al Abbas, Uma Fazal she is the wife of Al Abbas. He used to make arrows. He was sitting in pavilion around Kabbah sharpening arrows while Abu Lahab was sitting his back towards him, when one of the fighters from Quraish approached, Abu Lahab said, come up and tell us the news, what happened? The man came and he said. As soon as the fighting started, we handed ourselves over to them to be killed and to be taken captives, but I do not blame them for this because we were facing men in white clothes on horses between the heavens and earth and nothing can stop them. When Raffah heard that, he said, In the name of Allah, those were the angles. Abu Lahab turned around and punched him in the face. Raffah said, I started fighting back, but Abu Lahab was stronger than me, I was the weak man, he was sitting over me and beating me hard then Umma al- Fazal came with a rod and she hit Abu Lahab on the head and told him, you are taking advantage that his master is not around. Then Abu Lahab left. Raffah says, Abu Lahab was inflicted with a disease and died a week later. This particular disease terrified the people of Quraish. Nobody wanted to go near him. Abu Lahab died and remained in his house for three days, until body started decomposing and nobody wanted to bury him. Quraish went to two of his sons, told them you should be ashamed, the body of your father is decomposing and you do not want to bury him because you are afraid of the disease. They ended up dragging him and placing him next to a wall and covered it by stones. This is the humiliation he suffered even after his death. People of Quraish prevented to cry publicly for their dead, there was no vailing allowed. Also they refused any body to investigate the issue of ransom for prisoners. Ibne Kathir says he observed, Allah is forcing them to forego mourning for their dead this was part of the totality of his punishment of those who remained alive for that time. Mourning for the dead contributes for the grieving hart. Ibne Mutlab was inflicted with the loss of his three sons. He was an old man, already blind and he was not allowed to mourn for the loss of his three sons.

One night he heard a woman weeping, he sent someone to find out, if mourning has become permissible, and now Quraish are allowed vailing for their dead. Perhaps he will be able to redeem the loss of Abu ul Hukum, his elder son, because he was in great pain. They found out that woman was crying because she had lost a camel. His lines of poetry said, is she crying because a camel of hers has gone astray, so samia is keeps her from sleeping. Do not weep over young camel but over Badr that ruined our hopes over Badr and the alit of Banu Hasces Mukhzoom and the tribe of Abu ul Waleed, and weep if you weep at all for Abu Akeel and Abu Harris -the lion of lions -weep for them all and do not for that for there is none like Abu ul Hakeem. After that – had it not for Badr they would have come to me. This poor man was not allowed to mourn the loss of his three sons. Quraish wanted to pretend that they are brave and do not care. Surah IN fall, was revealed after the Ghazwa Badr, the first verses of surah IN fall, reveal that was Muslims of Badr when they disputed the issue of booty, spoils of war. Muslims were in three groups First group, they were protecting the Prophet pbuh, second group, they were pursuing the enemy and third group was collecting the spoils of war. The ones, who collected, they said, these belong to us, but the ones who were protecting the prophet pbuh, they also wanted their share and the ones who were pursuing the enemy said, without us you would not have spoils of war, they disputed and were arguing. Allah revealed the Ayat of Surah In fall, O' Muhammad, they ask you about the bounty of war, say, the decision concerning bounty is for Allah and his messenger, therefore everything was brought to the prophet pbuh. All of this belongs to Allah and the messenger of Allah. Allah says fear Allah and amend that, which between you, and obey Allah and his messenger, if you should be believers, this Aya is teaching the fighters that they should Trust in Allah. (Taqwa). You cannot fight for the sake of Allah without taqwa.

Amend between you and you have to have unity. For fighters for the sake of Allah, Aya one and number three. Obey Allah and his messenger. Must have discipline. fighters without discipline are not going to succeed. And obedience of the leader. These are three qualities, Taqwa, Unity and Obedience of the leader. Then Allah gives the rulings, how the spoils of war will be divided. Allah says, Anything as war booty. Indeed, for Allah 1/5 of this and for the messenger and his near relatives and the orphans, the needy and the stranded traveler. If you believe in Allah and in that we sent down to our servant on a day when the two armies met. Allah is competent over all things. The rulings as regards the spoils of war is as follows, they are divided in to five portions, five equal portions. Four portions are distributed among the fighters, meaning 80% is divided among the fighters. The foot soldier receives one share and horse man receives three shares. The remaining 20% is further divided in to five portions. First portion to Allah, one portion to the messenger of Allah and one portion to relatives, one portion for orphans and final fifth portion for travelers.

The share of Allah and the messenger of Allah goes to projects like Mosques and other social needs like roads. It is up to the Imam of muslims to distribute. These are the rulings regarding the distribution of the booty. Another issue dealt in Surah in fall is prisoners of war. There were seventy (70) prisoners of war. The Prophet pbuh invited companions and held conference for different opinions. Abu Bakar spoke, his opinion was, these are our relatives and from our tribes ask

for ransom. This will strengthen us and also this will strengthen Islam and may be these people will become muslim in future. That was the opinion of Abu Bakar Allah may give them guidance. Umar bin Khattab said, O' Messenger of Allah. They exiled you and called you a Lier, give them to their close relatives and strike their necks. This was the opinion of Umar Allah be pleased with him. This way Allah will know that we feel no leniency towards non-believers. Abdullah bin Rahwa spoke, he said O' Messenger of Allah, I suggest, find a valley with many trees, make them enter and then set fire to it, burn them. The Prophet pbuh went in came back and said, Allah softened the hearts of men concerning him, so they become softer than soft, and Allah hardened the hearts of men so they become hard as stone. Abu Bakar, you are like Abraham, who said, whoever follows me is from me and whoever disobeys, then to Allah, you are forgiving and merciful. Abu Bakar, you are like Eisa pbuh (Jesses) who said, to punish them, they are your servants and you forgive them, you are all powerful and wise.

Umar, you are like Nuh pbuh, who said O' Lord do not leave on earth any place for non-believers prophet Nuh pbuh made supplication to Allah, to obliterate and destroy all kuffar, and also Umar you are like Moses pbuh who said, O' Allah destroy their wealth and make their hearts hard, for they will not believe until they see the painful punishment. The Prophet pbuh said, let non be exempt from ransom or having their head smitten. The prophet pbuh was inclined to adopt the opinion of Abu Bakar and was willing to accept ransom. One day Umar bin Khattab came and saw, The Messenger of Allah and Abu Bakar were crying, Umar says, I went to the prophet pbuh, early in the morning, he was with Abu Bakar they were weeping. I asked O' Messenger of Allah and your companion, why are you crying ? If I find the reason, I shall weep otherwise I shall weep any way. I shall make myself weep. The Prophet pbuh said, I am weeping, how your companions proposed to me that to me to accept the ransom for prisoners of war. You proposed punishment that was closer than that tree. Meaning, Allah was not happy that Muslims have accepted ransom. why ? Allah revealed in Ayat 57 to 69 in Surah In-Fall. Allah says, it is not fitting for a prophet to have captives of war until he inflicts massacre upon Allah's enemies in the land. You desire the commodities of the world, but Allah desires for you hereafter. Allah is exalted in might and wise. If it was not for a decree from Allah that preceded, you would have been touched for what you have with a great punishment. The prophet pbuh should have executed them all, that is what would have pleased Allah. A newly formed state needs to show its strength in the beginning. Asking for ransom here is not. Then by decree of Allah, Allah has made ransom halal, therefore what Muslims did was halal. Otherwise they would have been punished. I hope this issue is clear.

THE BATTLE OF UHUD

There were several reasons, they were religious, social, political, and economical reasons. The religious reason, the people of Quraish wanted to stop the advancement of Islam. They wanted to stop people becoming Muslim. Allah says, "indeed those who, disbelieve they spend their wealth stopping people from way of Allah. They will spend, that will be their source of regret and then they will be overcome, they get together and mobilize the armies to fight the messenger of Allah. The social reason, the Quraish wanted to wash away the shame of Badr. The economical reason, now it was different. Allah says in Surah Quraish, "they were used to accustom security in summer and winter. The caravan of winter to Yemen and the caravan of summer to Syria. Now they refused to worship Allah, their security was gone. The Quraish, their trade was buying and selling products from Yemen to Syria and likewise, products from Syria to Yemen. Safwan bin Omiya says, "Muhammad (pbuh) and his companions have ruined our trade, while we do not know what measures to take against them. Muhammad (pbuh) was squeezing Makkah tightly. This was the planning and strategy of the Muslims to inflict damage against Quraish. Because they had thrown them out of Makkah and were against Islam and had taken over their property. Now, the defeat in Badr had weakened the authority of Quraish in Arabia status-quo was changing, before Quraish were noble, respected and powerful but not anymore. The Quraish wanted to regain their political status again. The Quraish mobilized an army of 3,000 strong and financed it from the caravan which Abu Sufyan saved. These were the causes of the battle of Uhud.

The Prophet (pbuh) was receiving information that there were intelligence units all over Al-Abbas bin Abdul Mutlab who was working for Muslims in Makkah. He sends a message to Prophet (pbuh), which was carried swiftly in three days. Full information their army was 3,000, they had 700 coat nails. Also, the number of camels, for full complete information. This was the first news of the intentions of Quraish. Aubia bin Kaab read the letter, the Prophet (pbuh) told him to keep it a secret. The messenger of Allah sent other people who brought the same information. Then the messenger of Allah sends out Annice and Mons, they brought the same information. The Prophet (pbuh) went to one of the chiefs of Ansar. Saad bin Rabia at his house, told him about Quraish and takes his opinion, this was secret discussion. After the Prophet (pbuh) left, the wife of Saad bin Rabia asked what the Prophet told you, and Saad bin Rabia says, "you do not need to know" but she says, "the Prophet (pbuh) said this and that because I heard him." Saad bin Rabia says, when a disaster happens Saad bin Rabia came to the Prophet and told him, that his wife knows this and if it comes out, do not think that Saad bin Rabia leaked it. The Prophet (pbuh) said "leave her alone." The Prophet (pbuh) held a Shura to discuss what to do? There were two opinions (i) we should fight within Madinah and use it as a fortress, fight in the streets, women and children will be able to participate from the roofs by throwing rocks at the enemy.

This was the opinion of the Prophet (pbuh) and Abdullah bin Abbey (ii) the majority opinion was to go out and meet the enemy in the battlefield. The reason was that it is shameful that we shall hide in Madinah and they will come and attack us in our own homes, we shall go out and meet them and would not allow them to come close to Madinah. This was the opinion of those who did not attend Badr. They did not want to miss. Another opinion was that they would not come into Madinah and it will be a missed opportunity to fight non-believers. This group put the pressure on the Prophet until he agreed with them. The Prophet (pbuh) went inside to put on his Armor, the group thought that we pressurized the Prophet (pbuh) and went to Hamza bin Abdul Mutlab to tell him to tell the Prophet (pbuh) we shall go along with whatever he says, Hazrat Hamza goes to the Prophet (pbuh) and informed him. The Prophet (pbuh) came out and said, it is not fitting for a Prophet of Allah to put on his armor and take it off, before Allah judges between him, the Prophet and the enemy. It means we have taken a decision and we shall go ahead with it. We are not going to change our mind. When a Prophet pbuh holds a Shura, he takes a decision, he will go ahead until Allah judges between him and the enemy. A leader should be decisive unless something changes or decision was taken on the wrong information. The followers or army soldiers, like a leader who does not change his decision often. They are following the leader.

The location was near mountain Uhud, which is few miles out of Madinah. The Muslim army marches out. The Prophet (pbuh) asked if anyone knew a way, that the enemy army would not see us. Abu Khaizam said, I will show the way. They traveled through agricultural land, rather than a traditional root out of Madinah, they passed through a farm owned by a Munafiqeen. Maraba bin Kayli, was blind and wanted to stop the Muslim army. He said, if you are messenger of Allah then I do not permit you to enter my garden. If you pass, I shall consider you are destroying my property. But the Prophet (pbuh) ignored him and his army goes forward. National interest is bigger than individual interest. That blind man picked up some earth in his hand and says, "by Allah if I know you, I shall hit you with this." This was very disrespectful, some of the Sohaba wanted to attack and to kill him. But the Prophet (pbuh) told them leave him do not kill him. This fellow is blind both in his heart and his eyes. They left him alone.

The Muslim army was 1,000, Abdullah bin Abbey pulls back 300 of his soldiers, the army is left with 700 soldiers. Abdullah bin Abbey gave the reason that Muhammad (pbuh) ignored his opinion and listened to youngster. He also said, "I do not think there will be any fighting," therefore he left. Now it is the battlefield which decides between Momin and Munafiq. Munafiqeen could be anywhere, do not know who is who. But Allah says, "Allah will not leave the believers in that state, Allah will separate evil from good." Surah Al-Imran, Allah says, "what struck you that two armies met at Uhud, by permission of Allah that Allah will make evident between the true believers and the hypocrites." Abdullah bin Abbey said, "if we knew there will be a fight, we would have followed you." They were nearer to disbelieve than to faith saying but something else in the heart. But Allah is knowing something else in the heart. Allah is knowing of what is in your heart. In fact, they were leaving because they knew there will be fight, there were two tribes, they were also on the edge of leaving. Banu Salman, but Allah made them steadfast. Allah says, "two parties wanted to leave but Allah was their ally." It is up to Allah whether a believer should rely. Because Allah says he is their ally that kept them firm. The Prophet (pbuh) refused assistance from the mushriqeen. The Prophet also turned back the underage. Araqa bin Fateej was turned back, and Abdullah bin Umar was turned back. But Arafa told the prophet, he is a good archer, and because of that he could join. His friend Samara went to his stepfather and started crying saying the Prophet allowed Arafa and I can beat him in wrestling. His stepfather took him to the Prophet and told him that Samara can beat Arafa in wrestling. The Prophet called them both and saw them wrestle in front of him and Samara defeated Arafa, the Prophet pbuh allowed him to join as an exception to the rules.

The Prophet (pbuh) divided the army in to 3 battalions, Almajroon the flag was given to Marain Dbair. Al-Auss and the flag was given to and the Al-Khazrj flag to Habab. The Prophet (pbuh) had the mountain of Uhud at the back, the Prophet saw the battlefield, and realized there was potential of an attack from the rare from the flanks, there was a small hill in front of them. The Prophet placed 50 men out of the 700. 50 Archers on top of that hill and gives them noticeably clear instruction. The Prophet of Allah said, protect our backs if you see us killed do not come to our aid. And you do not join if we are winning. Even you see vultures flying with us do not move until I send you the message. If you see us winning and trampling over enemy, do not leave until I send you a message, it was clear statement, whether we win or lose do not leave the place until I say so. It was a high sniper place, without that, the enemy could attack. The Prophet told the army do not start fighting until I order you to fight. The enemy was trying to disunite the Muslims. Abu Sufyan told the Ansar leave us alone to fight with our cousin because we have no purpose to fight with you. That was a lie and a trick. The Prophet held a sword in his hand and asked the Sohaba who will take this sword from me one of the Sohaba volunteered. But then the Prophet said who will take this sword with its rights. One of the Sohaba asked what are the rights of the sword, the Prophet said, "for you to strike the enemy with it until it bends." Abu Dojana came forward and said, "I will do it O'messenger of Allah".

He accepted the challenge. The Prophet gave it to Abu Dojana, Ibn Ishaque says, "when he took the sword from the Prophet, he took out a red head hand. He then started between two lines, and walks in front of the army with pride, one can see strength in his walk. The Prophet said that way of walking, Allah dislikes but in certain circumstances like this. Abu Dojana takes the sword and creates havoc in the enemy lines. Abdullah bin Zubair narrates a story of what he saw on the day of Uhud. He says, "every man he met Abu Dojana killed him among the mushriqeen. A man was killing whoever he wounded, this man and Abu Dojana came close to each other and I prayed to Allah to bring them together and they did meet, they exchanged few blows the Mushriq struck a blow but Abu Dojana used his shield which stuck the sword of Mushriq, then Abu Dojana struck and killed him. Kaab bin Malik says, I then saw a Mushriq well armored, saying to Muslims "come on you sheep, gathering for slaughter," then he saw a Muslim fully armored (did not know who he was) waiting for him. Kaab bin Malik says "I went behind and was sizing them up." The Mushriq were bigger, well equipped and covered with armor, one would expect that mushriq would win. I kept on waiting until they met. The Muslim struck a blow on his shoulder, the sword came right down to his thigh cutting him into two and then Abu Dojana said, "what about that Kaab, I am Abu Dojana," Abu Dojana knew that Kaab was watching. He was a proud man. The Muslims were winning and the enemy were fleeing the battle ground. The Sohaba said, "we could see the jewelry on the feet of the women, because they were tucking up their clothes ready to run away." The enemy were showing Muslims their backs. Banu Abdider, who was given the responsibility of holding the standard of Quraish that was the division of Authority in Quraish.

One family food and water to pilgrims, one had a key to the Kabba and one had key to Nadwa the parliament. One family to hold the banners of war, this family was Banu Abdider, they held in Badr and also in Uhud. Abu Sufyan told Banu Abdider you oversaw banners in Badr and you saw what happened to us. Men will fight for their flag. If flags are lost, they will drop. Either take care of the banners or give them to us and we will relieve you. This angered them and they returned the banners and said we shall meet in the battlefield and show you how we behave. Abu Sufyan charged them up, and that is the response Abu Sufyan wanted. Banu Abdider fought well they last 7 men one after another. They were all killed carrying their banner. Then one of their slaves, his name is Saab. He took hold of it and his arms were severed, still hugging the banner and said have I served well. After that, the banner fell and they left it on the ground. At that time, the Quraish started to flee the battleground. They were defeated, they lost. Allah says, Allah has fulfilled his promise to you when you were killing them by his permission. According to the Quran, the Muslims have won the battle of Uhud. But the tide was turning, the Archers who were instructed by the messenger of Allah to remain on the hill, even if you see vultures eating from our body, do not come down.

But as the Archers saw Muslims were gathering booty they wanted to go and join. But their Ameer Abdullah bin Jabeer said, "you know the instructions of the messenger of Allah, don't move until I tell you to move." They said the battle is over and they left. Out of the 50, 40 Archers defected, they disobeyed the order of Prophet, and this is a profoundly serious offence. Khalid bin Waleed was the head of cavalry of the Quraish himself and Akrama bin Abu Jahl, they detected the weak point that was exposed, they immediately took advantage of that and out flanked the Muslim army. Also, Muslims were not expecting that and were taken by surprise. It brought a chaotic state for Muslims and when the Quraish army saw that they returned and attacked. Muslims were attacked from both sides; the Muslim ranks became disorganized. At that time Muslims were defeated and were killed falling one after the other. It is said that only 12 men remained around the Prophet (pbuh). Allah says, "Allah has fulfilled his promise to you, when you were killing by his permission until you lost the courage and you dispute him and disobeyed the order of the Prophet after he had shown you that what you love in victory. Some of you who desired this world, Abdullah bin Masood say I did not know that some of us desire this world until this Ayat was revealed. This is how the Quran writes history, not only external but internal feelings of some. Then he turned you back. But Allah has already forgiven you. But is testing you on defeat, victory in Badr but defeat in Uhud. Ibn Ishaque says, "the Muslim ranks broke and enemy gained the advantage. It was a day of trial and testing where Allah honored some with martyrdom. At the enemy broke through to the messenger of Allah. He was hit with a rock and fell on his side breaking his front teeth slashing his face and lips. The Prophet was injured. In Bukhari Sharif, Fatima was washing him and Ali was pouring water. When she saw washing was increasing the blood flow, she took a piece of mat she burned it and then attached it to the wound. Hot ashes stopped the blood. Also, the Prophet's helmet was crushed into his head. Abdullah bin Abu Waqas hit the lip and lower tooth; the Prophet spoke a curse against Atiya bin Abu Waqas.

"O' Allah change may not come to him, he dies as non-believer, and no change came over him. He died as non-believer bound for hell fire. Annice bin Malik says, the Prophet (pbuh) while wiping blood from the face, said, "how any people could prosper, who wounded the Prophet of Allah and broke his front teeth. How could they succeed, who could do this to a Prophet who is calling them to Allah?" Allah revealed, "it is not for you O' Muhammad but for Allah to decide to cut them down or to forgive them or punish them. It is up to Allah." Some Muslims heard the rumors that the Prophet (pbuh) is wounded and killed. How did they the Muslims react? Some of them said we ask Abdullah bin Abbey to get us truce from Abu Sufyan. 'O, people, Muhammad (pbuh) has been killed, go back home before they kill you.' Some Muslims were defeated in the heart., but other Muslims one of the Muhajir passed by one Ansar. A man who was covered in his own blood and asked him, "are you aware that Muhammad (pbuh) has been killed?" The Ansar replied, "if Muhammad (pbuh) has been killed, he must have fulfilled his mission so fight on for your religion let us die as he died fighting for Islam." These Muslims cannot be defeated in heart even if they are defeated in the battle ground. Defeat will never get into their spirit.

Muslims had to retreat, not in orderly way. The messenger of Allah wanted to retreat in orderly fashion but the enemy had the upper hand and were attacking with full force. They were coming closer, the messenger of Allah said, "whoever will repel them, he will be my companion in paradise." That is how difficult it was. The Prophet (pbuh) was promising paradise. One of the Ansar volunteered. He would fire his arrows at the enemy until he was killed. Prophet pbuh asked for volunteer another Ansar comes up, he is also killed. And then It was an extraordinarily strong attack from Quraish Until 7 of Ansar were martyrs, 7 bodies lay there while defending the Prophet pbuh and this is the reason they are called Ansar. This honor from Prophet pbuh and in Quran, they earned it. May Allah be pleased with them. Ali bin Abu Talib says, "I never heard

Prophet pbuh say about both his parents to be sacrificed except Saad bin Abu Waqas." I have heard the Prophet to Saad bin Abu Waqas, "shoot, may my mother and father be your ransom," the Prophet (pbuh) was so pleased with him. Another hero standing next to the messenger of Allah was Tla bin Obaidullah. This is narrated by Annice bin Malik say Abu Tla was shooting from in front of the Prophet and shielding him with his body. When Abu Tla would shoot the messenger of Allah would raise himself to see where the arrow will hit. Abu Tla would raise his chest and say, "O'Prophet my parents be your ransom, no arrow will hit you. He said O' Prophet direct me according to needs and order me whatever you want." These were the companions of Prophet. The Prophet (pbuh) retreated to the mountain of Uhud itself. Tla had carried him because Prophet was injured, when they went up, the battle stopped because Quraish would not pursue the Muslims up the mountain. Also, cavalry cannot fight in such trains that had to be foot soldiers. Now the Muslims with the Prophet (pbuh) were up in the mountain and Abu Sufyan approaches them. He calls and asks if Muhammad is alive. There was no answer, then he asks if Abu Bakr is alive, no response, finally he asked if Umer is alive. Abu Sufyan is happy and tells his people that these men have been killed. Now Umer bin Khattab, stands up and says the three men you named are alive to upset you. Abu Sufyan says, "a battle for battle" i.e., Badr, one day you win and one day we win. And you will find some bodies mutilated. I did not order that but it does not bother me and starts chanting, 'raise up Hubble'. Prophet pbuh asked wouldn't you response, question what we say, say Allah is higher and glorious. Abu Sufyan said we have Al-Uaza, another idol and you have no Uaza. Prophet pbuh said, say Allah is our master and you have no master. Allah says about climbing up the mountain, Allah says, remember when you fled and climbing the mountain with looking aside anyone. The Messenger of Allah was calling you from behind so Allah repaid you with distress upon distress as you would not grief which has escaped you or that which had befallen you, Allah is fully acquainted with what you do.

Allah also says "indeed those of you who turned away when two armies met. That was Satan who caused them to slip because some blame they had earned." But Allah has already forgiven them. Allah is forgiving. Surah Al-Imran, Allah says, "the matter belongs completely to Allah they say, if there was anything we could have done, we would have not been killed. Tell them, even if they were inside their houses, they would have been killed it is so that Allah might test what is in your breast and what is in your hearts and Allah is knowing what is in their breast." Munafiqeen were saying why did we participate in this trouble why are we fighting Jihad. Why, Allah says "you were not killed because of Jihad, if you had stayed at home even then you would have been killed, it is a decree of Allah you will die when your time comes. The Battle of Uhud was a test from Allah. Do not blame for the deaths of Muslims. There were 70 martyrs on the day of Uhud. There are many Ayat and hadith, about martyrs on the day of Uhud. Hazrat Hamza bin Abdul Mutlab died on that day. According to the Quran, martyrdom is not death. But we are using the word. I hope everybody will understand. Two Sohaba went to see washi, who was old at the time, they wanted to share the story. How he killed Hazrat Hamza. Washi said, "I shall tell you, as I told the Prophet (pbuh), Washi says, I was a slave of Jabeer bin Matem, Taama bin Adey was his uncle who was struck down at Badr when Quraish went to Uhud, Jabeer told me if you kill Hamza, the uncle of the Prophet, in retaliation of my uncle's death, then you will be a free man. I went out with my warriors (he was from Abyssinia) and could throw the spear like my country men (he was good at it). He would rarely miss with it. When forces met in battle, he waited for Hamza bin Abdul Mutlab, laid in wait. He found him in middle of affray. He would tear apart anybody. I was hiding behind the bushes. I was close to him but Saba Auza got there before me. Hamza bin Abdul Mutlab saw him and said to him come here you son of a woman who does circumcision. He then struck a blow so quickly, that appeared to have missed his head. I aimed my spear carefully and when sure of it. I threw it at him. It struck him below his naval and emerged between his legs. He tried to move towards me but was overcome, I left him with the spear until he died. Then I went over to him to retrieve my spear and return to camp where I stayed. I had no other business. I did that to gain my freedom." The messenger of Allah heard the news of the death of his uncle, it was devastating. One of the saddest moments in the life of the Prophet (pbuh). The Prophet (pbuh) asked for a death spot? One of the Sohaba went with the messenger of Allah, when I saw his stomach was open and his insides pulled out.

Sahaba said this mutilation happened afterwards. This is when Hinda bin Atiya, wife of Abu Sufyan wanted to eat the liver of Hamza. This is the state in which Prophet pbuh saw his uncle, incredibly sad. Then Washi says, "he went back to Makkah and the Prophet (pbuh) opened Makkah, he had to leave Makkah and went to Tawif. When Tawif delegation went to meet the Prophet (pbuh) and to accept Islam. I did not know what to do. Wanted and thinking to go to Syria or Yemen then people said the Prophet pbuh would not kill anybody, who accept the truth meaning accept Islam. Then I went to Makkah and told the truth. When Prophet pbuh saw me asked me if I am Washi." I said, "yes O' messenger of Allah then I was told to sit down and relay to him how I killed Hamza. I relayed the same story," then the Prophet pbuh said

"O' Washi can you remove your face from me?" The Prophet (pbuh) did not want to see the face of Washi as it will bring back memories of his uncle. Washi later joined army that went to fight Muslima qzab, the man who claimed to be a Prophet. Washi says, "I took the spear with which I killed Hamza, when forces met, I saw Muslima standing, sword in his hand, while I was preparing to attack Muslima, another Muslim from the other side was preparing to attack Muslima. Washi with his spear and the other Muslim with his sword. I held my spear until I felt good then let it loose and it struck Muslima. While the other Muslim attacked with his sword and killed him." Washi struck first then the other Muslim, Allah knows who killed him, the other Muslim was Abu Dojana, Washi says, "if I killed Muslima, then I killed the best of men Hamza and the worst of men Muslima. It is said that Prophet pbuh told Washi go and fight in the path of Allah as you fought against Muslims. Good deeds erase the evil ones in Islam (this is a month of forgiveness).

The Prophet (pbuh) saw a woman rushing through dead bodies, the Prophet (pbuh) told Zubair to stop that woman, Zubair says, "that was his mother," the aunt of the Prophet (pbuh), Safiya bin Abdul Mutlab, Zubair stops her but she pushes him away. Ibn Qaim who shot the Prophet (pbuh) in the cheek. Ottba bin Abu Waqas who hit the lip and broke the lower tooth.

REACTION TO THIS DEFEAT

Annice bin Malik says, "while the Prophet (pbuh) was wiping the blood from his face, how people can prosper, when they injure the Prophet and break his teeth when he calls them to Allah. Allah revealed, "the fate of the people is not up to you it is up to Allah. The time between the battle of Uhud and battle of the Trench." The Prophet (pbuh) heard the news that forces of Banu Assad and other tribes were preparing to attack Madinah and Tla Azadi was their leader. This man started fighting against the Prophet pbuh then became Muslim and after the Prophet (pbuh) he apostates and claims to be a Prophet, and after that he changes his religion and becomes Muslim again and he fights for the sake of Allah (mujahid) now he was recruiting against Islam. But the Prophet pbuh Strikes first to surprise them, the Prophet pbuh sent a Muslim army led by Abu Muslma. Abu Muslma was injured in the battle of Uhud. But this Suraiya was successful and the booty was cattle. But his injury came back and he died, another tribe was getting ready to fight the Prophet (pbuh) this was Hodli, their leader was Khalid bin Sufyan, the Prophet (pbuh) said, "Khalid bin Sufyan was getting ready to fight so go and kill him." These orders were delivered to Abdullah bin Annice, and he said, "describe him to me, so I shall know what he looks like because I have never seen him." Prophet said, "if you see him you will tremble." Perhaps he was a powerful man. Abdullah bin Annice said I never tremble for the sight of anyone. But the Prophet (pbuh) said, "if you see Khalid bin Sufyan, you will tremble." Abdullah bin Annice was brave, he would not fear. This was a special sign, Abdullah bin Annice says he carried his sword and went out. Khalid bin Sufyan was gathering men in Arafat, close to Makkah, that area supported Quraish. Abdullah bin Annice says, "I was walking towards this man, when I saw him, I shivered. So, I knew this man was Khalid bin Sufyan. He was with some women from his family trying to find a camp."

Abdullah bin Annice walked towards him, it was Asr time (prayer time), Abdullah wanted to pray Asr salah, but how could he pray in front of this man. He will know that I am a

Muslim. Therefore, I was praying while walking towards him. My Rakat and Sajood was the movement of my head. When I reached with him. He asked who you are. Abdullah bin Annice said, I am a Badoo, Arab. We have heard about your plans to fight Muhammad (pbuh) and I came to join you. He said, "yes that is what I am doing." Abdullah bin Annice said, "I talked with him for a while, until I felt confident to attack. I attacked him with my sword and killed him. And left him dead with his women. I came back to Madinah, the Prophet pbuh prayed for success, I told him that I have killed him." The Prophet (Pbuh) said, "yes you did, you are speaking the truth. Then the Prophet pbuh called him into his house and gave him a stick, Abdullah bin Annice takes the stick and left. When people saw him with this stick, they questioned Abdullah about why the Prophet (pbuh) gave you this stick. He said, I do not know, but he gave it to me. The People said you should go back and find out why did the Prophet (pbuh) give you this stick. Abdullah bin Annice goes back and asks the Prophet (pbuh), "why did you give me this stick?" The Prophet (pbuh) said, this will be a sign between me and you on the day of judgment. Abdullah bin Annice says he tied the stick with his sword meaning always with him, when he died, he asked for the stick to be buried with him. It was wrapped in his shroud and was buried with him. Khalid bin Sufyan was assassinated to save the blood shed of other people, as there was no fighting once he was killed.

THE PROPHET (PBUH) SENDS 10 MEN UNDER THE LEADERSHIP OF ASIM BIN SABIT

The Prophet pbuh sent a group of 10 men the leader was Asim bin Sabit they reached a land of Banu Alayan but were ambushed by 100 archers and they were outnumbered 100 to 10. They fled to a small hill and there the 100 archers surrounded them. The archers said come down, we guarantee that we shall not kill you, the Ameer said, "I do not accept pledges of mushriqeen." He chose to fight. They fought, 7 were killed, the remaining 3 surrendered and were tied up, one was able to get his hands free and attacked. But he was killed, the other two were sold to the people of Makkah. Habab bin Art and Zahid, they were the remaining two who survived in the Suryia. Quraish wanted to kill them and took them outside the boundary of Makkah. Quraish asked, "would you like to be safe with your families and instead Muhammad (pbuh) would be in trouble they refused the offer. We would rather die. Abu Sufyan said, I have never seen people who would love more than the people of Muhammad (pbuh). The Sahaba love Muhammad (pbuh) more than anything, the love of the Sahaba for the Prophet was so true and deep, that it was known to the enemies of the Prophet Muhammad (pbuh). They were both killed so all 10 were killed.

A leader of a tribe came to the Prophet and said, "Islam is spreading in our area, we need some teachers," the Prophet pbuh sent 70 people, they would work during day and recite the Quran at night. They were given guarantee of safety by this man Abu AL bra, when they reached in his territory, his nephew Amer bin Tufail, invited his tribe men to fight these 70 Kuraz, teachers. His uncle refuses but he brought his force to attack those 70 men. Amr bin Tufail has met the Prophet (pbuh). He said to the Prophet, "you become king over the towns and I shall be the king over the Badoo people. Make me a Khalifa after yourself. If not, I shall attack with the army of 2,000 men." The Prophet (pbuh) refused; he was upset. 70 men were killed. The Prophet was greatly affected by this news. He was incredibly sad. The Prophet pbuh prayed for the people who were killed in cold blood, he prayed for them in every salah. Amer bin Sahara, one of the 70 was raised by angels. Asim bin Sabit swarm and flood. His skull was worth 100 camels, a woman wanted to drink from his skull. But the fourth year of Hijra, Omiya bin Bambry, saw men sleeping under a tree. He asked them, "who do you belong to?"

They told him they belong to so and so tribe. This was the tribe who killed the 70 men teachers of the Quran. He killed them thinking they belong to a treacherous tribe. It turned out that these two men had a peace agreement with the Prophet (pbuh). The Prophet (pbuh) said to Omiya bin Bambry, "I have to pay for them the blood money." Remember the Prophet (pbuh) had an agreement with the Jews that they support each other for blood money. The Prophet (pbuh) went with the Sahaba to Banu Nadeer a Jewish tribe and told them that these two men were killed mistakenly and we have to pay blood money so help as we have agreed. They said, we agree and we shall help you O' Muhammad. The Prophet (pbuh) was sitting under a wall of theirs, they pretended to go and bring money, but in fact they went to conspire to assassinate the Prophet and said, that they will never find a better chance than this. He is sitting under a wall, someone should climb up and throw a stone at him and kill him, to get rid of him forever. However, this is not new for Jews, they did that with Eisa pbuh (Jesus) and others, sometimes they succeeded and sometimes they failed.

The Prophet (pbuh) received revelations from Allah, Gabriel came and warned the messenger of Allah about the plot, the Prophet pbuh stood up and left without telling anything to the Sahaba. He just left, walked away. The Sahaba waited but the Prophet did not appear, they went to Madinah to enquire. The Prophet (pbuh) told the Sahaba that Gabriel came and told me that the Jews were planning to assassinate him. The Prophet (pbuh) sends them a letter. he told Muhammad bin Muslma (not the prophet of Allah, this man is a different person) to go to them and tell them. I am sent by the messenger of Allah, he is telling you to leave his land because you have betrayed our agreement, by conspiring against him. And I give you ten days to leave. Anyone seen after the ten days will be executed. Muhammad bin Muslma was their ally at the time of Jahiliya (ignorance). The Jews of Banu Nadeer, said, we would not expect you to come and deliver this message Muhammad bin Muslma responded and said Islam has changed us and our hearts are different. Now things are different, now we are Muslims and our covenant with Allah is more important than our former covenant with you. Our agreement with the Prophet is to help, support, him that is more important than you. Banu Nadeer, their initial reaction was to accept and leave peacefully. But Abdullah bin Abbey, he was the head, he told them if you stay and stay firm, we will not give up on you. If you fight, we shall fight along with you, if you are expelled, we shall leave with you. He told them, I have 2,000 men and there are other people sympathetic to our cause, do not leave. This was a powerful backing; Banu Nadeer changed their mind and they decided to stay and fight. When the Prophet (pbuh) heard the news, he said let it be so and laid a siege to their territory, Banu Nadeer were rich had fortresses and acres of agricultural land, palm trees. That was their livelihood, their plan was to remain in their fortresses until the Muslims get tired and leave them. They had food, water and money which could last for a long time, the Prophet (pbuh) used a strategy that baffled the Jews and probably the cause of their surrender.

The Prophet (pbuh) ordered to burn down their palm trees. The Jews thought how could they survive. And why fight, our existence is on farms and their trees take years to bear fruit. This took them by surprise, and said to the Prophet O' Muhammad, you used to criticize the destruction of trees, why are you cutting down and burning our farms. They made an offer; they asked the Prophet (pbuh) to allow them to evacuate and spare their lives and allow them to take their wealth with them. The Prophet (pbuh) agreed with these conditions. You do not take any weapons with you and are only allowed to leave with one camel load. If your property is more than that you leave it behind, and they agreed, Muhammad bin Muslma was to oversee that. Three men on one camel and one camel to take their property, Ibn Ishaque says they loaded their camels up to the limit. Some men tore down their houses and took with them. Some had a lot of money, Islam bin Haqeeq, filled a skin of a bull. He filled it with Gold and Silver and said this is what we have prepared. If we are leaving the palm trees behind, we shall find palm trees in Khaybar. Some of them went to Khaybar and some went to Shaam (Syria), Banu Nadeer were extraordinarily rich, immensely proud, and educated. They wanted to show the Muslims that they are not bothered. When they arrived in Khaybar, they were received by women, children, gifts and girls singing with pride. Abdullah bin Abu Bakr says, "they were well respected and were welcomed in Khaybar as heroes." Surah Al-Hashir was revealed. Al-Abbas used to call it the Surah of Banu Nadeer.

Allah says, "he who expels people of the scripture, non-believers they thought their fortress will protect them from Allah. Expectation on your side, that you cannot drive them out, their fortresses were strong and powerful, they had good numbers of fighters, they had wealth to finance war, their expectation that they wouldn't leave but Allah drove them out." Allah says, "He expelled at the first gathering. But the decree of Allah came where they did not expect it to come from and caused terror in their hearts, fear a soldier of Allah." Allah says, "if they didn't evacuate, their punishment would have been execution that is because they opposed Allah and his messenger, what you cut down that is by permission of Allah. What remains is also by permission of Allah. Because Allah will disgrace defiantly disobedient." The Prophet (pbuh) instructed that the trees should not be destroyed and women, children, and old people should not be killed. Also, monks should not be killed. But sometimes you have to go against the rules like this incident, the palm trees had to be burned down. Attacking at night, some people got killed. One Sahabi says, "he attacked 9 houses and killed people, including women, children, and old people, who went against the rules. This is in Muslim Sharif.

We also know that the Prophet (pbuh) ordered the execution of two women, one of them poisoned the Prophet (pbuh), these were incidents where old men were killed who went against the rules. The answer in Islam is a tolerant religion but has laid down rules for an engagement these rules are to protect innocents and other lives. But when enemy tries to take advantage of these rules and harms the Muslims, these rules are suspended. Any property received without fighting goes to the Prophet and he deals with it as appropriate palm trees and other property became personal property to deal with it as he wished.

The Prophet (pbuh) calls the Ansar, Al-Auss and Al-Khazrj and told them if you like, I shall split amongst you and muhajir will continue living in your houses and work on your farms or if you like I shall distribute this amongst the muhajir and they will leave your houses and will not take any share from your harvest. Ansar said, distribute it among, muhajir and also if they want share from the harvest, we have no problem. This shows the generosity of Ansar. Now muhajir move into the houses of Banu Nadeer. Now the difficult situation was lifted and the financial situation improving. Houses and land were given to muhajir, only two men from Ansar received share, Abu Dojana and another, because they complained of some poverty, now the Prophet (pbuh) also had some wealth.

The Prophet (pbuh) started as a Sheppard, then business, after Prophethood. He would live on money from Hazrat Khadija and his uncle Abu Talib when they came to Madinah. Ansar helped, but they would not accept Sadaqat (charity) but would accept gifts. Now from this faith money he would take year's expenses and distribute the rest. The Prophet pbuh says, my provisions come from beneath my spear (from fighting in the cause of Allah). That was the source of income of the Prophet (pbuh). Now the Prophet (pbuh) had money to give back.

ABOUT MUNAFQEEN (HYPOCRITES)

Allah says, "have you not considered those who practice hypocrisy they are liars," Banu Nadeer were hoping for help from Abdullah bin Abbey, they didn't come, but even if they had come, they would have lost.

THE BATTLE OF RICAYAH

The Prophet (pbuh) went out with 400 soldiers called battle of Ricayah. Ricayah means a piece of cloth Abu Sal Ashur said, we went for this Ghazve. I was one of 6 men sharing the same camel. Skin of my feet was peeling off and my nails were falling off. And we would wrap a piece of cloth around our feet that is why the name of Ghazve is the Battle of Ricayah, the enemy fled, they did not face Muslims but Muslims were careful when they prayed, salah of fear. Surah Al-Nisa if a group has prayed let them carry their arms and the other group carrying their arms, salah is compulsory. The Prophet (pbuh) appointed two guards Amer bin Yasir and Obadiah, they will take their turns, while Amer was sleeping, Obadiah was guarding, Obadiah was in salah one of the enemy shot an arrow at him, but he didn't move, second and third arrow, then Obadiah woke up Amer bin Yasir. Amer saw three arrows in him, he said, "glory be to Allah why didn't you woke me up?" He said, "I was reciting a Surah I didn't want to stop until I finished it." If he had not continued, or I had died, I would not have fulfilled my duty, this is amazing.

CONVERSATION BETWEEN JABBAR BIN ABDULLAH AND THE PROPHET

Jabbar bin Abdullah was riding a weak camel, Prophet pbuh asked him, "what is the matter?" He said, O'messenger of Allah this camel of mine is slowing me down." Prophet pbuh told him to make it kneel and the Prophet (pbuh) had his camel kneel. Prophet said to Jabbar, "give me your stick or get me one from a tree." Jabbar gave the stick Prophet pbuh plodded the camel with that stick and then told Jabbar to ride. Jabbar says, "my weak camel was competing with the fast camel of Prophet pbuh." Prophet asked Jabbar, "would you sell your camel to me?" Jabbar bin Abdullah said, "I shall give it to you," the Prophet (pbuh) said no sell it to me, and Jabbar said, "make me an offer." The Prophet (pbuh) said, "1-dhrm (currency)," Jabbar said, "no O'messenger of Allah you will be cheating me (jokingly)." The Prophet of Allah kept on raising the price until the Prophet (pbuh) offered an ounce of gold. Jabbar agreed, the Prophet (pbuh) is talking with Sahaba asked, "are you married?" Jabbar was young. He said, "yes," The Prophet asked, are you married to a virgin or a woman previously married, Jabbar replied, "previously married." Why not with young one, you could play with her and she could play with you?" Jabbar bin Abdullah said, my father was killed at the battle of Uhud and left 7 daughters, so I married a mature woman to bring them up well. The Prophet (pbuh) told him you did well. Hope from Allah, then the Prophet said when we get nearer we shall slaughter a camel she will "the wife of Jabbar) hear about us and dust off the cushions for us Prophet before entering Madinah would stay outside to let the family know wouldn't surprise them. Jabbar bin Abdullah said, "we don't have cushions, tough situation." Prophet pbuh told him; "you will have some when you go back act wisely." They came to Madinah, the Prophet, when he came out of the mosque saw a camel tied up, he enquired and found out that Jabbar brought it for the Prophet (pbuh). Prophet called Jabbar and told him, "cousin, take the camel" and he asked Bilal to give an ounce of gold to Jabbar, Bilal gave an ounce of gold and little more. Jabbar says, "my finances improved until the day Madinah suffered, very many people died.

Now Muslims won the battle of Badr, Quraish won the battle of Uhud, and they agreed, that they will meet again called the appointed Badr. Abu Sufyan left Makkah with 2,000 soldiers, but soon after, he said to Quraish, "this year is famine, we shall travel when there will be plenty of fruit in a good year. I am going back and you should do the same. It was a barren year, that was their excuse. The messenger of Allah, came to the appointed place, stayed for few days and then left.

THE GHAZVE OF JUNDAL

Another Ghazve, jundal about 450 kilometers north of Medina. Muslim army 1,000 travel through the night day, there was guide from Banu Ghazve. Prophet pbuh arrived in Doma Tul Jundal and found out that these people are gathering force to attack Medina. This was in fifth year of Hijra, this was a tribe of Qobar. They ran away when the Prophet (pbuh) arrived. The movement of the Prophet (pbuh) was secret travel, through the night and sleep during the day, no fighting. Another Ghazve Banu Mustaliq. It was tribe from Qaza took their livestock, children and women but no fighting (i) Muslim (ii) Jazia (iii) We will fight. Always three days' time to make up the mind. Ghazve Banu Mustaliq, Javeria. She was the daughter of the head of the tribe, Hazrat Ayesha says she made Maqatba with Sabit bin Qais. Maqatba is an agreement between master and slave, where slave can buy freedom. Hazrat Ayesha says she was incredibly beautiful, sweet girl, men liked her she came to Prophet (pbuh) for help and to prepare the document. Ayesha says, "I swear when she came to my door, I didn't like her and feared that the Prophet will see in her what I did." Ayesha was worried, that she is beautiful and if Prophet sees her, he may want to marry her. When she came, she said O' messenger of Allah I am daughter of Harris bin Abu Druid, the leader of the tribe. She has fallen to Sabit bin Qais. Now she has a Maqatba and needs help Prophet asked her would she prefer better she asked what? Prophet said, I shall take responsibility for your deed and marry you. She replied, "yes messenger of Allah, I agree." So, the Prophet (Pbuh) married Javeria and paid her ransom. News spread and army said, then these people are relatives of Prophet and released them. Because Javeria was the wife of the Prophet and they did not want her relatives to be slaves. Ayesha then said 100 of her relatives were freed, I know no woman who brought so much blessing for her people.

Umar bin Khattab had a servant, a muhajir fetching water, got into a fight with Ansar. Ansar was calling Ansar to gang up against mahajreen. And muhajir did the same and fight was to be erupted. Prophet heard about this and came and stopped such fittana. Now the news reached to Abdullah bin Abbey the head of Munafiqeen. He said, did they really challenge us they out number us in our own land. He said you fatten your dog and it will eat you. I (Abdullah bin Abbey) swear when we reach Madinah, the stronger will drive out the weaker. Now he was reminding them, that you allowed them in and shared your property with them. I swear if you had kept what was your own, they would have gone somewhere else. A young Sahabi Zaib bin Arqam. He heard Abdullah bin Abbey what he said and he goes to Prophet and conveys the news. Some Ansar, who were at present, told Prophet, perhaps the young man misunderstood or did not remember correctly, they were defending Abdullah bin Abbey. Hazrat Umar bin Khattab said, let me go and execute this Munafiqeen, Umar does not play around. Prophet said, how it be, how it will be Umar? That people will say that Muhammad (pbuh) kills his companions. Allah says they say, honorable will drive out the weak. But honor belongs to Allah and his messenger, but Munafiqeen do not understand Prophet ordered the Army to leave March on day and night and in the morning. When Prophet told them to stop, they were tired and fell asleep. That was to get them out of this argument.

AN UNFORTUNATE INCIDENT HAPPENED

Hazrat Ayesha relates the story of what happened. This is in all books, Bukhari Sharif Hazrat Ayesha says, "when the messenger of Allah would go on a journey, he would draw lots among his wives who will accompany him for the journey. He did so for the journey to Banu Mustaliq, my name was drowned and he took me with him, the women on such an occasion would eat light food and they would be light weight. Hazrat Ayesha, said, "I would sit in my hoodage while the camel is prepared or made ready when the Prophet completed, he ordered to go back to Madinah, when nearer to Madinah they will rest for the part of the night. Then everybody to start again, continue the journey. I went out to relieve myself. I was wearing a (Onex) necklace. When I finished my business, the necklace slipped and fell without my knowledge. When got into my mount, I checked the necklace, I could not find it, people were leaving, but I returned to where I had been and eventually, I found it. It was where she was sitting. But in the meanwhile, my camel came and they put the hoodage on the back of the camel. Since I was exceptionally light no one noticed and they moved on. When I returned to the campsite nobody was there, everybody had gone. I wrapped myself in my clock (sheet or shawl) and lied down. I was sure that they will return for me when they will miss me. I swear I was lying on the ground when Safwan bin Muatal came by, he had his own reason for staying behind. When he saw me, he approached and stood over me. He had seen me before the veil. When he saw me, he said, to Allah we belong and to Allah we return. I was all wrapped in my clothes. He asked, "what made you stay behind?" Allah's mercy be upon you; I did not speak to him. He then brought up the camel and said, "you ride, and stayed away from me. I mounted and be led the camel by the head." Moving swiftly to catch up with the rest. I swear we could not catch up nor did they miss me before the morning. By the time the force had halted and made secure the man appeared with me. Those who saw began talking and men were greatly perturbed. However, I swear, I knew nothing of this.

Now this man Safwan appears with me and Muslims saw that Safwan and Ayesha are coming alone. So, Rumors spread, why they were together? Accusing Ayesha, we then came to Madinah, and I soon fell seriously sick, and heard nothing of what was going on. All the talk soon reached the Prophet (pbuh) and my parents but they told me nothing of this. All I noticed that the Prophet was not kind as he used to be towards me. Whenever, I was sick. He had been kind, exceedingly kind and comforting to me but not on this occasion, I pretended not to notice. Whenever the Prophet came in, my mother was nursing me, the Prophet would only say, how is she? He would not even speak to her and he would add nothing more. Eventually, this coldness bothered me and I asked him, O' messenger of Allah, if you would allow me I would like to go to my mother, she will look after me," the Prophet (pbuh) said, "ok," so I moved in with my mother, and had no knowledge of the rumor, until I recovered 3 weeks later. She says we are Arabs and did not have toilets that foreigners use. We would go out and use open areas. Each night women would go out to relieve themselves. I went out one night accompanied by O' Masta, a daughter of Abu Adam Al-Mutlab, she was walking with me and slipped over her gown and swore at her son Masta. I could not understand this language against a muhajir and who had fought at Badr. Ayesha is saying, why are saying this against your son. The mother of Masta said, "the news has not reached you O' daughter of Abu Bakr," Ayesha says, "what news?" She then told me what those people were saying, Ayesha asked her, "is that so?" She replied "yes". Ayesha says I swear, "I couldn't do my business and went home. I cried so much; I thought my crying will burst my liver. I told my mother; May Allah forgive you for not telling me what people are saying about me. My mother said, do not take it seriously daughter, rarely a beautiful woman, and her husband who loves her. Rarely not to have co wives and others to speak about her." The Prophet (pbuh) had stood and tried to tell people but I knew nothing of that, praising Allah and then why people are giving me concern about my family. I swear I only know well about people and would not enter my house without accompanying me. The Prophet (pbuh) is saying I only know well of Ayesha and only know well of Safwan. The greatest blame lay with Abdullah bin Abbey. Some of the Khazrj and Masta and Hamna, the daughter of Josh. Hamna was the sister of Zainab, daughter of Josh, who also lived with Prophet. Zainab was the only Rival. Zainab was given protection through her religion. She only spoke well of me but Hamna spread rumors for her sister's sake and I suffered.

When the Prophet (pbuh) made this address Hsay bin Hrair stated, "O' Prophet if they were from Al-Auss we will deal with them for you if from Khazrj then give us order, they deserve to have their heads cut off. Hsay is from Al-Auss, Ayesha says, "then Saad bin Obadiah rose, stood up, he had been previously considered a fine man. He said, "you lie, I swear by Allah certainly not cut, their heads you made that statement because you knew they were from Khazrj. If they were from your own tribe you would never say that. Hsay said to Saad bin Obadiah, "you lie, munafiq arguing on behalf of munafiq people were angry and almost two tribes Al-Auss and Khazrj were to fight between them. Even after 4 to 5 years of becoming Muslim, the tribes will fight inside mosque then the Prophet (pbuh) stood down and came in to see Ayesha. After the Prophet (pbuh) settled the problem and came to see Ayesha, the Prophet called Ali bin Abu Talib and Sama bin Zaid and consulted, Sama spoke well of me and said Prophet, it is about your family all we know is good, these are foolish lies. Ali bin Abu Talib said, O' messenger of Allah there are plenty of women you can exchange them. Ask the slave girl and she will speak the truth. The Prophet called for Brerara to ask her. Ali went to her, struck her strongly and told her to speak the truth to the Prophet (pbuh). Brerara replied, "I swear by Allah I know nothing but good, I never found fault with Ayesha at all, except when I need dough and her to watch.

She may fall asleep and her pet lamb comes and eats it. Ayesha says, "then Prophet came to me. I had both my parents and an Ansari woman with me. I was weeping and so was she. The Prophet (pbuh) sat down, gave praise and thanks to Allah. The Prophet (pbuh) said, "you have been informed what people are saying about you. Fear Allah, if you have done wrong as people say then repent to him, Allah accepts repentance from his servants." "As soon as the Prophet said that my tears dried up and I could feel nothing of them. I waited for my parents to respond on my behalf but they did not speak. I swear to Allah, I felt myself too humble and unimportant for Allah to send a verse about me, the one will be sited for prayer. But I hoped that Allah will reveal something in his sleep to prove my innocence. Give some knowledge and information. But for a verse in Quran for me I swear I felt two insignificant for that. When I realized my parents were not going to respond for me. I asked, 'will you not reply to Prophet pbuh.' They said, 'by Allah we do not know what to reply.' I swear I do not know any household who suffered as the house of Abu Bakr in those days. When I realized they would not answer, I started crying again. If I say what people are saying to affirm it. Allah knows that is not true and if I deny it then you will not believe me." Ayesha then says, "I then tried to remember the name of Hazrat Yaqoob (pbuh) but I couldn't remember it, so I said, I shall speak as did the father of Yousuf, patience is fine and Allah's help is sought against what you describe. I swear the messenger of Allah had not left his seat before Allah sent down upon him what he used to send. He was wrapped up in his clock and a pillow of leather was placed under his head so the Prophet (pbuh) was now receiving Wahi (revelation) as for myself when I witnessed that, I was not alarmed or concerned. I knew I was innocent and Allah will not harm me. However, I swear in the name of Allah who has Ayesha soul in his hand. As soon as the Prophet (pbuh) came around I thought my parents will expire with fear, that confirmation what people are saying will come from Allah," Ayesha says, "having recovered, the messenger of Allah set up. He began to wipe off the sweat droplets from his face" "rejoice Ayesha."

Allah's glory has sent down confirmation of your innocence. Ayesha said "Alhamdullilah (praise be to Allah)." Then the Prophet (pbuh) went out and told people what Allah has sent down in the Quran on this subject. He then gave orders for Musta bin Hasa, Sabit and Hamna those having spoken openly and they received flogging prescribed by law. This is the story narrated by Ayesha. Another narration says, when the Prophet (pbuh) revealed the news, the mother of Ayesha told her to go and thank the Prophet, Ayesha said, no she will only thank Allah. An Ayat in Surah Noor, Allah says, "indeed those who came with falsehood are grouped among you. Do not think it is bad for you it is good for you for every person who has earned a punishment for a sin and he who took upon himself a greater portion, there off for him is a greater punishment, why? When you heard it the believing men and believing women did not think good of them and say this is an obvious falsehood why, who slandered, didn't produce any witnesses when they do not produce witnesses then they in the sight of Allah are liars, and if it had not been for the favor of Allah on you and, mercy hereafter you would have been in a great punishment. When you received it with your tongue and said with your mouth that for which you had no knowledge and thought it was insignificant, while in the sight of Allah it was tremendous and why? When you heard it, to say it is not for us to speak about this exalted, are you O' Allah this is a great slander. Allah warns you to the likes of this conduct. If you should be believers and Allah makes clear to you, and Allah is knowing and wise, indeed those who like immorality should be published and those who believed will have terrible punishment in this world and in the hereafter, Allah knows and you do not know. If it had not been Allah's favor on you and his mercy. Allah is merciful O' you who have believed. Do not follow the footsteps of Satan. Whoever follows footsteps of Satan, he enjoins immorality, and if not favor of Allah on you and his mercy, not one of you would have been pure but Allah purifies whom he wills Allah is hearing and knowing.

Allah is forgiving and merciful, indeed who falsely accuse the chaste, women are cursed in this world and hereafter and they will have a great punishment. On a day when their hands, their tongues and their feet will bear witness against them as to what they used to do that day, Allah will pay them in truth, full recompense and they will know that is Allah who is manifest truth. Allah is great.

All of these Ayat were revealed in defense of Ayesha (i) Saying against Ayesha is kufr, because that will be disbelieving the Quran (ii) Good came out of this, we learned a lot (iii) Muslims should care about the reputation of other Muslims (iv) We should not carry rumors around. (v) It should never happen again. (vi) We should never talk about immortality. (vii) Musta was a poor man, and Abu Bakr was taking care of his financial needs. He stopped after what Musta did. (viii), it is a serious sin to talk about a chaste woman. (ix) Muhammad (pbuh) did not know of the unseen. He suffered for a month. (x) If one accuses a Muslim, they should produce four witnesses or he will be flogged publicly eighty lashes as a punishment. One they are flogged; their witnesses are not accepted at court. This is to protect the community.

Others were flogged but not Abdullah bin Abbey, although he was at the forefront. Because punishment is a kaphara. He was only spreading rumors in way that was excusable. Also, this is established through witnesses there was perhaps no evidence against him. May be not to cause fitnah, may be all above.

THE BATTLE OF THE TRENCH

The next battle was the battle of the Trench, (Al-Ahzab) Al khandaq. A group of Jews brought some clans together against the messenger of Allah, they went to Makkah and to other tribes, they brought together a formidable army of 10,000 warriors, the agreement was that Ghutfan will supply 6000 soldiers and the Jews will give them the date harvest for one year. Ghutfan were in this for the money, but the real opponents were the Jews and the Quraish. Jews were educated people; they would go to Makkah and people would ask them as you are the people of the book tell us who is on the right side. Quraish or Muhammad (pbuh), Jews would tell them you are. Allah revealed, "have you not seen who were given a portion of a scripture to believe in superstition and worship some objects. And say for disbelievers these are better guides as to the way, those are the ones who Allah has cursed and those whom Allah curse cannot find helpers." The Prophet (pbuh) received the news that a big army is coming your way. Prophet held a Shura Salman Pharsi says, "in our land in Persia. If we fear a cavalry, we dig a trench. The Prophet (pbuh) and the Muslims liked the idea and the project started. It was decided to dig a trench north of Madinah. Madinah had natural protection east and west, volcanic tracks, in the south is dwelling and agriculture. The danger is from the north. Every 10 men were given 40 feet to dig. It was difficult. Muslims were hungry, poor, they had lack of food lack of numbers.

The Prophet (pbuh) went out and saw muhajir and Ansar busy digging, in a very cold morning. They had no slaves to work for them. When the Prophet (pbuh) saw, he prayed, "O' Allah their life is the afterlife." The Prophet (pbuh) participated in digging; the messenger of Allah was so hungry, that he tied a stone to his stomach. Spirit was high, they would chant, 'O' Allah without you, we to would not have been guided and not charitable nor would we have prayed, so send tranquility on us and make us stand firm when we meet the enemy. They have wronged us and we will meet them.' There were guards and Sahaba would take turns. The difficulties were increasing. This army made up of Quraish and Ghutfan coming forward, and there was a serious problem, at a very worst time, the dwellings of Banu Karewa, the last Jewish tribe remaining in Madinah, were part of the protection of Madinah. Their fortresses were used as protection against the Army coming from that area. The Prophet (pbuh) was receiving news that Banu Karewa themselves were breaking the agreement and were joining the enemy army. That was a serious blow to the Muslims. The Prophet (pbuh) sends Zubair bin Awam to investigate. Zubair bin Awam brings the information that they are bringing in their livestock and are paving the road, which is an indication for preparation of war. The Prophet (pbuh) wanted to investigate further and sends Saad bin Moaz, Saad bin Obeda, Abdullah bin Raukha and Fawad bin Jabeer, go and find out whether Banu Karewa has betrayed and broken the agreement with the Muslims, and if that is the case, do not leak the news and deliver the news to me secretly. If they are still keeping the agreement, then make the news public. Saad bin Moaz, Saad bin Obeda, Abdullah bin Raukha and Fawas bin Jabeer, go and came back with information and said two words, "Awa-Karewa," those people have killed Muslims. That meant that Banu Karewa has broken the agreement, the Prophet (pbuh) prepared for that, the Prophet (pbuh) sends two groups, 200 and 300 men as guards, and they would go around the area of Banu Karewa to show them, we are here and willing to fight. It was a show of strength. The Muslims were able to intercept 20 camels loaded with dates, figs and barley they were going towards the army of Al-Ahzab and it originated from Banu Karewa. It was clear that Banu Karewa had betrayed the messenger of Allah. They committed treason; they are now supplying the enemy army. It was difficult for Muslim Allah describes this to us, remember when they came at you from above and below and eyes shifted with fear and hearts came to throats and you assumed about Allah, various assumptions likes' doubts were created. Allah says, "when believers saw this, they thought this is what Allah and his messenger have promised us. Allah and his messenger spoke the truth, and it increased them in faith and acceptance. This was the response of the believers.

When believers saw all these dangers thrown at them that increased their Iman rather than decreased it. They knew Allah will test them it was a part of a test. But with Munafiqeen it made them doubt even more. Now one can see how one event brought different reactions from two camps believers and non-believers Musa (Moses) (pbuh) felt fear Allah says, "Musa felt fear in his heart. But with Musa, fear was only in heart but did not show up in his actions. His actions were full of Iman. This is a difference between believers and non-believers, positive and negative reaction. Fears increased for Muslims and some were saying Muhammad (pbuh), used to say we shall conquer treasures of kissara and Persia but now we are not safe even for going to the toilets. Munafiqeen would say, when we were digging the trench, the Prophet (pbuh) was giving tidings of conquering the Persian Empire and Roman Empire but now we are fearful for our safety. Allah says in Ayat, 13 to 14 in Surah Al-Ahzab and section of people said O' people of Yasrab there is no stability for you're here so return home and a party of them sought permission of the Prophet (pbuh) saying, indeed our houses are exposed, when they were not exposed but they intend to flee, and if they had been entered from surrounding regions and fitnah had extended they would not have accepted. This Ayat says Munafiqeen, if they are pressured a little, they will give up Islam. And they had already promised Allah not to turn their backs and ever the promise to Allah questioned, say, never fleeing will benefit you, if fleeing from death or killing and if you did you will not be given enjoyment for life except for little the Ayat says, 'Allah says death is determined upon you and running from it wouldn't change even a bit.

Allah says, "who can protect you from Allah, if Allah intends for you ill or mercy and they will not find beside Allah any protector or any helper then," Allah says, "Allah knows Munafiqeen, they say come to us and do not go for a battle except for a few, and when fear comes, their eyes are revolving like overcome by death. But when fear passes, they lash you with sharp tongs. Those who have not believed and Allah has not rendered their deeds, for Allah it is easy. They think the companies have not withdrawn and if companies come again, they want to be with Badoo, enquiring from for away," then Allah says, "and if they are with you, they will not fight with you except for a little." Muslims were suffering hunger, Bukhari Sharif, Annice bin Malik says, "they will bring a handful of barley and smelling fat, this is their food. Hungry as they were, this food will stick in their throats and smell bad, it was difficult and Muslims had to workday and night. It was stressful, Allah was testing them to the limit.

There was some fighting enemy trying to break through the trench from time to time. One incident happened challenge to come back one of the Quraish heroes, a strong and powerful man, he challenged the Muslims, and the one went forth was Hazrat Ali bin Abu Talib. Amer says, "who are you?" Hazrat Ali said, "I am Ali," he said "Ali bin Abdul Munaf" but Hazrat Ali said, "no, I am Ali bin Abu Talib." He said, "nephew, there are senior members amongst you. I feel sorry for spilling your blood. Hazrat Ali said, "but I do not feel sorry for spilling your blood," Amer wanted someone senior to come and meet him. Amer was very upset and drew his sword as a brand of fire and they exchanged blows. Amer hit with force and Hazrat Ali took it on shield but it was such a powerful blow that the shield but the head of Hazrat Ali, because it was so powerful blow the sword got stuck in the shield, and Ali bin Abu Talib struck Amer in the neck and he fell down, he dropped dead and the Sahaba make Takbir. God is great. At the time, the Prophet knew that Ali has won, Saad bin Abu Waqas was a good marksman. He had in his sight an enemy soldier who was holding two shields. He was teasing the Muslims and was moving the shields up and down, Saad bin Waqas aimed at the man fires his shot while the shield was down and hits man in his forehead the man fell down but his legs went up. The Prophet (pbuh) saw that and laughed, the way the man fell was funny. Ibn Moaz, Hazrat Ayesha says he was a tall and large man, he was wearing armored but his arms were not covered, Ayesha says, "when I saw him, I was worried about his arms.

He was shot in his arm and he was seriously injured, these were some of the fights that happened in the battle of Khandaq. The Prophet (pbuh) tried to break the coalition. This was part of his strategy. He tried to negotiate a deal with Ghutfan, these tribes came from Najaf, they were more than half, maybe around 6000, the Prophet (pbuh) met with two leaders of Ghutfan, the Prophet (pbuh) made a proposal, that if they should withdraw from coalition then we shall give you 1/3 of the harvest of Madinah. They agreed and prepared a document in writing but did not finalize and did not bring witnesses, the Prophet (pbuh) called Saad bin Moaz and Saad bin Obeda and consulted them, and they were revolt when the Prophet (pbuh) told them the proposal. They said, 'Prophet is it an order of Allah or you yourself want to do that or are you doing it for us? If it is from Allah then yes, but if you want this for us, then no.' The Prophet (pbuh) said it is for your sake. Saad bin Moaz said, "O' messenger of Allah we used to be disbelievers in Allah we used to worship idols along with others not knowing Allah at that time they would never eat a single date without purchasing or guest should we give them our property now when we are Muslims and believe in Allah through you. We will have none of this. By Allah all we shall give them is the sword until Allah decides between us and them," the Prophet (pbuh) said, "as you wish." Saad bin Moaz took the document from the Prophet (pbuh) and raised the writing on it and said, "now let them fight us." Allah was going help Muslims. If you have Taqwa in Allah. Allah will find the way out and will provide you from avenues you never expected. A man came to the Prophet (pbuh), his name is Naeem bin Masood this man is from Ghutfan, he came and said, "O' messenger of Allah I have accepted Islam but my people do not know of this. Give any orders you wish, only Allah knows his soldiers," the Prophet said, "you are only one man use trickery to relieve us from them if you can. War is deception," the Prophet told him to go back and weaken them. Naeem left and he went to the Jews of Banu Karewa he had good relations with Jews also had good relations with Quraish as he was from Ghutfan. Naeem told the Jews we know each other we are friends and I shall give you a sincere advice, what you have done is wrong. You have decided to fight Muhammad (pbuh) and you are living in Madinah while Quraish and Ghutfan are coming to fight but their property is somewhere else their families are not here. Now Quraish and Ghutfan are opportunists, they are trying to defeat Muslims, if that does not happen, they will pack up and leave and you know what will happen to you. Muhammad (pbuh) will attack you first. You are in Madinah; you cannot face alone against Muslims.

The Jews agreed and what should we do? Naeem said, "you should make sure that Quraish and Ghutfan will fight to the end until you achieve the objectives, Jews wanted to know how to guarantee that Naeem said ask them to leave some of their men with you as assurance, that was the practice in those days. The Jews liked the idea. Now Naeem left the Jews and he went to Quraish. He says to them, "you know about our friendship, my advice to you will be sincere to you, I shall tell you the truth, I am here to give you some secret information," then the Quraish said 'yes, we trust you' and Naeem told them that Jews have regretted that they broke the agreement with Muhammad (pbuh) and now they are trying to reestablish the agreement they have offered Muhammad (pbuh) to hand over to him some of your men to be executed as the sign of their truthfulness, therefore if Jews come to you asking for some hostages, do not give them any, then he goes to Ghutfan and tells them exact the same story. Now the siege was taking a long time and Quraish were upset. (Quraish did not come to lay siege in the first place) They came to fight but found the trench, their supplies were diminishing. Akarma bin Abu Jahl was the head of the delegation who went to meet Banu Karewa. He told Jews that we are tired of this long siege, our camels and horses are dying we want all-out war and you better get ready and we shall attack today. Jews said no because we do not fight in the Sabbath (Jews' holy day) and also, we are worried that you may not stay till the end. To make sure you stay till the end, you handover some of your men as a guarantee. Akarma goes back and conveys this information to Abu Sufyan. Abu Sufyan says, "this is it, Naeem told us about this." The Jews have betrayed us and want to handover our men to Muhammad (pbuh), Abu Sufyan answers and says, "we are not going handover even a single person," the Jews said, 'this exactly what Naeem told us, they are not serious and they will leave us.' The same happened with Ghutfan, one man was successful in breaking up this coalition. Allah solved this because Muslims had passed the test. Allah says, "O' believers remember, when armies came to attack you, we send upon them wind and armies you did not see, angels. Allah is watching over you whatever you do.

THE STORY OF HADEEFA AT THE TIME OF TABI'UN

The Muslims had a battle cry, they (the enemy), will not be victorious. Ahmed narrates; a man from Koofa asked Hadeefa, "have you seen the Prophet?" Hadeefa said, "O' nephew yes." He asked how you treated the Prophet (pbuh). Hadeefa said, "it was difficult for us, I swear by Allah but we tried our best." This man said, "I swear, if we lived during his time, we wouldn't have let his foot touch the ground, we would have carried him on our shoulders, we have heard the stories of Tabi'un." He thought, if the Prophet (pbuh) had come in their time, they would have treated him much better than the Sahaba. Now Hadeefa wants to tell this man what he does not know, and to tell him it is easier said than done. Now the Sahaba brought Islam to you and you know the greatness of the messenger of Allah and you see the Khalafa that he established. He does not understand that the Sahaba who were living with the Prophet (pbuh) had to fight their families, fathers brothers, and had to fight their clan, had to give up their wealth it was not easy.

Hadeefa said, "nephew, I swear by Allah I was with the Prophet (pbuh) at the battle of the trench, Khandaq, and after he had prayed for part of the night, he turned to us and said who would go in the enemy camp and get information and come back. The messenger of Allah stipulated that if the volunteer came back. He (the Prophet) will ask Allah for that man to be my companion in paradise. But it was very cold, hungry and fearful, no body volunteered. The Prophet saw no volunteer, he called upon me, and once he called me, I had no alternative but to do so. Then the Prophet told me to go infiltrate the enemy to find out what they are doing. But do not cause any trouble and come back to us." Hadeefa said, so I did, the wind was extraordinarily strong it was blowing everything. Abu Sufyan stood up and said O'Quraish, every man to check out the person sitting next to him. Abu Sufyan was worried that under conditions like that the enemy may have infiltrated in their ranks. At that time immediately, Hadeefa says I took the hand of another person and asked him his name. Hadeefa acted quickly before the other person asked him instead Hadeefa asked his name that was a smart move that saved his life. The man told me who he was. Abu Sufyan then said, we are not in a permanent camp, our horses and cattle are dying and Banu Karewa are at odds with us. And we have heard things about them that we do not like. Due to gales, we can't keep the fire burning, cooking pots are upside down, and tents are hardly standing. You should leave as I am about to do; they gave up. He then went to his camel, which was hobble, struck it to stand on three legs since he only hobbled it. Hadeefa said, he was within my range, I would have shot him but the Prophet (pbuh) had told me not to cause any trouble." Then Hadeefa says, "I returned and found the Prophet (pbuh) standing and praying covered with one of his wife's shawl. When he saw me, he asked me to come in and sit down. And threw part of his wrap over me, he then prostrated while I was under it. When he finished, I related the news to him. Then Quraish and everybody had left. This is a narration by Ahmed in Muslim Sharif there is another narration as well. The Prophet (pbuh) praised Allah who fulfilled his promise and gave victory to his servant.

There are some Miracles, i: when they were digging the trench, Jabbar bin Abdullah saw the Prophet (pbuh)'s food story. ii: when digging the trench there was a big boulder and the Sahaba were unable to break it. They told the Prophet (pbuh), who then said, "bismillah (with the name of Allah) and struck it. A spark came out and the Prophet (pbuh) said, "Allahu Akbar (God is great)". He then struck it again and another spark came out. He then said, Allahu Akbar." He then struck it again and a light came out. He then said Allah hu Akbar then struck it a third time, it disintegrated into dust and the Prophet (pbuh) said, "Allahu Akbar." Suleyman Pharsi asked the Prophet (pbuh), "what was that light and you said Allah hu Akbar?" The Prophet (pbuh) said, first time I struck it, I was given the glad tidying of opening the Roman Empire, and I could see the red palaces, of Syria from here. The second time I said Allah hu Akbar I was given the glad tidying of conquering the Persian Empire. I was able to see its white palaces from here. The third time I was given the glad tidying of conquering Yemen, and I was able to see the gates of Sana'a from here. The Prophet (pbuh) was giving glad tidying's at a time when the moral of the army was low everywhere, defeat was staining at the face, when they were besieged. But that was the whole purpose. Now we should give the news that this religion will reach as far as day and night can reach. Allah has shown the whole world to the Prophet (pbuh) and have told your Ummah will reach all over the world and it is coming. The third miracle; the Prophet (pbuh) saw a Sahabi, Ammar bin Yasir and told him O' Ammar you will be killed by the aggressing party. He was working hard. Ammar lived through the time of the Prophet (pbuh) and through time of Abu Bakr, Umar Usman and then during the time of Hazrat Ali. He was in the army of Hazrat Ali and was killed by the Army of Movia. This Hadith tells us that the party of Ali was on the righteous side and the party of Movia on the evil side. This was the news of Alghaib (unseen) from Allah, both parties are Muslim but one side are righteous and the other are on the wrong side.

Surah Al-Ahzab, Allah talks about Muslims at the time of difficulty. "There is certainly, a messenger of Allah, who a pattern for people who believe in Allah and in the last day (the day of judgement). When they saw, they said this is Allah and his messenger promised us. And Allah and his messenger promised us. And Allah and his messenger spoke the truth. It increased in faith and acceptance. Among the believers are men, true believers in Allah. Among them is he who has fulfilled his vow to death. Among them is he, who waits the chance and can't alter it." This Ayat is saying follow the example of Prophet. Surah Baqarah, Allah says, "do you think, you will go to paradise without going through what nations went through before you? They were tested by fear and hunger, by difficulty, until they and their Prophet say, when shall we see the victory of Allah. They were tested to the limits till they ask, O' Allah, when are you going to guide us to victory. The believers said in Khandaq (the battle of the Trench), Allah promised us in Surah Baqarah and that is happening as we were promised. The same event brought different reaction from believers and from Munafiqeen (hypocrites). Banu Karewa did participate along with Quraish and Ghutfan in the battle of the trench. Abu Yasir, Aiya discussed and their remarks. He is the true Prophet but I shall be opposing him as long as I live, their initial reaction, Aiya came to Kaab, Kaab did not want to see Aiya and told him we have a package with Muhammad (pbuh).

The battle of the Trench was over, the Prophet (pbuh) came home and takes off his Armor and took a bath. Ayesha says, "when the Prophet (pbuh) took off his Armor and took a bath, Angel Gabriel came and said, you have put down your arms, Gabriel said, 'go over to Banu Karewa." The Prophet (pbuh) and the Muslims suffered a lot during the siege at the Trench, they were exhausted, cold, hungry, and now finally they can take some rest. Gabriel came and said, "put your armor back on, pick up your weapons and go and fight with no rest. The Prophet (pbuh) realized the matter was very urgent. He told the Sahaba to not pray Asr unless at Banu Karewa, we have to leave now. The Sahaba left but sunset was approaching and they had not reached Banu Karewa. The Sahaba discussed the order of the Prophet (pbuh). Some of them said, we have to pray Asr now, because it is sunset and the Prophet meant that we should rush. The others said no, we are going to pray just as the Prophet (pbuh) said. Both parties wanted to do what they understood of the meaning of the Hadith. When they returned, they brought the matter up. The Prophet (pbuh) did not disapprove anyone. The Prophet (pbuh) laid siege to Banu Karewa. Allah says, "he brought down among those people of the book from their fortresses, and casted fear into their hearts. That party you killed and took another party captive and caused you to inherit their land, their homes and their property and land which you have never trodden, and Allah is competent over everything. The siege lasted for

25 or 27 days, there are multiple schools of thought. Kaab bin Assad, the head of Banu Karewa gathered his people and gives them 3 options, you are aware of the difficult situation in which we find ourselves. The three options are i: to believe in Muhammad (pbuh) and to follow him, by Allah we know that he is a Prophet sent by Allah. He is the one indeed described in our own book. If you do so you save your own lines and perfect your children.

The objective is that they said we will never abandon our book. ii: if you do not want this, I suggest we kill our own women and children so we can fight him and his army. We can fight much harder since we will not have any responsibility behind us. We can fight until Allah rules between us. If we win, soon we shall have women and children. The people said, 'what will be the purpose of our lives if we kill our women and children. He said, "if you reject this then, these are Sabbath nights, they will be easy, they wouldn't expect an attack and we take them by surprise and fight them to the bitter end." They said, you want to spoil and violate our Sabbath, that has never done before. Except by those whom you know and received the punishment. Then one of them said, "how you can take them by surprise, when you see they are getting stronger every day. In the early days of the siege, they were fighting during the day and retreating at night. But now they are maintaining the siege day and night. The element of surprise is not in our hands. Kaab bin Assad said, "none of you have made a firm decision since he was born." So, they are thinking about surrendering. They sent for Abu Labbaba who was their friend in the time of Jahiliya (ignorance), and they seek his council. Abu Labbaba came and met the women and children crying over the very emotional scene. When they asked Abu Labbaba what will Muhammad (pbuh) do? Abu Labbaba pointed to his throat; he made a gesture that he will slaughter you. As soon as he did that, he realized that the betrayed Allah and his messenger. He should not have done that. He rushed back and tied himself with a pillar in Masjid Al-Nabawi, and said, "I am not going to untie myself until Allah accepts my repentance." Abu Labbaba remains tied up for 6 days in the mosque. His wife will come and untie him for salat and after that tie him back to the pillar. This continues until one-night, the Prophet (pbuh) was at the house of Ummah Salma, and he smiled. Ummah Salma asked, "O' Messenger of Allah, what is it?" The Prophet of Allah said, "Allah has accepted the repentance of Abu Labbaba," Ummah Salma said, "shouldn't I go and deliver the good news to him."

The Prophet (pbuh) said yes if you want to. So, she opens the door and she delivers the news to Abu Labbaba. The Sahaba rushed towards Abu Labbaba to untie him. But do not do so until the Prophet (pbuh) comes and does that himself. When the Prophet (pbuh) came for Fajr Salat, he untied Abu Labbaba. Now there is pillar in Masjid Al-Nabawi called the pillar of Toba (repentance). Banu Karewa agreed to surrender knowing that Saad bin Moaz will rule over their case. Saad bin Moaz used to be their ally at the time of Jahiliya. Saad bin Moaz was given the full authority of their case. Saad bin Moaz was injured during the siege of the Battle of the Trench. He was shot by an arrow in his arm. Saad made a dua. 'My Lord if we are to fight Quraish again, spare me now for that fight. There are no people I like to fight in your cause, then those who have opposed your messenger. They rejected him and forced him out of his hometown. If you will, that will be the last encounter between us. I pray to you O' my lord, make my wound the way to martyrdom and do not make me die until I see our affair with Banu Karewa have a happy ending for Islam.' Saad bin Moaz was bitter at what Banu Karewa did when they betrayed at the bleakest time. The Prophet (pbuh) prepared a tent and called for Saad bin Moaz. They carried him to the gathering place. Al-Auss were telling him to be kind towards Banu Karewa. The saying is that Al-Auss wanted and said hand over Banu Karewa to us as you handed over Banu Kanuka to Al-Khazraj. Banu Kanuka were handed over to Abdullah bin Abbey and he set them free. The Prophet (pbuh) left the matter with Saad bin Moaz. Al-Auss agreed, Saad bin Moaz did not respond to anybody, he kept quiet. In the end, Saad bin Moaz said, "it was time to disregard any criticism while serving Allah. Meaning I am going to do what will please Allah." The Prophet (pbuh) said, "stand up for your master." Saad bin Moaz was a special Sahabi. He looked at Jews and said, "do you accept my ruling?" They said, "yes we do." Then he is pointing out to Muslims, he did not want to see as he was embarrassed. He had so much love and respect for the Prophet (pbuh), and he said to the Muslims, "do you accept my ruling?" Since the Prophet had asked him to do so. The Prophet (pbuh) said, "yes, we do." This was an important moment ruling over the entire tribe of Banu Karewa. It will affect the fate of Banu Karewa who have lived in Madinah for centuries.

Saad bin Moaz said, "I hereby rule that all the men of Banu Karewa to be killed, their properties to be divided and their women and children to be enslaved." The Prophet (pbuh) said, "you have ruled the same ruling as Allah from the top of the 7 heavens. This ruling of yours is the ruling of Allah, this will please Allah. This is the maximum sentences around 400 to 900, various narrations were killed because she killed one Sahaba by throwing a stone on top of him. This woman was sitting with Ayesha, she did what she had done. This woman was laughing and joking and then Ayesha says, "we heard her name, I asked why she said, because they want to kill me for the crime I have committed." Ayesha says, "I shall never forget," she was high spirited even though she knew she was to be killed. All of them were killed except some who became Muslim so their lives were spared. One of their women, her name is Rehana was taken by the Prophet (pbuh) as a slave. The Prophet (pbuh) invited her to Islam, the Prophet (pbuh) gave her the choice either to remain slave or to become Muslim, she preferred to remain slave until the Prophet (pbuh) passed away. One Sahabi asked for one man, who had done him a favor at the time of Jahiliya. Sahabi Sabit bin Qais went to the Prophet (pbuh) to appeal for Zubair bin Bata. He was an old man and he was blind. The Prophet (pbuh) agreed to spare his life but he told Sabit what an old man could do without his son and family. The Prophet (pbuh) released his wife, children and his property.

Then Zubair asked what happened to Kaab who's face would shine like a virgin. Sabit said he has been killed, then Zubair said what about Azal bin Shamal, our guardian. Sabit said, "he has been killed what became of two council," Sabit said, "they have been dispersed and killed." Then Zubair said to Sabit, "let me join my own people. I can't post phone joining my loved ones." Zubair asked what the purpose of living is, if my whole tribe is dead. Zubair was asking Sabit to pay back his favor by making him join his loved ones when that was the wish of Zubair. Sabit bin Qais went over and cut off his head. When this news reached Abu Bakr, when he heard the statement of Zubair, Abu Bakr said he will meet them in hell, by Allah they will dwell there forever, the men were killed and property was divided. Ibn Ishaque says, "this was the war, where eighty percent of property was divided among the fighters and the remaining twenty percent was left for the Prophet (pbuh)." Ibn Ishaque says, the Prophet (pbuh) sent slaves to Najaf, they were sold for horses and money. The Prophet (pbuh) had chosen a woman for himself,

Rehana. When he the Prophet passed away, she was still in his household. Prophet had suggested to her to accept Islam but she had refused. Eventually she did embrace Islam and this brought great pleasure to him. He suggested to free her and to marry her but she remained a slave but stayed until the Prophet (pbuh) passed away. Why was the punishment so severe? Why 400 – 900 men were slaughtered? And entire population women and children enslaved? The whole wealth taken as booty, why? The answer is in one word. Treason. Banu Karewa were the citizens of Islamic state and they committed Treason. Establish rule, punishment should be fitting proportionate of the crime they committed, which was treason against messenger of Allah. Saad bin Moaz refused to be lenient in his ruling. Because it is a sign of weakness. Saad bin Moaz makes a dua (prayer) to God, "my lord, if we are going to fight Quraish again, then spare me now for that fight. There are no people, I would like to fight for your cause, then those who rejected your messenger and forced him out his land, Saad bin Maaz head of a tribe wanted to carry on fighting Quraish, if there was any fighting left, and if you will, that this encounter be the last against Quraish, then I pray to you O' Lord, keep this wound of mine towards martyrdom." This shows Saad bin Maaz had no objective other than to live fighting Quraish in the path of Allah. Then he says, "do not let me die before I have seen the affair with Banu Karewa end in favor of Islam. Allah made him to rule over Banu Kraiwa affairs. Also, battle with Banu Karewa is a special Ghazwa for the following reasons (i) it was commanded by Gabriel (ii) Gabriel accompanied Muslims (iii) the execution of Banu Karewa was a command from Allah, delivered on the toung of Saad bin Moaz. For these reasons this Ghazva was special. This Ghazva drove out Jews from Madinah last tribe.

Saad bin Maaz was the head of Al-Auss after the ruling was delivered on Jews of Banu Karewa the injury of Saad bin Maaz which was almost healed. It was erupted again and caused the death of Saad bin Maaz. His dua was fulfilled, (i) no more fighting with Quraish (ii) He died as a martyr in Allah's holy cause (iii) he saw a happy ending to Banu Karewa. The Prophet (pbuh) called stand up for master. Prophet called him master. The only person for whom Sahaba to stand up, Prophet heard about Saad bin Moaz dying. He rushed with the Sahaba towards him walking so fast, that the Sahaba complained. But Prophet said, the angles will reach there before us. Angels were rushing towards Saad bin Moaz. When he died, his mother was weeping for him. The Prophet (pbuh) said every mourner is exaggerating, except the mother of Saad bin Moaz. He was such a good Muslim, when they carried the funeral of Saad bin Moaz, the coffin was so light. The Sahaba thought it was empty. But the Prophet (pbuh) said, "why it should not be light, when angels came down to participate in his funeral and were carrying the coffin alongside the Sahaba. Those angels never came down before. He was a great Sahabi and the greatest virtue of all. It is in Muslim Sharif, the Prophet (pbuh) said, the throne of Allah shook because of the death of Saad bin Moaz. Some scholars say that the thrown of Allah shook because of the commotion of Angels because of the death of Saad bin Maaz, Prophet never forget Saad bin Moaz even after his death.

One day the Prophet (pbuh) received a gift, it was pieces of cloth. The Sahaba never saw cloth like that before, the Sahaba wanted to touch it. When the Prophet (pbuh) saw gathering, the Prophet (pbuh) said, "the handkerchief of Saad bin Maaz in Jannah (heaven) are softer than this cloth." With all those virtues, when they were lowering his body in the grave, the Prophet (pbuh) was standing on top of the grave and suddenly his face changed, and then he said, "Subhan Allah (praise be to Allah)," three times, Sahaba repeated Subhan Allah (praise be to Allah) then his face returned to normal and he said, "Allah Akbar (God is great)," three times, and the Sahaba repeated after him again. The Sahaba asked for an explanation as to why he said Subhan Allah and Allahu Akbar. The Prophet (pbuh) said, "the grave squeezed the body of Saad bin Moaz, and if there has been any body, to spare of this, that would have been Saad bin Moaz, and then the grave released." Dear brothers, we ask Allah to spare us from punishment of the grave. Saad bin Moaz was a great Sahabi. He was 37 years old when died. He became Muslim before the age of 30. The Prophet (pbuh) said after the battle of the trench, "from now on we shall attack them, they will not attack us." This was a turning point in the life of the Prophet (pbuh). It moved from defensive Jihad to offensive Jihad. We ask Allah us, those who follow the Sunnah of the Prophet (pbuh) we ask Allah to save us from hell fire.

The new founded state posted for five years. Muslims were defensively battling with Quraish for survival. Now the tables are turned, Quraish will have to struggle to survive, and they will be on defensive. Quraish had attacked in Badr and also in Uhud. Also, in Khandaq (the battle of the Trench) that was their last attempt not because they had a change of heart but simply because they were exhausted. They were unable to carry on any further. Muslims had out done them in patients and pursuance and now they couldn't keep up with the Muslims. Allah tells the Muslims to be patient in Surah Al-Imran, the Muslims were patient and it paid off. The Muslims tired out the Quraish. Now the messenger of Allah says, "we shall attack them, they will not attack us. Abu Sufyan was never able to invade Madinah again. They had done their best with 10,000 soldiers in the Battle of

Khandaq (Trench). That was failure at the end because of the supernatural event that occurred. The wind and soldiers of Allah, only Allah knows his soldiers we don't know. Anything can be a soldier of Allah. A Mosquito killed Nimrod. An ocean killed Fir 'awn (the Pharaoh) and earth swallowed crowns. Wind and thunderbolts destroyed nations. Anything in the universe can be a soldier of Allah but we don't know. Although Muslims say that it started with Hijra but those were the difficult days, years of fear, years of hiding in Madinah, years of insecurity. Quraish, Jews and Badoo's to all angels, that was difficult time for Muslims. The Sahaba used to say, we would sleep with our weapons next to us, the first five years were exceedingly difficult but Muslims held on strong.

But now Muslims will move on to occupy new positions. The next five years were the years of expansion. They switched from defensive Jihad to offensive Jihad. Change had taken place. In the next five years, dear brothers and sisters, we shall see growth and expansion of Islam. We ask Allah to give us the ability to go through some important key events, we ask Allah to give us knowledge. (i) The peace agreement at Hudaybiyyah in the sixth year of Hijra. (ii) The battle of Khaybar in seventh year of Hijra. (iii) the battle of Mut'ah. (iv) The conquest of Makkah. (v) The battle of Honaine in the eighth year. (vi) The battle of Tabuk and fare well of Hijra in eighth year and finally the greatest calamity which fell on the Muslims, the death of the messenger of Allah. Also, we shall cover some smaller events in between. We start with events happened between the battle of Khandaq (Trench) and the peace agreement Hudaybiyyah in the fifth year of Hijra. We have already talked about the assassination of Kaab bin Ashraf. He was a Jewish leader and a rich man. He held an important position among the people of Hejaz. He was a poet. During the days of Jahiliya (ignorance), poetry was important.

This was the media of the day, and Kaab bin Ashraf would use poetry to defame Muslims, and he was talking about Muslim women. Muslims would and should stand up to defend the Muslim women.

The battle with the Jewish tribe, Banu Kaneka. It started where a Jewish man uncovered a Muslim woman in a shop, with a trick, tying her clothes with a pin, when she got up her body parts were showing and a Muslim man saw that, he killed the Jew who did that, in return Jews killed him. There was a battle, the Jews lose and a hypocrite had allowed them to leave. The Prophet (pbuh) said, "who will kill Kaab bin Ashraf?" Because he had harmed the Prophet (pbuh) because he had said bad things about the wife of Al-Abbas. The uncle of Prophet Muhammad (pbuh), Muhammad bin Muslimah volunteered for this special operation along with some other members of his tribe. This was Al-Auss who killed Kaab bin Ashraf, one of the Ansar said, and this is in Ibn Kathir. Descendants of Ansar said Al-Auss were like stations, competing in front of the Prophet (pbuh). All tribes were doing their part and wanted to be seen. But this competition was not for the world or money. In Islam, success in how close to Allah we are. For example, Owais al-Qarani. He was not known by people, and Umer bin Khattab asked from people who came as delegation from his tribe named Murad in Yemen. When Umer bin Khattab asked about him, the people were surprised that Amir al-Mu'minin (who was Umer bin Khattab at the time) was asking about such a simple person. Who is Owais Al-Qarani. Nobody knew him. He was not a leader or Ameer of a Jamaat. Simple man. But he was so special that the Prophet (pbuh) told Sahaba when a delegation comes from tribe of Murad from Yemen if you see that man then ask him to pray for you, that Allah forgives you. He is one of the Oulia of Allah. Prophet is telling the Sahaba the greatest generation who ever lived and Owais Al-Qarani is not a Sahabi. He is a Tabi'un. He never saw the Prophet (pbuh). He wanted to make Hijra, wanted to go to Madinah but his mother was ill, and he had to stay with his mother but the Prophet (pbuh) knew him told Sahaba to ask him to make dua. Ask Allah to forgive back you. These tribes would compete about Al-Akhirah. Who would serve the Prophet (pbuh) the best. In this case Al-Auss had the honor of killing Kaab bin Ashraf but Al- Khazraj did not want to be left out. They wanted to do something similar. They held a meeting and discussed the issue. They came up with Abu Rahafa anther enemy to perform they presented the idea to the Prophet (pbuh) and the Prophet approved of it.

Abdullah bin Attic was appointed to lead this group for special operation. They set out towards the land of Khaybar. This was before the battle of Khaybar and Khaybar was the strong hold of Jews. Abu Rahafa was living in fortress. The Sahaba Marched out and came to gates of the fortress of Abu Rahafa. They wanted to get in Abdullah bin Attic played a trick against the Jews. There are two narrations, in Bukhari Sharif. In one narration it says that these Jews lost a donkey, they opened the gates and someone came out to fetch the donkey. Abdullah bin Attic stood next to the wall and sat down looking like he was responding to the call of nature. The Jews saw him and thought he also came out because in those days they did not have toilets or restrooms inside and would go out, far away from their houses to respond to the call of nature. They thought when they went in servant of Allah, Abdullah, if you want to come in now is the time. He walked in normally, the trick worked. But his companions were outside. He was inside. He stayed in donkey stall, but watched the gatekeeper, where he would place the keys. In one narration they were left on wooden peg and in another narration, the keys were left in hole in a wall. Abdullah bin

Attic says, "when the man went to have his dinner with Abu Rahafa. Abdullah bin Attic stayed there until everybody left and lights were turned off. It was a dark night Abdullah bin Attic, picked up the keys. He would go in the rooms open them and locked the doors from inside. It would stop people coming in but also make escape difficult. Abdullah bin Attic made it to the inner chambers of Abu Rahafa. Now he is in the room, Abu Rahafa is sleeping and lights are turned off. It was dark, Abdullah bin Attic could not see anything, what would he do? He called out Abu Rahafa, one has to be brave to do that. But also terrifying for Abu Rahafa said, "who are you?" Abdullah bin Attic says he struck his sword at source of the voice. But the blow was futile. There was confusion, Abu Rahafa yelled out for help. Abdullah bin Attic played another trick, he changed his voice and responded to Abu Rahafa asking, "what do you want?" Abu Rahafa said, "woe to your mother, there is a man here who struck me with his sword." Abdullah bin Attic struck him again at the source of the voice. Abu Rahafa called out for help again, Abdullah bin Attic retreated again and came back, he changed his voice again and said what do you need? Abu Rahafa said, "woe to your mother there is a man here trying to kill me." This Abdullah bin Attic says, "he was injured and lying on his back." Now Abdullah bin Attic stabled him, found the bone and cracked it. He cut the spinal cord. Now Abdullah bin Attic retreated from inner chambers, which was on upper level and there was a wooden ladder, while coming down. Thinking it was the last step, Abdullah bin Attic fell down and broke his leg. He came out and told his group that he has killed Abu Rahafa. But he still wanted to make sure, so he stayed behind to hear the announcement of Abu Rahafa's death, while others were sent back to Prophet with the news that Abu Rahafa is killed. Later on, be heard that Abu Rahafa is dead, second narration, this is by Abu Rahafa, his wife came in and said, "he is dead," in the name of God of the Jews. Abdullah bin Atik says, "I swear, I never heard words, sweeter than that in my life."

Abu Rahafa was killed because Ibn Hijr says Abu Rahafa used to harm Prophet and used to assist against him. Also, he supported Ghutfan and other polytheists with money to fight the Prophet (pbuh). He supported Ghutfan and other polytheists financially and by words.

ZAYNAB BINT JAHSH

She was the sister of Abdullah bin Jaish, her mother is the sister of Hamza bin Abdul Mutlab (Abpwh) and she is the Aunt of the Prophet (pbuh), so Zaynab was the cousin of the Prophet (pbuh). The Prophet (pbuh) visited her and proposed marriage to Zahid bin Harsa. He was a slave. The Prophet (pbuh) wanted to break the barriers that existed. He wanted to start from his own family. But Zaynab bint said, "no," but the Prophet (pbuh) said, "yes," while they were talking it was revealed, it is not fitting for a believer man or woman when a matter is decided by Allah and his messenger to have any option about their decision. If anyone disobeys Allah, clearly, they are on a wrong path. After the Ayat was revealed, she accepted his proposal, but there was not compatibility. After a year they divorced. Zahid bin Harsa and Zaynab bin Jaish were both unhappy. The Prophet (pbuh) said, "fear Allah and keep your wife." But things didn't work out. Then the Prophet (pbuh) married her that created the gossip. In Arabia it was not known that a man would marry the wife of his adopted son. Before it was called Haram in Islam. Zahid was called Zahid bin Muhammad. All the rules applied and one of the rules was that a man cannot marry the wife of his adopted son. Allah wanted to break that rule, what can be better than the Prophet (pbuh) broke the rule himself. There are two rules, (i) a man can't adopt, (ii) can marry the wife of a former adopted son.

Allah says, "show the right way, call them by the names of their fathers. If a father is not known call them your brothers in faith. Intention is what matters and Allah is most merciful. Everybody should keep the name of their ancestor. Zaynab bint Jaish was very righteous, Hazrat Ayesha says, "only Zaynab bint Jaish would compete with me no one else. The Prophet (pbuh) said from his wives, "who will follow me quickly, the one who has got the longer arms." Hazrat Ayesha says, "we used to measure our arms. But in fact, what it meant that whoever gives more Sadaqat (charity), and that was Zaynab bint Jaish, and she died sooner than the rest of wives, after the death of Prophet." Hazrat Ayesha says, "I have never seen a woman, more fearful of Allah, more religious, and more truthful than her. And more attentive to family and giving more Sadaqat (charity). She was fast in these things; she would give full attention to deeds and any work she would do; she had a bit of a temper but would calm down quickly.

There are two particular marriages the non-believers would talk about, that is the Prophet (pbuh)'s marriage to Ayesha because she was of a young age and his marriage to Zaynab because of many tales and legends. But there two marriages were divine, they were commanded by Allah, Zaynab bint Jaish would say to others, "you were married by your parents, I was married from the top of the seven heavens." Allah says, "we married you, your marriage to Ayesha was because of dreams, and we know Ambia (the dreams of the Prophets) are true. Also, in this period Prophet married to the daughter of Abu Sufyan, Umm Habiba who was in Habesha at the time. Her husband Abaid-Allah bin

Jaish, he was one of the Muhajir, he was deceived by Satan. He changed his mind and became murtad. He used to make fun of Muslims and say you are looking with half of your eye open and I have seen the light, he is referring to Christianity. He died as a murtad. After his death, the Prophet (pbuh) sent Amer bin Omiya Gomri to Najashi with the message to marry her, Habiba bin Abu Sufyan. Her Wali (guardian) was her cousin Khalid bin Saad and representative of the Prophet (pbuh), he was performing the contract with Najashi. By this, Umm Habiba became Am-al Mu 'min and Movia became the uncle of the Mu'min, as he is her brother.

PEACE TREATY AT HUDAYBIYYAH

The messenger of Allah (pbuh) had a dream, in the dream he saw that he was doing tawaf around the Kabba with the other Sahaba (Abpwh), then they shaved their heads and shortened their hair. It had been 6 years since the Prophet (pbuh) had left Makkah along with Muhajir. They dearly missed the Kabba, Makkah was the greatest land of Allah. It was beloved land, because of religious reasons, also because it was their home. So, they wanted to go to Makkah and visit the Kabba. Some mufassireen (Islamic scholars) have commented that we have made the house of Allah, the Kabba, Musahiba, (the place where one wants to visit time and time again). An example is given like a young camel. it always wants to go and play, but it also always wants to go and see its mother, just to see its mother and to make sure and have the comfort of knowing its mother is fine.

The same thing happens to a believer, when a believer sees the Kabba for the first time, he is hooked for life, and he would like to go back time and time again. Even once foreigners visit it, they believe that it is their home. Even if they don't speak the language they speak at home, they still feel as if they are home.

The Prophet (pbuh) called on the people of Madinah and surrounding areas of Madinah, the Prophet (pbuh) invited everyone to come out and go with him to Makkah to perform

Umrah. There were 1400 people who responded to the call, and they started on a path to Makkah. When they arrived at Hanifa (the place where they changed into clothes for Umrah. The Prophet (pbuh) told the Muslims to put on the clothes and mark the animals which would be sacrificed, as it was a tradition that the animals which were to be sacrificed should be marked. The messenger of Allah had with him seventy camels, they started saying, 'Labaik, Labaik.' The procession was peaceful. The Prophet (pbuh) intended no fighting and therefore no arms were carried with them. Except their swords in the sheathes. Because Arab men would not travel without their swords. But this army was only going for ibadah, they were not going for fighting but the Prophet (pbuh) was incredibly careful and alert. He was careful to not be taken by surprise therefore he had twenty men on horses ahead of him for protection and to clear the roots and to check if there are any dangers on the way. Also, he sent spies to reconnaissance and gather information. The person responsible for this mission was Bashan ibn Sufyan. Bashan ibn Sufyan, the man appointed over horsemen was Obaida bin Bashan.

Umar bin Khattab was very alert man, very careful. He was known to attend to details. There is a saying about Umar bin Khattab. He said, "I am not a trickster but a trickster cannot trick me." Umar bin Khattab could not be taken by surprise and couldn't be tricked. Everybody knew that about him and that is reflected through his statements, words and advice he would give to the Prophet (pbuh). Umar bin Khattab told the Prophet (pbuh), "you are entering, where people are in a state of war with you and you are going without any weapons." The messenger of Allah agreed with Umar bin Khattab and sent for weapons from Madinah. But he kept the weapons separate from the group. Because it was a peaceful mission.

The man on Reconnaissance came back and told the Prophet that Quraish have in fact marched out and are preparing for war; the Prophet (pbuh) said to the Sahaba, "men give me your advice. Do you want me to head for children and women of those who wish to keep us away from the Kabba."

Ladies and Gentlemen, you know that Quraish had held a high status in Arabia because they were the custodian of the Kabba. But it was common knowledge people knew. This that no one should prevent any body from Hajj or Umrah. The Quraish are trying to prevent Muhammad (pbuh) and the Muslims from entering Makkah. This was unheard of.

The Prophet (pbuh) is asking his companions, 'should we head for children and families of those.' The Prophet (pbuh) is talking about tribes, who allied themselves with Quraish in this mission of trying to prevent Muslims from entering the Kaaba. Because Bishan had told Quraish and other tribes to mobilize. The Prophet (pbuh) said, "how about if we attack the families of these tribes." So that these people will have to come back to protect their families and then we can go ahead to deal with Quraish. By doing this we can broke the alliance and weaken the Quraish Army.

Abu Bakr replied with his opinion and said, "O' messenger of Allah, you have come to visit the Kaaba. Not to fight with anybody, we shall deal with anybody who blocks our way."

The Prophet (pbuh) agreed with him and therefore his plans to attack were dropped. The messenger of Allah said, "then proceed forward in the name of Allah."

Quraish sent out a force of 200 men, led by Khalid bin Al-Walid and Akarma bin Abu Jahl, when this information was received, the Prophet (pbuh) said, "who will take us on a path around them, so we do not meet them." A man offered to guide them through a back root. It was very rough and difficult path. Eventually they made it to the plan ground of Hudaybiyyah, in the south of Makkah and a one day long walk from the Holy city.

When Khalid bin Al-Walid received this information, he rushed back to Quraish. Now Quraish knew that the Prophet (pbuh) was only one day's distance away from them. When the Messenger of Allah, reached at Hudaybiyyah. His famous camel Qaswa sat down and they tell him about Duldul. This is when they wanted the camel to stand up and move. The camel refused to stand up so people were saying it has become refractory. Sometimes camels, horses, donkeys, and elephants do refuse.

The Prophet (pbuh) said, Al-Qaswa is not refractory and that is not in his nature. But she had been held back by he who held back the elephants (the story of Abraha and the elephants). When Abraha and his army of 40,000 were attacking Makkah, the elephants refused. But there is a big difference. At that time there was Abraha and non-believers, and now, the messenger of Allah and the Sahaba. Ibn Higer, comments and speaks. Ibn Higer Allah knew then and knows now that people of Makkah are going to become Muslim. Therefore, Allah prevented bloodshed now and then, then by destroying the army of Abraha and his followers and now by opening up the doors to peace. If the Prophet (pbuh) had proceeded, there could have been a lot of killing, but Allah held back the Muslims. The Prophet (pbuh) said, "in the name of Allah, I shall accept any requests which dignify the century of Allah, and families are honored." The Prophet (pbuh) made it clear that he wants peace.

There was a well in that place, but when the Sahaba went to drink from it, it was empty, they told the Prophet and the Prophet (pbuh) told them to take the arrow from his cover and drop it in the well and they did so, and water flowed Alhamdulillah (praise be to Allah). This is just one of the vast number of miracles the Prophet (pbuh) and other prophets have produced with the help of Allah.

The Prophet (pbuh) chose Kharasch bin Omiya to go to Makkah and tell Quraish that we are coming to perform Umrah peacefully. Kharasch bin Omiya is from Qazi tribe. Kharasch went to Makkah, how they dealt with him? Quraish killed his camel and almost killed him until the Habesh interfered and protected him. This is how they treated the envoy of the Prophet (pbuh). One can see that Quraish were in despair and were frustrated. Now they were humiliated and were losing their position in Arabia. Kharasch was only a messenger, so he left. Umar bin Khattab said his clan is not strong in Makkah and Quraish were aware about his opinion, therefore he was not a good choice to go as an envoy to Makkah. But if the Prophet of Allah insists then he will go. Umar bin Khattab gave frank assessment of the situation. If he goes to Makkah, he will be in danger. But if it was an order, then he will obey. The Prophet (pbuh) remained silent. Then Umar bin Khattab suggested another name. He suggested Uthman bin Affan because his clan was there. Uthman bin Affan belongs to Banu Omiya and Banu Omiya are from the major branch of Quraish. Banu Abdul Munaf, two families who held leadership in Quraish, these are Banu Makhzum and Banu Abdul Munaf, Abu Jahl is from Banu Makhzum who was the head of Quraish during his life.

After that, Banu Hashim, the family of the Prophet (pbuh) and Banu Omiya when Uthman bin Affan went into Makkah. He was given protection immediately by Banu Omiya. Abu Sufyan is also from Banu Omiya, but he was not there at the time, Aebn bin Sa'id bin As gave protection to Uthman. He had him ride on his camel and went in front of Quraish and said, "this man is under my protection." Usman bin Affan told Quraish the peaceful purpose of the visit and message was simple. Secondly, the Prophet (pbuh), told him to visit believing men and women and give them the glad tidings that Islam will be victorious. The Muslims will win. Uthman bin Affan told Quraish, "the Prophet (pbuh) has sent me to you, to call you to Islam and to enter in the religion of Allah because Allah will give victory to his religion and will honor his prophet." He told them let someone else take care of this affair. The fight if you win, that is what you want and if you lose, then like others you choose and also, war has exhausted you and the best among you are killed. That was a blunt, direct message. The Prophet (pbuh) is telling you that we have come for Umrah with sacrificial animals marked. We shall slaughter them and leave peacefully without any trouble.

Abyan bin Saied told Uthman bin Affan, if you want to do tawaf go ahead, no one can prevent you. Some companions were saying Uthman is lucky because he is making tawaf. The Prophet (pbuh) said, my expectation of him is that even he stays for years. He will not make tawaf until I perform tawaf, and that was the case. Uthman bin Affan said, "I will not make tawaf in the house of Allah until the Prophet (pbuh) makes tawaf first," this was out of respect for the Prophet pbuh. Quraish were sending their envoys. The first one was Audey bin Varka. He came to the Prophet (pbuh), he belonged to Qaza tribe, all believers and non-believers were sympathetic t Muslims. Qaza. They were advisers to the Prophet. In one narration it says, "Qaza would inform the Prophet, of anything in Makkah. Both Muslims and non-Muslims were bringing them information. This was the tribal alliance in the time of Jahiliya (ignorance). Qaza were allied with Hashim. Now the leader of Hashim tribes was the Prophet, therefore they carried on the relationship, they were considered close to Banu Hashim and close to Muslim. Information was help to their success, since they were living in and around Makkah therefore, they had inside information. Audhay bin Varka came to the Prophet (pbuh) and said, "Quraish have come out with camels with milk, meaning they have provisions and intending to stay for long time, if circumstance demand. Also, they have put on tiger skin meaning they are ready for war." The Prophet (pbuh) said, "We have not come to fight but to perform Umrah. Quraish were ruined with war fare. If they want, we can give them some time but they should give me access to people. If I prevail and if they wish to join, they can do so. Otherwise, they would be fresh after rest. I swear by Allah who holds my soul, I shall battle with them until I perish and Allah will prevail."

The Prophet (pbuh) said to them, "either you leave me alone or fight with me, I shall never give up. I shall win Insha'Allah." After the battle of Khandaq (the battle of the Trench), the Prophet (pbuh) said, "we shall win they will not." Now, Quraish are defensive Audhay bin Varka went back to Makkah, Quraish were quiet, nobody wanted to ask. Audhay bin Varka said, "do you want me to tell you what happened," Akrama bin Abu Jahl said, "we do not want to hear anything from you," then Sufyan bin Omiya and the others said, 'go on tell us what happened,' Audhay bin Varka gave the message but they didn't like what they heard.

Now they sent another man Makarsh bin Hash, when the Prophet (pbuh) saw him, the Prophet (pbuh) said, "this man is with double policy." Later on, that was proved true because he brought 40 men with him and circled around the Muslim camp looking for a loaner to capture him to make a prisoner. But it happened other way around, Muslims captured all of them except Makarsh who ran away. The Prophet (pbuh) intended peace. Therefore, he released them without any condition. Then the head of Al-Habeesh. He was an ally with Quraish, he offered to go and meet the Prophet.

The Prophet (pbuh) saw him and said, "this is from devoted people," Muslims showed him sacrificial animals as proof of their peaceful Umrah. As soon as he saw the animals, he walked away without meeting the Prophet (pbuh). He was moved for what he saw. He went back to Quraish and said, "all glory belongs to Allah and it is not right to keep these people away from the Kabba." Although he was Mushriq (non-believer) he didn't want to prevent anybody from the House of Allah. He said, "Allah will not forgive for other tribes from Yemen to come to the House of Allah and the son of Abdul Mutlab is being prevented from the House of Allah." He was angry but Quraish told him to calm down, let us get on with our business. All envoys were failure and then Urwah bin Masood, came and said to the Quraish, "Ascend you, my parents." Urwah bin Masood was from Sokeef. His mother was from Quraish. He was a great man of Arab. In fact, they questioned why the Quran was not revealed on a great man of two towns. Makkah and Taif. He said, "do you want me to go," the Quraish said "yes." Urwah bin Masood also said, "I have seen the previous envoys insulted by you, because they wouldn't come with the answers they were looking for. But Quraish told Urwah. We trust you, and you go." So Urwah bin Masood went to the Prophet (pbuh). He said, "hey Muhammad, have you not considered that you are ruining these people before you. And if that is not the case, I see people here, Hach, pouch, I see they are capable of fleeing and leaving you alone." Then Urwah saw that Muhammad (pbuh) is invading his own people. "Even if you win you will destroy your own people. That is unacceptable, secondly option you will be defeated." He referring to different tribes Quraish and different tribes Hach pouch. He considered them and class tribe.

Now the larger tribes were slow in accepting Islam. They thought Islam will take away their position as everybody is equal. However smaller tribes had accepted Islam. When Abu Bakr saw that it wouldn't go unnoticed. He swore at him and told him to get lost. We flee /and abundance the Prophet, that was a big insult. Abu Bakr insulted Urwah bin Masood. Urwah stared at Abu Bakr and said, "if it was not your favor towards me in the past I would have responded back. I stay quiet and by doing this, I have paid you back your favor." Abu Bakr had paid blood money i.e. 100 camels. He asked people to help with blood money, people gave 1 or 2 camels and Abu Bakr gave 10 camels, in time of Jahiliya (ignorance). The insult was so great that Urwah thought by staying quiet he had paid him his favor back. But Abu Bakr could not handle what he had said that Muslims will flee.

Ladies & gentleman, you can imagine the Sahaba's reaction, they were strong, loyal and united they had no weakness. When it comes to the defense of the Prophet (pbuh), Abu Bakr said, "we are going to fight for him and are never going to leave him alone."

There was a custom to ask, people used to hold each other. Beard for regards and favor. Urwah bin Masood was speaking to the Prophet (pbuh) often he would extend his hand to touch the beard of Prophet. Al-Mughira was standing near the Prophet (pbuh) as a guard. Al-Mughira had his sword and would strike the hand of Urwah every time he extended his hand to touch the Prophet (pbuh). Al-Mughira told him Urwah to keep your hand away from the Prophet (pbuh). Otherwise, it will not be returned to you. I shall cut it off. Al-Mughira was covered with his Armor from head to toe and only his eyes could be seen. Urwah didn't know who that man was. He told the Prophet (pbuh), you are rude, this is a wicked man who is armed. Urwah asked who this man (Al-Mughira) is. The Prophet (pbuh) smiled and told him this is your nephew. Al-Mughira was the nephew of Urwah bin Masood. The rough man was his own nephew. Then Urwah said, "I only washed away yesterday, what he was referring to, was that Al-Mughira was traveling with thirteen mushriqeen. He killed them all, stole their money and then ran away to Madinah to become Muslim. The Prophet (pbuh) told him that I shall accept you to become Muslim but I shall not accept this money. Because there was trust between travelers and he betrayed that trust, therefore money was not accepted. The Prophet (pbuh) did not apologize to mushriqeen. Urwah bin Masood had to pay it, being the relative of Al-Mughira. He also had to pay blood money. He is now reminding Al-Mughira that he took care of Al-Mughira and now this is how you treat me.

Ladies and Gentlemen, you can see how Islam changed the hearts and minds of people. For the love of the Prophet (pbuh), they would put away their personal matters and relations. Al-Mughira treated his uncle like that, because he was being disrespectful to the Prophet (pbuh). Now you can see the reactions of Abu Bakr and Al-Mughira for the love of the Prophet (pbuh). Sometimes it is difficult to understand, but put yourself in their shoes, you will appreciate the love the Sahaba had for the Prophet (pbuh) and it was sincere love.

Ibn Higer comments on the statement of Urwah. Urwah had said, "you will ruin your own people. Secondly, these different tribes' people will leave you and you will be taken as a prisoner."

Islam changes, if the Prophet defeats, his people that will be praise, if the Prophet (pbuh) loses, that is also praiseworthy because it is Fi-Sabeel. Allah says, "tell disbelievers what you are waiting for, what will happen to us. Both are good for us. Win or lose."

Urwah bin Masood had experience of a lifetime. He went back and told Quraish. "I have gone to meet kings, had audience with, Caesar, kissra and Nagis, and I swear by Allah

I have never seen the subjects any king to venerate him the way Muhammad's people venerate him. I swear, if he spits, it will fall on palm of someone and then he will rub it on his face or skin. If he gives them a command, they hurry to carry it out. If he speaks, they lower their voices in his presence and they never look directly at him out of respect. He has made an offer to you so accept it. These people will never abandon him so draw your own conclusion, says Zohri. He came with some ideas but having seen the reality he changed the idea. When the Prophet made Wudhu, the Sahaba would pick up the drops and rub them on their body, that was blessing for their skin. If any hair falls out, he will pick it up and hide it. The Sahaba thought everything came from him, had his blessing, this was the love and respect for the Prophet (pbuh) the Sahaba had for him." Urwah bin Masood was a seasoned man he knew. Later on, in his life, he chose the path of Islam and became Muslim.

This was the living example of Dawah. Dawah of words and Dawah of actions. Urwah bin Masood saw this with his own eyes. He said to Quraish, "there is no way you can defeat these people."

Uthman bin Affan was still in Makkah, rumors spread. Time of war time of rumors. Rumors spread that he has been killed. The Prophet (pbuh) headed for the camp of Banu Najjar. Every clan had their own camp. Ummah (Hamara), a woman from Banu Najjar, she says, "I saw the Prophet (pbuh) going towards our camp. So, I thought he needed something, the Prophet (pbuh) came and sat down."

THE BAY'AH (PLEDGE)

"Allah has commanded me to take the pledge from Muslims," and she said first man to give him pledge then Muslims were rushing to give him, pledge what were the terms of the pledge. The first pledge was the pledge to die. The second pledge was to never flee. The third pledge is the pledge to you for what is in your heart. This is amazing. Allah knows perhaps Sahaba didn't know but were pledging for whatever the Prophet will say.

This was the pledge of (Al-Rizwan), Allah was pleased with Muslims after this pledge, the reason for Bay'ah, pledge, was the rumors that Uthman bin Affan had been killed.

A few things to remember, the pledge Bay'ah was taken in the camps of Banu Najjar, Banu Najjar belongs to the tribe of Al-Khazraj and they are the maternal uncles of the Prophet (pbuh).

They were close associates and private soldiers of the Prophet (pbuh). When the Prophet (pbuh) made Hijra, he first settled with in the Kabba, but when he went to Madinah, he stayed with Banu Najjar and the men of Banu Najjar were surrounding the Prophet (pbuh) with swords for protection, private force.

Now he came to Banu Najjar camp, Ummah Hamara says, "my husband stood with his sword in his hand, and Ummah Hamara had her belt stuck knife with her and held a pole in her hand, and said I am ready to fight." Muslimah, gave his pledge three times, because he was asked. He prayed; 'O' Allah give me someone whom I love more than myself (soulmate).'

Now about Uthman bin Affan, someone claimed that Uthman did not attend Badr and did not give pledge at Al-Rizwan. In the battle of Badr he was told to stay behind because Uthman's wife, the daughter of the Prophet (pbuh) was not well. But this time the whole pledge was for the sake of Uthman. Secondly, he did give his Bay'ah. As the Prophet (pbuh) put one hand into the other and said this is the pledge of Uthman. It was even better.

Allah says, "we have truly sent a witness, a Warner, order you, O'people believe in Allah and his messenger that you may assist and honor him and celebrate his praise in the morning and in the evening." They really did not know. The hand of Allah is over their hands, if anyone violates his oath does it to harm his own sole and anyone who fulfils his covenant with Allah. Allah will soon grant him a great reward. These Ayat were revealed about the pledge of Rizwan. Allah says, "Allah is pleased with believers who have pledged to you under the tree that was the pledge."

Al-Abbas and Akrama say that in practice, loyalty is to fight in front of the Prophet (pbuh). But Uthman bin Affan was not killed and it was a false rumor. This must have caused a terror in the hearts of Quraish. This event was witnessed by the heavens. Allah revealed an ayah, "when the Sahaba finished the pledge, the Prophet (pbuh) told them you are the best people on the face of the Earth."

Another hadith, the people who pledge, their sins are washed away, except the person with red came. One man, Quays did not pledge to the Prophet (pbuh). One Sahabi said he saw him hiding behind the camel so he did not have to give Bay'ah (pledge). The best people, 10 people, who are given the glad tidings of paradise. Then the people of Badr and then who gave pledge at Rizwan, the Sahaba pledged to give their lives. This was the pledge of Rizwan.

The reason was Uthman bin Affan, Muslim are willing to fight and die for one man, the whole Ummah is one body.

Quraish sent Sohail bin Amr to negotiate with the messenger of Allah to negotiate truce. Sohail means easy, therefore the Prophet (pbuh) took a good omen from the name, he thought peace is on its way and Quraish are intending on an agreement. The Prophet (pbuh) and Sohail deliberated pros and cons of the agreement for some time. Quraish were very persistent on the point that the Prophet and the Sahaba (Muslims) should not enter the city of Makkah. This year was the pride of ignorance, they didn't want to say that the Prophet (pbuh) entered forcefully, the Prophet gave those reasons but they were stuck on this point. The Prophet (pbuh) wanted a settlement. The Prophet (pbuh) had said, "before that house of Allah (sanctities were glorified) the Prophet (pbuh) will accept it.

The terms of the agreement were spoken (verbally). The only thing left was to get them down in writing.

Umar bin Khattab was quite upset with what he heard. He went to the Prophet (pbuh) and said, "Are you not the messenger of Allah? The Prophet replied, "yes I am the messenger of Allah, Umar then asked, "are we not Muslims," the Prophet (pbuh) said, "yes," then Umar said, "are they not the kufr (disbelievers), the Prophet said, "yes. Then Umar bin Khattab said, "why we should demean our religion?" "We are lowering our religion by accepting their demands. Since we are on the right why should we agree with them and bargain with them."

The Prophet (pbuh) told Umar, "I am the servant of Allah. I am the Messenger of Allah; therefore, I shall not disobey him and he will not abandon me or forsake me."

Umar bin Khattab then went to Abu Bakr and told him that isn't he the messenger of Allah. Abu Bakr said, "yes, we are Muslims yes." Umar said, Quraish are kufr, Abu Bakr said, "yes," Umar then asked Abu Bakr, "why should we demean our religion?" Abu Bakr said, "follow him. He is the messenger of Allah and Allah will not forsake him." Abu Bakr knew the incident in Ghare Soure (the cave of Soure).

Although Umar bin Khattab had good intentions, he regretted the argument. He was overly sensitive when it comes to right and wrong. He distinguishes, that is why he is called Al-Farooq. He summits to Allah. He does not allow himself to follow the winds of heart (his story when he was Amir al-Mu'minin. He was an extraordinarily strong believer. He would control himself. But here he spoke because of Nasr (victory). For victory of the religion of Allah. However, when he realized the revelation from Allah and the will of Allah, Umar bin Khattab realized his mistake. He later said that he kept on fasting and giving Sadaqat praying, freeing slaves, for the fear of what he did on that day,

Allah says, "good deeds raise bad deeds. Now sin has been committed give or do lot of good deeds."

We all commit sins this is our nature. We can raise with good.

THE TERMS OF THE AGREEMENT

They both started to write the terms to the agreement.

1. Both parties have agreed to a complete truce for the period of 10 years. During that period all the people will enjoy peace and security and will not attack each other.
2. If anyone joins the Prophet (pbuh) without the authority of the chief from Quraish, he shall be returned to Quraish.
3. If anyone joins from the camp of Muhammad (pbuh) to Quraish, he shall not be returned. This was not

pleasing to Muslims. Both sides agree to harbor good intentions to each other.

4. No theft or treachery will be condoned.
5. Whoever wants to enter in alliance with Muhammad (pbuh), may do so. Also, whoever wants to enter in alliance with Quraish may also do so.
6. Muhammad (pbuh) will return home without entering Makkah this year.
7. Finally, after one full year, Makkah will be emptied and you, the Prophet (pbuh) may enter and stay for only three days, you will carry only necessary arms like swords in their sheathes. No other arms will be carried. Managed to escape

They wrote down these terms to the agreement and now is the time to sign it and have witnesses. (Quraish disliked the word Prophet). Suddenly, Abu Jandal appears. He is the son of Sohail who is writing the agreement. He was in chains; he was imprisoned in Makkah, he managed to escape and he fled from Makkah. He was Muslim and heard that Muslims are nearby. He made it walking through mountains and valleys and reached Hudaybiyyah. He was happy that he was in the Muslim camp. Sohail bin Amr says, "this is the first case and you should return him to me." The Prophet (pbuh) asks to keep him, but Sohail says, "either this or nothing. If you refuse to give back Abu Jandal, I shall refuse the agreement, we have not signed the agreement yet, but Sohail was insistent for the Prophet to either give back his son or there would be no agreement. The Prophet (pbuh) told Abu Jandal to go back. Abu Jandal was pleading the Prophet of Allah to free him and send him back to the disbelievers. The Prophet (pbuh) told him to be patient and endure your situation for Allah's sake. Allah will provide you and others suffering with you a way out of hardship. We have made a peace agreement with these people to give pledge by Allah. That we shall be faithful to the terms of the agreement. We should not violate our pledge. Umar was walking next to Abu Jandal while he was being dragged away and placed the handle of his sword pushing it towards Abu Jandal so that he can pick up the sword and strike his father. Umar bin Khattab says, "Abu Jandal wanted to preserve his father and issue was over." Umar was whispering to Abu Jandal that these people are disbelievers, their blood is no more than the blood of a dog. But Abu Jandal did not take any action. The Sahaba had dignity, honor and trust in Allah. For them to see a Muslim brother taken back to non-believers was disastrous. This incident of Abu Jandal was very difficult for Muslims to take in.

The Prophet (pbuh) did this because it was an order of Allah. Allah will provide the way out for them. This was a revelation, a promise from Allah. It was not a forecast by the Prophet (pbuh) but a Wahi (revelation). Allah will provide the way out and solution to these problems. But it was exceedingly difficult on Muslims. Normally when the Prophet (pbuh) ordered something, the Sahaba would rush to complete it, but when the Prophet (pbuh) said, slaughter sacrificial animals and shave your heads, no one moved. Some mufsreen have said that the Sahaba were not disobedient but delayed in the hope that perhaps the Prophet (pbuh) will receive revelation to change the situation. Maybe there is hope to go to Makkah they were very eager to make Tawaf, around the Kaaba, they came in with that intention, and now had to go back empty handed, they were waiting for a change. But the Prophet (pbuh) went back angry and told Ummah Salma that Muslims are ruining themselves because I gave them an order and they disobeyed. Ume Salma, a wise woman, said O' Prophet do not talk to them about it. They are under great pressure because the trouble you have taken to achieve peace settlement. Also, because they have realized that they have long way to go home without achieving their purpose. Also, she said, if you want them to follow, then go and do it in front of them. The Prophet (pbuh) called his barber and slaughtered his animals and the Sahaba immediately followed the orders but were incredibly sad, they returned home, on the way there were two questions. About tawaf, the Prophet (pbuh) said to Umar, "did I tell you that you will make tawaf this year?" Umar said, "no," and then the Prophet told him you will make tawaf. The second issue was how the Sahaba can return Muslims to them. The Prophet (pbuh) said, "Allah will provide the way out, and if someone leaves us and goes to them then Allah will rid us of them. Why should we keep them with us? If he has given up Islam and has run away, we do not need him."

There was an exception to this rule regarding Muslim women are not to be returned and an Ayat was revealed to clarify that issue. Allah only knows what this Ayat does to the agreement. But Allah says in this Ayat, "O' you who believe when a believing woman come to you, examine and Allah knows best. If you are certain that they are believers, then do not send them to unbelievers. They are not lawful wives to non-believers. Nor non-believers are lawful husbands to them. But pay what they have spent and there is no blame to you. Ask the non- believer what they have spent. Such is the command of Allah. Allah judges between you and Allah is full of knowledge and wisdom.

THE STORY OF ABU BASIR

After the Agreement was complete, a man called Abu Basir, who belongs to the tribe of Banu Sokeef, they are from Taif. But he was an ally of Banu Zora, and Banu Zora is one of the clans in Makkah. Abu Basir was a Muslim and fled from Mushriqeen and he came to Madinah. Three days later two men came asking for his return. These men are from Banu Amer bin Luwai. One of the branches of Quraish. The other man was a servant who came with him to guide him. They had a letter that was presented to the Prophet (pbuh). The letter said we have an agreement and you have to return this man to us. The Prophet (pbuh) told Abu Basir to go back. Abu Basir said, "O' prophet of Allah you are sending me back to disbelievers to test my religion. The Prophet (pbuh) told Abu Basir, "we have an agreement with these people and it is not appropriate for us to betray. Betrayal is not allowed in our religion." The Prophet (pbuh) is doing this because these are the rules of Islam. Muslims are bound by the laws of Allah with Muslims and non-Muslims we follow the rules of Allah in everything we do. And Prophet (pbuh) told Abu Basir like Abu Jandal, that Allah will find the way out for you. Abu Basir left with these two men. When they reached a place called D' Allifa. It was Zohar time, there is a mosque which Abu Basir pointed at. He prayed two Rakat and he had some dates with him, and he called the other men to join him. They also had bread with them and they all had meal together. A man (Amer) pulled his sword, and said I am going to kill Al-Auss and Al-Khazraj men with this, day and night. Abu Basir asked, is it a good sword? He said yes, I have tested it. Abu Basir said can I see it. The moment the sword was in the hand of Abu Basir. The man was dead. He killed him. The other narration is that they were sleeping and Abu Basir' hands were tied and he pulled out the sword with his month. Cut the ropes, freed his hands and killed the Amri man. The other man ran away. Al-Waqidi (a Scholar) says, he ran so fast that rocks would fly from beneath his feet. He was running towards Madinah. Abu Basir chased him but he ran fast and came to the mosque. When Prophet (pbuh) saw him, the holy Prophet said that the man is terrified. They asked him, "what is the matter?" He replied, "this man has killed my companion and wants to kill me too." He was seeking help; he was told to calm down. Abu Basir came holding the sword in his hand and told the Prophet (pbuh), you have fulfilled your pledge to them. You have handed me over to them and you have done your part. It is in Bukhari Sharif the Prophet (pbuh) said, vow to his mother he will incite war if he had men with him. It means that Abu Basir is capable of starting a war if he has men with him. Abu Basir from this statement understood that the Prophet (pbuh) will hand him over if he stays. He decided to leave and he left, Al-Waqidi says that Abu Basir brought the belongings of Amri and gave them to the Prophet (pbuh) to be divided as spoils of war.

The Prophet (pbuh) refused to take them because that would violate the agreement. Abu Basir cannot go back to Makkah, because he fled from Makkah and killed a man, where could he go? He went to the coast alone. He had only hand full of dates. He ate for three days that was the only food he had. Al-Waqidi says Allah provided him fish. He would eat from that dead fish which come to the coast. Subhan Allah, the story of Abu Basir is amazing. He was alone, and people are looking for him (Quraish). He was in a fearful situation. But Allah provided him way out and gave him victory, Abu Jandal heard about that. He fled from Makkah and joined Abu Basir and also some other believers who were living under tyrants they all joined Abu Basir. This would make Abu Basir first Muslim in the history of Islam to wage a Gorilla style war. Al-Waqidi in one of the scholars of the Seerah. Although his narrations do not stand up to Hadith, take your pick. He narrates that Umar bin Khattab had a letter writing campaign to Muslims who were living with Mushriqeen, to join Abu Basir and he mentions in a letter that Prophet said vow to his mother he would incite war if he just had men, what Umar meant, that you living under Mushriqeen should join him and fight. Now there were enough men and they started to raid caravans belonging to Quraish. News of these operations spread around and other young men from other tribes who wanted to fight, that way were joining with Abu Basir and now he had an army of three hundred strong. These three hundred men would attack any Quraish caravan, kill people with caravan and take away the goods. This situation was unbearable for Quraish. The Prophet (pbuh) did not interfere with that because he was responsible for Medina and not for the coast. Sohail bin Amar when heard about the killing of Amri was very upset because that man belonged to his tribe. He put his back against Kaaba and said he is not going to move until the blood money is paid for this man and Muhammed (pbuh) should pay it. Abu Sufyan said this is insane. Muhammed (pbuh) had nothing to do with it. He played his part and didn't allow Abu Basir to stay in Madinah. Muslims are doing what is required under the agreement and the Prophet (pbuh) is not going to stop Abu

Basir nor would they pay blood money. Suhail bin Amr said then Quraish should pay his blood money. Abu Sufyan said, why Quraish? But Banu Zora sent him. Sohail accepted that Banu Zora should pay it. The head of Banu Zora refused to pay and Sohail received nothing. The Qadr (predestination) of Allah was working in the favor of Muslims and Abu Basir. At the time of the agreement, Quraish saw it as a victory for them, but now things were unbearable for them.

Their caravan just started after a long break, and now Abu Basir. Before the peace agreement at Hudaybiyyah, Muslims were threatening their caravan. The battle of Badr was because of the caravan of Abu Sufyan. Also, many of the Suraya were to threaten the business roots of Quraish. Now, because of the peace agreement, Quraish were able to do business again. Now, they sent messages to the Prophet (pbuh), they were begging the Prophet (pbuh) to change the terms in the agreement. All praise to Allah. They were saying in the name of our relationship. They wanted to change the terms and also to call these people back. The Prophet (pbuh) sent a letter to Abu Basir to come back to Madinah and asking other people to go back to their people.

The letter arrived to Abu Basir in his last moments when he was dying. He died with letter of the Prophet (pbuh) on his chest. Allah provided a way out for him. And Abu Jandal with other Muslims returned to Madinah. This was the promise of the Prophet (pbuh) that Allah will find the way out for you. Muslims have to follow the commands of Allah, and Allah will find the way out for them. Surah Al-Fatha: This Surah was revealed on the way back from Hudaybiyyah. It was then revealed in its entirety. When it was revealed. The Prophet (pbuh) send to call Umar when Umar realized that the Prophet (pbuh) is calling him. He was frightened that revelation may have reprimanded him for what he did. Then the Prophet (pbuh) told him that he had received an Ayat. Those are better than anything in the world this narration is in Bukhari Sharif. Umar bin Khattab said, "is it opening?" The Prophet said, "yes." In the name of whom, my soul is in his hand it is opening. The meaning Fatha and meaning of Nasr. Fatha is opening. In Arabic when something is locked and opening is Fatha. This meaning was borrowed when a land is opened because the land is locked against the army and now is opened. You have to fight to open enemy land. Therefore, the word Fatha is used for victory for taking over land. Nasr could be used to refer a victory in a battle like victory in Badr. We can't say we opened Badr. But we can say Fatha Khaybar and Fatah Makkah. These are the meanings for Fatha and Nasr.

Now, question is, how could be Hudaybiyyah be called Fatah? There is no land involved. A scholar once said, 'it was called Fatah, because this is the event which led to opening of Makkah. Because of Hudaybiyyah, Makkah was opened.' Hudaybiyyah was Fatah because the Prophet (pbuh) came to Hudaybiyyah in force of 1400 when finished, people were meeting each other, and people learned about Allah and who ever wanted to become Muslim was able to become Muslim. Now there was no fear or threat for Muslims. After two years, Muslims entered Makkah with the Army, troops of 10,000. In two years, Muslims multiplied. Thirteen years in Makkah, and then six years before the peace treaty of Hudaybiyyah, total of nineteen years. The number was 1400 and in just over 2 years the numbers jumped from 1400 to 10,000. This is the blessing of the peace treaty of Hudaybiyyah, that gave the chance to Muslims to practice Dawah. There is no risk for becoming Muslim and Muslims can travel freely. While in Makkah, Muslims were not fighting and were persecuted that was difficult time. Now Muslims had the ability to speak to people and were free to listen and accept Islam.

Allah says, "verily we have granted you a manifest victory. That Allah may forgive you your faults in the past and those to follow. Allah gave victory to his messenger and forgave him. Prophet (pbuh) any faults? Let us put them in to prospectus. The status of messenger of Allah is extremely high to us everything is a good deed." But Umbia, prophets have high status therefore anything falls short of that high status. These are the things which Allah will forgive. It is different than sins. I hope this is clear. The Prophet (pbuh) is guided by Allah and revelations will continue. And Allah may give you great victory. This great victory is opening of Makkah. And what came after that, all of the other victories. Muslims enjoyed because of the agreement of Hudaybiyyah. It is Allah who sends tranquility in the hearts of believers. Muslims came to perform Umrah and at a particular moment they gave their pledge to die. They were mentally prepared for a fight and there was no fighting. And now had to go back without Umrah. There were some changes, which were difficult to bear. This was a kind of insecurity that Allah replaced with tranquility. That was the promise of Allah that we shall come back with victory. Allah says 'reminding the believers that the forces of heavens and the earth belong to Allah. Anything can be a soldier of Allah. Angels are soldiers of Allah that came down at the battle of Badr. Wind is a soldier of Allah that was sent down on the battle of the trench. Rain is a solider of Allah that was sent on Muslims in Badr. The faithful Muslims are (Mu'minin) when they heard the first Ayat of Surah Fatha, Allah promising to Muhammad (pbuh) the victory. They were happy for the Prophet (pbuh) but wanted to know what is for them, Allah says 'Allah will admit them, Muslims, men and woman in the gardens of paradise where rivers flow underneath their feet, where they can dwell forever and remove their illnesses and that will be highest achievement for Muslim men and women. Allah has told us what he will give to believers. Now he tells us what is in store for the kufr. Allah may punish hypocrites, men or women. The forces of heavens and earth belong to Allah and Allah is powerful and wise. We have truly sent you as a witness, as a bringer of glad tidings and as a warner. Here we see three characteristics for the messenger of Allah. He is a witness. Witness is someone who approves or disapproves a claim that is made by someone else. This is the role of the Prophet (pbuh) to approve the believers and disapprove the disbelievers. He brings the glad tidings and brings warnings. Barely those who pledge to you they pledge to Allah. The hand of Allah is over their hands. Mushriqeen say that no Sahaba violate their oath whoever fulfills. The covenant with Allah will soon grant him with a great reward. And that is the reason who gave pledge under the tree have extremely high status. The Arab! Who log behind. The one who did not come with believers in Sulah Hudaibia. Why did not they come they thought Quraish are extraordinarily strong and Muslims will be killed so they stayed behind. Allah says those who deserted, Arabs will say we were busy looking after our herds, flocks and our families. This is their excuse. Now, Allah be praised, the 1400 who went they also had families, this is not an excuse in the eyes of Allah. Then they ask the Prophet for forgiveness but they say with their tongues, but this is not in their heart. Say to them who can intercede with Allah. Allah is well acquainted with what you do. Allah says about them. Nay, the reason is that they thought that the Prophet (pbuh) and the believers will never return to their families. For those who do not believe in Allah and his messenger we have prepared a blazing fire for them.

To Allah belongs the dominions of the heaven and the earth. Allah forgives whom he wills and punishes whom he wills, and Allah is forgiving and merciful. Those who log behind and that they say, now Allah has promised victory, now they want to join for spoils of war (booty). They want to join for the world but for Allah they do not want to join. As a punishment for them they were prevented to join in Khaybar. When they were told not to join in Khaybar, they said you are jealous. You want to take the spoils of war for yourself. Little do they understand such things. Khaybar was declared victory for the Muslims. But say to those that you will be allowed to fight against others. Who are very tough in fighting? If you fight, Allah will reward you, if not then Allah will punish you.

These tough enemies, some Mushriqeen says about Muslima Kazab, some say, Persian and some say Romans. God only knows, there is no blame on the blind or lame or on the sick these are excused from fighting in Jihad. But who submits to Allah and his Prophet (pbuh), Allah will give them Paradise (Jannah) and he who turns back, Allah will punish him with grievous penalty. Allah says once again who pledged under the tree, they will enjoy Allah's good pleasure that is why it is called pledge of pleasure. Allah knew those believers who pledged, and Allah rewarded them with a speedy victory, this tree was known afterwards, and some Muslims would come and pray next to that tree. Because what happened there, and this tree is mentioned in the Holy Quran. Umar bin Khattab ordered that tree to be cut down because Umar bin Khattab was worried that this could lead to Shirk. Although the Prophet (pbuh) sat under the tree, in Islam it is the substance and not the symbols that count. Many other gains were achieved, and Allah is full of wisdom. Allah promised the bounties and first of them was Khaybar and many other gains will be acquired. And Allah has given you beforehand, and he may guide you to a straight path. Other gains are not with in your power but Allah has power over all things. If disbelievers fight you, they will turn their backs. No help or protection to them.

Believers will win. They might lose a battle but eventually they will win. This is Allah, believers will win. The end belongs to who have Taqwa (trust in Allah). Allah says, "Allah will make your feet firm. Muslims lost in Uhud but eventually, they won the war against Quraish. The Muslims perhaps lost some battles against Romans but eventually they have won. The Muslims perhaps lost some battles against Persians but ended up conquering the entire Persian empire. This is a promise of Allah as long as they are fulfilling commands of Allah. Allah showed a vision to his messenger that he will enter Makkah, perform Umrah. Although it did not happen this time, but it happened in peace e.g., last Hajj.

During the sixth year of Hijra, there were some men from tribe of Judah. These narrations are in Bukhari Sharif and Muslim Sharif. Also mentioned by Ibn Ishaque and Ghamdi in books of Seerah. It is authentic. There were eight men they were extremely poor. They are non-Muslims, and they came to the Prophet (pbuh) from outside Madinah. They accepted Islam and were asking for Sadaqat they stayed with Ahl-e-Sofa. A place in the back of Masjid An-Nabawi, which was shaded from sun. It is where homeless and poor who had nowhere to stay, would stay in that space. Some people would bring food or invite them to eat. These men were feeling unhealthy. At the time, the climate of Madinah was unhealthy.

Hazrat Ayesha says, "when they first moved to Madinah, they suffered fever, the area of Bethan was stagnating with water, god knows whether it was Malaria or infection. The disease was endemic in Madinah.

We have talked previously about the lines of poetry from Abu Bakar and Bilal. When they came to Madinah, they were ill with strong fevers. These 8 men didn't like the climate of Madinah and told the Prophet (pbuh) that they are not urban people but we are shepherds and Madinah is unhealthy for us. The Prophet (pbuh) gave them permission to go out with the shepherd. The Prophet (pbuh) advised them to drink the milk and the urine of camels. They drank the milk and urine of the camels; they became healthy and their neutral color came back to them. Once they were healthy, they killed the shepherd of the Prophet (pbuh) and they stole the camels and became murtad, they gave up Islam, and fled. This was in return of the hospitality shown to them. The news came to the Prophet (pbuh). The sun had come out and they were caught and brought back. The Prophet (pbuh) prayed against them to blind them and to make their path narrow. They were lost and brought back.

In Another narration, when the news came to Prophet (pbuh), he was sitting with twenty young men from Ansar, these are the ones the Prophet (pbuh) dispatched to bring back these thieves. It is in Bukhari Sharif that the Prophet (pbuh) ordered that their eyes be branded by hot nails and their arms and legs were cut off. Then, they were left in an area which was next to Madinah's volcanic tracks, they died.

THE SEVENTH YEAR OF HIJRA

The Prophet (pbuh) came back from Al-Hudaybiyyah. Musa bin Uqba, is an author of the Seerah. Scholars say that his narrations are among the best. Musa bin Uqba says, "after twenty days of the Prophet's arrival to Madinah from Hudaybiyyah, he set out to Khaybar, Hudaybiyyah was a truce between Quraish and the Prophet (pbuh). The agreement was to stop fighting for ten years.

The problem was that some Jews were conspiring against Muslims. The Prophet (pbuh) wanted to stop those Jews from conspiring against Muslims. Khaybar was a very strong area for Jews. On the way, Amr bin Aqwa was asked to read poetry like the non-Muslim ways. This had an effect on the camels. The camels would become active, stronger and faster. About the Prophet (pbuh), Amr said, "without you, we could not have been guided rightly. Nor we would have given up our arms nor prayed to Allah. You forgive us for anything wrong, may we be sacrificed for you."

When the Prophet (pbuh) heard these beautiful words from Amr bin Aqwa, he said, "may Allah have mercy on him."

The Sahaba had the understanding that when the Prophet (pbuh) prays like that for one he would die as Shaheed (martyr). Umar bin Khattab said, "it has become inevitable, I wish you had allowed us to enjoy his company more."

The Muslims reached Khaybar and surprised the Jews, they had gone out on farms with equipment ready for work. They saw the Muslim army. They came back alerting everyone that Muhammed (pbuh) is here with his army. These Jews used to brag about, that fighting us is not like the rest of the Arabs. But when they saw the army of Muhammed (pbuh) they fled and ran away, that is because Allah puts fear in the hearts of enemy, the news about the siege spread and the Arabs knew the strength of Jews in that area one of the envoys from Makkah at Hudaybiyyah. When he went back, he said, "he knew that Muhammed (pbuh) and his army will be victorious." Urwah bin Masood took the impression when he met Prophet (pbuh) at Hudaybiyyah. Some people of Quraish had a different opinion and had a bet with Urwah bin Masood they were saying that Jews will win because of their reputation. The bet was one hundred camels. During the attack, one fighter of Jews, Marhab. He came out asking for a dual, Amr bin Aqwa he came out to meet him they exchanged few blows with their swords then Marhab struck with his sword, the sword got stuck in the shield then Amr had the opportunity to strike. He did strike but his sword was short and came back and injured his leg above the knee and Amr bled to death. Now some people were saying that Amer lost his good deeds because he committed suicide. Muslima was the nephew of Amr. He was terribly upset and was depressed about what people were saying about his uncle. The Prophet (pbuh) saw him and asked what is the matter? He said, he was sad because people say that his uncle lost all his good deeds. The Prophet (pbuh) said, "who ever said that he lied". He will receive a double reward and raised two of his fingers to signify the reward. He was a mujahid who did his best and few Arabs mocked him. The earlier prayer of the holy Prophet (pbuh) had been successful. There was one particular fortress, which was giving Muslims hard time. The Prophet (pbuh) would appoint people to open it and one after another they all failed. Then one evening the Prophet (pbuh) said, I shall give the banner to a man tomorrow who loves Allah and his messenger and Allah and his messenger love him. Allah will open this fortress for him. Next day in the morning all the Sahaba went in front of the holy Prophet (pbuh) because everybody wanted that honor for himself. It is in Bukhari Sharif.

Please listen to what Umar bin Khattab said. He said, "I never loved position of authority except on that day, Muslim Sharif, everyone wants and loves the position of authority. In Islam that is discouraged." Hazrat Abbas is the uncle of the prophet (pbuh) asked to be appointed in authority. The Prophet (pbuh) said, "we do not give this authority to someone who asks for it or who is eager to have it."

This is the way of the Prophet (pbuh) and this is the way of Islam. It reached to the level that Umar bin Khattab did not even desire it. Except that day because of the honor that Prophet (pbuh) said he loves Allah and his messenger and Allah and his messenger love him. Hadith in Tirmizi: If two hungry wolves go to a sheep, they will not corrupt the sheep more than the eagerness a person as for wealth and position of authority for his religion. The meaning if a person is eager to have wealth and power. These two things are dangerous like sending two hungry wolves on a sheep. They will ruin it. You will regret the love of authority on the Day of Judgment.

The Prophet (pbuh) said, "Where is Ali?" The Sahaba said, he has a disease in his eyes. The prophet said bring him. Ali came but his eyes were closed, they had to hold him by hand and brought him to the Prophet (pbuh). The Prophet (pbuh) put some of his saliva in his eyes and they were immediately cured. This is one of the many miracles of the Prophet (pbuh). The banner was handed over to Hazrat Ali (Abpwh), Ali asked a question to the Prophet (pbuh), "should I fight them until they become like us?"

This is interesting, Ali did not say until they become Muslim but like us, meaning Islam and the Sahaba were the same. The Prophet (pbuh) told him, this is in Bukhari Sharif, "go to them, in front of them and then invite them to Islam and inform them about their duties towards Allah." Then Prophet (pbuh) said, "in the name of Allah, if Allah guides even one of them through you, it is better for you than great Ghanima (spoils of war), the purpose of Jihad Fi-Sabillilah (war for the sake of Allah) is to spread the truth. Invite others to the truth, save them from Jahannam (hell fire) through faith in Islam. Everybody should have heard; people will be dragged in chains into Jannah (heaven). Now this is it. People who fight against Islam and if they lose and are forced to accept Islam, they are being dragged into Jannah (heaven). Ali (Abpwh) posted the banner in a pile of rocks under the fortress. Jews looked at Ali bin Abu Talib from the top of the fortress and said who are you? Ali replied proudly, "I am Ali (Ali means 'to ascend' in Arabic), the son of Abu Talib." The Jews knew that and said, 'you will ascend.' By the time he returned Ali bin Abu Talib had opened the fortress. Some examples from the battle of Khaybar.

One of the Sahaba, a very good fighter for Muslims was doing a good job. The Prophet (pbuh) said, "he is the friend of fire," the Sahaba were surprised. Because he was a good mujahid and the Prophet (pbuh) said he is in hell fire. He was a strong fighter. One man was following him to see where he goes. And then the man was injured. It was painful. He didn't have patient. So, he took an arrow from his Quiver, and slit his throat. The Sahaba went to the Prophet (pbuh) and what was said happened to be true. The Prophet (pbuh) told him to go and announce that only a believer will enter Jannah but Allah can give victory to his religion through a corrupt person.

Another example, there was a worst non-Muslim. He became Muslim, then he went out with the Prophet (pbuh) in the battle of Khaybar. The Muslims won. There was a great booty, which was divided among the Sahaba and after a long time they had something to live off from. The Prophet (pbuh) told that give the share of the non-Muslims to him. He said, "what is this?" He was told that this is your share of the booty. He went to the Prophet asked what is this, he was told your share. He said this in not the reason that I became Muslim and followed you. He said I came in to be hit in the neck and will be killed and then I shall enter paradise, look at his fittara (purity).

The Prophet (pbuh) was a shepherd and also a businessman before Prophethood but after the Prophethood, his Rizq (provisions) came from booties of war. He gave full time to Dawah. He survived through his share in Ghanima (it is halal). Hadith: 'I was sent with the sword before the hour and my sustenance comes from under the shade of my spear. That is the best of Rizq. The Prophet (pbuh) said, "if you are true with Allah, he will fulfill your desires. Allah will be true with you."

In another battle he was hit exactly in the place where he pointed with his finger. He was brought to the Prophet. Prophet (pbuh) said is that him? He was replied, "yes".

The Prophet (pbuh) put his own garment over him to be put with him in his grave, and Prophet (pbuh) made a Dua (prayer) for him, this was a long dua. 'O' Allah, this is your servant he came forth. He was a mujahid struggling in your path and he was killed as a Shaheed (martyr) and I am a witness of that." Allahu Akbar (God is great).

ABU YASIR

Abu Yasir was a companion of the Prophet (pbuh). He said, "one day I was with the Prophet (pbuh) in Khaybar. We saw a sheep belonging to Jews, the sheep were going into their fortress and we were besieging that fortress. The Muslims were hungry, the Prophet (pbuh) said, "who will feed us from this sheep, Abu Yasir said, "I will O' Messenger of Allah."

The Prophet (pbuh) said, "go ahead, run like an Ostrich." Abu Yasir narrates this story. 'When the Prophet (pbuh) saw me running, the Prophet (pbuh) said, "O' Allah let us enjoy his company." I reached the sheep when the first one had entered the fortress; I was able to catch the last of them. I carried two under my arms and came back running as I was carrying nothing until I reached and dropped them under the feet of the Prophet (pbuh). Abu Yasir was the last of the Sahaba to die, why? Because of the Dua of the Prophet (pbuh). When they opened the fortress in Khaybar they found dried fat of animals, they would cut it in to pieces and dry it in the sun for future use. There was a sack full of it. Abdullah bin Mukhful grabbed it put it on his shoulder and started walking with it. Other Sahaba said, bring it here so it can be divided. Abdullah bin Mukhful refused and they were pulling the sack from both ends. The Prophet (pbuh) saw this and smiled, then the Prophet (pbuh) told to those Sahaba, "leave it and let him take it."

Abdullah bin Mukhful was embarrassed but took it away to his companions and they ate it all. Scholars say, "you are allowed to eat then and there. But the punishment for taking from Ghanima is very severe. Then, she says she came to the Prophet (pbuh) with some women from Ghaffar. Ghaffar were non-Muslims, they were close to Madinah and they were famous for stealing from pilgrims. That was their reputation before Islam. They would attack pilgrims and rob them. Many of them became Muslims. Abu Zar Al-Ghaffari guided them and they became Muslims, Allah guides whoever he wants. This woman came to the Prophet (pbuh), and said we want to go with you to attend wounded and assist in other work.

The Prophet (pbuh) told them to go with the blessings of Allah. The women came with the army and this girl was riding with Prophet (pbuh). She was sitting behind the Prophet (pbuh) on the luggage. They arrived, the camel sat down, she came down but there was some blood on the luggage. She sat next to camel and was very embarrassed. The Prophet (pbuh) told her to take water and salt and clean the blood. She did that and participated in the battle. When the booty was divided, Ulma says children and women are not given the share. But Umar can give them as he sees fit. The Prophet (pbuh) called that girl by name.

She said, "the Prophet (pbuh) had a necklace with him and gave me the necklace. The Prophet (pbuh) said, 'it is yours,' and the Prophet with his own hands put it around my. " She says after that she would clean herself with water and salt. And left in her will, that she be washed with water and salt. She said, "in the name of Allah, I shall never part with this necklace." When she died the necklace was still on her neck.

THE STORY OF TWO JEWISH WOMEN

There was a Jewish woman, her name was Zainab bin Thara. After the battle of Khaybar and the defeat of Jews, she held an invitation, she hosted the Prophet (pbuh) and some of the Sahaba. She roasted a sheep, she filled it with poison. She asked which parts of meat the Prophet (pbuh) likes best she added the poison in those pieces of meat. The Prophet (pbuh) accepted the invitation and came with Sahaba. She offered the dinner and they started eating. The Prophet (pbuh) was the first to take a bite from the meat. The Prophet (pbuh) had the meat in his mouth but hadn't swallowed it yet. Then the holy Prophet (pbuh) dropped it and said, "this bone is telling me that it is poisoned." He then called the woman and asked her if she had poisoned this meat. She said yes. The Prophet asked her, "why did you do so?" She said, "if you are a king you will be killed, and we shall be at rest because we have ridden ourselves from you. But if you are a Prophet, Allah will tell you and you will know about this. The prophet (pbuh) said, "Allah will not give you the ability to kill me."

The Prophet (pbuh) forgave her. His companions wanted to kill her, but the prophet (pbuh) said forbade them. But then Bshr bin Bra died because it was a powerful poison. In some narrations, the Prophet (pbuh) Bshr bin Bra killed. After three years, in the Prophet's final days, he had a fever. This hadith is in Bukhari Sharif. Ayesha said, "the Prophet (pbuh) would say in his final days that, O' Ayesha, I still find the taste of the food I ate in Khaybar. This is the time my hoita will be cut because of the poison I had in Khyber.

Ibn Shaam says, "Muslims see that Prophet (pbuh) died as a Shaheed (martyr) as well as a Prophet." But some scholars say that it is contradicting that Allah said he will protect the Prophet. But Allah promised him, Allah will protect him from fittana and defeat and Allah will protect him before he fulfills his mission.

When Allah revealed that Allah has completed your religion for you. Now it was time for the holy Prophet (pbuh) to leave this world and meet his lord. When the Prophet died, it was because of this poison even three years later. But the Prophet (pbuh) told the woman that she will not have the ability to overpower me. But the pain and effect of the poison came three years later. But his was the appointed time for Prophet (pbuh) to pass away. The next woman was Safiya bint Hay. She was also a Jewish woman. She recalled an incident when she was an incredibly young girl, when Muhammed (pbuh) made Hijra from Makkah to Madinah and he was welcomed by Ansar. Whenever her father and uncle see her, they used to express joy. One day she went and both of them were sitting under a tree, they didn't welcome her as they usually do, then she says, she heard her uncle asking her father is that him? Her father said yes. He asked are you sure, that is him. Her father said yes. The Uncle asked what was he going to do?

Or what do you think of him? The father said, "I shall be his enemy as long as I live."

He lived up to it. He was the enemy of the Prophet (pbuh) until he was killed that happened at the time of Hijra, three years later. Muslims laid a siege at Banu Nadir. And Hay was their leader, they were evicted, and they moved to Khaybar. At that time, Sofia was a young girl. Five years after Hijra, Hay bin Akhta who convinced the third and last tribe Banu Kriza to betray the Prophet (pbuh) and break the agreement they had. The Prophet (pbuh) had an agreement with Jews from the time when he entered into Madinah. He is the one who incited them to commit treason and we know the story; they were defeated and were executed including Hay bin Akhta

Safiya grew up in Khaybar and married one of her cousins, Kenana bin Al-Rabi. At that moment in time, the Muslims had recently defeated the people of Khaybar. The agreement was that all of their Properties will be confiscated by Muslims and they were to leave Khaybar, gold, silver, women, children and houses, all of this were transferred into the hands of the Muslims. But then, the Jews pleaded the Prophet (pbuh) to allow them to remain in Khyber and serve as workers, farming, and cultivating the land.

The narrator of the story says that the Sahaba did not have time to take care of land themselves. As a result, if the Jews leave Khaybar, there is no one to work on the lands and the land will stop producing crops. Because the Sahaba were busy with knowledge, call to Islam and Jihad, the Prophet (pbuh) agreed.

The terms of the agreement were that they will remain in Khaybar and the harvest will be split in half. Jews were not to conceal anything from him (the Prophet). All the currency in their possession had to be handed over to Muslims, and they agreed. The Prophet (pbuh) told them, if you conceal anything that will be punished as seen fit. And we shall be free from any obligation. They agreed. When they handed over their property to the Prophet (pbuh), some was missing. The Prophet (pbuh) had some inside information about a treasure which was taken by Hay bin Akhta from Banu Nadir to Khaybar. The Prophet (pbuh) asked where is the treasure of Hay bin Akhta? Kenana said, "it was spent on war and provision."

The Prophet (pbuh) said, "that was a large amount of money and couldn't have been spent and this happened recently." Kenana insisted that there is nothing left. There was an old Jew, he said he had seen Hay bin Akhta roaming around this particular area, where no one lives. When the Sahaba dug that area, they found part of the treasure. The Prophet (pbuh) asked Kenana where the rest of it is, but Kenana refused to admit. The Prophet (pbuh) handed him over to Zubair bin Al-Awam. The Prophet (pbuh) told him to rough him up until you take what is left. Zubair was able to extract the information where the rest of the treasure was. The Prophet (pbuh) ordered that Kenana was to be executed. The husband of Safiya, Kenana bin Al-Rabi was executed. Safiya was among the captives Dahiya Al-Kalbi. One of the Sahaba came to the Prophet (pbuh) asking for a slave. The Prophet (pbuh) handed Safiya over to him. That was the rule at that time. When Muslims came on the international scene that is how things were, women and children, if they fall after war they were automatically enslaved. The Prophet (pbuh) told him to go and choose a woman and he took Safiya. She was described as a very beautiful woman. One of the Sahaba came and told Prophet (pbuh) that Dahiya Al-Kalbi has taken Safiya, the daughter of a noble man of Jews and she is only fitting to be yours, O' messenger of Allah. The Prophet (pbuh) called Dahiya and told him to hand over Safiya and go and take someone else. Dahiya did so. When the Prophet (pbuh) saw Safiya, he offered her freedom as a dowry and would marry her. The Prophet (pbuh) did not take her as a slave. He freed her and married her. She is counted as a wife of the Prophet (pbuh) and not a woman in bondage.

Prophet (pbuh) saw some blue marks on her face. He asked her what these marks are? She said, "one day I was sleeping, my head was in the lap of my husband and I saw a dream. I saw the moon falling in my lap. When I woke up, I told my husband the dream and my husband slapped me in the face and said you desire the king of the Arabs." So, Kenana interpreted this dream to mean that she is desiring to marry Muhammed (pbuh), but that was not a desire that she had. But this dream was a vision from Allah telling her what will happen in the future and it happened. She married Muhammed (pbuh), those blue marks on her face were the traces of the slap from her husband Kenana.

Anas bin Malik narrates this part of the story. Safiya that gives us glimpse of the private life of the Prophet (pbuh).

The camel is a large animal when one is sitting on camel it is high. It is higher than riding on a horse. When people ride on a camel, even when the camel is sitting it is high. Anas bin Malik says, "I saw the Prophet (pbuh) sit down on the ground, a foot on the ground and then raised up his knee and told Safiya to step with her foot on his knee in order to climb on the camel."

One can imagine, the humbleness and kindness. He is being described as the king of the Arabs. The Prophet (pbuh) refused to be a king. He chooses to only be a prophet. The Prophets were the greatest men who ever set foot on this earth. Sits down on the ground and has his wife step over him in order to climb on to the camel. Sofia's father and her husband and her uncle were all killed. The Prophet (pbuh) wanted to soften her heart. they were all killed by Prophet (pbuh). She also saw complete annihilation and eviction of her people. All these events in front of her eyes. She must have had some hard feelings. She says that the Prophet (pbuh) was the most despised person to her. "He killed my father, my husband and my uncle. He apologized and said, your father is the one who mobilized Jewish people against me."

This is how the pain from her heart was taken away and her heart was won. She was mu'mina. May Allah be pleased with her. The end of the story of Safiya.

There was a servant of the Prophet (pbuh). He was struck by an arrow, and he died. The Sahaba congratulated him for dying as a martyr. But the Prophet (pbuh) said, "no, by the name of the one in whose hand my soul is, the cloak (cloth) he has taken on the day of Khaybar from Ghanima, is burning on him. He is in flames."

This is in Bukhari Sharif, a single piece of cloth. He was a Muslim, mujahid and a momin. He also died, Fi-Sabeel Allah but the Prophet (pbuh) refused to pray Janazah (funeral prayer) for him. The Prophet (pbuh) said, "he is not a Shaheed (Martyr) because of that cloth." This is how dangerous it is to take anything from the ghanima.

Also, in the battle of Khaybar when the Muslims were laying siege to the fortress. They were very hungry. They slaughtered donkeys and were cooking them. The Prophet (pbuh) asked them what they are boiling in the pots. They said we slaughtered some donkeys. The Prophet (pbuh) said, "throw it all away, that is when donkeys became haram to eat. Arabs used to eat donkey meat but Islam made it Haram.

The Jews remained in Khaybar, serving in the land and Muslims would send someone to collect their half of the harvest. Abdullah bin Rawaha went to collect, but the Jews tried to bribe him. He was angry and told them that he would not betray the Prophet (pbuh) no matter what the offer is.

The Jews remained in Khaybar until the time of Umar bin Khattab when he became Khalifa. Maqdad, Zubair, and Ibn Umar went to Khaybar to collect their share. The Jews attacked Abdullah bin Umar at night. He was sleeping on a roof they pushed him. He fell and dislocated his hands Umar bin Khattab said to the Muslims, "O' People, the messenger of Allah had an agreement with the Jews that we shall evict them if we wished, they have attacked Abdullah bin Umar and dislocated his hands as you have learnt. They also attacked one Ansar before him. We have no doubt that they have done it. We have no enemies here except them. Those who have property in Khaybar should proceed, I am going to evict them.

They were forced to leave, and they went to Sham (now called Syria). Umar bin Khattab did this because of a Hadith, that no two religions should live in Arabia, therefore the Jews and the Christians were forced to leave. Although Umar bin Khattab did not hear this directly but investigated and found it authenticated and true. He acted upon it and told the Jews of Khaybar to leave. Three hundred years later, the descendants of those Jews wrote a document. It stated that this is an agreement between the Jews and the Prophet (pbuh) and that they are free from tax. Ibn Kathir says this document has fooled some of the scholars and they left it. But Ibn Kathir had investigated and found that this is fabricated there is no such document this is three hundred years later. Seven hundred years after Hijra, they came up with same document perhaps with some alterations. Again, it was proven to be a lie while the Prophet was in Khaybar he received four delegations.

First, delegation, Lashari, people from Yemen, from the coast on the red sea, Abu Musa Ashaari, this is a Hadith in

Bukhari Sharif: we heard the news of the Prophet (pbuh) in Yemen, we went out to him, my brother and I (Abu Musa Ashaari) were the youngest along with fifty-two or fifty-three other people. They took a boat, but boat went off course, it ended up not in Medina but in Abyssinia the land of Najashi. They found Jaffar bin Abu Talib. He told us that he has in instructions to remain there, we stayed there and came with Jaafar, when the Prophet (pbuh) had opened Khaybar. Next delegation Jaffar bin Abu Talib from Hubisha. Prophet (pbuh) embraced and kissed Jaafar on the forehead. Evidence of hugging and kissing. The Prophet (pbuh) said, I don't know, which has brought more happiness, opening of Khyber or Jaffar from Habisha.

Hadith: Hijaj owed some money in Makkah, and he told a lie that Jews have won. This wrong news was spreading this is what Al-Abbas hear. But the secret meeting told good news, Al-Abbas after three days told the truth. Jews were defeated, but Hijaj told a fib.

Suryia of Abu Bakr Siddique. They went too Bini Kasara, after Khyber, this is in Muslim Sharif: Salma is the narrator. He says I saw them running away from us, women, men and children or only men. They were running towards a mountain. I was following them. I was worried that they will reach the mountain before me. I took an arrow and stuck it between them and the mountain. Abu Salma did not want to kill them. He wanted to take as captive. Arrow between the mountain and them to let them know that they are within the range that was a warning to stop. When they saw this arrow, they stopped Abu Salma brought all of them back to Abu Bakr. There was a Badoo woman wearing worn out leather clothes she had girl with her she was a beautiful girl. Abu Bakr gave me that girl. When we came back to Medina. I met Prophet (pbuh) in the marketplace. Prophet (pbuh) said, O'

Salma, hand over the girl to me. I told the Prophet (pbuh) that I like her. Prophet (pbuh) left them, next day they met again in the marketplace. Prophet (pbuh) told Muslma again that hand over the girl to me. Salma said O' messenger of Allah I like her, but I shall give her to you. Prophet (pbuh) sent her to Makkah in exchange for some Muslim prisoners.

Next Suryia Abdullah bin Roha, went to Yasir and told him that Prophet (pbuh) wants to appoint you as governor of Khyber. At first, he resisted but Abdullah bin Roha convinced him. He came along with thirty (30) Jewish men. On the way back Yasir regretted the agreement and tried to pull the sword of Abdullah bin Anees and was able to get away from Yasir. Muslims saw that and turned around thirty (30) Muslim men against 30 Jewish men. Every Muslim had a Jewish companion riding on the same camel. All of Jews were killed except one who managed to get away the leader Yasir was also killed.

The story of Muallim bin Jasama. He was a Muslim, they were traveling. A man by the name of Amr, passed by them and said, Asslam Alaikum. The Muslim greeting Mualam bin Jasama. Rushed out and killed this man; because he knew him from Jahiliya and there was problem between them. He sought revenge even the man said Asslam Alaikum. The chief of the tribe of that murdered man came to Prophet (pbuh) for the blood of Amr. And the chief of Mualm also came to Prophet (pbuh) asking for leniency. Prophet (pbuh) wanted to prevent fittana between these two tribes. There were two options. (i) Asking for execution (ii) to accept blood money which is one hundred (100) camels. Prophet (pbuh) wanted to convince them to accept blood money in order to prevent fittana. The chief said, in the name of Allah, I am not going to rest until his women taste the sorrow as my women has tasted. He must be killed. Prophet (pbuh) said, take fifty (50) camels from me now and fifty (50) when we return to Medina. Initially they refused but Prophet. Kept on trying until they accepted the blood money. People of Mualam told him to go to Prophet (pbuh) and ask for forgiveness. Mualam came dressed in garments for execution. He came to Prophet (pbuh) this was a tall and heavy man. He came and said I am Mualam, ask Allah to forgive me, Prophet (pbuh) prayed O' Allah do not forget Mualam. He asked second time and covered his face to hide his tears, this is to show the sanctity of Muslims.

Allah revealed the Ayat. O' you who have believed when you go forth to fight in the cause of Allah investigate and do not say, that you are not a Muslim for worldly goods when he says Salaam. There were times when you were disbelievers, then Allah conferred his favors on you, so investigate indeed, Allah is acquainted with what you do. Mualam, who killed Amr, had taken his camels after killing him. One year has passed since the signing of the agreement Sulah- Hadibya. And Prophet (pbuh) wants to go for Umrah. Muslims who were with him at Sulah Hadibya, join him now for Umrah. The Prophet (pbuh) had an agreement that they will only have traveler's arms swords in the sheeds. But Prophet (pbuh) and his people brought with them other weapons. Bows, arrows and spears. And when they reached close to Makkah. News was carried that Prophet (pbuh) has other weapons. So, he must be preparing for war. Quraish said, we have not broken the terms of the agreement why Muhammed (pbuh) is attacking us? Some came to the Prophet (pbuh) and asked O' Muhammed (pbuh) you are not known even when you were young and old, to betray. You want to enter into Harem, with weapons Prophet (pbuh) said I shall not enter with these weapons. This is what you are known for faith. Keeping your word. This is a witness of Quraish that he is a man of truth.

They entered into Makkah, Quraish had jealousy, hatred and amnesty, and they couldn't even stand being around Muslims. They evacuated Makkah for three days to allow Muslims in there. They went on top of the mountains surrounding Makkah. They were looking at Muslims. They used to say that Muslims will be weak, because of fever in Median. Prophet (pbuh) wanted to give an image of strength. He told the Muslims to uncover their right shoulder and do Rummy around.

Kaaba it's like marching, walking fast with strength. Muslims would do that. But in between corner Ruken-e-Yemeni and Black stone and they would walk because Kufuor could not see them from that side. Now when Muslims go for Umrah, they would do that Sunna. But the area which was covered by Kaaba from Kufuor. They would walk normally for first three rounds. Prophet (pbuh) did not want to exhaust the Muslims but at the same time he didn't want that kufr would take the impression that Muslims are weak. Therefore, Rummy on three sides of Kaaba and on fourth side they would walk. If it wasn't for exhaustion the Prophet (pbuh) would have liked it for seven rounds. Even it was done for that objective, but we still do it as a Sunna until today.

The Prophet(pbuh)sent one Sahaba(as messenger), He wanted to get married to May-Mona bin tharaf, she agreed and she said, my Wali responsible to sign the contract would be Al-Abbas. Al-Abbas was married to her sister Am maul -Fazal, and Prophet (pbuh)wanted to hold the walima in Makkah. But three days were over. Quraish came and said in the name of Allah and as per agreement, we ask you to leave. Prophet (pbuh) told them, I married a woman among you and it will not harm you if I finish my wedding. We will prepare a feast and you are welcome to join us. They said we ask you in the name of Allah to leave. When the Quraish came

Prophet (pbuh) was sitting with some of the An-sar people. Quraish said we want you to leave from our land Saad bin Abada, Responded and said, this is not your land or the land of your fathers. Prophet (pbuh) calmed him down and said we would leave and they left and celebrated whatever ceremony was left of the wedding outside Makkah in place called Sarah. May- Mona died in the same place where she married to the Prophet (pbuh), when Prophet (pbuh) was leaving Makkah, daughter of Hamza. Young girl she came running saying, O' uncle O' uncle, Hazrat Ali grabbed her and handed her over to Hazrat Fatima and said take care of your cousin. Take her back to Medina. Jafar said, no, I am going to take her, Ali ibn Abu Talib said, I am her cousin. Jafar said I am her cousin too. Then Zahid came in and said she is the daughter of my brother. Because of this conflict, Prophet (pbuh) came in as well to judge, who will take care of the daughter of Hamza. Prophet (pbuh), he handed her over to Jafar because Jafar was married to her Aunt. Zahid was the adopted son of Prophet (pbuh). Hamza is the uncle of Prophet, but also the brother of Prophet (pbuh) because of breast feeding. The same woman breastfed both Muhammed (pbuh) and Hamza. That makes the daughter of Hamza, the cousin of Zahid. Then Prophet (pbuh) told Hazrat Ali, you are from me and I am from you. And told Jafar bin Abu Talib. You are similar to me in manners and in looks and told Zahid bin Harsa, you are our brother and our companion. Then Hazrat Ali asked Prophet (pbuh) wouldn't you marry Hamza's daughter. Prophet (pbuh) said she is the daughter of my brother from breast feeding. That makes Prophet (pbuh) Mehrm for her and cannot marry. This is the end of seventh (7th) year of Hijra.

NOW WE MOVE ON TO (8th) year of Hijra. In this people who became Muslim included Khalid bin Waleed, Amr bin Auss, Usman. Also battle of Motha. This was the first proper battle between Muslims and Roman Empire, and Fatah Makkah and great battle of Honaine and siege of Taif. It is a remarkably busy year.We start with the story of accepting Islam of Khalid bin Waleed and Amr bin Auss. Amer says I fought against the Prophet Muhammed (pbuh) in battle of BADR and Allah saved me. And then I fought against the Prophet in battle of Aud and Allah saved me. And then I fought in the battle of the trench and Allah saved me. Amr bin Auss is saying this, after he became Muslim. And he is looking back to his memories. He is thinking and says I was fighting the messenger of Allah, what in the world was I doing? At that time as non-believer, he was thinking differently but now looking back, he says hang on wait a minute, I was fighting the messenger of Allah. These are the Sahaba who loved Prophet more than anything in the world. After every battle he says Allah saved me meaning, if I had died then I would have been in hell fire. So, he is going through his life history. He said, I fought in BADR, Aud and in Khandaq (the battle of Trench), and I was beginning to feel, no matter what Muhammed (pbuh) will win. His army is getting better and better, his invitation (Dawah) spreading more and more. We Quraish are being restricted and narrow in our movement day after day. Amr bin Auss was beginning to feel this conflict and depression that a kefir would have when he feels the victory of Islam. Built up hatred, jealousy, suborned the hearts of the kufr. But Satin is always dominating the heart of disbelievers. All these feelings are bottled up in the heart of Amr bin Aase. He had enough. He decided to leave Makkah and go and stay in a place called Al-Wahid. He took his family and wealth and went there. He says I stayed away from people and then when the agreement of Hydbia, came in to force, when Quraish were forced to admit that Islamic estate exists, they were forced to admit the authority of the Prophet (pbuh).

When people, Sahaba started to complain about And. Prophet (pbuh) reminded them, that now Quraish have accepted your terms, that was a great development, also we have said Hydbia, a great victory for Islam. At the time of Hydbia Amr bin Auss said tomorrow Muhammed (pbuh) will enter into Makkah. It is inevitable Muhammed (pbuh) will come in, the circumstance were such that Quraish were unable to fight with the Prophet(pbuh) when he was at the doorsteps of Makkah and they accepted to sign(signature) a treaty with him. This was a sign, the fact that sooner or later Muhammed (pbuh) will enter into Makkah. So, he ruled out staying in Makkah or in Taif these were the two major cities of Hajaz. He called some of the members of his clan. Amr bin Auss was a man who was respected among his people. They used to listen to him and accepted his advice and guidance. He called those people who trusted him. He told them I can see the affair of Muhammed (pbuh) is rising above all others in a horrible way. He is seeing the events unfolded in front of his eyes through his wisdom and intelligence he can read, through these events in history and see that Muhammed (pbuh)and Islam slowly but surely rising and rising against everything else. He is a disbeliever but can sense and feel that Amr bin Auss told his people therefore it is not a good idea to stay in Makkah, but we should go and stay with Najashi in Abyssinia (Habisha), Amr bin Auss had good relationship with Najashi. If Muhammed (pbuh) is victorious then we are away from him and if he loses and Quraish win then Quraish already know who we are and what our position is. Amr bin Auss said about himself that even though all Quraish become Muslim, I shall never become Muslim. That is the kind of hatred he had in his heart towards Islam. Even every single one becomes Muslim I shall not. His clan agreed with his assessment and opinion and they decided to leave Makkah

and travel together to Abyssinia. The driving force behind
Hijra is the hatred against Islam. He took some gifts for the
King Najashi, Najashi loved leather goods. He himself and
his people gathered best leather goods to present as gifts for
government officials and Najashi himself, with all that they
went to Najashi in Abyssinia, they went to visit Najashi. And
found coming out of kings court another Amr bin Omiya
Bembry (Quraish). Who came to Najashi with a message from
Prophet (pbuh) to perform the marriage of Prophet (pbuh) to
Umma Habiba the daughter of Abu Sufyan, and also to call
the Mahajreen Muslims to go to Medina? Amr bin Auss saw
him coming out of the court of Najashi. Amr bin Auss entered
alone. Rest of the companions had to wait outside. He went
and made Sajood to the king Nagas as was the tradition. He
was very well received by the king Nagas. Najashi said well
come my friend. Have you brought me any gifts from your
land?

Amr bin Auss said, yes. O' king I have brought you some
Hyde. Then he presented the king the pieces of Hyde he had
brought. The king was incredibly happy and pleased with it.
He distributed some of the gifts to his officials and friends.
The rest he ordered to be registered and recorded deposited
and kept in a safer place. Amr bin Auss was carried away
with the reception. He told the king, O' king I have seen a
man coming out of your palace, who is the messenger of our
enemy, who has killed the nobles among us would you hand
him over to me. King Nagas immediately hit Amr bin Auss in
the face. Amr bin Auss thought that his nose was broken and
blood started flowing from his nose he covered his nose with
a cloth he wished that the earth would swallow him because
of the embarrassment and fear he felt from the king. Then
Amr bin Auss said if I knew you dislike what I had said, I
wouldn't have said it. Then the king Najashi said Ya Amr. You

are asking me to hand you over the messenger of the man who receives Angel Gabriel that you may kill him.

Amr bin Auss said, right then and there I had a change of heart and told myself, Arabs and non-Arabs recognize the truth and I do not, and that is when my heart changed. The way, Allah guided Amr bin Aus. He lived in Makkah for thirteen (13) years with Prophet (pbuh). And knew him. But he did not become Muslim but became Muslim in a foreign land in the court of Najashi. Najashi said I testify in front of Allah and then Najashi said, O' Amr listen to me and follow him, the prophet is with the truth In the name of Allah he will prevail over his enemies just like Moses prevailed over Pharoah and his soldiers. Najashi in faraway land this is his testimony about Prophet (pbuh). Najashi was man of truth. The man who understood religion the man who understood history. He was a man who understood the lives of the Prophet and he is giving Dawah (invitation) to Amr bin Auss. Amr bin Auss who knows about Prophet (pbuh), knows about Islam, and knows about Muslims. Receiving Dawah from Najashi. The way Dawah works, it defies all logics. Therefore, we should not have any fixed believes. We know from the Dawah of Prophet (Pbuh). Abu Talib does not become Muslim but we have Abu-Zr-Ghaffari becoming Muslim. Abu Lahab the uncle of the Prophet (pbuh) does not become Muslim but Suliman Pharsi becomes Muslim guidance comes from Allah. Do not guide to the ones you want; this is Allah who guides whom he will. Amr bin Auss said, I gave him my biya, baiet, pledge at the hand of Najashi, who took the pledge that I obey Prophet (pbuh).

Amr bin Auss came with the intention an objective but now coming back totally different human being. Nobody knows about the soldiers of Allah, but he Najashi is a soldier of Allah and through him this great man. If you read the history of Amr bin Auss you will know what he did for Islam. One of the greatest Muslims. His acceptance of Islam came through Najashi. He was such a great enemy of Islam, now he becomes a Muslim. Then Najashi ordered some new clothes for Amr bin Aase because his clothes were soaked in blood. Then came out and when his companions saw him with new clothes they were incredibly happy, that things are working well. Before he went in he told them that he will ask Najashi to hand over to him the messenger from Medina. Amr bin Omiya, Bambry so that I could kill him. Because that will gain good reputation with Quraish.

Now they asked him what he did. He said, it was not good to propose to the king at first meeting but I shall do that at next meeting. They said, that is a good idea. Amr made an excuse to go for a business but did not tell them his plans. Amr bin Aase left and took a boat and went towards Medina. He simply left without a word. He came with some people to get away from Muhammed (pbuh) but now he leaves them and goes to Muhammed (pbuh). Amr bin Aase reaches a place called Shuba and then goes and reaches Marha da Drohan, when reaches at this place Marha Drohan. He was traveling towards Medina. He saw two men. One was in the camp and other was tieing the camels. Who were these two men? Khalid bin Waleed and Usman bin Tilla. He walked up to them and said what are you doing? Where are you going? Khalid bin Waleed said, there is no one worthy left and Muhammed (pbuh) is prevailing.

So, we want to go and become Muslims. Amr bin Auss said, I am here for the same reason. The striking thing is that these were the leaders, who were fighting Islam. Amr bin Auss and Khalid bin Waleed who belongs to the family of Banu Makhzum were enemies of Islam. Abu Jehail belongs to the same family and Usman bin Tilla, also very noble family in Quraish, this family carried the banner in war and also holds the keys of Kaaba until this day. The Prophet (pbuh) said the key should remain with you until the Day of Judgment. No one will take it from you but a transgressor. These three men belong to prominent families in Quraish, and they are especially important figures, they all meet, what a coincidence. But this is not a coincidence. It happens with the Qadr of Allah.

Now we are talking for 20 years fighting Islam. Now they meet going towards Medina. They will travel together and enter Medina together they reached out skirts of Medina. They hear someone saying. Yaruba, Yaruba, Yaruba that means Prophet. Amr bin Aase says we took it as a good Omen. And then someone saw us and spoke. Alqd. Makkah has handed the rains over, after these two men. He was referring to Khalid bin Waleed and Amr bin Aase, who is left in Makkah after these men. These men are second generation of leadership that was fighting Islam. The first generation. There were Abu Jahal, Abu Lahab, Omiya bin Khalaf, Abu Sufyan, Alwaleed bin Mughaira, Ottaba bin Rabia. These men were leading against Islam. Early days up to the battle of Badr on the day of Badr the forces of evil were crushed. The entire first generation of leaders were terminated. Abu Sufyan was the only one alive.

The reason he survived because he did not attend Badr. The whole reason the battle of Badr was fought because of his caravan. Quraish wanted to defend, Ottaba bin Rabia, Sheeba, Waleed, Abu Jahal, Omiya bin Khalf, they were all killed some others already died like Abu Lahab. He died in Makkah. The next generation who took over the leadership people like Khalid bin Waleed, Akrama bin Abu Jehail and Safwan bin Omiya. And Amr bin Auss they represented new blood, the new leadership in Makkah. For these men to

245

become Muslim was such a devastating blow to the people of Makkah who were against the Prophet (pbuh) of Allah that is why, it was said, that Makkah was handing over the reins of leadership to Prophet (pbuh). After these men accepted Islam.

They came to Medina Prophet (pbuh) was eagerly waiting for them, smiling all the time walking towards him. The beaming smile on the face of Prophet (pbuh). He was so happy for their Islam. That was true Dawah, the Prophet (pbuh) did not have anything against them. Even though they had spoken against him, they had harmed him. They had driven him out of his land.

Prophet (pbuh) was looking at the interest of Islam, also happy because these men were becoming soldiers of Allah. Amr bin Aase said O' messenger of Allah I pledge my allegiance to you with the condition, that Allah forgives me all my past sins against Islam. He later on says, I forgot to ask him to forgive my future sins. The Prophet (pbuh) told Amr bin Aase O' Amr don't you know Islam wipes out anything before and Hijra raises everything before it and Hajj raises everything before it.

Amr bin Aase said, Prophet (pbuh) took good care of us. Prophet (pbuh) used to put us ahead of many companions. Abu Bakr also took great care for us, in the time of Umar bin Khattab. He took great care for me and would appoint me in especially important places. But was disapproving some of the actions of Khalid bin Waleed. This is the story narrated by Amr bin Aase. Next, we shall see the story by Khalid bin Waleed himself.

KHALID BIN WALEED, Khalid said, I have attended all of the battles against Muhammed (pbuh). Every battle I attended I left with the feelings in my heart that I am putting my efforts in something which is wasted and in the end Muhammed (pbuh) will prevail. He had this deep feeling in his heart, what he is doing is wrong.

Then Hadibya came I led a contingent of kufr two hundred (200) men and at one time, I came face to face with Muhammed(pbuh). The Prophet (pbuh) was praying salah. That was my opportunity to attack them in salah. But I was reluctant to do so. This coming from Khalid bin Waleed is strange because he was not a reluctant person. He was a very decisive man. So for Khalid to say, he was reluctant to attack. Allah saved him. He was reluctant because Allah wanted something good for Khalid. He wanted to attack at salah -ul- ASR. He was waiting but Prophet (pbuh) was already praying salah- ul -khauf. Where 1/2 of army prays and other half protects. Khalid says I knew this man is being protected (protected by Allah).

Khalid says, when Prophet (pbuh) came the following year to do Umrah. His brother Alwaleed bin Waleed came looking for him. (He was a Muslim). Khalid bin Waleed was with kufr who vacated Makkah for Muslims. They did not want to see them. His brother came looking for him, when he could not find him he left a letter for him. What did the letter say? Bismillah, In the name of Allah who is most merciful and most compassionate, I know nothing more strangely than your empathy for Islam. Being as intelligent as you are, could disregard anything like Islam. Prophet (pbuh) has asked me about you, where is Khalid, I replied, Allah will bring him. The Prophet (pbuh) then asked could any one disregard Islam. If he would put his energy and bravery to work with Islam, it will be better for him. We shall give preference to him before others, take note brother, of what good things you are missing. Prophet (pbuh) is asking where Khalid is and then sending him a message through his brother. He is telling him it is not appropriate for someone like you as intelligent as you are to stay away from Islam, and if you become Muslim we shall put you ahead of many others. Respectable listeners. Ladies and gentlemen, this is true Dawah (invitation to Islam). The fact Prophet (pbuh) is asking about him, cares about him. Khalid says, the fact Prophet (pbuh) asked about me, made me think, influenced me and helped me to become Muslim. The fact Prophet (pbuh) asked for me and considered me intelligent.

It is a fact that Prophet (pbuh) had Khalid in mind and thought about him. To say about Khalid that he is intelligent how he doesn't understand Islam. Yet he was a kefir at that time. Also, to put him ahead of others. The status in Islam is how soon one accepted Islam. That was the status of the Sahaba. The earlier one becomes Muslim the higher he is held. That is just and fair because that shows the state of the heart. Because of the status of Khalid. Prophet (pbuh) had therefore he could put ahead. His intelligence, his abilities. This is important for a leader. Everybody has different qualities and abilities, people are different some are strong, and some are weak. People have different strengths; leadership is the ability to put the person in the suitable place.

Khalid bin Waleed decided to become Muslim. He had a dream. He saw himself in a very narrow and constricted place and He walked out from that place in a very vast and beautiful area. Later on, he asked for the interpretation of that dream. Abu Bakr told him that you are leaving Shirk and coming into Islam. He wanted to consult his close friends. He went to Safwan. Khalid told Safwan bin Omiya. I want to become Muslim would you like to join me? Safwan said, if nobody remains and only I am left I shall not become Muslim, Khalid said, this is a man whose father and brother were killed by the Muslims. Then he went to Akrama bin Abu Jehail. Told him our situation with Muslims is like a fox in a hole you drop a bucket of water over it and fox will come out running. He is explaining that Muslims are surrounding us and we are like a fox. All they have to do is dose us with water and we shall come out running. We have nothing left. What do you think of becoming Muslim? Akrama refused, Khalid told him do not tell anybody about it.

Then Khalid talked to Usman bin Tila but before talking to him he was double minded because Usman had lost his family in the battle of Audh. Family members of Usman were killed under the banner. But then he thought that talking to Usman would not make much difference as he was going to leave anyway. He went to Usman and gave him the idea of becoming Muslim. He found him very co-operative and was ready to go immediately. This shows that we should not pre-judge anybody. We do not know who will be guided and who would not be guided. Allah only knows. We should not lose hope and should not close the gates. Even though he had (Usman) lost seven (7) members of his family because they were the banner holders for Quraish in the battle of Aud. We have to do our part but Allah controls the heart of men. Khalid and Usman arranged a meeting place, they traveled and then they met Amr bin Aase we have already talked about that, when they reached out skirts of Medina. Khalid said, we will stop, change our clothes and put on our best clothes. That is how they wanted to meet Prophet (pbuh) they were dressed up. That was the greatest moment in their lives, they met Prophet. After the pledge Prophet (pbuh) called Khalid and said Alhamdullilah, (praise be to Allah), who guides people. The Prophet (pbuh). I used to think that you are intelligent and your intelligence will guide you towards Islam. Khalid bin Waleed said the Prophet (pbuh put me ahead many of the Sohabas. The Prophet (pbuh) took great care. And I can see the manifestation of that.

Mohammad L. Raja

Ghazva of Motta

The Prophet Muhammed (pbuh) appointed army of three thousand (3000) strong to attack the lands of Romans in Sham. This was the first encounter between the Muslims and Christians there was something unique in the appointment of Ameer, Officials. The leaders of this army, usually the Prophet (pbuh) would appoint one Ameer for the army and that is it. This time it was different, Prophet (pbuh) said the Ameer is Zahid bin Harsa. If he is killed then Jaffar bin Abu Talib and if he is killed then Abdullah bin Roha. God knows whether it was the risk or danger of this encounter that Prophet (pbuh) appointed two extra leaders or it could be that Prophet (pbuh) knew beforehand that they would be killed. We do not find in the history of Seerah that Prophet (pbuh) had appointed back up Ameer in any other situation. This is something unique what we refer to Ghazva at motha.

BATTLE OF MOTHA

There are two unique things in this battle. Where the army is not led by the Prophet (pbuh) it is not called Ghazva. But Ghazva Motha, usually a Ghazva is where the messenger of Allah participates and a Suryia in which Prophet (pbuh) does not participate. (1) Three Ameers were appointed that is unusual and (2) the Prophet (pbuh) was not participating it is called Ghazva Motha. That is how it is in the books of Seerah. So, when it is Ghazva, we know Prophet is there and when it is Suryia we know Prophet is not there, but with Motta it is called Ghazva. All the books Bukhari Sharif, Muslims, Wagdi. In all the books it is Ghazva. Some scholars say, because of its huge importance it was given this honorary title of Ghazva even though Prophet is not there, and this is the largest of all Suryia. Normal Suryia is smaller numbers some time only four or five (5) but here we have three thousand (3000) army. There is a Hadith in Tirmzi, but this is a weak hadith. There is a strong Hadith, Not the same words but talking about the same issue.

Hadith in Tirmzi says that Prophet (pbuh) sent out an army and among the members of this army was Abdullah bin Roha and this army was to leave on Friday and Ibne-Kathir mentions this Hadith as evidence that Muslims left Madinah for Ghazva Motha on Friday. Abdullah bin Roha thought about this that I am a single person. If I stay and pray

Jumma, with Prophet (pbuh). I shall be able to catch up with the army as I am just one person. Army as a whole is slow, and one person can catch up. The Prophet (pbuh) spotted him in salah and said how come you stayed behind, Abdullah bin Roha responded and said, O' messenger of Allah, I wanted to pray Jumma with you. Prophet (pbuh) told him, if you spend all the money on earth you would not catch up with them. These few hours, where Abdullah stayed behind between Fajr and Jumma. The Prophet (pbuh) is telling him if you spend all the money in the world, you will not catch up with them in terms of reward. We are not talking about him if he stays behind, all together but catches up with them, these hours he missed he will never be able to make up if he spends all the money in the world.

The stronger authentic hadith, which I was talking about is, that the Prophet (pbuh) said, leaving early with army or coming back with them is better than the earth and everything in it. Now, let us think over it for a while Abdullah bin Roha, did not stay behind for fear. He had the right intentions, he wanted to seek knowledge, and he wanted to seek knowledge from the Prophet (pbuh) himself not from a sheikh. He wanted to stay behind to seek reward for Jumma. Nevertheless, Prophet (pbuh) is telling him what you did is wrong. Those few hours you missed; nothing can make up for them. Prophet (pbuh) was teaching the Sahaba that you are not excused for staying behind. We know fighting Fi-Sabil Allah can be by yourself, it can be with the wealth, can be with your tongue. However, fighting with non-believers only with tongue is not enough. Otherwise, it would have been sufficient among the great scholars. Sahaba to sit behind in Medina and not go out with the Prophet (pbuh). We know scholars like Maaz bin Jabil and the poet of the Prophet (pbuh) Hassan bin Sabit they all went out in Ghuzvat, and their knowledge was not enough to stay behind. In fact, the Prophet (pbuh) himself, for learning the revelation, he did not stay behind. He wished to join every army that leaves Usman bin O'Fan and Abdul Rehman bin Auf they use to finance the armies with their wealth this was not sufficient for them they had to go out themselves.

The army reached in Jordan (at that time) that was called Sham and received intelligence that the Romans have heard of the marching and have mobilized an army. The news that (Muslim army) heard was not that good. If they had heard that they would be meeting an army of their size that would have been good. Even if they had the intelligence news that Roman Army is ten times bigger like thirty thousand (30,000) that would have been okay. These were the Sahaba of Prophet, courage, bravery, Amaan and Tawaqal of Allah. But the news they received was that they are facing army of two hundred thousand (200,000) strong. One hundred thousand professional roman soldiers and in addition to that one hundred thousand (100,000) Christian Arabs. They were the allies of the Romans. This is a disastrous news, 3000 facing 200,000, so far Muslims have never ever heard such numbers. In the past the biggest army they faced for example in battle of the trench was 10,000. Battle of the trench (Khandaq). Here they will be facing well equipped professional army of two hundred thousand (200,000). We are talking about the soldiers of Roman Empire. The Romans and Persians had reputation of having very strong force, well trained, armed, professional soldiers. We are not talking about tribes men. We are talking about professional army.

Therefore, this issue demanded Shura consultation (conference). The Zahid bin Harsa, consulted prominent Sahaba. What should we do? Some of them suggested send a messenger to Prophet (pbuh) and seek advice and wait here. By now Abdullah bin Roha was there and he said, Men! What you dislike what you have come for martyrdom. Once again listen. Men what you dislike that is what you have to seek. Abdullah bin Roha is reminding them with their original intentions. You are companions of Prophet (pbuh). Every single one of you have come to die Fi-Sabil Allah that is our ultimate desire if that is what we want how come we are disliking it. What is the reason for waiting and not facing the army? Is it fear of death? We all came here with the intention of dying Fi-Sabeel Allah. He is reminding them. Because reminder will benefit the believers, we are not fighting by numbers or strength. We are combating only with the religion. With which, Allah has honored us. Go forward, it will result with only two good out comes. Either victory or martyrdom. This is what every Muslim looks up to. Win against the enemy in world or die Fi-Sabeel Allah.

That encouraged them and they said by Allah Abdullah bin Roha is right. They decided to go forth disregarding the consequences. This tells us the spirit of Sohaba. Their concern was with Al-Akhara. They were concerned with Al-akhara and world. We are facing Allah, let us go on the other side of world we shall be meeting Allah. This deliberation happened in Jordan area called Aman. The army went forward. Now they were moving forward towards the planes of Motha. Motha is also in Jordan, with this army there was a new Muslim Abu Huraira. He became Muslim in Khyber. Abu Huraira speaks about his experience in this battle. Abu Huraira, said, I attended the battle of Motha. When the Mushriqeen came close to us. We saw what no one can face weapons, preparations, gold, eyes were dazzling. Abu Huraira is a new Muslim and there are things a Muslims learns by experience Abu Huraira is coming from a Jahiliya background. An army of 3,000 facing an army of 200,000. Something you will find in no religion and no tradition.

The Arab tribes men cannot think about that and anybody who is coming from any other tribe or culture cannot comprehend, cannot understand. Why should we do that, this is death not only with fear some numbers. But now when they faced the army before they heard it now they are seeing it. Hearing is not like seeing it. Then these armies play on the psychology of the enemy. The show of force plays an important role. It demoralizes the enemy they came in a show probably drums were beating, powerful show Abu Huraira says that preparations and weapons we could see, the gold and badges silk, thick silk cloth. The army was dressed in all that that puts the fear in the hearts of the enemy. Abu Huraira says I was dazzled it was like lightning. My eyes were struck with lightening was it confusing was it fear was it surprise? Whatever it was could be seen on the face of Abu Huraira. Sabbat bin Arqam saw what was happening. He told Abu Huraira. It seems you are looking at a huge force. Abu Huraira said yes, definitely looking at them. Are we supposed to fight this force? Sabbat bin Arqam an experienced Muslim handing down his experience to a new Muslim. Sabbat bin Arqam is deep in Islam. He told Abu Huraira; you were not with us at Badr. We are not getting victory through numbers. Here he is handing down a lesson to Abu Huraira which is learned through experience. You were not at Badr. We Muslims forget about the laws of nature, war, when you were non-Muslim, now forget about that, we Muslims view the world differently. We Muslims see things differently you were not at Badr. The numbers in Badr were nothing like this but Badr was the first encounter. Then Muslims saw interference by the soldiers of Allah. They saw angels came in and help victory. It was not our numbers. Muslims were little over three hundred (300) and the Quraish were one thousand (1000). That is three times the numbers. But now three thousand (3000) against two hundred thousand (200,000), it is now a totally different ball game. But he is telling him it is not the numbers, but the trust in Allah, which gives victory. Some Ayat were revealed after the battle of Badr. "You did not throw, that was Allah.

The battle started with Zahid bin Harsa. The leader is the head of the army, he is carrying the banner. His courage leading his army, giving them an example moved forward carrying the banner in his arms and it says in the narration until he was lost among their lances. Zahid bin Harsa went forward until he was last in enemy army, and then Zahid bin Harsa was no more and then the banner was carried by Jaffar bin Abu Talib. Who had come back from Abyssinia. Prophet did not keep him with him Prophet but sent him with the army. Jaffar bin Abu Talib carried the banner and in the heat of the battle Jaffar bin Abu Talib felt that his horse is a hindrance. He dismounted and killed his horse. This was used as evidence by Imam Abu Hanifa that you are allowed to kill your animal because enemy is taking advantage the rule is that we should not kill animal wastefully. If you are not going to eat it why kills it. But used as evidence if enemy is taking advantage then it is allowed. Jaffar killed his horse and moved on foot. It is said that his right arm was cut off so he carried the banner with left hand and then left arm was cut he held the banner with his body and whatever was left of the arms until he was killed. He was stabbed from all sides Bukhari Sharif. Abdullah bin Umar used to call him the man with two wings. Because Allah replaced his two arms with two wings after his death to fly with wings in Jinnah. To fly wherever he wants.

Then Abdullah bin Roha took over and became Ameer of the army. He was handed a piece of meat to strengthen himself. So, he started to eat that piece of meat then he heard uproar from certain corner of the battlefield. He said to himself that you are still living and he jumped ahead and was killed Fi-Sabil Allah. Now the three leaders appointed by Prophet were killed. Sohbat bin Arqm. He carried the banner and said, to Muslims choose a leader from among us to lead us. They said you lead us, but he said no. Muslims gave the banner to Khalid bin Waleed and asked him to lead. Muslims army choose Khalid bin Waleed. He was also a new Muslim. This was the first battle he would lead.

The messenger of Allah received the news through Gabriel. He was in Medina and received the news from battlefield in Jordan. Prophet said, Bukhari Sharif. Prophet the banner was carried by Zahid bin Harsa. He was killed and then it was carried by Jaffar until he was killed and then it was carried by Abdullah bin ROHAH and he was killed then the banner was carried by sword, from the sword of Allah. Khalid bin Waleed is sword of Allah and Muslims need a sword of Allah. They needed sword of Allah. Khalid bin Waleed carried the banner that was fighting leading the Muslims. He was a new Muslim but spirit of Islam was strong Khalid bin Waleed said, he broke 9 swords on that day and then a broad sword Yemen sword survived with Khalid bin Waleed. The question was whether a sword can survive with Khalid bin Waleed. Nine swords were broken in one day. He was killing the enemy and at the end of the day only a broad iron sword survived. Prophet said about three leaders of the army. Zahid, Jaffar and Abdullah bin Roha are happier in akhara than in world. They do not want to come back with us they are happy where they are, it is mentioned in one narration Khalid bin Waleed at night fall when the fighting stopped Khalid bin Waleed was doing a slow retreat. He did not want to do a fast retreat because enemy will take advantage and could destroy.

The army it was a slow retreat they were holding on until night fall encouraging Muslims to hold on at night he switched the right flank to left and the left flank to the right. In the morning Romans saw different people in front of them Right and left. The Roman were deceived to feel that Muslims have received the reinforcement. They were thinking if Muslims were able to hold grounds when they were only 3000 what they will do after receiving reinforcement. This convinced Romans and they retreated or stopped fighting, and this is the victory that Prophet is talking about in Bukhari Sharif. This is the opening, Prophet said, when Romans stopped fighting Khalid bin Waleed immediately retreated and they came back to Medina. Prophet visited the children of Abu Jaffar. The brother of Hazrat Ali cousin of Prophet, told their mother to bring the children, asama had washed and cleaned them. Prophet hugged them embraced them and tears were swelling in his eyes. Asma asked something happened Prophet said yes. Jaffar was killed. She screamed and Prophet said I am their Wali in world and akhara. I shall take care of them.

The wife of Jaffar a widow, later married Abu Bakr and after his death married ALI BIN ABU TALIB.

Poetry, she said I swear my soul sad over you. Hazrat Ali spoke to her and asked who said my soul will be said over you. And my skin will always wear dirt. She had a son, Mohammad with Abu Bakr when she married with Hazrat Ali. He son brought up by Hazrat Ali. He always supported Hazrat. He was appointed governor over Egypt by Hazrat Ali.

The total Muslims men killed in the battle 12. Two armies of conflicting faith. Muslims 3000 the other disbelievers total 200000. 100000 Romans and 100000 Christian Arabs could battle and resulting deaths. Only 12 Muslims genuinely great, and large numbers of non-believers were killed. Khalid alone stated Al-Amran 12. Allah gives victory to whom he wants. SURYIA AMER BIN AAS. This was the first for Amr bin Aase. Prophet pbuh, put them in the position of leadership because they were capable men. Amr bin Aas was sent to the land of Bali. This is an Arab tribe, because of the situation Amr bin Aas asked for reinforcement. Prophet sent him Abu Abida, Amr bin Aas said I am the Ameer but mahajroon said Abu Abida is the Ameer, Amr bin Aas SAID, Prophet pbuh appointed me and Abu Abida is reinforcement. There was an argument. Then Abu Abida said the last advice from Prophet was to agree with each other and do not disagree. Abu Abida said you are the leader.

Suryia ABU ABIDA, 300 hungry, and found a dead fish ATE from this for a month, Rizk sent by Allah. PROPHET PBUH STOOD ON THE MAMBER. and said I want to send some messengers to foreign kings. The letter to foreign kings to follow him. Telling them to apply the laws of Allah. THIS was a major step and an important event Prophet wanted to warn the Muslims that this should not cause dispute among you. Like Banu Israel disputed about Hazrat Eisa. The son of Marry. At the time of Hazrat Eisa. Banu Israel were living under kings. Now Prophet PBUH was inviting the kings they were not different from the kings of yesterday.

Sahaba said we shall never disagree about you. It was an extremely dangerous for a Sahaba to go and enter the kingdom and tell the kings to fallow the Prophet Muhammad PBUH. It was not easy thing to do Prophet is giving the Sahaba warning. Prophet appointed Khalifa Kalbi to carry the letter to the great emperor of the day Hurcle of Rome the Roman Emperor of Eastern Empire in Sultanate of Ghazahapian. But they used to call them Roman. Roman had divided into Western and Eastern Empire. Western from Rome Eastern from Istanbul.

Hurcle was military commander in, cartridge is in Tunis. He became emperor and supreme military commander. The Roman Empire in 610 AD. He became emperor when Roman Empire was going through exceedingly difficult time. That was the time when Persian Empire was pounding them. Romans were receiving hit after hit. City after city. Persians were rolling on, and Romans were suffering defeat after defeat. Hurcle was a good strong military commander. But the empire was falling back. In 613 AD, Damascus fell a year later Jerusalem fell, and Persians took over the true cross. This is a wooden cross believed by Christian on which Hazrat Eisa was crucified. But we Muslims do not believe this. But the Roman believe it the most important relique sign. Roman were Christians. Great cross true cross or holy cross. Persian took over the true cross the important relique. In year 621 AD Hurcle led the campaign and started fight back the Persians and he took back one city after another and not only he regained what was taken but also attacked Persia in their land and took some part of Persia.

Allah says in Quran about this story, the story of Dawah in Makkah. Quran says Romans were defeated but they will win between 3 and 9 years. Even it was impossible to see Roman come back, but now they are rolling back. Hurcle was winning he got back Damascus and Jerusalem. This campaign took him few years. Hurcle in 630 AD, reaching the height of his power. He fulfilled his vow to march barefoot the pious Christian pilgrim into Jerusalem. In 630 AD he marched into Jerusalem barefoot.

He restored the true cross to the holly sepreka. He was given a grand reception and grand celebration to celebrate the return of true cross to its place.

THE LETTERS TO FOREIGN KINGS. Now this is the time when HERACLE receives the letter from Prophet pbuh that started interesting chain of events. He suffered defeat after defeat. He last Syria, Jerusalem, Lebanon, in fact entire Eastern Empire would fall to Muslim later on. The closing chapter was the fall of Qustustonia, Istanbul. The Ottoman Empire.

When Hurcle received the letter from Prophet, letter was not delivered by hand by Yaya Al kalbi. He was a Sahabi very handsome, there is saying he was from Kalbi tribe whenever Gabriel visit Prophet. The form of man he would transform in Yaya Alqalbi that has something to do that Prophet chose him as Ambassador.

The letter was given to one of the Governors of Hurcle and this governor in turn handed it over to Hurcle. Hurcle read the letter and told one of his deputy. He told him to turn Shaam upside down until you find and bring someone who is from the place of Muhammad. They found Abu Sufyan and other merchants they were in the country Shaam. The soldiers stormed in asked, "Where are you from ?" They said we are from Arabs. The soldier said come with us. They ended up meeting the emperor himself.

Abu Sufyan is narrating the story; he says my companions were told to stand behind me. Because Hercules asked who is the closest to Muhammad amongst you they answered Abu Sufyan. He was asked, what is your relationship to Muhammad Abu Sufyan said he is my cousin. He is the closest. His name is Abu Sufyan ibn Imia ibn Abid Shams son of Abdul Mannaf Muhammad PBUH bin Abdullah bin Abdul Mutlab bin Hashim. So the grand fathers are cousin. Hercules said to others stand behind him, and if he tells a lie you will have to point out to me. Make a sign or gesture that he is not telling the truth. Stand behind so you do not feel embarrassed in front of him Abu Sufyan. Heracle wanted to confirm the information. Abu Sufyan said later that I have never met a man more intelligent and Astute than Heracle. Heracle is going to question Abu Sufyan. Abu Sufyan says he knew the companions will not refute me even if I told lie, they were loyal to him. But I was a man with dignity and honor and would have been ashamed to lie. Also, I had a feeling that if I told lies, they may report it to others and people would talk about me in Makkah. So I didn't lie to him, these men even in Jahlia, they had dignity, honor and virtues. He didn't want to lie.

The questions started, Heracle to Abu Sufyan who is Muhammad Abu Sufyan said, he is a magician and a liar. Heracle said I do not want to heir curses. I want you to tell me about him. I want some objective answers leave these curses aside. Give me some valid news, valid information do not give me curses, question began, first question, what sort of family lineage he has. Abu Sufyan his ancestry is distinguished one.

Q2. Was any of his forefathers king? Q3. Has anyone among you come up with the similar claim? Q4. Majority of people who follow him are aristocrat or poor people. Q5. The followers are on the increase or decrease. Q6. Has anybody turned away after accepting? Q7. Have you ever known him to tell lies? Q8. Is he given to treachery? But we have an agreement with him and we do not know what he will do in these period. Abu Sufyan says this was the only thing he was able to sneak in without telling lies. Abu Sufyan wanted to tell lies but he is bound by his word not to lie. Q9. Heracle asked have you ever fought him? Answer yes. Q10. How did the fighting go? Answer. Sometimes he wins and sometimes we win. Q11. What kind of commandments does he give you? Answer. He tells worship Allah alone without ascribing divinity to anyone else. He tells us not to fallow our fathers. He tells us to pray and be truthful and be chased and kind to our fellow human beings.

Heracle said you have mentioned that he enjoys distinguished ancestry and this is the case with all Prophets and messengers. Since you say that no one has claimed before, I cannot say that he is imitating anyone. You also deny that any of his forefathers was a king that means he is not claiming a kingdom. You also say that he is not known to tell a lie before he came out with this message. I know that he will not start lying to Allah. You have stated that the poor are his followers and this is the case with all messengers from Allah. The fact that the followers are on the increase this is a phenomena with truth. Until it completed you have also said that no one turns away from his religion after having embarrassed it. This is a character of faith its light shines in people's hearts. You also deny that he is treacherous. You also said he calls on you to pray one Allah be truthful and chaste. If what you have told me is true, then he will have supremacy right here where I stand. I knew that his time is due. I don't think he would belong to your people. If it was in my power I would certainly like to meet him and wash his feet.

In these words of Heracle we see the intelligence and understanding of history and understanding of religion and understandings of the laws of Allah and understanding to distinguish between true Prophets and false Prophet. The Heracle is telling something to Abu Sufyan. The man who was leading the war against the Prophet. Heracle the Emperor of Rome in telling Abu Sufyan himself, that if I meet Muhammad I shall wash his feet.

Now, these words had an effect on Abu Sufyan. The letter was brought and it was read from Muhammad the messenger of Allah, to Heraclius the Great one of the Romans, peace be to those who fallow the guidance. I call you to believe in Islam, adopt Islam you will be safe and Allah will give you double the reward. If you decline you should bear the responsibility of RCG. These are the farmers. Romans were farming people. Prophet is telling him that you will be responsible for their disbelief. The letter was read.

Abu Sufyan said, what he said Hercules. After the letter was read the noise became loud we were driven out, I told my companions this Ibn Abu Qabsha, the name they use to call Muhammad PBUH. His affair has reached at a level where he scares the king of pale skin. There after I was convinced that Muhammad PBUH will prevail and Allah drew me in to Islam.

Roman were themselves really worried about Muhammad PBUH. These are the people of the scripture. These are the people who understand.

Prophet pbuh used the title to address Heracle was the great one among the Roman. Ibn Hajar says he was not given the King or leader. Islam does not recognize his kingdom or his authority and does not recognize the authority of any disbeliever. But he was given a title a great one of Romans. Then the letter says peace be to those who follow guidance. Prophet did not give him Salam directly Ibn Hajar says Abu Sufyan said, when he was reading the letter or when the letter was read to him Abu Sufyan says he saw sweat following down his forehead. That is how heavy the letter of Prophet was, he knew that this was the truth but he did not want to follow it.

There is a story that Heracle called his patriates that we should become Muslim this is a Prophet we have been told in our books, they all roared and became angry. Then Heracle told them calm down I just wanted to test your faith. Heracle wanted to become Muslim but when he saw the reaction of his people. He said I was only testing you.

But he told the messenger if I could have reached Muhammad PBUH I would have done so but he feared for his Kingdom. This is the story of the letter to Heracle. THE NEXT

LETTER TO KISRA. The Persian Emperor. This letter was sent with Abdul ibn Adefa. According to one narration the letter was read in front of Kisra. In the name of Allah, the merciful and beneficent from Muhammad PBUH the messenger of Allah to Kisra the great one of the Persians peace he upon him who believes in the guidance of Allah and his messenger and declares there is no Deity but Allah. The only God who has no partners and Muhammad PBUH is his servant and messenger. I wish to convey to you Allah call that I am Allah's messenger to all mankind sent with the task to give warning to all those who are alive that doom will fall on non-believers. If you summit to Allah you will be safe if you refuse you will bear the responsibility for that.

Kissara was angry. How dare you write this kind of letter to me. When he is my slave and then he ordered his governor of Yemen to send two able bodied men to arrest Muhammad PBUH stop and look at this man's arrogance and pride and look how they used to view, Arabs as their slaves as they are not people who have great kingdom like them. He sent this letter to. He Persian ruler of Yemen. Badan sent two men one of them the name was Abu dhow, and other Khrkhra to arrest Muhammad PBUH they did not bring army but went alone. Their reputation was sufficient they did not show force. Just the two of them traveled and reached Taif they asked where was Muhammad PBUH. They told them that he is in Medina. But people of Taif and Quraish of Mecca were incredibly happy about this. That is, it, this will be the end of Muslims, and these two men came to Medina. They delivered their instructions to Muhammad PBUH. They said, Khosrow, the Kisra the king of kings. Shahan Sha has written to Badan of Yemen commanding him to send us to take you to him. If you comply Badan will write to the king of kings on your behalf. This will spare you a great deal of trouble. If you reject his order, you know how powerful he is. He is sure to destroy you, your people and your country.

The messenger of Allah responded and told them, who ordered you to shave your beards. Prophet disliked that and they had long mustache. They said our lord, Prophet told them but my lord has commanded me to have beard and trim mustaches, and then he told them to wait for the next day. This particular narration is from seerah. It is not from Hadith.

Next day, when they came Prophet told them, My Lord has killed your lord this night. They said, do you realize what you are saying. Your arrest has been ordered for much more trivial than this. Do you still wish us to write it down and inform king Badan. What you have just said, Prophet said yes. Also tell him on my behalf that my religion and my kingdom will replace that of kissara and will sweep all before it tell him also if he accepts Islam, I shall give him, what he has under his authority and will make him a ruler in the area that he now governs. The Prophet gave them gifts and ordered them to leave. Whenever a delegation is received the tradition is to give them something as a gift. They went back to Badan and told him everything. Badan said these words are not of a king but of a Prophet. But let us wait and see about any news about kissara. It takes a long time for message to be dispatched. A while later, they received the information that kissara was killed on the same night which was told by Prophet. Badan, became Muslim. He knew that this is a miracle from Allah and Muhammad PBUH is a messenger of Allah, and that was the beginning of Islam in Yemen. The new kisra now ruling, he has killed his father he sent a letter to Badan because what he had done to our noble men and I would stop you doing anything regarding the Prophet PBUH, who my father send you a letter to arrest him.

What kissara had done, after receiving the letter from Muhammad PBUH he tore the letter. Prophet said Allah will tear apart his kingdom and that is what happened that Muslims conquered the entire kingdom of kissara.

THE NEXT LETTER WAS SENT TO ALMOQAQAS. The ruler of Egypt. This letter was sent with Hatif bin Alibaba. The letter read, in the name of Allah the merciful the beneficent. From Muhammad bin Abdullah to Almoqaqas the great of the kops peace be to those who follow right guidance. I wish to convey to you the message of Islam. Accept Islam and you will be safe. Accept it and Allah will double your reward should you turn your back on it. You will have the responsibility for kaafs, people of the book, let us share common agreement that we shall not worship anyone but Allah and that we shall never ascribe divinity to anyone else and that none of us will give status to others as lords alongside Allah. If they refuse say to them that we witness that we summit to Allah.

Almoqaqas said, I have questions for you and would like you to help me to reach understanding. Almoqaqs said tell me about your master. If a Prophet he is indeed. Then why he does not pray for the destruction of the people who evicted him people of Makkah. Hatif said, about Jesses son of Marry. You do not witness that he is a messenger of Allah Almoqaqas said yes I do. Hatif said then when people took him to crucify him? Could be not have prayed for the destruction for his people. When Allah raised him up for the lower heaven. Almoqaqs said you are wise man, who has come from a wise man there are presents I am dispatching with you to Muhammad PBUH and send a guard with you who will conduct you to safe heaven. His response was polite but he did not become Muslim.

He sent with Hatif some say 2 girls and some say 3 salve girls, unbelievably valuable slave girls. One of them was Marria, whom Prophet, married and she gave birth to Ibrahim. The son of Muhammad PBUH. He died at a young age. The other one was given to Hussain bin Sabit. He also gave for the Prophet, Bughla, Meul named Duldul. He also sent some other valuable gifts these were the letters sent.

Also, a letter was sent to Najashi and another letter sent to king of Gasan.

These were the letters sent to the surrounding areas and response was different. Response of kissara was the worst one and the response of Najashi was the best. Since he accepted Islam. Then Heracle and Moqaqos were polite but did not become Muslim. We ask Allah to benefit us all.

During the time of Jahlia. A man from Banu hazrami who was an ally with Banu Bakr. He was traveling in Hajaz when he was deep in the land of Hajaz. There was a tribe named Khazha. They killed him and took his money people of Banu Bakr took revenge by killing a member of Khazha. Khazha then targeted 3 from Banu Aswad Ali and Banu Aswad belonged to the tribe of Banu Bakr. They considered themselves above everyone else and also considered to be the noblest. In fact, they used to charge double the dea (Dea is blood money) the children of Banu Aswad, would take double the blood money. Khazha killed three of them, then Islam came and one will call from Sulah Hudaibia one of the terms of the agreement was that whoever wants to enter into agreement with Quraish can do so and whoever wants to enter into alliance with Muhammad PBUH, can do so. Banu Bakr entered into alliance with Quraish and Khazha entered into alliance with Muhammad PBUH. Khazha were in alliance with Banu Hashim in Jahlia. Now they became allies with Muhammad PBUH, the leader and the son of Banu Hashim. Although some of them were mushriq and some of them were Muslim. But they were all loyal to Muhammad

PBUH. Because of tribe tradition not because of religion. They were the allies with Banu Hashim in Jahlia. Now Banu Bakr wanted to revenge the three people and some of them Nobel among them. One of the leaders of Banu Bakr Movia bin Nofal. He was one of the leaders, in tribal society have several chiefs of clan.

Movia bin Nofal, who is from the branch of Banu Bakr they had lost three men, he attacked some people from Banu Khaza. There are stone marks marking the land of Haram. These attacks were awfully close to Haram. But were outside the Haram and told his people to attack, the rest of Banu Bakr refused to attack only Movia bin Nofal and his men attacked and not all Banu Bakr. It is important to keep this in mind because of the implications of it. Like when to wage war on an enemy.

It is clearly stated that not all of Banu Bakr attacked and therefore were not involved in this betrayal. As we know there is a peace treaty and this a betrayal. Sulah Hudaibia was between Muhammad PBUH and Quraish and Banu Bakr and Khazha are part of the treaty. Because they are in alliance with two parties of the agreement. Movia bin Nofal is breaching this agreement, breach of the truce of Sulah Hydbia. Therefore, many of his tribe refused to join in, and other chiefs of the tribe did not participate in this Movia bin Nofal attacked and killed some people of Khazha and Khaza entered into Haram. Now they were within the sacred bounds and Haram is recognized by the people of Jahlia. It used to be considered a great sin to kill anybody inside Haram or to kill anybody during the holy months. There were four months of the year where no killing should happen and there are boundaries surrounding Makkah where no one should be killed that is throughout the year. While for 4 holy months there should be no killing in the Arabia.

Now people of Khazha are within the boundaries of Haram. So, the people of Banu Bakr are killing with Movia. They told Movia. This is Haram and were amazed at Movia what he was doing they told Movia we have entered Haram. Your God, your God, O' Movia.

But Movia responded, there is no God today O' Banu Bakr seek your revenge. In the name of Allah, you are stealing from inside Haram and would not you seek your revenge there in. Movia is justifying what he is doing and telling them, you already steal from inside of Haram. How can you complain now inside Haram. Now, we have a point in killing and we are seeking our revenge. People of Khazha fled from Movia and his men until they entered into Makkah itself and they wanted refuge in the house of Warqa bin Osei. This is a man from Khazha who used to live inside Mecca. They went in his house to sought refuge from this crime. That was committed against them. Amer bin Salm Qazi, immediately went to Medina to convey the news what happened to Prophet pbuh and he delivered the news to Muhammad PBUH in lines of poetry. Reminding Muhammad PBUH of their alliance and reminding the alliance with great grandfather Hashim.

What was the response of the Prophet Muhammad PBUH. When Amer bin Salam presented it to Muhammad PBUH. Prophet gave him clear, direct and decisive answer. Told him just one word. Prophet told him you are being helped. He did not tell him how but gave him his promise of help Then a cloud passed over and Prophet said this cloud is giving me the glad tiding of support and help to the people of Banu Khaza, people of Khazha. Ibne Ishaque says Movia bin Nofal went out with his people. He was their leader but not all of Banu Bakr followed him. Even though Prophet considered sufficient for the covenant to be ended and war to be announced against the people of Makkah. But it was a secret. Three conditions for

Quraish. The blood wit of the murdered men of Banu Khaza should be paid. The Quraish should repudiate their alliance with Banu Bakr. It should be proclaimed that the truce of Hudaybiyyah stands terminated. Quraish. Accepted the third condition repudiation of Sulah Hudaybiyyah. Prophet kept the idea of attack secret Prophet pbuh made Dua, O' Allah conceal the idea and blind their eyes from seeing us or knowing about our attempts. But Prophet pbuh did not want any bloodshed. And that is what happened people of Makkah only knew about the Muslim army when they were out skirts of Makkah. Prophet started preparations.

Abu Bakr visited his daughter Aysha and saw she was sifting wheat to prepare food for Prophet for the trip. Must have been some special food. Abu Bakr realized that Prophet is preparing for Ghazva. But did not know where. In one narration Abu Bakr asked Ayesha is Prophet planning for a conquest, and she said yes. Abu Bakr asked her is that Romans? She did not answer. She was keeping it secret.

In another other narration he asked her but she did not know then Abu Bakr waited till Prophet came then Abu Bakr asked Prophet and Prophet told him. Abu Bakr is the most prominent adviser to Prophet. He shares his secret with him. Prophet told Abu Bakr that I am going to attack Makkah. Abu Bakr I can see, Abu Sufyan coming to see you and ask for a renewal of the agreement that is exactly what happened Abu Sufyan After what had happened started towards Medina. Banu Bakr were killing Khaza. It is said that they are meaning Quraish provided support to Banu Bakr. Under the darkness. They provided arms and some say they participated in the killings. They said this is night and dark and nobody will know about our participation, that Quraish. They are ignorant of the fact that Muhammad PBUH is a messenger of Allah and he is receiving Wahi, messages from Allah. The news was delivered to Muhammad PBUH. Abu Sufyan now, became extremely worried that Prophet might attack. He traveled to Medina to beg Prophet to renew the agreement and to increase the time limit. The period after Sulah Hudaibia is 17 to 18 months. Sulah Hudaibia was for 10 years now just after a little over a year Quraish have committed breach of the agreement. Now they want to apologize for what has happened.

Abu Sufyan on the way met with Budbill bin Warqa is the man in Makkah in his house, Khaza went to seek refuge. Abu Sufyan asked him where did he go or who did he meet. Warqa said, he visited some people of Khaza on the coast Budbill bin Warqa had gone to Medina and was coming back from Medina after having told Prophet what had happened. Muslims and Khaza were going to Prophet seeking his help. Abu Sufyan was not convinced what Warqa was telling him. He waited for Warqa to leave and then went to the place where his camel was. He took some of the droppings of the camel and crushed in his hands and he found in it crushed date seeds and that food is fed to camels in Medina. Please note that dates are not grown in Makkah and in place where people of Khaza resided therefore Abu Sufyan knew that Warqa had been to Medina. Abu Sufyan went to Medina and he went to the house of Umma Habiba. She was his daughter and the wife of Prophet when he entered into house, there was a rug on the floor Abu Sufyan wanted to sit on that rug. But Umma Habiba pulled it away and raped it. Abu Sufyan asked his daughter I do not know whether you pulled it away because it is not befitting for me or I am not good enough for the rug.

Umma Habiba said, this rug belongs to Prophet and you are nonbeliever mushriq, and I do not want you to sit on that rug. This is a loyalty towards Prophet. She is speaking to her father but she understands kufr is dirty Najasha. Abu Sufyan was also the leader of Quraish. Abu Sufyan was shocked and said, O' my daughter evil have befallen on you and then Abu Sufyan went or Prophet on the way he met Abu Bakr. No response and Umar bin Khattab asked him for help but he said he wanted to kill him. However, went to Prophet and said wanted to continue the agreement and wanted to extend its time. Prophet asked him have anything happened at your end the agreement is for 10 years, Abu Sufyan said, everything is OK. Then Prophet walked away from Abu Sufyan. Abu Sufyan then went to Abu Bakr and wanted him to speak to Prophet. Abu Bakr told him I would not do that then Abu Sufyan went to Umar bin Khattab. They all knew Umar bin Khattab but thing is when Muslims were in Makkah and only after few years they are being humiliated Abu Sufyan asked Umar to intercede on his behalf, Umar bin Khattab said, you want me to intercede on your behalf if I find nothing to fight with I shall fight with ants with you Abu Sufyan left and went to Ali bin Abu Talib. Hazrat Ali said, once Prophet has made up his mind nobody can change it Abu Sufyan was in the house (this is before vailing) Hazrat Fatima was with her son Imam Hussan.

He was a child at the time. Abu Sufyan asked Hazrat Fatima, O' daughter of Muhammad would you ask your son Hassan to give us protection. He will be a leader until the end of the time. She said in the name of Allah my son is too young to do that and then she said no one can give protection in the presence of Prophet. If he has made up his mind no one can change it. Abu Sufyan is wise, strong leader but now he is frustrated and he is confused. He asked Hazrat Ali for advice. Hazrat Ali said by Allah I cannot suggest anything but you are the leader of Kanana. Go to mosque and go back to your land. Abu Sufyan said would that do me any good. Hazrat Ali said no but I find nothing else to tell you. Even then Abu

Sufyan went to mosque stood there but people ignored him. Abu Sufyan left and went back to Makkah and reported what happened in Medina.

Now Prophet is planning to attack Makkah. He told the Muslims to prepare but keep it a secret. One day Prophet summoned Hazrat Ali, Zubair bin Awam and Maqdad bin Aswad. He told them to go to place called Radtke you will find a woman and she is carrying a letter bring that letter to me. They went on horses and reached the place that Prophet told them, they found the woman told her to give us the letter you have. She said, I do not have any letter. Hazrat Ali told her to give us the letter or we shall search your person because Prophet has told us that you have a letter that means you have the letter when she realized that it is serious she pulled out the letter from her hairs. The letter was from Hatib, one of the Sahabi who fought in Badr. He wrote the letter to Quraish informing them of the plans of Prophet to attack Makkah, what Hatib did was extremely dangerous. He is telling Quraish of a secret plan of Prophet, when Prophet saw the letter and knew the contents Prophet called Hatib and asked him what is this? Hatib said, this hadith is in Bukhari Sharif. Hatib said Prophet do not hurry in deciding about me I do not belong to Quraish.

Your companions have families in Makkah who would take care of their families and property but I do not have any relatives in Makkah to take care of my family and my property (In one narration his mother was in Makkah and he was worried about her). I wanted to do a favor to Quraish that they will not harm my family and will protect my family. I did not do this to relegate my religion nor did I do this to choose anything other than Islam. Hatib made it clear. Prophet said he is telling the truth. Umar bin Khattab said, O messenger of Allah allow me to cut off his head this is a Munafiq. Prophet said, he has witnessed the battle of Badr. Allah has forgiven the people of Badr whatever they do. It shows the high status of people of Badr. Also, Prophet did not disapprove Hazrat Umar. It is in Bukhari, Allah revealed, O' you who believe take not my enemies and your enemies as friends offering them, love even though they have disbelieved in the truth, which has come to you and who so ever Muslims does that indeed he has gone away from the strait path.

Initially when marching towards Makkah Muslims were fasting, when came near, Prophet told them to break the fast. Prophet drank water in front of them. The army was 10,000 strong. This was the largest army assembled by Prophet pbuh so far. All Mahajreen and all Ansar and many surrounding tribes around Medina. All tribes participated. These were the Sahaba who witnessed the great battle of Fatah Mecca. THE CONQUEST OF MAKKAH.

Muslim army reached area called mehrhadran. There were trees of Iraq that is a tree where msawaq (toothbrush) is taken from. Msawaq is good the root of this tree. Also, the tender branches tree is called Al Iraq. The fruit is exceedingly small. It is audible and have taste of miswak, sohaba, were plucking the fruit. Prophet told them take the black one because they are the best ripe one. It starts as green then yellow and red then black. Aliraq does not grow in Makkah. It is outside of Makkah. Sahaba told the Prophet you must have been a Sheppard of a sheep. Because usually Sheppard eat it. It is out of Makkah. Prophet pbuh said yes and every prophet has been a Sheppard of sheep. We have talked about this, because of wisdom behind it. We have talked about this in one of the topics in Makkah, Abdullah bin Masood was exceptionally light and this is not a high tree Abdullah bin Masood was climbing to get the Kabatth the fruit. His legs were showing. They were very slim. Some of the Sahaba were laughing at his skinny legs. Prophet said you are surprised at the thinness of Abdullah bin Masood. In the name of Allah, they are heavier on the scales on the Day of Judgment than the mountain of Audh, Abdullah bin Masood is very heavy on the Day of Judgment. Deeds are very heavy. Prophet pbuh gave this secret. Virtue to Abdullah bin Masood. When they were walking, suddenly a rabbit jumped and one of the Sahaba caught it, they took this to Abu Talal. Who slaughtered it? Then they sent a piece of it to Prophet and he ate it. So, Rabbit is Halal. Until that moment Quraish had no idea of the movement of Prophet pbuh. Huge army 10000 strong but Quraish were blind and deaf, concerning the movement of Prophet. On the other hand, when Quraish made a move Prophet pbuh would be alerted. The intelligence gathering was much higher level Than Quraish that was blessing from ALLAH. Even though the resources were much less, kufr in that area were much move. The number of Muslims was in and around Medina. Rest of the Arabs were non- Muslims. Nevertheless, Prophet had trained the Sahaba to be alert. But Quraish until this moment had no clue about what was going on. Another reason was that loyalty of Muslim that they had for Prophet. We know the case of Hatib. That was a single case and Prophet was alerted to it by Wahi (revelation) from Allah. Sahaba would never disclose information about the movement of Muslims. Prophet was in this area of Marha Doran Abu Sufyan the Quraish leader along with Warqa. Hakim Bini Azam came out of Makkah, searching for information, asking the travelers.

At night, they were close to the Muslim army and they saw the lights of the Muslims, Abu Sufyan says who are there, they are Khaza, preparing for war. Abu Sufyan said Khaza are much less than that they cannot have these lights, they cannot be Khaza. They are humbler and few to have these lights Abu Sufyan. Bodel and Hakim were overseeing the Muslim army. Muslim guards were alert they arrested three of them and took them to Prophet pbuh. Another narration is that Al-Abbas found them, we go with the narration that they were arrested and taken to Prophet. In one narration Umar bin Khattab saw Abu Sufyan and Umar bin Khattab wanted to kill him. But Al-Abbas has Abu Sufyan ride on the camel of Prophet and he was rushing to go to Prophet before Umar bin Khattab kill Abu Sufyan. Until they entered the place where Prophet was and Umar bin Khattab wanted to have Abu Sufyan killed while Al-Abbas was appealing for Abu Sufyan, to Prophet for his life. The argument carried on. Then Al-Abbas get angry and said O, Umar. If that was from Banu Adi. Hazrat Umar's clan then you would not say that. Quraish is a tribe but then there are clans. But you know he Abu Sufyan is from Banu Abdul Mannaf that clan is the family of Prophet and the family of Abu Sufyan. They are both descendants of Banu Abdul Mannaf.

Umar bin Khattab told Al-Abbas Waite O' Abbas. Your Islam is more beloved to me than the Islam of my father Khattab. If he had become Muslim. Because I know Prophet pbuh will become more pleased by Islam of you than if my father had become Muslim, Umar bin Khattab is making clear to Al-Abbas. This is not the way how we Muslims think. We do not think on tribal level. That is not our way of thinking. I am happier for your Islam because you are the uncle of Prophet and it is pleasing to Prophet. What pleases me is what pleases Prophet and what makes me angry that displeases Prophet. Umar bin Khattab is teaching Al-Abbas, how Muslims think. We do not think on family basis if a person is close to Allah. We Like him if he is away from Allah we dislike him.

Any way Prophet pbuh told them to leave and come back in the morning, according to that narration and when they met in the morning Prophet pbuh accepted the Islam of Adeel bin Warqa and Hakeem bin Hazam. Prophet pbuh told Abu Sufyan is there time to recognize that there is no God but one Abu Sufyan said to Prophet you are merciful and you are gene rice. Then Abu Sufyan said if there was another God that would have defended us Abu Sufyan accepted that there is no God but Allah, worthy of worship. Prophet told Abu Sufyan is it not time to testify that I am the messenger of Allah. Abu Sufyan said O' Prophet there is something in my heart against this at the moment. I accept there is only one Allah but I find it difficult to accept that Muhammad PBUH is messenger of Allah. Al-Abbas told him vow to you Abu Sufyan, become a Muslim before your head in chopped off. Before you are executed. Abu Sufyan said, I have witnessed that Muhammad PBUH is the messenger of Allah. And he became a Muslim (He was a good Muslim). Prophet instructed Al-Abbas to hold back Abu Sufyan from leaving and have him wait at the Mountain pass Prophet want Al-Abbas to hold back Abu Sufyan for a reason.

Prophet wanted him to see the strength of the Muslims when Abu Sufyan would see the overwhelming forces of Muslims that Prophet have bought together to invade Makkah that will bring an end to any desire or willingness to resist. Because even Abu Sufyan is a Muslim but he is a new Muslim and he is a leader of Quraish. He might have some interest and Quraish might fight. Prophet wanted them to see with their own eyes because hearing is not like seeing and Prophet did not want any bloodshed in Makkah. He wanted them to see how strong the Muslims are and would surrender. Prophet had divided the army in battalions and every battalion had a Riya, and they were divided according to their tribes, they were all separate. They were passing this mountain area. They were passing one after the other. Whenever these battalions pass through the mountain pass Abu Sufyan would ask who are they? Al-Abbas would say Al Ghafar. Abu Sufyan would say I have nothing to do with Al Ghafar. Likewise, other tribes as well.

Until one battalions, you can sometimes sense the strength of what you see Abu Sufyan saw, one of the battalion caught his attention. He asked who are these Al-Abbas told him these are the Ansar. And the banner was with Saad bin Abada, who is the leader of Alkhzraj, when Saad bin Abada saw Abu Sufyan. He told Abu Sufyan today is the day of great battle today is the day of sanctuary of Al Kaaba will be violated Saad bin Abada a great Sahabi leader of answer one who gave Nasra, Victory to Prophet. He was over enthusiastic and uttered these words. Al-Abbas, Abu Sufyan, Umar bin Khattab carried these words to Prophet. Prophet pbuh said Saad lied (He is mistaken) today is the day. Allah will glorify the Kaaba. Kaaba will not be violated Prophet ordered that banner should be taken from Saad bin Abada and to be given to his son Qais bin Abada. This was for two reason (i) Prophet wanted to avoid bloodshed in Makkah and at the same time Prophet did not want Saad bin Abada will accept the orders from Prophet but he might be upset therefore the banner was given to his son. Prophet pbuh entered Makkah peacefully there was no resistance but in the area where Khalid bin Waleed came in there was some resistance from Banu Bakr. Banu Bakr and Orio, were outside Makkah. They do not live in Makkah. They put up a fight Khalid bin Waleed destroyed them. They all ran away, that was the end of resistance. There is a difference of opinion amongst scholars. Whether Makkah was entered by force or by an agreement. The implications of this are, that if land is opened by force then all the property belongs to the winning force. Even the people, so all the property could be taken away by Muslims. But if by agreement then no property is taken and people are free, they are not slaves. There is some difference of opinion amongst learned people.

Prophet pbuh entered Makkah, this is an absence of 8 years when Prophet left, he left secretly. There was a plot to kill him. Prophet had to flee from dangers that existed in Makkah. After 8 years Prophet is entering Makkah victoriously. Mahajroon suffered in Makkah for 13 years. All types of harm one can imagine. Now it is time for revenge, and great chance of celebration of victory as different armies do whenever they conquer a new land but how did Prophet pbuh entered with humbleness and he was reciting Sura Al- Fatah the Sura of conquest. His head was lowered so down the beard was touching the royal of the camel. He was reciting the Ayat. He had black turban and a white banner and entered into Makkah in state of humbleness. Thanking Allah and praising Allah for what he has given him. Prophet pbuh then made tawaf around Kaaba, Prophet called Usman bin Tilla to bring the key of the Kaaba the key belong to Banu Abdedar. Great great grandfather of Prophet when he passed away, all the powers were in his hand when he died. The family of Prophet had the responsibility of providing water to Hajaj zam- zam that would call providing water.

Then the family of Banu Abdedar, they were the custodian of Kaaba and held on to the key. Key was with them. Usman was Muslim Prophet told him to go and get the key. Usman asked his mother at first she refused but he took the key and brought it to Prophet. Prophet pbuh opened the Kaaba. He entered and saw pigeon made out of wood, Prophet pbuh destroyed it there were images of angels on the walls of Kaaba, and Ibrahim holding Divining arrows which is one of the biddah of jahlia. Prophet pbuh said May Allah kill them, they portray our elder meaning grandfather Ibrahim as using the divining arrows then Prophet asked Umar bin Khattab to wipe off all the images from inside of Al-Kaaba. Umar bin Khattab soaked a cloth in water and cleaned out all these images, when Prophet entered Kaaba it was all clean from all innovations from jahlia and kufr.

Then Prophet pbuh came out of Kaaba and stood at the door of Kaaba which was high by now all of the people were gathering around him. Then Prophet spoke to the crowd. The people of Quraish all came out to listen to Prophet pbuh.

Let us go back some years when Prophet received initial revelations from Allah and was commanded to deliver the warning to his people. Warn your close relatives or your clan that was in the beginning. Prophet stood on a mountain in Makkah and he said(wa subha). This is call when there is an emergency situation. It is a serious call and everybody responds. All of the people came and those who could not come, they sent their representatives to listen. Prophet said, "I am delivering a warning to you before a swear punishment be fall on you. When Prophet said that Abu Lahab said, he had a doubt in this. May you be cut off; this is why you have summoned us Abu Lahab was in the business of buying and selling. He left his shop and came to listen, what Prophet had to say if that was the message. Abu Lahab was upset and angry. And the crowds left and from that moment onwards nobody wanted to listen what Prophet had to say. One can imagine how difficult it is to deliver to people when they do not want to listen.

But now, Prophet pbuh is leading an army and has strength and he is a head of state everybody came voluntarily to listen. Prophet did not call anybody this time, but when he came out of Kaaba and turned around all the people of Makkah were under him and were listening, waiting for him to speak. Also, people were watching every move of the Prophet PBUH when Prophet went to the well of zam- zam to drink and made Wazu the Sahaba were rushing to grab the water that would drip and they were rubbing on their body, people of Quraish were saying we have never seen a king such as this before. Now they were watching every single movement of Prophet and were reporting it. That is how we know about this incident they have reported this to us. Prophet is the same Prophet as he was then, but in the beginning Prophet did not have strength and no one wanted to listen to him at that time.

Now Prophet pbuh delivered a short speech from the door of Kaaba. Prophet said, all praise to Allah, praise be to Allah, who has fulfilled his promise and he has helped his servant and alone he has defeated the opposing parties then Prophet is instituting some new laws in Makkah.

Compensation for those who are killed by queasy intent by whip or 'kugel' shall be compensated by 100 camels. This is blood money, shab, and al-Umar. Then Prophet told them all privileges of ancestry and pride that existed in the jahlia are finished. These are the foundations of the society of jahlia. The foundations, the customs and the laws of the Arabs in jahlia were based on this. In this one statement, Prophet pbuh is bringing a new era, and he is telling the people who are listening under his feet. Telling them the time of jahlia the rules of jahlia. The customs of jahlia. They are all behind, finished. Prophet is telling the kufr the kufr is over with. I am not going to accommodate you I am not going to accept your laws. In another narration Prophet said both ancestry and pride are under my feet.

Prophet did not try to win the heart of Quraish, by accepting some of their rules and customs. The people of Quraish would fight for their customs and would die. They fought against Prophet for 20 years. For no other purpose than protecting the old ways. They were not religious people. Even they had 360 idols in and around Kaaba. They are not known to be religious people. But it was the status quo they wanted to keep. Prophet did not try to win them over by accepting some of the jahlia traditions. The first statement made it clear that your ways are under my feet.

Now the keys of Kaaba are in the hands of Prophet pbuh, Ali bin Abu Talib from the family of Banu Hashim told Prophet and prayed to Allah to combine the honors of providing water to pilgrims and holding the keys to Kaaba. But Prophet called Usman and said, take it forever and no one will take it from you but transgressor. These things were great honor for Quraish. No one will take keys but a tyrant. Until today the keys of Kaaba are with the same family. Now they the descendants are called Banu Sheeba. The key has been passing from father to son until this day. Then Prophet riding on his camel going around Kaaba. In one narration holding on to his stick, in another narration holding on to his bow. He was pointing towards these idols these glorified idols sacred idols for the people of Quraish people are watching Prophet is going around poking these idols in their eyes and in one narration he was only pointing towards these idols and they were falling one after the other. If Prophet points on the face it would fall back on its back but if pointing on the back of an idol it would fall on its face. Prophet did that with 360 idols surrounding Kaaba and Quraish are watching. It was a monumental moment when all their Gods have been there for centuries. They are watching them falling down in pieces.

Prophet was saying that truth has come and error has gone, error is bound to disappear error or evil is bound to disappear. The Prophet pbuh told the people what do you think I shall do to you. The people of Quraish said, what they believed the case with Muhammad PBUH they know him. They said you are a noble brother and son of a noble brother. Prophet told them you can go you are the freed one, meaning you are under my hand you could he killed but you are free. That is the reason people who became Muslim are called freed one, Prophet freed them. You are released one. Prophet released them but there is a blacklist. This list included the names of Abdullah bin Khatal, Abdullah bin Abbsrha, Maqees bin Sbaba, Khuaz bin Naqeef and Sara, Kurtz, Aneeb and Arnr (4 four men 3 women).

Prophet said execute them even you see them hanging to the door of Kaaba. Question why these were excluded from the people of Makkah. Abdullah bin Khatal. He became Muslims made Hijra and then Prophet sent him to collect sadqa, charity. He had a servant with him on, the way he was upset with the servant. In one narration, he ordered the servant to prepare lunch and when it was lunch time, he asked him where is the lunch ? Servant told him I forgot and he killed the servant. He knew he will be punished for that. In Islam there is justice for everyone. Therefore, he ran away to Makkah and he committed apostasy reverted back. He had two slave girls he would teach them to sing against Prophet. He was excluded because of Rida, and blasphemy against the Prophet PBUH. His two slave girls Fritna and Arnb. They were included because of the blasphemy against Prophet, Abdullah bin Abu Srha. He was a Muslim and would write Quran for Prophet. Prophet would ascribe. The Ayat and he would write them down Abdullah bin Abu Srha ran away and became murtad(reverted back). And he was telling Quraish, that I would change the Quran. Muqees bin Sbaba. His brother was a Muslim. In the battle of Banu Almustliq. He was killed by mistake by a man from Ansar. Muqees He made Hijra and became Muslim just to collect the blood money of his brother. Prophet paid him the money he then ran away and became murtad. Forf bin Naqees. When the daughters of the Prophet, Zainab and Fatima were going to Medina. He provoked the camel they both fell and Zainab had a miscarriage, these were the actions of this man Al- Khafeef, Sahira was a slave girl in Makkah she used to sing against Prophet. Everyone on this list was excluded for one or two reasons. Either they had committed Rida or because of blasphemy.

These two things are unforgivable Abdullah bin Khatal was seen hanging on to the door of Kaaba. He was executed on the spot one narration is that Quartan was killed but Arnab became Muslim and was forgiven, Abdullah bin Abeesar, sought refuge with his brother from breast feeding Usman ibn Affan, Usman bin Affan took Abdullah bin Abeesr to Prophet. He said I came to give you allegiance, Prophet was quite He said 2nd time I came to give Bia Prophet did not respond the third time he said I came to give you Bia. Prophet accepted his Bia. When he left Prophet pbuh told the men who were there. Is there no wise man among you who could have got up and killed him when you saw I was remaining salient? Ansar said O' Prophet could you not have given us some signal Prophet said prophets do not kill by making signals. It is not appropriate for me to give signal, you already knew my ruling. In another narration one of the Ansar had his hand on the sword ready to execute the man but he was waiting for signal from Prophet.

That was the Qadr of Allah to spare the life of Abdullah bin Abeesr. He became a good Muslim and story is that he died in Sajood in salah ul fajr. Also, he held some position of authority in the time of Umar bin Khattab and Usman Ghani. Naqees bin Sbaba was killed by his cousin Harris bin Naqeeba was also killed, Sahira she was forgiven.

Ayhana is the sister of Hazrat Ali ibn Abu Talib two of her in-laws sought refuge with her. Hazrat Ali came in and said I shall kill them Ayhana had them hide in her place and then went to Prophet who was bathing and Fatima. She was cleaning him, from a container which still had marks of Dow. Prophet pbuh welcomed her and greeted her well and said what has brought you here she said the son of my mother has said, that he will kill the two men I have given protection. Prophet pbuh said we give protection to whom you have given protection Ayhana. Prophet gave the protection and spared the two lives of her in laws. And Ayhana saw Prophet pray 8 Rakat and each 2 Rakat separate.

The scholars have different opinion. These is 8 Rakat salat ul zuhr or salat ul Fatah. Some of them said this is the salat of conquest because no one else has said on this day other than Amr Hana. That was the day of opening Makkah some say, that is the salat ul Razbha. Because he prayed them at the time of Razbha.

ABU KOHAFA, the father of Abu Bakr. He told his younger daughter to take him on top of mountain. Qubaisi this is a mountain in Makkah. His sight was very weak. She took him on top of the mountain. He asked her daughter to describe him what she sees. She said I see a black mark. He told her those are the horsemen. He asked her what else you see, she said I see a man going to and fro. He said that is the man who gives instructions to cavalry then she said I see black mark dispensing. He said the orders have been given to cavalry let us rush back. They met the cavalry on the way. One of the soldier saw necklace in the neck of the daughter of Abu KOHAFA. He ripped it apart. Abu Bakr went and brought his father to meet the Prophet. When Prophet saw the old man Prophet told, Abu Bakr why did you not leave the Sheikh at home, I would be the one to go and meet him. Abu Bakr said this is more fitting that he should come to you rather than you go to see him. This shows that respect Prophet pbuh had for Abu Bakr and vice versa. Then Prophet pbuh put his hand on the chest of Abu Kohafa, he wiped his chest and said

Aslim, and he became Muslim. Then Prophet pbuh told them to change the color of his hair it was like a white line. Prophet said change the color but do not make it black. Therefore, the Ulma have derived the ruling that the old man should not dye his hair black but should change to any other color Hana color, which is red. Some scholars say if a person is young. They can change black, the sister of Abu Bakr she told her brother that her necklace was taken away.

Abu Bakr asked O' people has anyone taken the necklace of my sister, no one responded. She was told to seek Ajar from Allah. Because trust is little in the people today. Ibn Kathir says Abu Bakr said that because army was large probably he took it thinking it belongs to the people of war. So it is ghanima, Abu Bakr said there is little trust meaning for that day. In Bukhari Sharif, Osama bin Zahid asked the Prophet where are you going to spend the night. Did Akeel leave any property for us? Akeel had taken all property Prophet had nothing left. Then Prophet said the disbeliever does not inherit from believer, and believer does not inherit from disbeliever and this is the Hukum ruling regarding inheritance. The Prophet said, tomorrow we are going to spend the night Insha Allah in Khaif. The place they have vowed on disbelief. Prophet wants to replace the kufr by spending the night and bringing the spirit of Imaan to that place. Prophet pbuh when entered in Makkah. He chose the Moazan someone to call the Azaan, and particular choice was Bilal, Bilal had to Climb over Kaaba to deliver the Azaan. According to Younis bin Mukhera, Prophet ordered Bilal to give Azaan to anger the polytheist. Non-Muslim, because Bilal was seen as a slave now he is calling for salat and climbing over Kaaba to do it. Therefore, some comments made by the people of Makkah, showing their displeasure with fact that Bilal was the one who is calling the Azaan. One of them said, do you see that black crow, barking from on top of Kaaba like that derogatory terms made by Mushriqeen.

Prophet intended to show them that new era that Islam is bringing where class and cast of jahlia do not matter anymore and this Taqwa makes a person high or low. According to how close, They are to Allah, Their Taqwa it is following of Islam. According to Saeed bin Moeed that particular day when people entered into Makkah. It was not a day of celebration or a day of partying. When the people entered into Makkah upon conquest they remained in Takbir, Tahaleel, Tahaleel means saying, La Ilaha Illala, and takbir means Allah ho Akbar, and circling Kaaba. They had been away from Kaaba for a long time. Now they are pleased and happy Allah, allowed them to enter into Makkah and worship Allah according to rules of Islam, while Islam is domineering in Makkah, people were making tawaf around Kaaba all the way until morning. All night long there was Ibadat. Wherever you go in Makkah can see people making Takbir making Tahleel and making tawaf around Kaaba, House of Allah.

Abu Sufyan went back to his wife and said do you think this is from Allah. This affected even Quraish in Makkah, who little while ago, were kufr.

Abu Sufyan told his wife do you think this is from Allah she said yes this is from Allah. Then Abu Sufyan went to Prophet and Abu Sufyan was told by the Prophet. That you Abu Sufyan told your wife HINDHA do you think this is from Allah and she said yes. Said yes this is from Allah. Abu Sufyan said I testify that you are the messenger of Allah because no one overheard our conversation there was no one there other than me and my wife.

Prophet said as it is narrated in Bukhari Sharif, Allah has made MAKKAH a sanctuary holy place since Allah created heaven and earth. It is sanctuary made by Allah and it will remain as such until the judgment day, conflict was not made permissive before myself nor for anyone after me. And this only for a short time, in it, game may not be hunted its trees may not be cut down nor may it's vegetation be up rooted and items found in here will be finders after the announcement of that, Al-Abbas bin Abdul Mutlab wanted to exclude from this rule plant called (Alher) because people use it for its fragrance, tree has a nice smell to it. Also, because it is used as fuel for black smiths. Prophet said except for (Alher tree) Prophet allowed to cut down this tree but nothing else.

Makkah and Medina are AL haram they are sanctuary and hunting is not allowed there in and uprooting of trees are not allowed.

Hadith by Abu Huraira:

A long time after Fatah Makkah a delegation went to Movia, when Movia was CALIPHA that was during the month of Ramadan. Ramadan when people prepare food for each other. That also shows the social life of Sahaba and Tabyaeen. These were the delegations and rather to have their meal alone. They would invite each other.

Abu Huraira invited in his place. Abu Huraira would invite most people. One of the Tabyaeen wanted to invite Abu Huraira, they were not permanent but visitors so a visitor wanted to invite Abu Huraira. He says I prepared the food and then met Abu Huraira and told him invitation is at my place to night. Abu Huraira said, you beat me to it, visitor said yes. Abu Huraira when arrived he wanted to make it a beneficial gathering.

He said shouldn't I tell you Hadith which belongs to you O' people of Ansar. He talked about the story of the conquest of Makkah. He said, when Prophet pbuh came to Makkah, he sent Zubair, on one of the two wings of the army and Khalid bin Waleed commanding the other wing of the army. Abu Abada was commanding the foot soldiers, so they entered into Makkah, Prophet saw me Abu Huraira, Prophet called me and I said present. Prophet said, no one but Ansar should come to me. This was a private gathering Prophet wanted to have with Ansar. Abu Huraira went and called Ansar. They came and surrounded the Prophet from every direction. Prophet told them that Quraish have gathered a force from outside Makkah to fight but they did not risk themselves going into the fight. Quraish mobilized this force and said if they win then we shall join in. If they lose then we are safe. One cannot win this way, if you do not want to participate they had no hope of winning. They were hiding and sending other army to fight. Those people who were supposed to fight for Quraish. They were defeated Prophet said, ordered to fight these people many of them were killed and then the fighting stopped. They ended up meeting on Safa when they met Prophet. Prophet said, whoever enters the house of Abu Sufyan he is safe Prophet announced that but the house of Abu Sufyan is not big enough to house all of the Quraish. Prophet wanted to give this honor to Abu Sufyan to draw him closer to Islam, but also, whoever is seen in the streets he will be killed like curfew. No one is allowed to leave his home. After this Ansar felt that Prophet is back in Makkah in his home he might leave them. Now he is with his clan and might stay behind with his relatives. May be the end. But Prophet called them and asked them did you think like that or said so Ansar said yes. Prophet said I am the servant of Allah and his messenger I made Hijra to Allah and to you, life is with you and death is with you. Ansar they came crying to Prophet and said, we only said, what we said because of our eagerness and our desire to have you with us. We love Allah and his messenger Prophet said, Allah and his messenger believe you.

SUFWAN BIN OMIA was one of the leaders of Quraish he fled, because he thought he has done so much against Islam so Prophet will kill him Amer bin Wahab. A close friend of Safwan. Remember Safwan sent Amer bin Wahab to assassinate the Prophet in Medina when he arrived in Medina. Prophet told him of his plan that he was there to kill the Prophet and he was shocked Prophet knew the details of his plan and he ended up becoming Muslim. Now Amer ibn Wahab heard about Safwan running away he followed him. Safwan went to Jeddah to ride a boat and go to Yemen.

Amer bin Wahab told Safwan, I have come to you from Prophet, Amer bin Wahab met Prophet and said Safwan bin Omea is one of the Quraish leader therefore he should be granted immunity. Prophet said, I shall give him immunity, Ameer bin Wahab said, give me a token then Prophet gave him his turban. That was a sign that Prophet is giving Safwan bin Omea, immunity Ameer bin Wahab took the turban and went to Safwan and Safwan said stay away from me. Ameer said, I have come to you from most merciful and compassionate man, and most forgiving. His kingdom, his honor is yours, he is telling him he is your relative whatever good happens to Prophet is good happens to you. And Prophet has given you immunity Safwan said you are lying but then he produced the turban of Prophet. So Safwan came back with Ameer bin Wahab. Safwan went to Prophet and said, this man is saying that you have forgiven me and given me immunity. Prophet said yes, Safwan bin Omea said give me two months to think before I become Muslim Prophet gave him four months. Safwan bin Omea eventually became Muslim. Prophet has destroyed the idols and kufr of Makkah. Prophet wanted to spread the sovereignty of Islam in surrounding areas.

KHALID BIN WALEED went to a tribe close to Makkah. This is in Bukhari Sharif, Prophet pbuh sent Khalid bin Waleed to Bini Jzaima. He invited them to Islam, they were not educated enough to say we become Muslim. Quraish, kufr, whenever someone became Muslim, called him subbaha that was in the time of jahlia it was a derogatory term, against anyone who would become Muslim. Khalid bin Waleed told them to become Muslim. They said subbaha. In fact, they wanted to become Muslim but were not learned enough to use the term Islamna They had picked up that word and were repeating it. Khalid bin WALEED Killed them and captured some and handed one prisoner to each fighter in his army. Then Khalid bin Waleed gave instructions to his army to execute his prisoners Abdullah bin Umar was in this army and said, in the name of Allah I am not going to kill my prisoner, and none of my companions are going to kill theirs.

Abdullah bin Umar saw, this was a clear mistake on part of Khalid bin Waleed. These people have become Muslim and then they are killed, and taken prisoners, now ordered to kill them, I am not going to do it. It was clear disobedienous of the orders of the Ameer the leader, Abdullah bin Umar, knows that Ameer had to be followed but also knows that we should follow the orders of the Ameer, when it is Halal If it is not Halal, then there is no obedience. Although it is considered as mutiny. Abdullah bin Umar not only he did not obey but also stopped other people with him. The issue was raised with Prophet pbuh. Prophet told Abdullah bin Umar what you have done is correct. Prophet approved Abdullah bin Umar in his disobedienous to the Ameer. Then Prophet pbuh raised his hand and said, O' Allah I declare that I am free of what Khalid has done. Prophet made it clear that what Khalid has done is wrong. These people should not have been killed.

The lesson is that we should not follow any illegal orders. Another incident there was a man among them who did not really belong to that tribe but he was there because his woman was from that tribe that was the only reason, he was arrested his hands were tied up, he asked the guard that he wanted to speak to a woman (he pointed). Asked Muslim guard to allow him to have a final word with the woman and then do whatever you want. Muslim allowed him, he went and spoke to women to become Muslim before death she agreed. Then they were killed (mistake) when story was told to Prophet. Prophet there was not a merciful man among you and sent Hazrat Ali to pay blood money for all those who were killed. Because they were all Muslim. They made a mistake by saying Sabha na in fact they went Islam na. They were paid for everything. Hazrat Ali paid them even for their belonging which were missing. There was some money left over Hazrat Ali gave them just in case. This is how Prophet dealt with this situation. These were Muslims killed by mistake were paid blood money.

Ibn Kathir says, Khalid bin Waleed killed many and also killed prisoners. But nevertheless, Prophet pbuh did not sack him from his position. But Prophet kept on appointing Khalid bin Waleed in responsible positions as Ameer. Even Prophet cleared Khalid from what had happened, and Prophet paid for mistakes of Khalid either in blood or wealth. In this the opinion of one of the scholars is that when an Imam makes a mistake money is not paid from his pocket but from the treasury of the state. Then he says that is why Abu Bakr Siddique did not change him after becoming Khalifa in the days of Rida. Apostasy, also Abu Bakr, excused him when he, Khalid, killed Malik bin Manjra, who was supposedly Muslim and took over his wife (married her) I shall explain this in detail when I shall bring to you the life of Abu Bakr Siddique. Umar bin Khattab was angry with Khalid bin Waleed and advised Abu Bakr to change him. Because his sword is swear powerful. Abu Bakr said I am not going to shied a sword which was given by the messenger of Allah against mushriqeen. This was a sword drawn by Allah on kufr. I am not going to put it down.

Therefore, we can learn from this the Sunna, in dealing with in stakes in battle. These were Muslims and were compensated for the mistake of Khalid bin Waleed. He was not imprisoned. He was not fired from his position, why? The reason is that he did not assume them to be Muslims. But if a leader kills knowingly then that is a different situation.

The issue was clear with Abdullah bin Umar but not with Khalid bin Waleed and nobody should assume that Khalid bin Waleed killed them believing that they were Muslims. That is impossible and that is not the case. Khalid bin Waleed considered them to be kufr. A Muslim is never handed over to non-Muslims and is never betrayed. Because Prophet pbuh says Muslim is a brother of a Muslim. A brother does not give him nor he betrays him nor press him. Prophet disagreed with that and paid blood money.

Prophet pbuh sent Khalid bin Waleed to destroy AlUZA the big idol. AlUZA was one of the great God of mushriqeen in those days. These are the famous Aluza, Hubal, Idols they belonged to mushriqeen. Prophet pbuh destroyed the false Gods surrounding Kaaba. Now Prophet pbuh wants to destroy Aluza, which was outside of Mecca Khalid bin Waleed went there and the custodians of al- uza ran away. They did not stand to fight. In fact, one responsible for Aluza put sword around the neck of Aluza and told Aluza to defend himself against Khalid and said if you do not defend yourself then you deserve what will happen to you Khalid bin Waleed came to Uza and destroyed it. Khalid destroyed the idol when this narration and came back (this narration is in Biaky). Prophet asked Khalid, what did he do? Khalid bin Waleed answered I destroyed Al-Uza. Prophet pbuh told him you did not destroy it. Did nothing, go back. Khalid bin Waleed went back and now he found a necked woman her hair were messed up and she was throwing dirt on herself and she was yelling. Khalid bin Waleed killed her with his sword, and when went back. Prophet asked him what did he do?. Khalid replied I found a naked woman and I executed her, Prophet said, that was Al-Uza. You have killed her. So, Al-Uza was some kind of jinn or Satin. It was idol from outside but a jinn or Satin living inside this Idol, and that Satin came out in the form of this necked woman, when Khalid bin Waleed executed her that was the end of Al-Uza.

There were some kind of superstitions because some spirit was living there. That jinn or Satin played a role of deceiving people. Prophet pbuh said, there will be no more Al-Uza after this day.

Prophet pbuh stayed in Makkah for 18 days after conquest and in some narrations 19 days. During this period Prophet did not fast and shortened salah. Some scholars have taken the ruling from this that the travelers can break the fast and shortened the salat. 18 days is in Bukhari Sharif but there is a difference of opinion. Some say for 3 days, but ibn Tamia says as long as you are traveling you can shortened the salah.

AN OTHER INCIDENT, a woman from Bani Makhzum who was caught stealing. Bani Makhzum are prominent family in Quraish. Family of Khalid bin Waleed leaders of society. This was a noble woman committed the act of steeling. Prophet ordered the punishment of cutting the hand to be applied to her (it says hands but they start with cutting a finger from hand). Her people and Quraish they were overly concerned about that they were used to the fact that weak and slaves, people who do not have protection, they are punished. But if one belongs to nobility then there are way outs. Sort out a deal find a way out of that so they appealed against the punishment people wanted somebody to speak to Prophet the person they choose was the son of Zahid bin Harsa, O' Sama, ALLAH he pleased with him. They knew O' Sama is awfully close to Prophet. Prophet used to love his father greatly and used to love O' Sama. Zahid bin Harsa was a martyr in the battle of Motha. Because of this strong relationship, Osama was chosen to speak to Prophet. The face of Prophet pbuh changed and said you speak to me in Hudood for punishment among the punishment of Allah Osama said, O Prophet I seek my forgiveness on that day Prophet stood and gave Khutbah. Delivered a speech.

Prophet pbuh after praising Allah said, the thing that destroyed people before you is that when the noble men among them feel that they will leave him (the Prophet) and the weak among them steels they would establish the punishment against them. In the name of Allah my soul is in his hand if Fatima the daughter of Muhammad PBUH would steel I shall cut her hand, and Prophet ordered that hand of that woman be cut.

HADITH, that woman repented after that and got married. Aysha would say that she would visit me if she wanted anything from Prophet and I would speak to Prophet on her behalf. Prophet is giving us a law that governs the men, if a particular society there are double standards justice where the weak are punished while the strong go free Allah will destroy such a society.

There is a Hadith to apply Hudood of Allah is better than rain of 40 days.

Before the conquest of MAKKAH, Hijra was mandatory after conquest of Makkah people would come to Prophet ask about Hijra. Prophet would say there is no more Hijra. Hijra is over and people who did it will receive the ajar, reward. Now Jehad-Fi-Sabil Allah, Bukhari Sharif.

IBN KATHIR, hadith; Amr bin Muslma belonged to another tribe not from MAKKAH. He says, whenever the travelers pass by we ask them about this man. News about the Prophet was all over Arabia, and that was the news of the day, any news. They reply that the Prophet claims that Allah has sent him and receives revelation these travelers would mention some of the Ayat from Quran Amr bin Muslma was a child at that time he would heir this conversation and would memorize the Ayat of Quran. Even though the people were non-Muslim at that time, people although non-Muslim but were carrying the Ayat of Quran, for away but that was news for them that Prophet pbuh received this. That was news the words of Quran would enter into his heart and brain and would stay there. The Arabs were waiting for the conquest of Makkah and to become Muslim Arab knew that Quraish and Muslim two parties were at war, and they were waiting to see the results. That is the situation with many people they do not search for the truth but are waiting for the winner, and they follow that victorious party.

People, Arab, would say it if the Prophet wins against these people, then he is a messenger and truthful. But this is not a correct attitude. But that is what people used to say. HADITH; from Prophet that there are some Prophets who do not have any followers. Does that make them wrong? No. There is Hadith; Prophet says on the Day of Judgment there will be prophets with different quantities of followers like 10, 20, 3, 1 and non-followers. That does not mean that they did not know how to invite people to Islam they knew.

Allah says you do not guide whoever you want but that is Allah who guides. The Prophet who has no followers that is the Qadr of Allah but he did his job in conveying the message. Any way they Arab waited and Muslims defeated Quraish, obviously people who accepted Islam earlier their reward and their level in the eyes of Allah is much higher than those who became Muslim after the victories of Islam it is in Quran that people who accepted Islam before the conquest of Makkah. Their status is higher than those who accepted Islam afterwards, people who spent and fought Fi-Sabeel Allah have much higher status. Amr bin Muslma said, when Prophet opened Makkah. Every tribe was rushing to become Muslim. He says my father became Muslim before my people, when he came back he said I came to you from the messenger of Allah. He is truly a messenger of Allah. He told us to pray salat different salat at different times. Prophet gave the father of Amr bin Muslma, instructions how to pray when the time of salat approaches one of you should give Azan and the one who knows more Quran should be Imam.

When they searched Amr bin Muslma says no one knew Quran more than me Amr bin Muslma, because what I learned from travelers. They made me their Imam. He was a child under 10 and became Imam. He knew that most Quran among them. Amr bin Muslma says I would lead them in salat. I was wearing a barda. A square garment and he says when I made Sajood this garment was too short, and his behind would show. One woman said would you not cover your buts from us.

Another narration, that barda, had a big tear from behind and when in Sajood it would show. The woman made embarrassing statement, but he was a child. Then they bought a new robe shirt. Imam was incredibly happy with that Amr bin Muslma said nothing has made me happy as that shirt did. This is the end of Fatah Makkah. This hadith is in Bukhari Sharif. The messenger of Allah opened Makkah the strongest resistance. Now there was another tribe, which held prominence in the land of Hijaz. In fact, when kufr were questioning the Prophethood of Muhammad PBUH. They came up with suggestion that who should be the Prophet why this Quran was not revealed on one man from two villages. What they mean by two villages was Makkah and Taif. The tribe of Saqeef lived there. Tribe of Soqeef are branch of Auazam. Auazam is a big mother tribe and then many such tribes, that descend from Auazam. They used to see themselves prominent and important like Quraish. There was some sort of competition between the two tribes. Because of jahlia. They did not want a man from Quraish to take over their land and rule over them. Now this is what they saw coming. They felt since Prophet has opened Makkah. Now we are going to be next. Taif was awfully close also they had a savior history, how they treated the Prophet. When Prophet PBUH went to them to invite them to Islam. That was awfully bad evil they showed no generosity. The way they treated the Prophet was bad even *THE BATTLE OF HONNAINE,* by the standards of that time. That was an exceedingly difficult day on the Prophet PBUH.

Malik bin Ouhf, a nasery. He tried to mobilize various tribes of Auazam. Some of the tribes accepted his call some did not. However, he managed to build up a very strong coalition powerful strong united army. These were good fighters. Prophet heard this news and marched out of Makkah an army of 12000 strong. 10000 the original army came to Makkah and 2000 more Talqa. The released one, they were those whom Prophet released on the day of conquest of Makkah. People of Makkah became Muslim. The Muslim army was large Hazrat Abu Bakr and some others said, we are not going to defeated due to the lack of numbers. Our numbers are great. But soon you will see the consequence of this belief.

When Malik brought out his army and they set out. They were accompanied with an incredibly wise old man. This man was incredibly famous. A man well known a knight. A fighter in his youth and a very prominent poet among the Arabs. His name is Dreed ibn Sama. He was blind at that time, He was old and frail. A conversation between Dreed and Malik. Dareed asked where we are. Response we are in Oates. He Dreed said it is a fine place for cavalry. Neither hilly with rocks nor a soft ground. He liked the location. Then he said why is it that I heir grunting of camels the braying of donkeys the bleeping of sheep and crying of babies.

Malik bin Ouhf what he had done, he brought along with the army, their women, their children their cattle's, almost everything. The reason for this was that he though this will prevent the army from running away. Because if they run away they will lose everything and Muslims will take over. They told the old man this is what Malik did he brought all his wealth. The wisdom of an old warrior is showing through this conversation Dreed ibn Sama, but Malik a young man who wants victory for himself. He is taking large and unnecessary risk.

O' Malik this day has great consequences for feature. This day will determine our feature, why did you do? What you have done. Malik said, I brought them with us so every man will fight for his family and his wealth.

He said you sheep grazer, anything would return in retreat. If the battle is to go well it will be only men with swords and lances they will do you good. If the battle goes bad it will be disgrace for you your family and your wealth anyway. He said nothing will turn him back a man who is in retreat. They will not think of anything they will just flee away.

There were two other tribes of Auazam club and CAB, what happened to them? None of them came then the old man said, skill and courage are absent. If it were a day of fine deeds, cab and clab would not have missed it. The old man is saying, I wish you had done the same as them. Then he said who is with you, they said Auf bin Amr and bin Amr, two tribes, old man said they would not do well nor any harm. Then he said to Malik you have not done well by sending main force of Auazam in front of cavalry. He though as suicide. Then he gave his recommendation the old man said O' Malik, take away the families and cattle to the high land of Auazam take them to mountains of our land and then meet the appestats. This is the name they used to call the Muslims. Meet the appestats on horse backs. If it is for you than the rest would come, if it is against you, then you have at least protected your families and your wealth.

Malik responded in the name of Allah, I am not going to do that you are an old man and your knowledge is becoming old. He said, O' Auazam follow me or I am going to jump on the sword. He had sword stuck in the ground with blade pointing upwards. He meant he will kill himself. Malik did not want Dreed to have any involvement. Dreed's opinion was rejected, and he made it clear that I am not part of this and not responsible for consequences. O' men, army when you see the enemy brake the sheeds and attack them as one man i.e., united. All of you attack at the same time.

Prophet pbuh had sent Abdullah bin Kharj to gather intelligence for Muslim army. Abdullah bin Kharj came back and told the Prophet PBUH what he saw, he infiltrated the enemy army, brought the number of the army. He saw family's cattle of Auazam army. He reported back Umar bin Khattab did not like what he heard so he rejected it. Abdullah bin Kharj told him, you are rejecting the truth. Prophet pbuh said to Umar you were once misguided and Allah guided you.

Prophet wanted additional arms and spoke to Safwan bin Omea, Safwan one of the leader of Quraish and wealthy among them. He had good pile up of weapons. Prophet pbuh asked him to give weapons. Safwan asked the Prophet are you taking them, by force or you are barrowing them. Prophet pbuh said, no I am barrowing them and I shall return them to you. Safwan agreed, just remember Safwan is still non-Muslim. But he is a citizen of Muslim state. After the battle, some pieces were lost. Prophet pbuh gave him back his weapons and also said I can pay you for the missing weapons. Safwan said no do not do that, because I have found in my heart what I did not have before? Safwan is talking about Islam, that he is closer to Islam and closer to Allah. He refused to take compensation for the missing pieces, which were lost.

One the way Muslims passed by a tree. Mushriqeen used to hang their swords on this tree to get Burka blessing this was one of the rituals of Jahlia. But in Muslim army there were some new Muslims. They did not know about Muslim faith or belief. They said O' messenger of Allah, we would like to have something similar for blessing like the non-Muslims. Prophet pbuh said, in the name of Allah my soul is in his hands, you have said something similar as the people of Moses. O' Moses, we want to have a God as they have God Bani Israel when they crossed the sea, they asked Moses, they want to have Gods like the Mushriqeen. Allah says Moses told them you are ignorant people. These are the ways of the past; you will follow them one by one. You will follow the ways of disbelievers before you. The difference is that the evil in the Umma of Bani Israel was prevalent it overcome the good and became dominant while with the Umma of Muhammad PBUH. They will never cease (stop) the people on the truth or for holding firm to the religion of Allah and this is how, the religion of Allah will carry on until the Day of Judgment.

Prophet pbuh wanted someone to guard them this night. Prophet said who will be our guard this night one of the companion. Abu Arkab. The Prophet PBUH told him right, He was on horseback he came to Prophet. Prophet pbuh told him face this valley or mountain pass until you reach the end of it and then Prophet told him that we do not want to be taken by surprise from your direction. This is your responsibility this is your part; this is your duty we do not want to be attacked from your part (Every Muslim should be protecting Islam from his direction).

In the morning, this narration is from Abu Dawood. Prophet pbuh went to Muslma to pray Fajr. He prayed 2 Rakat then the Prophet said, how you felt about night. Answer came no nothing then Prophet started salat Fajr while Prophet was in salat. The Prophet was looking towards the valley when finished the Prophet PBUH said, bare the glad, tiding your knight has arrived the Sahaba kept on staring towards trees and couldn't see anything. Prophet pbuh saw first the knight (fighter) then Sahaba saw his movements, he was on horse. He came to Prophet gave salaam, and said I was in the place where you instructed me and in the morning I saw from the top of two mountains and I did not see anyone. Did you descend at any time, knight answered no only for prayer and for the call of nature? Prophet told him ALLAH will grant you Jannah and you do not have to do anything more. This is a great reward for guarding.

Fi-Sabil Allah. It was a very hot day; they took nap wherever they could find shade under the trees. Prophet pbuh called Bilal bin Rabia. He stood up from a shade of a tree. This shade was like a shade of a bird. Shade was useless, but this was the climate. They had on that day. Army marched on in this mountain terrain, hat and rough terrain.

They the Muslim army, was taken by surprise and shocked by this sudden attack from horse men of Auazam right from front. Attack by archers of Auazam from the sides. It says in the books of seerah that people of Auazam were good archers, arrows were falling on Muslims from each direction and the horses were attacking from the front. Muslim army was caught by surprise, the front of the army was Banu Sleen, a tribe next to Medina, they retreated, and they could not handle the shock, attack. They started fleeing from the battlefield then behind them were Atlqa. The ones who were released (new Muslims) their trust Tawaqal on Allah was weak they also retreated they numbered 2,000 and then it says in the narration that camels were stumbling on one another.

It was very chaotic (no discipline) stage. Camels were crowding and the alignment of the army had gone. The organization of different battalion had gone. There were two groups in front and they were fleeing from their positions and chaos in the army and everybody was fleeing away.

Prophet pbuh was calling them, where to O' people, come to me, I am the messenger of Allah, I am the messenger of Allah, I am Muhammad the son of Abdullah. The narrator of the Hadith. Jabbar Abdullah says, Prophet is calling them to no avail, they are running away Abu Sufyan, when he saw this, said, the defeat will not end except at the sea, meaning, they are going to carry on running away until they reach to the sea. And Qala bin Haml said, the magic is gone. Magic of Muhammad worked until this day. But this is the end of magic. No more magic. These new Muslims when they saw what was happening they last their trust in truth. They saw that Muslims are defeated. Safwan a non-Muslim until now, did not like what he saw and said I rather be ruled by the man from Quraish. Rather than by people of Auazam although non-Muslim but held better position than Abu Sufyan and

Qala ibn Haml. After having heard their remarks he said, I rather have Muhammad PBUH win than the Badoo of Auazam. There was some background between Quraish and people of Soqeef.

Salma bin Aqwa. Narrates this is in Bukhari Sharif. He said, when retreat started, I was fleeing running away we have spoken about Salma bin Aqwa more than once. He was brave hero, of Islam. But now he is fleeing we have talked about the story of Zulqraj, where he fought the mushriqeen alone. We have talked when Prophet pbuh praised him. Best of our soldiers on foot. Salma bin Aqwa, we are talking about the best fighters not someone who is weak. Salma bin Aqwa, said, I was fleeing, I had two garments on me and they were united, I tide them together and started running, I passed the Prophet. Prophet pbuh when he saw me said, the son of Aqwa has seen something terrifying, frightening. Prophet saw the face of Salma and saw the way he was running. It was a dayer situation. It was difficult situation. The entire world around you could he in a mess. Allah can give you tranquility and can give peace in the heart even in difficult times like this. on the other hand, things could be great around you things could be peaceful. Nevertheless, Allah will put exactly opposite feeling in the heart feeling of despair depression one cannot judge the affairs from outside but the judgment is based on what is in the hearts.

Ladies and gents if we follow the rules of Allah even though we go through some moments of difficulty. But Allah says after difficulty there is ease, peace, with difficulty comes ease, it is a promise from Allah.

In the battle of Badr the first battle between Muslims and kufr. At first it was difficult it was a difficult moment for Muslims. They did not know what will be the outcome. What they were seeing the enemy more in numbers and better in preparations and Muslims were few. At that difficult time even though difficult feelings in the heart, nevertheless Allah says and then slumber came to them and they slept peace fully, they felt feelings of drowsiness and sleepy in the difficult time, and here in the battle of Honaine.

We have seen the situation with Salma and also Prophet pbuh was calling and no response, everybody was running away.

After this difficulty what happened?

Allah says, Allah revealed tranquility on the messenger of Allah and on the believers and supported them with soldiers which they did not see what are the soldiers of ALLAH. Angels, there is one narration we saw a black cloud falling from the sky when it landed on the ground we saw numerous ants, like a carpet of ants and we thought these are the angels came from Allah. (ALLAH knows best) How authentic this might be, it could mean anything?

But regardless, Allah says we have provided than with soldiers. This changed the situation and it changed in a way which is unimaginable as we know what Abu Sufyan said and what Qala ibn Haml said and we have seen the response of the Sahaba, they fled only a small number of Sahaba remained with Prophet officially only few, Al-Abbas. Sufyan bin Harris and one of the sons of Al-Abbas bin Abdul Mutlab and Ayman the son of Umma Ayman who was the nurse of Prophet, only these were surrounding Prophet, and holding on to his mule rest had fled from their location.

At this particular situation Prophet told Al-Abbas because his voice was very powerful. Prophet told him to call Al-Ansar. So, Al-Abbas bin Abdul Mutlab made his call to Al- Ansar and then Prophet pbuh told Al-Abbas to specify Al-Kharj so he called Al-Kharj, they were special fighters strong powerful narrator says they turned around like cows in groups, and they surrounded Prophet. pbuh

Prophet pbuh was surrounded by 100 men. These 100 men stood in front of an army some people say 40,000 and in another narration 20,000 any way the number was huge. 100 standing in front of army of that size. The Prophet PBUH was marching ahead alone and Hazrat Abbas says we were pulling his mule to slow him down. Prophet was facing this army. It is said that there was one man from Auazam carrying an exceptionally long spear on top of the spear there was a banner. If he is heading that army his spear will be used and if has companions reach with him then he would raise it up as a banner. This front row of the army of Auazam was crushing the Muslim army. They were just ruling over Muslim army. Now Prophet is facing them alone and Al-Abbas is saying that we are trying to pull-back his mule. Until Prophet had number around him between 80 to 100. This is when the real fighting started. Before this there was no real fighting. It was initial shocking attack where Banu Sleen and Atlaqa fled and chaos started they were slammed by arrows from every direction but now real fighting with swords began.

Prophet pbuh said now the fire of battle is waging. This is when the fire is becoming hot. Then Prophet staired and prayed and with his blessed hand took a handful of dirt and threw it in the air towards the direction of Auazam and said this hand full of dirt in the hands of Prophet was a soldier of Allah. Because it is narrated that every enemy soldier felt something in his eyes. And also, they had feelings in their hearts. One of the fighter who became Muslim later on would describe the feeling that they had when Prophet threw single hand full of dirt towards them. When that man was asked how did you feel? He said take rocks and throw them in iron pan and you will hear all that clattering sound. This is how we felt inside. This clattering sound this terror is what we felt in our inside. HADITH. Imam Ahmad stated that relating to him by Abdul Wahab bin Ziyad and others Abdullah bin Masood from his father Abdullah bin Masood says, I was present with the messenger of Allah, at the battle of Honnaine. The men retreated from him 80 of Ansar and Mahajroon remained with him. We drew back some 80 feet but we did not turn our backs to the enemy. These men upon whom Allah sent tranquility. The Prophet still going forward on his mule, which Sheard to one side, he slipped out of his saddle, I called out to him up you get, May Allah raise you up. He replied get me a hand full of dust with this he struck them on their faces and filled their mouth. Then he asked where are the mahajreen and Ansar. They are close by I replied call for them. He said, they came with their swords in their right hands shining like stars. Then the mushriqeen turned their backs in retreat. This is the story by Abdullah bin Masood. The day of the battle of Honnaine.

Some events that occurred in the battle of Honnaine, Prophet said, whoever kills or defeat enemy gets his possessions. Abu Qatadah, this narration is in Bukhari Sharif and also in other books, Abu Qatadah says, one Mushriq, who raised his hand to strike a Muslim, I came from behind and attacked with my sword the sword dug deep into the armor. The blow was strong enough to go through the armor and dig into his shoulder. The man turned around and embraced me so hard that I felt death immensely powerful embrace of this man. But then he full down dead. Then the retreat occurred, I saw Umar bin Khattab and I said, what is happening? Umar bin Khattab said this is the decree of Allah.

When Prophet announced that the one who kills he will keep the possession of this man. Abu Qatadha says I was scarring for a witness that I killed that man. But nobody came forward to witness that. He did it again, no one stood up. He asked for third time, who will give witness. But no one gave witness. Then one man from Quraish stood up and said O' Prophet I am the person who took those possession. Ask Abu Qatadha to allow me to keep them.

Abu Bakr Siddique interfered and said, no, in the name of Allah we are not going to have a lion amongst lions to loose and give it to a hyenas from Quraish, Abu Bakr Siddique is talking about Abu Qatadha and describing him as a lion and Abu Qatadha is a lion we have talked about him. Abu Bakr does not want Abu Qatadha to loose for the sake of perhaps a new Muslim and Abu Bakr called him a hainnoha. Eventually Abu Qatadha took his possession Abu Qatadha says he sold that and bought date palms (only some) and he says that was the first wealth I owned in Islam. Abu Qatadha did not have any property and the first property came through ghanima. Abu Tla saw his wife Umma Saleem carrying a dagger asked what is this she said I am going to rip open any kufr who comes near me. Abu Tla said, O' Prophet did you hear what she said, Prophet laughed. Then she said, O' Prophet kill all those released ones, they were the reason for our defeat. She is talking about new Muslim from Makkah, Quraish, Prophet pbuh said Allah has taken care of us we do not need to kill anyone. There was a group of men, Prophet pbuh asked what is this? there was a dead woman, killed by Khalid bin Waleed. Prophet pbuh said this woman was not in combat (fighting) Prophet pbuh sent a message to Khalid bin Waleed. Not to kill women children or sick and old people. This is the order for intentional killing. We close this with the Aya. This was revealed at the battle of Honnaine, the name of the place. Auazam is a tribe. Translation, Certainly, Allah did help you in many battlefields on the day of Honnaine behold, the great numbers availed you not and you turned back in retreat. You felt confident with great numbers and that is where the problem is. If we feel that we shall win because of our numbers or training or technology, arms we are mistaken, Muslim win because Allah helps them to win if we attribute winning to anything other than Allah. We will be defeated. The help of Allah will not be with us.

What counts, Imaan trust in Allah, Tawaqal dependence on Allah. Allah says; the great numbers did nothing for you, even the land became too constrained for you. You had to flee, then Allah pore his calm on his messenger and on the believers and sent down forces which you did not see. Allah punished the non-believers. Thus, Allah rewards. The people of Auazam were defeated by the core group of the Muslim army. The total Muslim army was 12,000 but after big retreat, the one who stood fast, the number was 80 to 100 Sahaba these were a core group, who never retreated. Only moved forward. These are the Messenger of Allah, his uncle, his cousin and two or three other men next to them who were guarding the prophet pbuh, then the prophet pbuh called for Ansar and then for Al Kheraj and then called for Banu Najjar. These were the supporters of the prophet throughout. Now defended the prophet and defeated the huge army. Their leader Malik bin Ouf and main army retreated to Taife. Taife was a fortified city, they went in and closed the doors. Another branch of the army went to a place called O'TAS. The prophet pbuh, also split his army. Major body led by the prophet fallowed Malik bin Ouf to Taife, while a smaller group led by Abu Amer ul SHARI went to O'TAS, a smaller Suriya to attack disbelievers who went to O'TAS.

Dreed bin USMA, the old and blind man, he went with their army. He was incredibly old and Well-known poet, also very experienced and seasoned fighter. He had a discussion with Malik bin Ouf, where he told Malik, that it is a mistake to bring out the families and wealth, also told that nothing will bring back a man who is retreating. It eventually turned out that the words of Dreed were true. Dreed bin USMA was with a group who went to O'TAS, one of the member of Muslim army, his name is Rubia bin Raffah, he found a camel with a compartment on it, which is usually used for women. He was leading this camel thinking, there is a woman in the hood. He took that as captive, when he had the camel kneel down, he looked inside the compartment, to his amazement that was not a woman but an old man. He pulled out the old man, old man asked him what you want to do with me? He said I want to kill you. He old man asked, who are you? He said I am Rubia bin Raffa. Then he pulled out his sword and struck Dreed bin Usma, strike was not fatal Dreed bin Asma told him your mother did not arm you night, and then said take my sword from the saddle and hit over the spine and below the skull, that is how I used to strike men, and when you go back to your mother, tell her I killed Dreed bin Asma. I swear, many times I defended your women. Dreed bin Asma is talking to a man who is also from Auazam. But Dreed is non-Muslim and other follow is Muslim. Dreed is telling him, there have been days when I fought and defended your women. But other is a young man does not know any history.

He struck him as he was told and Dreed fell down dead, when he fell his body parts were exposed this young man said the skin higher between his thighs was like a apartment from having ridden his horse bare back often we do not know the Qadr of Allah. Look at Hazrat Abu Talib who supported Prophet, all his life and died as non-believer, and then person like Abu Sufyan who was fighting Prophet all his life dies as a believer at an old age.

Here we have Malik bin Auf who is the one who caused this disaster on the people of Auazam who insisted to follow his wrong opinion rejected the opinion of Dreed bin Asma, which was wiser, Malik bin Auf ends up becoming Muslim and we shall talk about this and Dreed bin Asma with good opinion dies as disbeliever. That with good opinion dies as disbeliever. That young man went to his mother and told her what Dreed said, told his mother I killed Dreed bin Asma. She said I swear he freed three of your mothers. Abu Ahr the leader of Syria. He was shat in his knee Abu Mal Ashari came and said, O' my uncle who shat you. Abu Ahr pointed the man who shat him. This is in Bukhari Sharif and Muslim Sharif followed the man that man when he realized that he is being followed he fled. Abu Mosul is running behind him and telling him are you not ashamed of yourself wouldn't you stand and fight. Are you not Arab man, when he heard these challenging words? He turned around and came to fight Abu Mosul. They turned around and came to fight Abu Mosul. They exchanged few blows and he was killed Abu Mosul killed this man and went back to his uncle Abu Ahr and told him O' my uncle I have killed the man who shat you. Abu Mosul pulled the arrow out bleeding increased Abu Ahr knew he was dying. He said give my Salam to Prophet and ask him to ask Allah to forgive me and then he passed away. Abu Mosul went to Prophet and told him the story. Prophet was sleeping on a bed made by ropes, made from dry leaves of date palms, there was no mattress on it. When Prophet wake up Abu Mosul could clearly see the rope marks on the side and back of Prophet. Prophet asked for some water made Wazu, and then raised his hands Abu Mosul could see the arm pits of Prophet was deeply involved in his prayer and said O' Allah forgive this servant of yours, O' Allah forgive the sins of your servant Abu Ahr, and make him above many of your creation, that was a great dua, made by Prophet for Abu Ahr, shaheed on the day of judgment. A great honor that is what matters the Day of Judgment.

A Badoo made Dua, O' Allah make my deeds the best the last of them and make the best of my day the day I meet you. This is important because the most important day is the Day of Judgment. That is equal to all of our days. The Day of Judgment is 50,000 years long. Best payer. When Abu Mosul saw Prophet making this dua for his uncle. Abu Mosul wanted to take advantage of this great opportunity that opened up for him. He said, Prophet make dua for me. Prophet said O' Allah forgive Abdullah bin Qais. His real name, O' Allah forgive the sins of Abdullah bin Qais. O' Allah give him a noble entrance on the Day of Judgment. Narrator of the Hadith, Abu Burda say, one due for Abu Ahr and one Dua for Abu Mosul. This is the story of Oates.

We move on to the two main armies. The Book of Seerah: Prophet put an extremely strict sage on Taif. Ibn Shaam says, student of Ibn Ishaque sealer and righter of Seerah. He ibn Shaam says I was told by the one I trust. The first one in Islam used and threw catapult. Is the Prophet PBUH. This was an equipment that was used to hurled stones at the walls of Taif. This was the first time it was used when stones are thrown at the wall or inside the fort, it is not known where the stone hits, and we are talking about the whole city inside there walls. It can hit anywhere, it could cause collateral damage which is not originally intended stone can hit women, children, although this is not the intention. It is out of sight, where it falls. It is not like arrows which one can target. But catapulting is like modern weapons.

Although, capital was being used they did not surrender and had their archers and the wall and in one narration Muslims army was within range. Therefore, they had to move and go ant of their range.

Then Sahaba used another technique to have a wooden box that will protect from arrows and would reach to the wall.

But people of Taif had a defense to it, they would use hat iron pieces to through at wooden boxes and burn the wood. This weapon was proving in effective and Sahaba had to retreat. At that time Prophet ordered to cut down great grape orchards and some were cut down. This similar when there was siege of Nuna deer well, when enemy sees that their livelihood is destroyed that weaken their moral. This is from Imam Ahmad.

Prophet said whoever shoots an arrow that reaches its target will receive one level in paradise. Each arrow gets one level that is how great the reward is the narrator of the Hadith. Abu Bakhaya he said I shat 16 arrows they all reached their target that is 16 levels in Jannah. The Prophet says whoever grows one gray hair in Islam, it will be life. Whoever frees a slave, equal hones will be free on the Day of Judgment. The siege carried on for 15 days the people of Taif were still firm and strong in resistance of the siege.

After 15 days Prophet held Shura for advice, Nofal bin Movia said, O' messenger of Allah, they are like a fox in a hole, if you stay you will take it and if leave it would not harm you anymore. What Nofal is saying eventually it will fall Prophet said, Insha Allah we leave tomorrow, this was a heavy news for Sahaba going back without opening Taif. We should not until we open the city.

Sahaba had success in Mecca Auazam they wanted to succeed. Prophet said OK. Then tomorrow we go and fight. Next day they want and fought, if was extraordinarily strong fight and many of them because injured on this day Prophet said we shall leave tomorrow by the will of Allah, Hazrat Umar said they were quiet and Prophet laughed. Yesterday Sahaba did not want to leave but today, the received some injuries and were willing to leave. During the siege announcement was made that whoever surrenders will be freed even if they are slaves. One who came down was Abu Bakra, he became writer and narrator of the Hadith Bakra means if one slides on rope with a piece of iron. He came like that and he was given the name Abu Bakra, and Prophet freed him. He was free man some other also surrender on that day.

Abu Bakra said, he heard Prophet say, anyone who accepts someone his father other than his real father will he denied paradise.

Ladies and gentlemen Taif was the last Ghazva, Prophet fought with Arabs. This was the end of wars with Arabs. After that only small skirmishes but no more Ghazva. From now onwards new frontier with Roman and that is the Ghazwa of Tabuk. Imam Ahmed narrates with authentic chain of narration. Prophet there are equal narrations in Bukhari and Muslim with some changes in wording and in other books of Hadith.

It is narrated by Abu Saeed Alkhdri when Prophet gave out the booty of Honaine to Quraish and Arab tribes. The spoils of Honaine were huge remember Malik bin Auf took everything with him, women, children and livestock. It was all there, as soon as they fled, Muslims took everything with them huge number of camels and gates, sheep, Prophet had just finished from Fatah Makkah and had large army with him included people who came first time some other tribes in Ghazva were rare because this was a major expedition. Prophet mobilized all Muslims to join him. Prophet starts giving their spoils of war to Quraish and other Arab tribes. Prophet gave Safwan bin Ameer from Quraish and people like Iqra ibn Abs and Ghalina bin Hassan. Those were the leaders of some Badoo tribes he gave to Al-Abbas bin Mardas the head of Banu Sleen. Prophet gave to everyone but left out Ansar. The ones who fled were given and the ones who fought went empty handed and Ansar were saddened by that at the time of fighting Prophet calls us and at the time of giving he gives to others. We are the ones whom Prophet called when Prophet was standing and everybody else was running away, who did the Prophet called for he told Al-Abbas to call Ansar, and then told him to call Al-Khazrj there are the ones who came to fight, some were injured and some were killed and now when it is time to split the ghanima.

Prophet is giving everyone but them. So, there was some talk going on among the Ansar. They were sad by this. Even Saad bin Abeda had to go to Prophet to bring up the issue. He went to Prophet and said, O' messenger of Allah these people Ansar are sad because you have given to your people (Quraish) and have given them great portion to the leaders of the Arab tribes people were given 100 camels to Al-Abbas bin Mardas were given 50 butt later increased to 100. Camels were awfully expensive and 100 camels a lot of big portion great amount of wealth. The Ansar empty handed. Prophet asked Saad bin Abeda where you stand O' Saad bin Abeda said O' Prophet I am a man but from my people this is a highly intelligent way to say, I have the same question to ask. He came and presented the opinion of his people. Prophet said bring all your people to this pavilion.

Saad bin Abeda went and gathered all his people in the appointed pavilion. Some mahajreen came and were allowed and some mahajreen were turned back. This was special meeting for Al-Ansar. Some important mahajroon were allowed rests were turned back. A private meeting when they were all there. Saad bin Abeda told Prophet that Ansar have gathered. When Prophet came they were all there Prophet praised Allah and thanked Allah. Then Prophet spoke to Ansar these words did not come to you when you were misguided and Allah guided you through me. I came to you when you were poor Allah enriched you through me I came to you when you were enemies and Allah brought you together. Ansar said all favors belong to Allah and his messenger. All of things you have said all the favors you have mentioned belong to Allah and to you the messenger of Allah.

Then Prophet told them would not you answer back. They said what should we say, all favors belong to Allah and his messenger. Prophet said in the name of Allah, you may say, and you will be telling the truth if you do, you came to us rejected and we believed in you, you were betrayed and we supported you, you were a fugitive and we provided you with a home. You were poor and we enriched you O' people of Ansar, are you upset because of a small material gain. That I am using to bring people closer to Islam, while I have trusted you to Islam O' people of Ansar, are you not content that people will go back with sheep and camels while you will go back to your home with Prophet. In the name of who has the soul of Muhammad PBUH in his hand? If it were not for Hijra I would be a man from Ansar, and if people take a road and Ansar take another road, I will follow the road of Ansar. O' Allah forgive Ansar the sons of Ansar and the grand sons of Ansar. Abu Saeed Khudri says they cried they started crying until their beards were wet, and they said we are pleased with Prophet as our share. Ansar are special Prophet told them that you are different than other people. I am giving this wealth to other people to bring them closer to Islam. I trust you Iman that you do not need this thing to bring you closer to me, Islam and closer to Allah you already have in your hearts.

The Ansar when they first met with Prophet, what was the deal between then and Prophet. We support you and we will fight for you what do we get, in exchange, Al-Jannah Prophet did not promise them world. From day one Ansar were in it for right reasons Prophet is reminding them that blessings of Allah when he arrived in Medina. They were misguided kufr.

What is a greatest disaster than being a kufr? They were guided through Muhammad PBUH and what is the greater blessing than that, nothing when you compare blessings of had Ayat. The most frequent dua we ask is to guide us to the strait path. That is letter than everything then they were enriched the economy of Medina was based on agriculture which was going down because continuous war before the Hijra of Prophet also through ghanima. Before they were enemies. Alauos and Al-Khazrj were fighting all the time. But Allah brought them together. They agreed that all favors belong to Allah and His messenger. Then Prophet told them you could say I was rejected by people of Quraish, we believed you were betrayed and we supported you also a fugitive, had nowhere to go and there was bounty on you and we provided with home and base to spread Dawah also you can say, I was poor and you are the one who hosted him. But Ansar would not say that they would not brag for what they had done. Because they considered everything is a blessing from Allah.

Then Prophet is telling them this is a small material gain, and I am giving them, not because I love them but to bring them closer to Islam. Then Prophet told them something special, they understand the greatness of Prophet. He told them people are going back with camels and sheep while you are going back to your, home with Prophet. I am going back with you I am not going to stay in Mecca.

Also, Prophet is telling them if it was not that I am a mahajir. If it was not for Hijra I shall count myself as a member of Ansar. Then Prophet is telling them if all the people will take a road and you take a road I shall follow your road to be with you. Then Prophet mode this wonderful dua for Ansar.

O' Allah forgive Ansar their children and grandsons of Ansar. When they heard Ansar cried and said we are pleased with Prophet.

There are different narrations in Bukhari Sharif and Muslim Sharif in one of them, one statement Husham, who is Tabyaeen narrating this hadith, asking Anees bin Malik whose Kenyan is Hazrat Hamzaro, Anees bin Malik was with Prophet most of the time. The stay is that he used to dream about Prophet every night.

Hadith. Where Prophet gave 100 camels to some of the leaders and only 50 to Al-Abbas bin Mardas. He spoke some poetry saying who how could be my share less than so and so when my father and his father were on equal footing. Prophet asked are you the one so and so and mentioned a sentence but it the words were misplaced and Hazrat Abu Bakr corrected and also said but you are not a poet.

Prophet did not say the line correctly and Abu Bakr said this is not how he said it. But in the name of Allah. You are not a poet and it is not appropriate for you to be one. Then Prophet asked what he said, so Abu Bakr mentioned the line as it should be Prophet said they are equal and it does not matter which are is mentioned first.

The reason for bringing it up is to show Prophet was not a poet. He did not follow the meters of poetry as they were followed at that time.

Because Allah has kept Prophet away from poetry. Al-Abbas said yes and Prophet said cut away his toung meaning given him another 50 camels to bring them to 100 as others and he will be quite. He was given 100 just like Alakhra. Then would not go around and speak those words. Safwan bin Amiya, authentic narration. He said Safwan says Prophet kept on giving me from the booty of Honaine and he was the worst of the creation to me until Allah has not created anything that was more beloved to me than him. So there given to them to soften their hearts to make them to love Prophet.

Ladies and Gentlemen when you see the seerah of Prophet. Prophet was master in dealing with peoples. Prophet was blessed by Allah with ability to draw together the hearts of the community and forgoing together an Umma. Allah told him, if you were sent to bring all that what is in the world all the hearts together you would not be able to do so but that is Allah who did so. Allah has brought these people together. Prophet was the means to bring them together. Allah is telling Prophet it is not you but Allah. The point is that we need to learn his Sunna and follow it.

Sometimes we have limited understand, the way Prophet dealt with people is Sunna. The way he made Dawah is Sunna, the way Prophet fought is Sunna these are all parts of Sunna. Prophet was giving Safwan bin Omiya who was an enemy until that moment. Prophet put everything behind him and was giving Safwan until Safwan was pleased and happy and he admits that Muhammad PBUH was the most disliked person to me and now I love him more than anybody else.

Bukhari sharif, Amr bin Talha, says Prophet was distributing money women and children. He gave to some men and left others Prophet was told the ones he left were upset that they were left out. Prophet praised Allah and then said, in the name of Allah I would give a man and I would leave out another man the one I leave out is more beloved to me than the one I give. But I am giving to people I see greed in their hearts and I trust others that Allah has blessed them with containment and good their hearts and one of them is Amr bin Talha. Amr bin Talha says in the name of Allah I love their words of Prophet more than all red camels. The red camels we have mentioned before red camels are most valuable camels what Amr bin Talha is saying that I would leave all the red camels for the honor a bage of honor.

Prophet gave Safwan more and he loved Prophet but Amr bin Talha would love to Prophet for the words spoken for him. But some people they were not only greedy but were complaining. For example: Bukhari Sharif, Abu Saeed Alkhdri narrates we were with Prophet when he was distributing a booty and he was approached by a man from Banu Tamim he said O' Prophet be just. This man is speaking to the messenger of Allah and he is telling him he just. He was a disbeliever until recently he was making Sajood to an idol. Now he is telling the best of the creation be just.

Prophet said now to you, and who would be just if I am not just Umar bin Khattab said, O' Prophet allow me to cut of his neck. Prophet said, leave him because he will have companions, you will be little your salat to their salat and you will be little your fasting compared to their fasting. They would recite Quran but it will not leave their throats. They would leave their religion just like an arrow would leave its target.

You will look at the blade and there is no blood on it, and then you will look at binding and you will find nothing on it and rest of the arrow, the shaft clean. This is an example O' Prophet gave how fast these people will leave their religion. They will leave religion so swiftly that no one will recognize. This example is remarkably interesting as they pray and Prophet is saying they are praying more than Sahaba and they are fasting and fasting more and they recite Quran but does not leave their throat because they are not following the meaning, than Prophet said a dark man with one arm, the other is only a trunk of an arm and it looks like a breast of a woman. Abu Saeed Alkhdri said, I testify that I heard these words and I testify that Hazrat Ali is the one who fought them and I was with him. He ordered that we search for one armed man now him and the description of Prophet fitting exactly.

Some words from Ibn Higer on this hadith. we learn the fighting the Khawarj is priority over fighting the disbelievers and the wisdom behind that is that fighting the Khawarj is capital, while fighting the disbelievers is Prophet, protecting the capital is to securing profit. This is the rule for fighting the murtadeen because they are eating the Umma from within protecting the capital takes precedence over profit. There is a warming in this hadith, for going to extreme in religion and going to extreme in worship in ways that Islam does not allow.

Our religion has encouraged us to be rough with kufr and soft with the believers and Khwarj did the opposite of that as we have seen. Prophet gives us an especially important sign off the sign of Khwarj. The sign is that Khwarj kill the believers and leave the disbelievers.

Abdullah bin Khab son of Khab bin Ark. He was traveling with his wife and was stopped by Khwarj they asked him who are you? He replied that I am the son of Khab bin Ark. He was a companion of Prophet. His wife was pregnant, Khwarj killed them both and opened up wife's stomach and pulled out the fetus. They took some belongings, belonging to a Christian or Jew. They returned them. But as for Muslims they killed the son of a companion of Prophet. This is the important quality of Khwarj.

Khwarj hate Muslims. This incident started the war between Hazrat Ali and Khwarj. Because Hazrat Ali said leave them alone. Until they kill or rob and then we shall fight them. When they killed Abdullah bin Khab and took his belonging then Hazrat said they should be fought. They are fighting against who revolted against just Imam, just leader, they fight for a false belief. Fight against who commit corruption on earth and commit robbery, there is evidence that they should be fought. Al-Higer says, it is important then ones who revolt against oppressive leader (He is not saying disbelieving leader) who wants to take over his wealth, kill him or to abuse his family then he is excused and he is allowed to fight him. If a leader is non-believer then can fight. A Tabri narrates with authentic chain from Abdullah bin Harris a man from Bini Ndr from Hazrat Ali said about Khwarj if they go against just ruler they should be fought. If they go against unjust ruler then do not fight them because they have evidence.

That is what we should say happened with Hazrat Imam Hussain and people of Medina when they revolted and Abdullah bin Zubair and who revolted against Hijaj. But Allah knows best there are examples of who revolted against unjust leaders.

The people of Auazam sent a delegation to Prophet. Asking Prophet to give them back their property because they had lost everything their women children and their live men are left everything else is taken away from them.

It is in Bukhari Sharif when Auazam came to accept Islam. They asked Prophet to return them their wealth and their women and children. Prophet said the most beloved words to me are truthful (accepting Islam). So, choose one of two either women and children or your wealth Prophet told them I cannot give you both back, either woman and children or wealth, and said I waited for you before distributing the ghanima with the hope that you would come to use old I shall give them back to you. Now it is divided now it is the property of individuals. I cannot take it back and give it back to you. But gave them choice one of the two. They said if you are giving us the choice then it is obvious we will choose our women and children. Prophet told them I am going to give them to you but I have to appeal to Muslims.

Prophet stood up in front of Muslims and praised Allah and then said your brothers have come repenting, they because Muslim and I want to give back to them their women and children who ever among you allow to give them what belongs to them, he should do so whoever wants to be compensated then I shall compensate them from first ghanima that we get. In Bukhari Sharif, mahajreen and Ansar gave back but Ibn Ishaque says Akra bin and his tribe said we will not give back what we have also other including Al-Abbas bin Mardas said we shall not give back what we have. But his tribe Banu Sleen said no we shall give up what we have Al-Abbas bin Mardas said you have disgraced me. But they did the right thing. Prophet appealed to the people to give it back. But Prophet said, I will not know who has given back and who has not. Prophet said the leaders should report to me. The women and children were returned livestock was split; it is said that everyone received 40 sheep. It was an exceptionally large ghanima. Malik bin Ouf received message from Prophet. That if you become Muslim I shall give you back and on top of that I shall give you 100 camels. Snecked out of Taif, and accepted Islam and led an army of Muslims from his people and led them against the people of Taif. He started the fight with Prophet now he is fighting the people he led because he became Muslim. First he was fighting against Muslims now he is fighting for Islam well it shows how Prophet was winning the hearts of people. Kaab bin Zaheer also became Muslim, Kaab bin Zaheer was the poet he used to pay poetry against Prophet. His brother sent him a message that Prophet is executing the poets who spoke against him. So, you come here as a Muslim a flee before you are killed. Kaab bin Zaheer was very worried about this.

He was concerned that he might be killed and went to Prophet and Prophet did not know him. He came and said Kaab bin Zaheer is responding and wants to become Muslim. Do you accept his Islam? Prophet said yes, let him come. He said I am Kaab bin Zaheer. Then gave his acceptance to

Prophet. Then he stood and read a beautiful poem praising Prophet. The story goes that Prophet told Sahaba to listen to his poem and then gave him his cloak and it is this Burda shirt which ended up in the hands of Khalifa of Banu Abbas. It was considered blessed because it belonged to Prophet and it was handed down from one Khalifa to the next. In the same year Prophet sent Sahaba to destroy the remnants of jahlia. The false idols of insane destroyed and this was bringing an end to idol worship in the land of Hijaz rest of Arabia.

Allah says O' you who have believed indeed the polytheists are unclean so let them not approach Masjid ul Haram after this their final year and if you feel deprived, Allah will enrich you if he will indeed Allah is knowing and wise. The people of Quraish for centuries, their livelihood was based on doing business, they had influence of people coming for Hajj and Umrah throughout the year that was the foundation of their business. They used to trade with people who were coming into Mecca throughout the year. That is all they knew how Mecca to do trade, they were not into anything else. Prophet announced to the non-believers that after this year, which was 9th year of Hijra. No mushriq will be allowed into Masjid ul Haram into Mecca. To the people of Quraish this was catastrophe disaster. They were dead because not all of the Arabs had become Muslims. Some people were Muslims but other parts of Arabia had not accepted Islam yet. A major part of Arabia were non-Muslim and they used to come for Hajj and Umrah and OK their business depended on the livelihood. Now Prophet is banning them from coming in and that was had for the economy. Even at that time financial concerned was of the people, and lot of the decisions politicians make are based on economic reasons. So, people of Quraish were thinking on those lines and thought that this is not a wise decision. How shall we live? The Ayat revealed by Allah that polytheist are unclean and that is the reason behind this decision. This announcement was made in 9th year of Hijra.

Allah says if you fear privation. Allah will enrich you from his bounties if he wills, indeed Allah, is knowing and wise. This is Tawaqal in Allah. If something is Haram we stop people from it and if it is Halal we encourage people to do it. That is how we lose our decision, Islam came to change the way people think, people usually think in financial terms, and decision and laws are mode in that sense, Allah is telling if you have trust in Allah. Allah will provide for you. It was difficult for Quraish because they did not know any other way how to earn money. The land in Mecca is not suitable for agriculture. It is very infertile day land. Rocky tracks and no rain. They Quraish were worried. But who ever have Taqwa on Allah. Allah will provide them sources they never expected. It is a promise from Allah.

How did Allah provided for people of Mecca, the next verse 29, Allah says fight those who do not believe in Allah or in the last day, who do not consider what Allah and his messenger have made lawful, who do not adopt the religion of truth from those who are given the scripture fight until they give jazia tax willingly while they are humbled. This is how Ibn Kathir starts the events of the 9th year of Hijra and this is how he opens up for the battle of Tabuk. The order from Allah in verse 123 of Sura Toba. Allah says. O' you who have believed fight those who are adjacent to you of disbeliever and left them find in your harshness and know that Allah is with righteous, who were against to Muslims at that time. They were Romans because Roman Empire reaches to the boundary of Hejaz. So, the first people mentioned in the Ayat are Romans because all the people of Hejaz are Muslims. Prophet started mobilization of the greatest army in Islam. Usually, Prophet would keep the target secret in order to ambush the enemy and take them by surprise. However, in this incident Prophet made it public from day one. The reason was they were facing a new and powerful enemy Roman Empire. Different people not as before the people we already know. This was something unknown. It was a foreign power and Roman had such a great reputation all over the world for its strength and power and this reputation was centuries old. Therefore, Prophet made it clear from the day one that we are going to fight Romans. The second reason for making it public was the distance. A lot of traveling will be involved

Prophet wanted the army to prepare accordingly.

Also, wrong time of the year summer very hat and puts were ready for picking, dates were ripening. Mainly life in Medina was based on agriculture and especially dates, and people would like to stay behinds people wait for whole year for the harvest and to travel right at that time, when fruit is ready. Difficult time to set out. But the battle of Tabuk is the last major trial before the death of the Prophet PBUH. Also, the battle of Tabuk represents the peak of Islam and represents most difficult test so far. Also, the battle of Tabuk brought down the Ayat which are talking about Nafaq and Iman. This was a test between the true believers and the Munafiqeen. This is a closing chapter in the Jehad of Prophet.

Now the final laws of fighting will come. These are the Ayat which will abrogate the Ayat before and the Ayat which will expose the Munafiqeen will come down even though the phenomena of Nafaq is few years old by now. Because Nafaq appeared in Medina right after the battle of Badr. We are talking about the span of 7 years of the appearance of Nafaq. Nevertheless, Surah Toba speaks about it openly. Surah Toba was revealed in the 9th year of Hijra in this year the battle of Tabuk occurred. Most of the Ayat of Surah Toba are relating to battle of Tabuk. We are talking about the final stages and there are final and most important ones. Although in the battle of Tabuk there was no fighting but it was an epic event great event. Also, it is important in Sharia and in every aspect of Islamic knowledge. We shall be going through a lot of Ayat, so many Ayat were revealed in Surah Toba about the battle of Tabuk.

Allah says O' you who have believed fight those adjacent to you disbelievers let them know your harshness and Allah is with the righteous one. The battle of Tabuk represents trial from Allah because there was no fighting involved. It was a best. Also represented difficult battle so far. That is the reason this battle was given the name Jase al Ussara. The army of difficult because of financing of the army was difficult the gathering of the army was difficult the travel was difficult the weather was difficult, and the enemy we are facing is difficult and that is why it is call the battle of difficulty Jase al Ussara. Army of difficulty, Allah has called in Quran, the hour of difficulty.

The mobilization Prophet called the people who are in Medina surrounding tribes and Mecca Muslims from all over. There has been no mobilization like this before Prophet wanted to recruit every able body Muslim and Ayat of Quran to support this and to lay down laws fighting Fi-Sabeel Allah. Sura Toba verse 38. The call was difficult therefore people were finding it hard to convince themselves to come out.

Ladies and Gentlemen: Quran speaks to the heart; Allah exposes the heart and tells about the illness that is in the heart whether you know it or not That is something unique about Quran. Because it is from Allah. It is a word of Allah, who created you and everything else Allah know what is good for you and what is bad for you. Allah knows what happening inside the heart. Those things one may not recognize himself. Allah is telling the people why they do not want to go out because people might give many reasons they might say the Fiqa may not say that they have to go.

Some might say that there is a difference of opinion, some might say it doesn't make sense, some might say it is not wise. But Allah tells us why? O' you who have believed what is the matter with you, that when you are told to go for the cause of Allah. You adherence heavily to earth that is the reason, it is love of world. It is adherence to the earth. Are you satisfied with the life on this earth rather than the life hereafter? But what is the enjoyment of this world compared to the life hereafter, but extraordinarily little. This Ayat mentions the cause and the cure. The disease is the attachment to world. The cure Allah is reminding us that this life is nothing compared to life hereafter the first Ayat in Surah Bakra where the first command was given. Allah says fighting has been prescribed on your while you dislike it. Allah told us this is something that we dislike. We even dislike to talk about it.

Allah tells us what will happen if we do not fight in his cause. Allah says if you do not go for it Allah will punish you with a painful punishment and will replace you with other people. You cannot harm Allah at all and Allah in confident overall things. Allay says, if you do not aid the Prophet PBUH Allah has already aided him, meaning Allah will help the Prophet. Allah has aided his messenger when those who disbelieve had driven him out as one of two Prophet and Abu Bakr when they were in the cave, Prophet is speaking to Abu Bakr. Do not grieve indeed Allah is within and sent down tranquility upon him and supported him with angels you did not see and made the word of those who disbelieve the lowest while the word of Allah is the highest. Allah is halted in might and wise, Allah says to all Muslims go forth whether light or heavy and strive with your wealth and your life in the cause of Allah, that is better for your if you only knew.

Light or heavy, Al-Qurtbee says opinions of sealer the said, young or old busy or not busy wealthy or poor. Every needs are to go out. Sahaba said it was such a burden there was no excuse everybody had to go out, and that is when Allah revealed the Ayat. There is not upon the weak or upon the ill or those who do not find anything to spend and any discomfort when they are sincere to Allah and to his messenger there is not upon the well off. Allah is merciful and wise. But everybody else has to go out.

Abu Qatada, the knight of Prophet. He was seen on a horse he was old and his eye broughs were covering his eyes. Also, he had gained a lot of weight. He was told you are one of the excused, why are you going out? He said Sura Toba has left us no excuse that was the understanding of the Sahaba. Wealth and life fighting consumes money therefore wealth is mentioned first. That was the case then and that is the case now. Any Sadqa in multiplied by 10 except when it is in cause of Allah, any contribution for fighting in the cause of Allah is multiplied by 700.

Prophet started fund raising, donations, stand up and ask people to give. But it was difficult time for resources, people did not have much specially before the harvest. But they were still bringing. Hazrat Abu Bakr and Hazrat Umar they brought. Then Prophet was asking for more and then Hazrat Usman Ghani, brought 100 camels ready with their saddlers ready. Then Prophet asked for more Usman bin Onan brought 100 camels again, now 300 camels altogether. Prophet asked for more than Hazrat Usman brought some gold coins and pored them in the lap of Prophet. But the fingers of Prophet were in the coins. And Prophet said Usman does not do any more after this day. Whatever he does after today he is forgiven because what he has done today. This shows the virtue of spending

Fi-Sabil Allah then there were those who were looking for excuse to get out.

Allah says when this Sura was revealed in joining them to believe in Allah and to fight with his messenger those among them ask your permission to stay back leave us with them who sit at home who are asking this, there are the wealthy ones. This shows the fittana of money. Money in itself in not evil but if it causes a person to forsake. Their duties towards Allah and his religion, that becomes on evil instrument. In the Ayat, these people came to Prophet and said excuse us.

Allah says they were satisfied with those who stay behind women and children and their hearts are sealed over and they do not understand. There people have heard Quran and sat in the Khutbah and the lectures of Prophet. They do not understand the difference between the life in world and life hereafter. Then Allay says about the ones understand, the messenger and those believe with him fought with their wealth and their lives there will have that is good and those are successful. Allah has prepared for them gardens beneath which rivers flow that is. Where they will be allied internally that is great attainment. Allah says those with the excuses among the badoo they had some valid excuses there are different opinions.

Allah says who have lied to Allah and his messenger at home. There will be strike among those a painful punishment. The next Ayat talks about the Sahaba who came to Prophet. They said, O' Prophet Carry us provide us with some transportation, we have nothing, because part of the preparation you need to have your camel or horse to travel. It is a long distance. These were extremely poor Sahaba but sincerely wanted to go. Prophet said, I cannot provide you with anything. They were incredibly sad that they were deprived from the honor of joining this army that left with their tear flowing on their cheeks. The difference is that some people had wealth but were happy to stay behind and on the other hand these poor Sahaba were eager to go when they were prevented they cried. So, there is difference between the hearts of people. Allah says, nor is the blame on those who came to you, that you might give those mounts and you said, I can find nothing for you to ride upon. They turned back with their eyes flowed with tears out of grief, that they could not find anything to spend in the cause of Allah.

The cause for blame is only upon those who ask permission from you while they are rich. They are satisfied with those who stay behind Allah has sealed over their hearts that they do not understand. In the previous Ayat, they had no Fiqa and in this Ayat. They have no knowledge. They have no understanding and they have no knowledge. Allah says about Munafiqeen. Had it been an easy gain and a moderate trip, meaning if there was a lot of ghanima, and the distance was not for away, the hypocrites would have followed you. But distance was the journey.

They will swear by Allah, if we were able we would have gone forth with you, destroying themselves through false oaths and Allah knows indeed those are liars. Allah says to Muhammad PBUH that you should not have excused them, Allah says, May Allah pardon you O' Muhammad; why did you give them permission to remain behind? You should not have until you knew who were the truthful and who the liars were.

Then Allah tells us who are the true believers and who are not. Those who believe in Allah on the last day, they will not ask permission to be excused from fighting with their wealth and their lives and Allah is knowing them who fear Allah. The ones who have Taqwa the ones who believe in Allah. They are not trying to find excuses but you will find them eager to support the religion of Allah and support for it.

But the ones who are looking for excuses Allah says about them, only those would ask permission from you who do not believe in Allah. On last day, whose hearts have doubted and they are in their doubt and are hesitating and this is a fact those who misinterpret the concept of fighting Fi-Sabeel Allah. Those who are trying to get out of this they are always hesitating. They are in state of contradiction. On one hand they say they support the religion of Allah; on the other hand, they want to find excuses to get out of it. It is a contradictory says about them they do not have true believe in Allah on the last day. Someone who has true believe in akhara and someone who has true believe in Allah. First of all, true believer will fear Allah more than anybody else, and because of Imaan will not have any value of this world on the last day.

The Allah says the criteria for those who are really excused and those who are not. Allah says; and if they had intended to go forth they would have prepared for it. Ladies and Gentlemen anything important need preparation.

Then Allah is telling Muhammad PBUH it is better that their people do not come out, why? Because this is what they will do, had they gone for with you, they would not have increased you except in confusion, because they are confused. Then Allah says, they would have been active with you seeking to cause you fittana. Allah is speaking to Sahaba and there are those will listen and Allah knows, there avoid listeners. That is why there is a warning about munafiq. They are so elusive. It is difficult to tell who is a munafiq, they could be extremely sweet tong, they could him very knowledge they could be very prominent, they could be very Cras emetic. If you look up to them and listen to them their words make sense to you, one becomes avid listener to them. But in reality they are deceiving.

Allah is giving this warning to Sahaba about Munafiqeen. Ladies & Gentlemen it is important to study the Ayat of Sura Toba and study about Munafiqeen in Sura Toba. We are not munafiq and we do not fall prey to Munafiqeen. It is so confusing that Hazrat Umar would make sure that he is not a munafiq. He would go to Adeefa. Umar would ask him in the name of Allah to tell him. Did Prophet mentioned his name in the Munafiqeen Adeefa said no, and said, I am not going to answer this question other than you the munafiq, they had already desired the sanction before and had upset matters for you O' Muhammad, until the truth came and the ordinance from Allah, Abdullah bin Abbey was a munafiq. But he was the leader of his people. He was the head of Al-Kharj. He would stand up before Khutbah and would say Muhammad PBUH is a messenger of Allah and listen to his words. When Hazrat Umar asked Prophet to kill him in one narration Prophet said there are many men who might fight for him. Abdullah bin Abbey had great following and people who were deceived by him might not handle it well and that is why Prophet refused to execute him.

Prophet told Al Jedda bin Qais one of the Munafiqeen. Asked him, are you ready to fight with Roman Al Jedda bin Qais said, O' Prophet my people know, I am a man who love women so much and I fear for myself if I go with you, that I might fall into fittana because of the women of Banu Aloud. Al Asfar is the name given to Romans as for means yellow. He showed that the reason wanted to stay away was because of fittana, this was his excuse. Allah says and among them is he who says permits me to remain at home and do not put me to trial. Allah says they are already in trial and hell fire is waiting for them. In other words, if they go they will be out of fittana if they stay home them in fittana. Allah says the ones who struggle in our cause Allah will guide them. If good becomes to you they are depressed if harm comes they say we took we took our matter in hand and turned away rejoicing. Allah says we wait for two best things. Victory, martyrdom and say wait either Allah will inflict you or by our hands wait and we are waiting with you. Muslims have two objectives either victory or martyrdom. These the best things to wait for. And two things will happen to you, either punishment from Allah or through Prophet when he would go out, he would appoint someone to take care of Medina and his family. Prophet when going for the battle of Tabuk appointed Mohd bin Muslma to be the Ameer over Medina and appointed Ali bin Abu Talib to take care of his family. Some Munafiqeen as usual started spreading rumors around how Prophet left Hazrat Ali behind, saying he is a burden that is why he is left behind. Hazrat Ali went to Prophet and told Prophet what people were saying Hazrat Ali bin Abu Talib wanted to go out. He did not want to miss out on such a Ghazwa.

Prophet told Hazrat Ali O' Ali doesn't it please you that you are to me what Haroon to Musa. Except that there is no prophet after me.

When Musa went to speak to Allah. He left behind Haroon. He appointed him to take care of the affairs of Israel Prophet is telling Hazrat Ali. I am doing the same to you. You are to me as Haroon was to Musa. Except no Prophet after me but Haroon was Prophet.

There are great virtues to Hazrat Ali. We the people of Sunna believe. We believe Prophet did leave Hazrat Ali behind and this is an authentic narration. Hazrat Ali held a special status with Prophet.

The army left some of the Munafiqeen, speaking among themselves, debate questions and answers, like do you think fighting the Romans is like fighting, the Arbs, Muslims will come back tied in ropes. Speaking like this about the army which is going out is not good this demoralizing and put fear in the hearts of soldiers and terrify them about their enemy. Although this conversation was private but Allah exposed them to the messenger of Allah. Prophet told Amr bin Yasir go to them men and ask them what they have said because they have burn themselves, catch them because they have burned themselves. If they do not admit tell them what they have said. So, Amr bin Yasir went and told them, this is what you have said, they came back apologizing.

Allah revealed the Ayat, when they came to Allah they said, O' Prophet we are just joking. Allah says you are asking them, they will say we are only conversing only playing. Say, is that Allah his messenger and his verses, you were mocking, make no excuse. You have disbelieved after you had believed, if we pardon when section from you, we will punish the other section because they were criminals there are verses 65-67 of Sura Toba. There Ayat make it clear, joking and mocking anything of religious value is Haram and it could reach the level of kufr. Because Allay says you have disbelieved after believe. Now look at what did they say. This tells us that in Islam making fun of Quran or Hadith or Prophet or joking in a way which is disrespectful to the divinity of Allah all of this is extremely dangerous it can lead to kufr and it is a sign of naffaq. Also tells us Islam in secret and should he held in high esteem and sanctity that it deserve. We should not be little our religion. There stern warning were to Munafiqeen who were making fun of Muslims.

Even today we should not spread rumors that will weaken the Muslims we need to uplift the Umma we must encourage the Umma and we should remind the umma that you are the best nation brought forth to mankind i.e., Islam is the best religion. We did have a bright past and as Muslim have bright feature. For example, the life hereafter, the end belongs to people of Taqwa.

The army left Prophet made general mobilization all the Muslims had to come out. But some people stayed behind they would come to Prophet and give reasons. Prophet would say leave him out. If there is any good in them Allah will make them follow us and if there is no good left in them then Allah will give relief from him. People came and said Abu Zar Ghaffari is not with us. Prophet said the same leave him if there is any good in him he will follow and if not then Allah has relieved you from him Abu Zar Ghaffari was following but his camel was slow. That slowed him down too much. He picked up the belonging and jumped off the camel and left. Abu Zar Ghaffari was walking in the heat of the sun in the desert with his belonging and Muslim saw him in horizon appearing for behind walking alone. They came to Prophet and told that there is a man following us Prophet said be Abu Zar, when the man came he was Abu Zar, Prophet said, May Allah have mercy on Abu Zar. He walks alone will die alone and will be resurrected on the judgment day alone years passed and Abu Zar was living in the extreme wealth of the Muslim and Muslim Khalifa. Abu Zar was brought up in the tough desert who believed in Islam when things were tough.

Abu Zar accepted Islam when Prophet was in Mecca. When it was hard. Abu Zar was a very dark man, well-built big man. But he was hot tampered he was extremely strict man. He was Zahid. He would follow strict form of austerity discipline. He had the belief that Muslim should not store wealth and keep it. They should give their wealth to needy and for good causes while predominant view, and this is the view adopted by the Ulma, Alim. If a person pays Zakat on his money than the rest of his money is Halal people can save money and can leave behind otherwise there would be no point to have laws of inheritance in Quran. But Abu Zar would follow strict austerity. For this reason, he was not getting along with authorities and also not with many people. He was in Shaam at the time of Movia and Shaam was a very wealthy place. That used to be capital of Roman Empire and the land of Shaam itself is a very blessed land. The Muslims were very wealthy over there. He was not happy with that Movia sent a letter to Hazrat Usman. He was the Ameer and Movia was the Governor in Shaam. He sent a letter saying Abu Zar has ruined, messed up Shaam for me. So, Usman ibn Adnan sent for Abu Zar to come back to Medina came to Medina Usman bin Adnan told him to stay in Medina. But he said I have nothing to do with world and leave me alone. Allow me to go to a small town in the middle of the desert Usman bin Adnan gave him permission go to Rabea. He went there and lived there. Hazrat Usman wanted to give him some camels as provision. But he said, he had nothing to do with them. I shall survive on my own. He left with nothing. When he was on his death bed, alone only his wife and servant. Abu Zar great Sahabi a scholar. He used to be a Mufti during the time of Abu Bakr and Umar. He was on his death bed, his wife started weeping. He said, why are you crying? She said how come you do not want me to cry. When you are dying here and I do not have anything to use as your coffin funeral. And I have no strength and ability to busy you. He said be happy and do not cry. Because I heard Prophet to say to a gathering that included me. One of you will die in flame, on empty land and his burial will be witnessed by a group of believers, then Abu Zar said, all those people in the gathering died and I am the only one left.

The all died in a group, I am the only one that fulfills that Hadith. Go and check out the road, she said what road, you are talking about the pilgrims have already left and roads are not used. But he told her to go out. She would go out any body and would go back to nurse him until one day she saw a group of men riding on their camels coming in the origin they are described as looking like vultures. Birds probably, in desert at a distance that is how they would look. She waved to them and they cause to her O' servant of Allah what do you need? She said, there is a man over here who is dying I want you to take care of him, they enquired who is he? She said Abu Zar. They said companion of Prophet she said yes. They scarified their parents for him, they used to help Abu Zar they came in when he was at his last moments. He said I give you the glad tidings Prophet told me that you will die in an empty land and your burial will be witnessed by believers. Then he told them if I or my wife had a garment suitable for burial, I would have used it but I have nothing. Abu Zar was living with nothing. He was visited by Abu Musa once. He was doing housework he came to help him. But Abu Zar told him leave me alone Abu Musa said, I am your brother. Abu Zar said you are not my brother. You used to be my brother before you took the position of leadership. He was living a difficult hard life. Now is the time for funeral he has nothing. He said to those people, I do not want you to give me anything if you have been an Ameer a policemen or a postman. If there is one who has not used their positions, he can give me a coffin. All of these men had assumed there rules at one point in their past. Except one Ansari. A young man among them. He said I am going to give you two garments made by my mother Abu Zar died alone they prayed Janaza used those clothes and that is the end of the life of great Sahaba of Prophet. Another Sahabi when Prophet left he was still in Medina. He had two huts. In summer if pore some water on the roof and the keeps it cool. Each of his wife was living these, they prepared some food and cold water. He came in and sow. He said Prophet is in the hat weather and wind and Abu Kheeta in a coal shade, prepared food and beautiful wife, this is not fair. In the name of Allah, I am not going to enter into the hut until I follow Prophet. So prepare my provisions. He mounted on a camel and followed Prophet. He arrived with them when they were at Tabuk. He came to Prophet and Prophet said warned Abu Kheetma. Abu Kheetma told Prophet what happened and Prophet made dua for him. Prophet said do not enter the dwellings of the people who transgress against themselves, except you are going to weep, otherwise you will be inflicted with the punishment that inflicted them. Then Prophet told them to throw away the water they have got and the Dow they have made with that water to feed to the animals. Prophet wanted nothing to do with smooth people, previous generation, their land and their water. The reason Prophet told us either remind yourself and take a lesson and weep because what happened to them otherwise, we should stay away to save ourselves from punishment like them.

We should have no pride of the civilization of non-believers. Because they were punished by Allah. How can we have pride in Babylon and pharaoh and all these non-believers when they did not believe in Allah?

Prophet wanted to make Wazu and he was late, Muslims made Ecama and Abdul Rehman bin Auf led the salat. Prophet got back while still in prayer Abdul Rehman wanted to retreat but Prophet wanted him to carry on, and Prophet prayed behind Abdul Rehman bin Auf. The only Sahabi Prophet prayed behind him and this is a great virtue for Abdul Rehman Auf.

Abdullah bin Masood says that during the battle of Tabuk. I saw a torch during the night, I followed it and he saw Prophet, Abu Bakr and Umar and Abdullah had died and they dug a grave and Prophet descended into his grave while Abu Bakar and Umar were lowering the body to Prophet body of zulbjadeen. He was an extremely poor man, unknown simple and Prophet Abu Bakr and Umar were preparing his Janaza. Abdullah bin Masood was watching Prophet putt him with his own hands into the grave and Prophet said O' Allah. I am pleased with him and O' Allah he pleased with him Abdullah bin Masood said, he wished that he were the one in that grave. To have the blessing of Prophet, making dua for him. When the army reached the land of Romans Shaam. Prophet sent Khalid bin Waleed to Dommand Jandal. The king of Dommand Jandal, Prophet told Khalid bin Waleed to bring him, capture him and bring him. O' Kader, the king, was living in a very strong fortress in Dommand Jandal. Prophet told Khalid bin Waleed, you will find him hunting bulls. O' Kadar used to go for hunting Bulls. O' Kader used to go for hunting. HE would go on horse with large group of his men, they would travel and spend extended period searching for the bulls. He had trained heroes especially for that. Prophet sent Khalid bin Waleed with some men to capture him and bring him. It was a full moon might and O' Kader was with his wife, on the roof of his palace. They saw the bulls came right to the gates of the fortress. The bulls were scratching their horns with the walls or gates of fort. They never seen anything like it before incredible scene. Normally people had to travel long distance to find them (the Bulls) and here they are outside the gates. His wife asked O' Kader have you ever seen anything like this. He replied no never, she asked him, is this something you could pass on, he said no. He immediately came down, ordered his soldiers to prepare his horses. He took few of his followers along with his brother. They rushed out to hunt down these bulls, they were rounded up and surrounded by Khalid bin Waleed. The brother of O' Kader fought and was killed.

The rest and O' Kader surrendered and were arrested by Khalid bin Waleed. They were brought to Prophet O' Kader agreed to the terms, paying Jazia tax and was allowed to go back. There was no fighting. Because Romans when they heard the advance of Prophet. Allah put fear in their heart and they did not come forward. Even though they had letter preparations, large numbers stronger weapons. But they were afraid to meet Prophet in actual battle. Prophet stayed their and waited for them but nobody came during that time. Prophet opened few cities and made agreement with others and took jazia from them. It was a very successful Ghazva, but no fighting was involved it was very difficult test for Muslims. Allah says Allah has already forgiven the Prophet and mahajreen and Ansar who followed him in the hour of difficulty. Hour of difficulty is a battle of Tabuk. Because part of them had almost inclined to doubt then he forgave them indeed he is kind and merciful. Now, we are coming to closing chapters, because forgiveness comes to the end Prophet and Muslims are being told that Allah has forgiven Prophet and Ansar who followed him in the hour of difficulty, Allah has given them Toba and has accepted their Toba. When Prophet left Medina. He was invited to pray in a mosque which was newly built by some people next to Medina. When Prophet was going for the battle of Tabuk they asked him to come and bless the mosque with salat. Prophet told them I am traveling now, but when I shall come back I shall pray in your mosque. Surprise surprise when Prophet was close to Medina. Prophet was told the true intention of those people. There was a man called Abu Amr bin Nafail. This man belonged to Al-Kharj and was a prominent member of the tribe. He was given the name Abu Amr bin Raya in the time of Jahlia. He believed in

Allah and used to worship Allah, the way he knew. He learned from the people of the book, followed their religion. He was a religious person deeply devoted individual when Prophet came to Medina.

He was the worst enemy one would expect him the closest to Islam but he was Furtherest from Islam. We want to Quraish and encouraged them to fight against Muslims in fact in the battle of Audh, he is the one who dug the traps the holes. Prophet fell in one and broke his tooth, also some iron nails went through the helmet and injured the checks this was caused because of Abu Amr bin Fasil name was Abu Amr bin Rayb. A priest this name was given because he was religious. Prophet called him Abu Amr bin Fasik. Abu Amr corrupt. When he saw that Quraish are unsuccessful he went all the way to meet Heraculus. He asked Heraculus to send an army to invade Medina Hercules promised him off assistance. He Abu Amr bin Malik send letters to Munafiqeen in Medina, promising them that I am coming to Medina with an army to destroy the Muslim state. He conspired with them to establish a base where from they can spread the conspiracy. A place where they can hold meetings and plat against Islam and for this reason they built the mosque. That was a cover to plot against Muslims and to promote the agenda of kufr.

Prophet was given Wahi the revelation that exposed this plan. Allah says in version 107 to 109 of Sura Toba. Allah says, there are those hypocrites, who took for themselves a mark for causing harm, disbelief and division among the believers and as a station for who ever had a word against Allah and his messenger before. They will surely swear that we only intended the best. Allah testifies that they are indeed liars. Do not stand for prayer with in it ever a mosque founded on the righteousness from the first day is firm for you. Allah is referring to mosque quay, the very first mosque with in it men, who love to purify themselves and Allah loves those who purify themselves you should pray in a mosque which was established on taqwa on first day where people are believers. The one who laid his foundation on righteousness on fear from Allah and seeking his approval for better or one who laid his foundation on the edge of a bank about to collapse so it collapsed with him in to fire of hell and Allah does not guide the wrong doing people. The building which they built not to be a cause of skepticism in their hearts until their hearts stopped Allah is knowing and wise. Prophet ordered that mosque should be burnt down to the ground and that is what happened and the plat was exposed. This was mosque Drar. This story was established to promote kufr rather than Imaan. Mosque Quba and Mosque Al-Nabi were made from the first day to promote the truth Prophet was told by Allah. Any mosque does not promote the truth is mosque Drar. Prophet entered Medina and was greeted. Ibn Qeem in his book Zain Maad, he says the benefits the story of Kaab bin Malik. Battle of Tabuk, hadith, from Kaab bin Malik, authentic narrated by Al-Bukhari other books of hadith and books of Meera. This Hadith has special significance because it represents a bad moment in the life of an exemplary man a companion of Prophet and it is loaded with lessens for us because it is a story of someone who struggled to do good and being a human being he went through a moment of weakness but was able to get out of it. Because of his good deed and good tramming learning, knowledge and because of his Imaan. We must study this hadith deeply and must learn the lessons relevant to us as a momin. It is in Bukhari. It was narrated by the grandson of Kaab bin Malik, he heard it from his father when he became a guide to Kaab bin Malik when he became blind. Father is telling the story to his son. Kaab bin Malik says I never stayed behind any battle of Prophet with the exception of the battle of Tabuk but I also missed the battle of Badr. Prophet did not senser went for the battle of Badr with different intention. It was intended an attack on caravan, therefore Prophet did not count anybody for staying behind. Caravan was led by Abu Sufyan. They missed the caravan and ended up meeting with the army of Quraish. They met the enemy without prior appointment. However, he says, I have attended with Prophet the sight of Aqba. This was in Mecca when Ansar gave the pledge of allegiance to Prophet and promised help and support. Kaab says he attended that he was one of the group of Ansar. He was one of the twelve leaders of Ansar, who represented the Ansar giving the pledge to Prophet. Kaab bin Malik says he would not have attended Badr instead of Aqba.

Although Badr has special reward and very famous and first battle in Islam. Kaab is saying the right of Aqba is such an important event. That he would not exchange it with attending Badr then he says Badr is very famous and with special rewards and reputation. However, the right of Aqba was very special and he attended that.

Now he is telling the story what happened on Tabuk. He says never before I was stronger and better of them the time of Tabuk when I missed it. Never before, I owned two riding camels but I owned them during the battle of Tabuk. He is accepting that he had no excuse. He was strong and had financial capability. He had two camels.

Prophet would never send out an army to fight a particular enemy but he would talk about a different destination. Prophet does this to instead the enemy. He would not disclose the destination. He would do that to surprise the enemy and catch them off guard. That was the practice of the Prophet PBUH. But with the battle of Tabuk it was different. It was in time of very hot weather. It was a long journey and a numerous enemy therefore Prophet made the announcement public Muslims were told that we are going to such and such place and we are facing the Romans. So that appropriate preparation can be made for this battle. This shows that Tabuk was different and special. Muslims were in numbers and books of seerah say they were 30,000. This is the most authentic that Muslims were 30,000. It sur passes any number before in Fatah Makkah. They were 10,000 and in Battle of Honnaine Muslims were 12,000. Now jump to 30,000.

Prophet called on all tribes, Muslims to join in the battle of Tabuk. Because of special circumstances Kaab bin Malik says but there was no dewan. That is a register names were not written. Therefore, if someone wanted to stay behind. He might assume that he will be disclosed. Because of the large numbers one can assume that Prophet will not miss him. Difficult to keep track of any individual Kaab bin Malik says Prophet went out at a time when fruits harvest was ready and shades were lowering. Kaab bin Malik is being honest. He is telling us the true reasons and hidden reasons which are going in the mind and in heart shades were lowering hat weather, fruits were ready and there were the temptations for staying behind. Then Kaab bin Malik says, Muslims with Prophet started making preparation. I started also preparing but retired accomplishing anything. Nothing, he had the intention to prepare but did not do anything. This is a usual habit of human if no commitment or discipline. Delaying todays work for tomorrow. That in what Kaab bin Malik doing. Then he tells us, he would tell himself that I am able to do it. Unless there is discipline things will drag down. If one leaves, himself to go with the wind. Nothing is going to be done Kaab bin Malik speaking to himself, thinking I can do it. Eventually did nothing.

People were busy with their preparation and time was passing by. Then Prophet and Muslim army were ready to leave. But he had done nothing. He thought he will get ready within a day or two and will catch up with them. The army left and I decided to get myself ready. But the next day the some did nothing. That was the case until the army had left and it was over. This caravan will continue until the Day of Judgment. Prophet says another hadith, enemy will be fighting until the dajjal comes out, and fighting Fi-Sabeel Allah the caravan is moving on any delay will make it more difficult to catch up. Kaab bin Malik says he was still thinking of setting up and catching them, and he says I wish I did that but it was not distant for him. When the army left and he was left in Medina. He would go out walk around go to market. He says whenever I went out mixed with people the only men I met the people suspected of hypocrisy or those who were excused by Prophet because those were in poor health. There were the one who stayed behind. Prophet made no mention of me until they reached in Tabuk and then Prophet remembered him Kaab bin Malik. Prophet in gathering said what did Kaab do?

A man from Bini Muslima said, Prophet he was covered with his two clothes and looking at the beauty of his clothes. This man was from Al-Kharj the same tribe as Kaab bin Malik. This is a very degrading statement. To say he was held behind by his clothes and string at clothes. In other words like a women stayed behind looking at clothes how beautiful they are. It is not a manly behavior looking in the mirror admiring clothes when people are in the battlefield. Maaz bin Jabal, who is also from Ansar from the people of Kaab bin Malik. He responded to that statement and said, what a statement you have made (they were speaking in Arabic). He said O' Messenger of Allah, we know nothing about him but good.

The messenger of Allah was quite when Prophet remains quite that would mean that Prophet is approving what is said or done, otherwise Prophet would respond to what is being said.

Let us examine this who is Kaab bin Malik? Kaab bin Malik was a man who was with Prophet from day one Kaab bin Malik is a man from Ansar who came to Prophet and invited him to Medina knowing well the consequences of their action considering those times. They knew Arabs will fight them, they will have to scarify themselves, their wealth for Prophet and he is one of the twelve men who put their hands into the hand of Prophet and gave him the pledge of allegiance. Kaab bin Malik was with Prophet in the battle of the trench every dry. He was in the battle of Audh. He was at Fata Mecca. He was in Khyber he was in Audhba. Battle of Honaine. He was present in every important moment in the history of Islam. But he missed cut on the day. Nevertheless this man from Banu Muslima made a statement that he is looking, staring at his clothes.

Ladies and Gentlemen the actions of Kaab bin Malik made him a target of these words. Regardless of whether the statement is right or wrong but Kaab bin Malik put himself there because of his actions. Maaz bin Jabal spoke for Kaab bin Malik and Prophet was silent. But it was apparent that Kaab bin Malik did not show up.

Kaab bin Malik says, when I heard the news that Prophet is on his way back I was very anxious and was thinking about lying. He was trying to fabricate an excuse to get out of the anger of Prophet when I meet him. Then he says he was seeking council advice from his family whom he trusted (language Arabic).

Kaab bin Malik says when he was told that Prophet is almost back in Medina. All those thoughts and falsehood left my mind. I realized if I told a lie I shall never be able to get out of this mistake. So decided that I am going to speak the truth. Kaab bin Malik fell into a deep trouble. A righteous man. But committed a serious mistake. But because of his Imaan and training practice. He was able to pull himself out of this hale through his good deeds. The decision to tell the truth and not to lie as we shall see saved him.

Prophet arrived in the morning, when Prophet would come back he would go to the mosque and pray two Rakat salat and then Prophet sat down for the people so people can meet him in the mosque people who stayed behind came to give their reasons and excuses for staying behind making the oath in the name of Allah that we are speaking the truth. Prophet accepted their reasons and excuses and took their words at face value and took their pledge of allegiance their Beja and prayed for them asked Allah to forgive them. And left inside of their hearts to Allah. This was a general rule that Prophet would take the face values. We judge people according to what we see. We see Imaan and believe they are believes even they are disbelievers in their hearts. And if they appear disbelievers outwardly we believe them disbelievers even they are believers in their hearts. That is the rule rest Allah knows. In world the rules are what is apparent and not what is hidden. Both for believes and non-believes.

Kaab bin Malik says, he came in and gave his Salam Prophet smiled but it was a smile of an angry person. Prophet said come here I came walking to him. Sat in front of Prophet. He asked me why you stayed behind. Didn't you buy your mount Kaab bin Malik said yest? Kaab bin Malik, if I was sitting in front of someone else it was possible perhaps to get out of the anger. I could speak and had the ability to argue. Kaab bin Malik was a very famous and important poet of Medina. He defended Islam and Prophet with his, poetry. He was one of the three sabot, what he is saying that I can give

349

excuses, which will be convincing and would sound valid. But Kaab knew that telling anything to the messenger of Allah will be exposed. Likewise, people with knowledge can produce Ayat from Quran, and can give convincing arguments and excuses that will save them from Allah on the day of judgement. But no truth has to be told or it will come out any way. Allah says, if one has to go out he has to prepare or he is only paying a lip service.

Kaab bin Malik said, if I speak the truth, even though it may not sound good but there is forgiveness of Allah in truth. He said, I have no excuse. He made it clear to Prophet, he had no excuse for staying behind. I have never been stronger and able to go but stayed behind. Prophet said, this man has spoken the truth now leave to Allah for judgment. Kaab bin Malik left. He says, some men from my clan followed me and told me. We never know you have committed a sin before or this is a first time. Why didn't you give an excuse to Prophet just like everybody else did? It would have been enough that Prophet have asked Allah to forgive you as he did for the others. That would have wiped off your sin. They convinced me to go back to Prophet make an excuse and he will ask Allah to forgive you. And I agree. But Kaab bin Malik asked did anybody else said the same thing what I did? They said yes two men Merara and Halal, said the same. And then what was the answer of Prophet Kaab bin Malik was told the same as to yourself. Then I said, those two men are the righteous ones and I decided not to go back. It shows when we find company that gives us support. It must be good company. Man has been created weak. We need company. Prophet says religion is an advice.

Three of us who told the truth were singled out for boycott. Not to speak to us, the rest of them who gave excuses were fine. This was a test from Allah, people stayed away from us.

It was had, like the land become unknown to me. He was from Medina lived there all his life. But people changed and he felt the land changed. That carried on for 50 days. The other two gave up sat at home weeping. But Kaab bin Malik says he was youngest and tough he would go out even in to market, but no one would speak to him. The society was strong, an order from Prophet not to speak to us and nobody would speak total obedience to Prophet. We know the Hijra was powerful. Boycotting was very powerful. I would go to gathering of Prophet, would give my Salam and would see if the lips of Prophet move in response. But Prophet would not answer him so he would stove at the lips of Prophet to if he would respond quietly. When I would go for salat, I look at Prophet and when I concentrate at my salat Prophet would stare at me when I move my eyes to look at Prophet he would move away. When it became too long I went to the house off Abu Qatada and climbed the wall. He was my cousin and beloved person to me. I gave him Salam but he did not respond back. I said, O' Abu Qatada. In the name of Allah, do you know me a person who loves Allah and his messenger? He was silent I asked him again he was silent and I asked him again and again he said Allah and his messenger know the best, my eyes were swelling with tears and I came out. Kaab bin Malik says when he was walking around the market in Medina. A merchant from Jordan, he had something to sell he was asking people to point out Kaab bin Malik. People guided him towards me. He came to me and handed to me a letter from the king of Ghassan is a Christian who hated Muslims and disliked Prophet. It is in the book of Seerah that he wanted to draw an army and asked. Heraculus for support as he was proxy of Heraculus.

They had big names like king, but they were traitors and agents for Hercules. He wanted permission from Heraculus to attack Medina. That was Heraculus who told him to stop and hold tite. Because Heraculus knew that the Prophet Mohd PBUH is a messenger of Allah and did not want to have confrontation with him. Heraculus was wiser than the king of Ghsan who was an Arab and should have different attitude towards the Prophet. The king of Ghsan sent a letter to Kaab bin Malik. That shows some spying was going on and what was happening in Medina. King off Ghsan found out what happened to Kaab bin Malik. The letter stated I have heard that you friend has forsaken you, and Allah would not like you to be humiliated in that place so come to us we will take care of you. They intended to break the Muslims ranks and draw a prominent member of a Muslim community. King of Ghsan disliked Muslims and wanted to weaken then Kaab bin Malik said, when I read the letter I realized this is a trial from Allah. And threw the letter in the fire Kaab bin Malik said a messenger from Prophet came to me after 40 days and said Prophet is ordering you to leave your wife. I asked shall I divorce her the answer was no but to stay away from her and Prophet sent the same messages to other two companies as well. Kaab bin Malik told his wife to go and stay with her family until Allah judges in this affair.

Kaab bin Malik said, the wife of Halal bin Umiya came to me and said, Halal bin Umiya is an old man who is last can I serve him. Prophet said, no but do not let him touch you. She said in the name of Allah he has no desire for anything. Since this affairs started he has been weeping until this moment. The stayed behind but their hearts were there. A believer realizes his mistake. After 50 days when I prayed salat in the morning, I was on a roof of my house. I was sitting in way described by Allah and his messenger my soul because constrained the whole earth became difficult, feeling difficult. I heard someone yelled out to me from the mountain of Salat with top of his voice, O' Kaab bin Malik rejoice, I immediately made sajood. And I knew that the problem has been revealed. Prophet was told by Allah that our Toba have been accepted people came out with good news. Some people went to others and two men came to give me the glad tidying one of them climbed the mountain and the other one took a horse but the sound was faster to reach. It was a tradition that person who delivers the good news one gives him a gift. The person who shouted from the mountain I gave him two clokes, which I had and then I borrowed two other to put on and went to meet Prophet. Then people were meeting me in groups and greeting me, congratulating me that my Toba has been accepted by Allah. I went to mosque, Kaab bin Malik says I went to Prophet gave my Islam. Prophet told me when his face was beaming with happiness rejoice with the best day ever since your mother gave birth to you. Kaab bin Malik asked Prophet. Is it from you or from Allah? Prophet said it is from Allah. This came down from Allah, when Prophet was happy his face was like full moon. Prophet was very happy because of acceptance of Toba of Kaab bin Malik and his two companions. Then Kaab bin Malik said part of my Toba will be that I give all of my money for the sake of Allah and his messenger.

Prophet said, leave behind some of your wealth it is better for your Kaab bin Malik said I shall hold on to my share from battle of Khyber. He said O' messenger of Allah, Allah has saved me because of my honesty, speaking the truth and part of my repentance is that I promised to myself that I shall always speak the truth as long as I live. When Kaab was narrating this hadith. He I have been blessed by Allah since that time I have not spoken any word but the truth. Ladies and Gentlemen, Allah has revealed two Ayat of Surah Toba the second Ayat is about Kaab and his two companions.

Allah says Allah has already forgiven the Prophet PBUH and mahajreen and Ansar who followed him in the hour of difficulty, after hearts of a party almost inclined to doubt and then he forgave them indeed he was kind and merciful. This represents the peak of Muslims and the towards the end of the life of the Prophet PBUH. Allah is accepting their Toba repentance.

Then Allah says, also forgave the three who left behind and regretted their mistake to the point the earth closed in on them in spite of its vastness and their souls confine them and they were certain that there is no refuge from Allah except on repentance Allah accepted Toba from Kaab bin Malik and his two companions.

Let us see what Allah says about those who gave convincing excuses and lied. Allah says in verse 95 and 96 of Sura Toba. They will swear by Allah to you, when you return to them, that you would leave them alone, leave them alone indeed they are evil.

Their refuge is hell as recompense for what they have been earning. They swear to you that you might be satisfied with them. But if you are satisfied with them, Allah is not satisfied with disobediently defiant people. The consequence of truth and consequence of lying is very clear. Some benefits mentioned Ibn Qeem in his book, Zaid ul maad, he says. A Muslims should not bring into open any sins if Allah has concealed them, leave the sins concealed. But sometimes there are some shortcomings and Kaab bin Malik saw some benefit in that firstly they were known and there are some lessons to be learned. He spoke about then and he was honest in his narration.

Secondly, it is allowed that one can speak some good things about himself but this is open ended. A person should not praise himself. However, Kaab bin Malik has said some good that he has been in every battle except battle of Badr and that he attended Aqba. However, it is allowed if it is not elevating himself. The pledge of Aqba is one of the best events or the best event of the Sahaba. We use to see as equal to Badr. Be hasty and take up the good opportunity that open up for you.

Ladies and Gentlemen Allah at some moments during the life would open up doors of opportunity to do goo. These doors of opportunity come and go and some time if they go they go for good, and one misses them. He misses their opportunity forever.

Kaab bin Malik had an opportunity that opened up for him, to take part in Tabuk. He missed it. The lesson is do not sit behind and say I wish I had done so. Take advantage of the good that comes your way from Allah.

Allah says in verse 24 of Surah Infal, O' you, who have believed in Allah and his messenger, when he calls you to that which gives your life and know that Allah intervenes between a man and his heart. And to him you will be gathered, Allah may intervene between you and your heart and may prevent you from joining next time. Do not delay or stay behind. Take advantage of the opportunities that open up for you.

Allah says in Quran and we shall turn away their hearts and their eyes just as they refuse to believe in it at the first time.

Allah says when he deviated when an opportunity opened up and they deviated Allah caused their hearts to deviate. Verse 115 Sura Toba, Allah will not let people go astray after he has guided them till he makes clear to them what they should avoid. In deed Allah is knowing all things.

Next lesson, the only ones stayed behind are Munafiqeen or the ones who are excused or the ones who are appointed to stay behind by Prophet one is allowed to speak in favor of

Allah and his messenger for Allah's religion. When a man spoke against Kaab bin Malik from Bini Muslima that was the intention. Also allowed to respond like Maaz bin Jabal. It is allowed not to respond to slam of person who has committed. After the life of hypocrisy and plotting against the Prophet PBUH. Abdullah bin Abbey was on his death bed. Mohd bin Ishaque says the Prophet PBUH visited him. Prophet saw signs of death on his face. Prophet told him in the name of Allah I used to warn you from loving the Jews. Until last moments, days Abdullah bin Abbey had split loyalties. This shows the hypocrisy. This is a sign repeated in Quran more than once. The ones who have disease in the heart these are the Munafiqeen.

In Bukhari Sharif when Abdullah bin Abbey passed away Prophet wanted to pray on his Janaza. Umar bin Khattab came and stood in front of Prophet and said Prophet are you going to pray for him when he said this and that on such and such days. Umar bin Khattab is going through the past of Abdullah bin Abbey reminding Prophet with positions that Abdullah bin Abbey was taking Prophet PBUH, responded and said oh Umer leave me alone. If I know, that if I ask Allah for more than 70 time and it will be accepted by Allah. I would do that.

Prophet is referring to verse 80 Sura Toba ask for forgiveness for them O' Mohd, or do not ask for forgiveness for them. If you ask for forgiveness for 70 times. Never for Allah to forgive them. That is because they disbelieve in Allah and his messenger and Allah does not guide defiantly disobediently people. This shows the striking quality of Prophet. The messenger of Allah has suffered personally again and again from Abdullah bin Abbey, directly and indirectly the plot and plans, the deception and lies of Abdullah bin Abbey are countless. Nevertheless, Prophet is still willing to give him a last chance to pray on his Janaza and ask Allah to forgive him. But then Allah revealed the Ayat verse 84 in Sura Toba, Allah says and do not pray over them who has died ever or stand on his grave. Indeed, they disbelieved in Allah and his messenger and died. They are defiantly disobedient. Now the issue is the clear and clarified that no salat should be offered on Munafiqeen. This the final.

This is one of the occasions where Quran supported the opinion of Umar bin Khattab. This was the Hikmet of Allah that Abdullah bin Abbey would not survive. The messenger of Allah Mohd PBUH. He died before the Prophet. Abdullah bin Abbey was living with the hope with aspirations that being patient and not facing the Muslims directly, he will go through the temporary phase and at the end, he himself, his people and his ideas will survive. That was his thinking, sitting tite and waiting they will have a chance. Islam is a temporary thing, it is a phase which will pass and people will be back to normal. He thought that Muhammad PBUH stripped him of his power and kingdom. As it is in the books of Seerah, his people were planning to appoint him king over them, and that is the time when Prophet made Hijra and his plans were shattered Abdullah bin Abbey died before Prophet. And Islam survived and was flourishing the way of the Munafiqeen dies and they face Allah on the Day of Judgment. They will have to face Allah's wrought Prophet appointed Hazrat Abu Bakr Siddique the 9th year of Hijra to go and perform Hajj. Abu Bakr had to lead the delegation of Hajj. Prophet did not want to perform Hajj while the false Gods are lining up around Kaaba the idols had been destroyed but their followers were still coming for Hajj. As shirk was still surviving in some parts of Arabia also people had tradition making tawaf. They used to believe because of their imparity they cannot come with their clothes on. They would take off their clothes and barrow some clean clothes from Quraish.

They used to view the clothes from Quraish. Special clothes but some people didn't have the status and money and means to harrow. Therefore, they would end up making tawaf nocked. This was a dual problem non-Muslims and naked tawaf around Kaaba. Therefore, Prophet did not want to perform Hajj under the circumstances. Hazrat Abu Bakr led the Hajj delegation, the numbers were around 200 Sahaba who went with Abu Bakr. After they had left for Hajj. Prophet received the first part of Sura Toba. Prophet wanted to send these Ayat to Makkah. So that the people will hear them, opinion was that these Ayat should be sent to Abu Bakr. But Prophet said no. Only a man should announce these Ayat who belongs to my household. And Prophet called Hazrat Ali ibn Abu Talib told him to go to Mecca and announce the following Prophet told. Hazrat Ali to go with the Ayat from Sura Bra and declare these to the people when they are gathering in Minha. Tell them no disbeliever shall enter into paradise and no polytheist shall make Hajj, after this year and no naked person will perform tawaf around Kaaba. The house of Allah, whoever has a contract of security from Prophet then his contract will be fulfilled until the end of its duration.

Then had to read the Ayat of Sura Toba. This is a declaration of disassociation from Allah and his messenger those of you, have made a treaty with the polytheist notice that the Surah Bra and Toba the only Surah which does not start with Bismillah the name of Allah the merciful and this is a strait forward disassociation from kufr, there it does not start with Bismillah Al-Rehman Al-Rahim. It starts with Bra disassociation this is first word Bra. Disassociation O' disbelievers travel freely in the land during four months but know that you cannot cause failure to Allah. And Allah will disagree the disbelievers. This is the announcement from Allah and his messenger to the people on the day of the greater pilgrimage that Allah has disassociated from disbelievers and so is his messenger. If you repent, that is best for you but you turn away, know that you will not cause failure to Allah and give glad tidying to disbelievers of painful punishment.

Accepted are those with whom you made a treaty among the polytheist and then they have not been deficient towards you in anything or supported anyone against you so complete their treaty until their term has ended. Indeed, Allah loves the righteous people who fear him, and when the sacred months have passed then kill the polytheists where ever you find them, capture them besiege them and sit and wait for them at every place and ambush them. But if they should repent establish prayer and give Zakat, let them go on their way. Indeed, Allah is forgiving and merciful. There are the Ayat, and more that Hazrat Ali ibn Abu Talib announced at the time of Hajj at the 9th year of Hijra, and it was the last year when non-believers are going perform Hajj. This was the last year that traditions and rituals of disbelievers are going to show in Makkah. Allah says when the victory of Allah has come and the conquest and you see the people entering into the religion of Allah in multitudes then exult him with praise of your lord and ask for forgiveness from him. Indeed he is ever accepting of repentance. When the victory of Allah has come and the conquest the result will be that people will enter into Islam. It is mentioned in the books of Seerah, the tribes of Arabia were watching the conflict between Prophet and Quraish, and they were waiting to see who will win. When Prophet defeated Quraish, the Arabs then came in multitudes accepting Islam. Quraish were seen as the religious authority. They are the keepers of House of Allah. They manage the affairs of people in Hajj and Umrah. They live in Mecca and Mecca is the religious center off Arabs. So people used to look up to them. When Prophet announced the Prophethood, the war between Prophet and Quraish, started many of them wanted to sit on the sidelines and wouldn't take sides. But watch where this conflict is heading. After Mecca was opened soon after that tribes around Makkah were accepting Islam. The two large tribes Quraish and Saqeef accepted Islam. After that people were flooding Medina accepting Islam.

The 9th year of Hijra was called Aloud the year of delegation; these tribes would send their representative to Medina. They would pledge allegiance to Prophet and this pledge was also a pledge to an Islamic state, they were become part of the entity of Muslim state in Medina. Because the Bia is to the head of state Prophet. So they were accepting his rule.

Ibn Kathir they mention many delegations. We shall try to go through some of them. We have keep in mind even though these delegations become Muslim and are accounted as Sahaba. But people who became Muslim before the conquest of Mecca have higher status than those who became Muslim after the conquest of Mecca. The reason is that after the conquest of Mecca it was very clear that the victory in world is for Muslims. But before people became Muslim knew they will have to go through hardship and will have to make sacrifices. Earlier it was very difficult for Muslims, Allah says Surat Al Hadeed, Not equal to you are those who spent before the conquest Fatah Makkah and fought and those who did so after Fatah Makkah.

The people Saqeef came to Prophet and accepted Islam. The story is that they tried to negotiate with Prophet to leave their major Idol for one year Prophet refused. Then they said leave it for one month. They were worried that the commoner among the people will be shocked and may not be able to handle to see, their so-called God, fall in to Rebel. Broken to pieces they wanted to take it slowly. They did say that we shall accept Islam but we do not want our Idol to be destroyed for one year, so we can take step by step with people, Prophet refused they said for one month Prophet refused then a week, Prophet refused even for one day Prophet refused, they tried their best but Prophet made it clear that he is not going to approve such a thing. False God to stay for an additional moment was unacceptable. Well they if this is the case we will not bring it down ourselves you have send somebody to destroy it. Prophet sent Abu Sufyan and Masheera bin Sheeba. He is from Saqeef they both went to destroy the main idol, people started saying you wait, there will be diseases wait for leprosy, people had their superstitious, that these things will happen, people were threatening and people seriously thought, that Mugheera will be destroyed by their false God, we Muslims say false Gods but those people who used to worship them for them they were true Gods, people believed in them.

But Mugheera wanted to make fun for what people were thinking. He struck the Idol with his Axe then he deliberately fell down to show people that the idol has struck him back. People started shouting and people were happy that the idol God has struck him hock. Then Mugheera stud up and said you are foals it is nothing but a peace of stone and he started to break it into pieces. Delegation from Banu Tamim come to Prophet and Prophet gave them glad tidying good news.

It is in Bukhari accept the glad tidying, Banu Tamim, O' Prophet, we have heard that now give us the good news we do not want give us something. Prophet did not like that and people had come from Yemen, Prophet told them accept the glad tidying since Banu Tamim di not accept them. They said we accept the glad tidings Prophet whenever a delegation came Prophet would appoint a leader, when Banu Tamim came they had two leaders names Mabid bin Zarar and Akra bin Habs. It says in Bukhari that Hazrat Abu Bakr suggested to Prophet to appoint Kaka bin Mabd as their leader Umar bin Khattab no appoint Akra bin Habs. Abu Bakr became angry and said to Umar you said that just to go against my opinion. Umar bin Khattab said no I did not do that to go against your opinion. They started arguing with each other.

Their voices became loud; that is the time when Allah revealed, O' you have believed do not put yourself before the messenger of Allah and fear Allah and indeed Allah is hearing and knowing. That was the first Ayat then there a delegation from Banu Abdul Qais. There is the eastern part of Arabia.

Prophet told them I command you with four and I command you to believe in Allah and do you know what it means to testify that there is no one worthy of worship but Allah, establish salat pay or give Zakat and Fast in Ramadan month and to give 1/5 of the booty. And the rule is that whenever you gain any spoils of war give 1/5 to the leader. Then Prophet said I warn you from four things that is they used to use 4 different types of containers for drinking (Alcohol). They were told not drink and not to use those containers to get them out of the habit of drinking. The incident of Yamama, this is mentioned among the delegations even though it does not belong there because Yamama did not come to Medina but he was arrested captured. Secondly this happened before when Makkah was not opened. But Ibn Kathir and books of Seerah put it in this Sequence (Although Makkah is Muslim now). Most off the delegations are brought in a section and the timing perhaps not the same. As they say about Tafseel bin Amraroosi, even though he came in Makkah. Prophet sent an army to Najad, they arrested a man from Banu Hanifa. His name is Tamama, they bound him with a pillar in mosque.

Prophet went to him and said what do you have to say? He said I have good to say, if you kill me then you kill a man who is very worthy among his people and important person. The other interpretation is that if you kill me (you kill a man who has blood on his hands therefore there is no blame on you). But if you release me, then you release a person who is grateful and if you want money ask me what you want. Prophet left him and Prophet came to him next day asked what you have to say. He said the same thing. I have what I already told you, if you release me I am grateful, then Prophet Cause to him the next day, asked him what you have to say Tamama. Again he said I have to say what you have already heard. Prophet said release him. He left As soon as he came out of the mosque. He took a shower bath, then entered into mosque and said Kalma Shahadat, I have witness that these is no God but Allah and Mohd PBUH is his servant, messenger. He did not want to do that when he was tied up but now he is grateful. He was free, he could leave if he wanted but he became Muslim and said O' Mohd PBUH, there was no face on the face of the earth that was more despised to me than your face now your face is most beloved to me. There was no religion that was more despised to me. Now this religion has become most beloved to me. There was no land more despised to me than your land and now your land is most beloved to me. Your horsemen have captured me but I want to go for Umrah. What do you think, I should do, Prophet told him to go and make Umrah. When he came to Makkah, people to go and make Umrah. When he came to Mecca, people told him you have become apostate that is what they used to say when people change to Islam.

He would say no, but I have become Muslim. And said not a single grain of wheat will come to you from Yamama. Until Prophet allows it. This is the evidence used by people who accept the procedure of boycott as a valid weapon of war. Delegation from Banu Hanifa that included a man called Muslima

Ibn Abbas says Muslima Qazab the lair came to Prophet. He said if Muhammad PBUH appoints me to lead after him, I shall follow him Prophet came to him along with Sabit bin Qais. Prophet had in his hand a stick from a palm tree Prophet said, if you ask me to give this stick to you I would not give it to you. Let alone to give you the leadership of Umma after me. I would not give you this stick. Then Prophet told him you are not going to surpass what Allah has destined to you. If you leave, you will be destroyed, Also Prophet pbuh said referring to him what Prophet saw in his dream and here is Sabit. He will speak to you and Prophet pbuh left.

The dream Prophet pbuh is referring to is, Prophet pbuh said while I was sleeping I saw two Bracelets of Gold on my arms, and Prophet was told in his sleep to blow them away I blew them and they flew away I interpreted as two liars who would come after me. One of them is Al-Asdi and the other is Muslima. Muslima would write a letter to Prophet and this is 11th year of Hijra the letter was sent by two messengers who came to meet the Prophet. Pbuh.

Letter read, from Muslima messenger of Allah to Muhammad the messenger of Allah, peace be upon you, I have been involved in the affairs with you. Half of it belongs to us and half belongs to Quraish. But Quraish are people who transgress. He is saying that kingdom should be split in half.

Prophet pbuh wrote back to him I begin with the name of Allah who is merciful and beneficent, from Muhammad the messenger of Allah to Muslima Qazab peace he upon those who follow guidance, earth belong to Allah and he will give it to whomever he wills and the end belongs to the righteous.

Then Prophet pbuh asked them, this is narrated by Abu Dawood do you testify that I am the messenger of Allah they the messengers said, we testify that Muslima is the messenger of Allah.

Prophet pbuh said, I believe in Allah and his messengers and if I was going to kill a messenger I would have killed you. Abdullah bin Masood said, it became Sunna that messengers are not killed the carries of letters the messengers should not be killed. Even if they are coming from enemy or people of war. As long as they are messengers then they are not to be killed.

A delegation came from Najran. It is in Sura Al-Imran also Tafseel of Ibn Kathir, A long debate and dialogue between Islam and Christianity. Prophet pbuh received a revelation about 80 Ayat from Sura Al-Imran talking about this the people from Najran they were Christian. Bukhari says, the Aqib and Saeed. They wanted to do a debate, where Prophet would come out and Christians would come out and ask Prophet to send his Wrought on the liars. But Christians refused to do it because they said if he is truly a messenger then that would be end of us and they did not accept that. But they had to accept the order of Prophet pbuh even though they did not become Muslim but they will pay Jazia tax.

They the Christians said, send someone with us who is trustworthy, and only send someone trustworthy. Prophet said, I shall send with you a man who is truly trustworthy man of this Umma. Then we have Amir bin Tafseel and Bin Riba, Arbid these men are from Najad, people told Abu Amir, and people have become Muslim why don't you become Muslims. He said I have taken a vow, that my life will not end until Arab will follow me, and now you want me to follow this young man from Quraish. They came to Prophet pbuh and wanted to strike a deal. They saw that Muslims are a force to be reckoned with, and if they wanted to have any authority in Arabia they had to have a deal with Prophet pbuh.

They are assuming that Prophet is like other tribe leaders. They wanted to negotiate something. They did not know this is a Prophethood and somewhat different. They came to

Prophethood and somewhat different. They came to Prophet and said we would like to split the affair between you and us. Prophet refused. In the name of Allah I am going to fill Medina with men and horses. He is known as numerous strong fighter. It is not only a threat there is some truth in that. He could fill Medina with men and horses. But Prophet pbuh told him Allah will refuse that and sons of Akela. Akela is the mother of Ansar. Al Auose and Al-Khazrj, Prophet pbuh is saying Allah and sons of Akela will refuse. This is the confidence in Ansar. Prophet has tested them and lived with them for 9 years now. Prophet pbuh has seen their strength their sacrifice and loyalty to wards Prophet pbuh. Now Abu Amir and Arbid, said since he refuses to deal with us let us kill him meaning Prophet. Abu Amir said he would talk to Prophet and Arbid will come from behind and strike with his sword to kill the Prophet.

One narration says that the hand of Arbid got stuck to the sword and he could not move it. The other narration says that whenever he would try to strike the Prophet. The messenger of Allah disappears and Arbid would only see Abu Amir in front of him. Later on Amir said what is the matter with you. In the name of Allah I would fear no one but I used to fear you. Now I see you as nothing, Arbid said what, do you want me to do? Every time I want to strike him only you are in front of me. Do you want me to kill you this is a miracle from Allah? However, they left empty handed, and the threat they made to Prophet, Allah took care of them. On the way back Abu Amir met a woman who belonged to his tribe and slept in her house when he got up, there was big swelling on his neck. It was a disease which kills he did not want to die in the house of this woman even though he was in pain. He went on his horse and kept on wondering until he died on his horse back. That was the end of him.

Arbid on his way back, he was struck by lightning which killed him along with his camels. This is the fulfillment of Surah.

Allah says it is he who shows you lightening as to aspiration fear and generates heavy clouds and thunder exults Allah with praise of Allah and angels as well from fear of him and Allah send thunder bolt and strikes there with whom he wills while they dispute about Allah. His Allah is swear and soft that was the end of these two.

A delegation one man as representative of tribe this man's name is Tmama bin Taliba. It is in Bukhari Sharif and in other books of Hadith. This narration is by Imam Ahmed, narrated by Abdullah bin Abbas. Tribe of Banu Saad bin Bakr sent Tmama bin Talbia as a representative to Prophet. He came he tied his camel and walked into the mosque, while Prophet was sitting with Sahaba. He was a strong man and long hair in two braids. He said who among you is the son of Abdul Mutlab is. He didn't say son of Abdullah but Abdul Mutlab as he was famous in the whole Arabia.(Abdul Mutlab)

Remember when Abra came with his army and elephants to Makkah Abdul Mutlab was the leader and met Abra, Abdul Mutlab had very high status and was well known. who is the son of Abdul Mutlab. Prophet pbuh said I am the son of Abdul Mutlab, are you Muhammad Prophet pbuh said yes. He said I am going to ask you strate questions and do not be angry. Prophet said, I am not going to be angry, ask whatever you want I ask you in the name of Allah. You're God, and the God of ones before you and the God of the ones after you. Did he send you as a messenger? Prophet said yes in the name of Allah, you're Lord the Lord of the ones before you and the Lord of the ones after you. Did Allah told you to tell us to worship him and no one else, and to leave there Gods, we used to worship. Prophet said yes, in the name of Allah and

Allah of before you and after you. Did Allah order you, that we pray there five daily prayers. Prophet said yes, in the name of Allah, then he would repeat and asked about 5 pillars of Islam and Prophet said yes in the name of Allah. Then he said, I testify there is no one worthy of worship but Allah, I testify that Mohd is the messenger of Allah, I am going to fulfil these obligation and I am going to leave what you do not want me to do. And I am not going to add anything or subtract anything. When he lift Prophet said if the man is truthful then he will enter in to paradise. He went on his camel to go to his people. As soon as he came to his people he said Auza and other Gods are evil, people asked him what are you saying? You will be inflicted with leprosy or will become insane. He said vow to you, they do not harm and they do not benefit.

Allah has sent a messenger and revealed to him a book that will save you from what you used to do. I testify there is no one but Allah and no one is associated with him. And Mohd is his servant and messenger I came from him I am ordering you to do what he ordered me to do. I warn you against the things he warned me from. By the end of the day everyone in his tribe became Muslims. Abu Abbas says we do not know anybody more blessed than that man Tmama bin Tanya.

The story of Adhay bin Hatim. He heard about the Prophethood of Prophet. He was Christian. He did not like it. He was not happy about it and he heard about the expansion of the Islamic state and it was reaching closer to his people in the north east of Arabia. So he went to Roman Empire, he says when I reached there, I found the situation worse than our situation and he came back. In one narration he told his servants to prepare strong camels and then he said that whenever you see the banners of Muslims approaching tell me. His servants saw the Muslims banners coming he was informed. He took his fast and strong camels and ran away. Muslims came they took his aunt and in a narration his sister as prisoners of war and they were brought to Medina. His aunt told Prophet to free her. Prophet asked her who is she and she told him. Prophet freed her and she was free. Hazrat Ali advised her to ask Prophet for some transportation and Prophet did so Muslims were kind to her she went to Audhay. She told him what you did is shameful. You ran away and you left your family. She said I have come from a man, who is a truthful and messenger of Allah she praised Prophet. He decided to go and visit the messenger of Allah, now he was feeling safe, and he felt that Prophet is someone whom one can approach. This is a good quality. But non-Muslims of Arabia would heir false rumors about Prophet. But they heir from someone who happens to know him, they would learn that he is merciful, kind and approachable. That encouraged many people to come and meet the Prophet and see him. But there was some are cruel harmful then people would be reluctant to go and see the Prophet.

Adhay bin Hatim came there are different narrations but are narration says that he had a cross hanging from his neck to chest necklace. Prophet told him that people have taken other Gods beside Allah, Adhay though perhaps Prophet does not understand about Christian religion. Since he was the expert in his religion. He said we do not take them as Gods beside Allah. Prophet said, didn't they make what was Halal to Haram and what was Haram to Halal? He said yes, Prophet explained since you give them this authority. You allow them to be your Gods because this authority belongs to Allah alone. In another narration Prophet told him that I understand your religion more than you do Adhay bin Hatim questioned that, Prophet asked him don't you belong to a sect Requasia, he said yes.

Don't you take from your people from spoils, he said yes. Prophet told him that is not allowed in your religion Adhay says I knew that and as soon as Prophet said that I was humbled. In Bukhari, Adhay bin Hatim says we visited Umar bin Khattab in a delegation Umar bin Khattab call them in one by one and call them by their names, meaning Umar bin Khatam knew all off them by name. But Umar did not call Adhay and Adhay said, O' Ameer ul Momnin, you don't know me Umar bin Khattab said, yes I know you, you are became Muslim when they were disbelievers, you are the one who came when they left. You are the one who fulfilled when they betrayed, and you are the one who knew when they had rejected, you accepted. Then he said I do not care, he was pleased that the Ameer, knew about him and recognized him. Adhay bin Hatim was the son of an Arab who is very famous for his generosity, Hatim Tai. There are many tails and legends about the generosity of Hatim Tai. Adhay is his son. In Bukhari, Adhay bin Hatim is a noble man in the society. He came to Medina, he saw the situation in Medina, he was with Prophet and a man came to Prophet complaining about poverty and another man came and complained about bandits. They are preventing the travelers. Prophet noticed what Adhay is seeing. Did you see Alhra, a city in Iraq, I didn't see it but I have heard about it. If you live long enough, you will see a woman traveling from Alhra to Kaaba. Until she readers she will fear no one but Allah. I asked myself where the handouts are turning land into fire. Travelling from Alhra to Mecca they have to pass the land of Adhay. There are many arm robbers and handouts over there which makes it impossible for a woman to travel, now Prophet is saying she will fear no one but Allah. Then Prophet said and if you live long enough the treasures of Kissera, will become spoils of war for us. Kissera is the son of Hurmuz, is Emperor of Persia.

And if you live long enough you will find a man coming with hand full of gold or silver trying to find someone who will take Sadqa from him and he will find no one.

Prophet was telling him what will happen on the Day of Judgement, Adhay bin Hatim said the three things, Prophet told two have been true I have seen myself and third one will come true. Another narration Prophet was telling Adhay bin Hatim probably you do not want to follow me because we are poor many people go by what they see. They are affected by material aspects of things I they see people are wealthy, they are successfully they are impressed by that, this false and wrong one should look at assents of the message and not at the material things Adhay bin Hatim admitted this was turning him away from Islam because Muslim were poor people Prophet was telling him that time will come.

Then there was delegation from Yemen. In Bukhari Sharif it says, Prophet said people of Yemen are soft hearted. Imaan is Yemeni and wisdom is Yemeni. This was the praise Prophet gave to people of Yemen. This is when Abu Mossa AlAshari came to see Prophet. Then another delegation from Yemen Anees bin Malik says, he gave a garment a gift to Prophet that cost him 33 camels expensive gift and Prophet accepted this gift.

Then Jareed bin Abdullah came to Prophet, Imam Ahmad says Jareed tide his camel and entered into the mosque when Prophet is speaking and people were staring at me. He thought Prophet must have said something about him before he came in and that was the case. He asked someone next to him, did Prophet mentioned me and the man said yes, with a good mention that Prophet had said during his Khutbah that now a man will come in through this door and you will see on his face signs of a king, Jareed said praise be to Allah for that Jareed says Prophet never refused meeting me after I became

Muslim and whenever he would see me he would smile in my face, and he told Prophet I cannot stay firm on my horse Prophet struck me in my chest and said O' Allah make him firm and make him a guided man and guide through him Jareed a guided man and guide through him Jareed said, I never fell off from horse after that.

This is how Prophet pbuh, won the hearts of people. He would smile at them and meet them. He was close to his followers. Now another son of king from Hazar moat. He came to Prophet he met Prophet. Prophet hosted him and treated him very well. Then Prophet gave him a piece of land Prophet wanted to show him the land so Prophet sent with him Movia bin Abu Sufyan. Movia was a young man. He went with Weyl to show him the location of the land. Movia is walking while is riding Movia was perhaps barefoot, Movia told him I want to ride with you on your camel. He said you are not going to ride with a king. He refused to allow him to ride. In another narration Movia said, I want to ride with you on your camel Weyl said you are not a king to ride with kings Movia told him the ground is very hat, He said use the shade of the camel and walk in it. Movia wouldn't forget how badly he was treated days passed and Movia becomes Khalifa, King, who visits him Weyl when he arrived Movia had him sit with him on couch sofa, the couch of the king unlike, that Movia was not allowed to ride with him Movia reminded him what happened on that day, Weyl said I wish not only I had him ride with me but ride in front of me. On delegation a man told he had met Dajjal. We shall talk about this in detail in the series of life hereafter.

A delegation of 7 men came from Alaz they are relatives of Ansar. Ansar are descendants from Alaz, they came to see Prophet and Prophet was impressed by them by their books their character, they said we are believers Prophet smiled and said what is the reality of that they said they were believers.

15 choristertic, 5 of them commanded by your messenger to us, 5 of them you have commanded us to do and 5 of them are traditions from Jahlia except you want us to change them Prophet asked what those 5 are. Which my messenger ordered you we are ordered to believe in Allah. His angels, his books, his messenger and resurrection after death, what are the five commands that I gave you, you ordered us say, Kalma. Establish salat, pay Zakat, Fast in Ramzan and make Hajj who is capable.

And what are the five you have your character from Jahlia to be grateful in the time of ease, be patient in times of difficulty, to accept destiny, be truthful when the enemies meet, and to avoid malicious enjoy out of enemy. Not to go to extreme in order make fun of enemy.

Prophet said you are wise and knowledge and because of your knowledge you are almost Prophets. Prophet was very impressed by their wisdom. Prophet said I shall give you five more so that you will have so characteristics.

If you are what you say, do not collect what you will not eat, do not build what you will not live in, do not compete in something that you will leave tomorrow. Fear Allah to whom you will return to and to whom you will he presented to, and strife for what is ahead of you and where you will be living forever. They left and fallowed the advice of Prophet. We have covered only few delegation but that was a busy year people were coming from four corners of Arabia. This is towards the end of the life of Prophet. Now he is witnessing the fruits of his Dava.

HAJJ- ATUL WIDA

The Messenger of Allah PBUH, on his way back from the final Hajj said, "Ali (ABPWH) is a friend".. The reason was that some false rumors against Ali bin Abu Talib. The Prophet PBUH wanted to defend him in front of everybody. Ali is also a cousin of prophet PBUH, husband of Prophet's PBUH daughter, Fatima, and father of the only lineage from Prophet PBUH i.e.; Imam Hassan bin Ali, and Imam Hussain bin Ali. The Messenger of Allah is telling people, If I am your Mollah (helper) then Ali is also helper. If you love me, you also need to love Ali bin Abu Talib.

The Messenger of Allah returned to Madinah, now we are entering in to 11th year of Hijra, Osama bin Zaid, he is eighteen to twenty years old to lead an Army. At first, he was young. Secondly, he was a slave. This is in Bukhari, if you dispute his appointment. You should have objected the appointment of his father Zaid bin Harsa. He was suitable and one of the beloved to me, after him Osama bin Zaid.

In the month of suffer prophet pbuh had received indication that the prophet pbuh will die as other human beings. Allah revealed Ayat in Makkah, Allah says, The life hereafter is better for you than the first life, and your Lord is going to give you, and you will be satisfied. Therefore, when prophet pbuh was given the choice of living in this world or leaving this world, we shall see, what was the choice of the prophet pbuh.

The prophet pbuh had the promise very early in Makkah, that after life is better for you. Allah will give you until you are satisfied. Allah says, indeed you are to die and then on the day of Resurrection, you will be the first one. Surah Al-Ambia Allah says, we did not grant any man eternity, so if you die, that would be eternal. Every soul will taste death, and we shall test you with good and evil trial, and to us you will return. So the whole life is a trial of good and bad.

Allah revealed at Hajj Atul wida, I have completed your religion and have perfected my favor on you, and approved Islam for you as religion.

There is nothing direct but there is an indication of fulfilment of the mission. Allah says, Muhammad pbuh is a messenger. Other messengers have passed on before him. If he is killed or is to die, would you turn back on your belief, and he who turns back on his heals will not harm Allah, but Allah will reward the grateful. It is not possible for one to die, without the permission of Allah at a decree determined. Whoever desires the rewards of this world, we will give there off, we will reward the grateful. Allah says in Surah Nasser, when the victory of Allah, the conquest has come, you will see, the people entering in to religion of Allah in multitudes. Then exalt him with praise, praise of your Lord and ask him for his forgiveness, he is accepting repentance.

Again in these Ayat, there is direct indication of death of the prophet pbuh. Ibn e Abbas used to sit with senior Mahajreen and Ansar in the court of Umar bin Khattab, some Mahajreen and Ansar, questioned, why is this young man sitting here while our young ones are not invited? Umar bin Khattab wanted to point out, and therefore asked, what do you understand of Surah Nasser ? No one answered, and then Umar bin Khattab asked Ibne Abbass. He answered, the death of the prophet pbuh. Umar bin Khattab said, that is what I understand. Ibn e Abbas was sitting there because of his knowledge.

Victory of Allah is towards the end. The end result belongs to believers. After the conquest of Makkah, people were entering in multitudes. Repentance comes towards the end.

Hadith, Prophet pbuh said to Mazz bin Jubbal when sending him to Yeoman, told him "you may not see me after this". He cried. Another

Hadith, Prophet pbuh said at Hajj, learn your trials from me, I may not make any more Hajj.

The prophet pbuh said, Angel Gabriel used to recite Quran with me every year once, this year, he did this twice, and I see as an indication of end of my life. In the month of Suffer, 11ᵗʰ Hijra, Prophet pbuh sent for Abu Mohaiba, this was late at night and told him O' Abu Mohaiba, I have been commanded to ask for forgiveness for people in Jannat ul baqee (this is the smetery) of Madinah. this is beloved smarty, where companions of the prophet pbuh are buried. Prophet pbuh was ordered by Allah to go there and ask Allah to forgive them. The Messenger of Allah told Abu Mohaiba to go with him, they went together to the graveyard. Prophet pbuh is going at midnight to give company to his companions. Prophet pbuh said, peace be upon you O' people of the grave. Then Prophet pbuh told them congratulations. The people who are dead, that you do not experience what living people are experiencing, congratulations. You passed away, when hearts were pure, trials and tribulation come like dark portion of night, fallowing each other in succession, the last are worse than the first. (we are living in that period).

Then prophet pbuh looked at Abu Mohaiba and said, I was given the keys of treasures of this world and living in this world as long as it exists and then Paradise, and second choice, meeting My Lord and paradise. Abu Mohaiba said, choose us. Prophet pbuh said, no. I have chosen to meet Allah and paradise. Then prophet pbuh sought forgiveness for people of Al Baquee (THE GRAVEYARD) and then left.

When he arrived home, the illness of his death began. His concern in this world was his Ummah.

Ibn e Katheer, says, this world is so small in the eyes of prophet pbuh, that he left it without leaving anything behind.

Ayesha (wife of the prophet pbuh) says my head hurts, prophet pbuh said, no, I should say my head hurts, severe headache, also severe fever One of the companion, touched the prophet pbuh and said, I cannot remove my hand it is so hot, and you are going through severe illness, prophet pbuh said, yes, because we the prophets suffer double the suffering than anybody else, because Allah loves them and puts them through tougher tests.

One day prophet pbuh wanted to go to Mosque to give them a covenant, He said, bring seven buckets of water from seven different wells, and pour over me for coolness. People brought seven buckets of water, cold water and poured over the body of the prophet pbuh to cool down the temperature and give the prophet pbuh chance to go to mosque his head was raped because of headache. The prophet pbuh was carried into the Mosque. He could' t walk, he had to lean on son of Al Abas and Ali ABPWH into the Mosque, his feet were dragging on the ground because he couldn't pick them up. The prophet pbuh went to the Mosque, after praising Allah, advised, Prophet pbuh mentioned Martyrs of Audh, asked Allah to forgive them. Prophet pbuh lived for his Ummah and suffered for Ummah. Advised to mahajreen, you are increasing in numbers while Ansar are not because people are coming from all over to join you, and Ansar are the ones, they supported me in the beginning, so honor the honorable and forgive the ones who make mistakes. There is a servant of

Allah, among the servants, Allah has given the choice of living in this world or in other world (LIFE HEREAFTER) going to Allah, ABU BAKAR understood, who is the slave. ABU BAKAR started crying. Prophets of Allah are given the choice. Angel of death comes to prophets seeks their permission, before taking their soul

Prophet pbuh told everybody the most faithful person and his wealth is Abu Bakar for me, informing people the status of Abu Bakar, the most faithful, his friendship and his wealth. If I was to take anybody as a dear friend, other than Allah, I would take Abu Bakar. However, I do have his companionship and his love. Every door in the Masjid should be closed except that of Abu Bakar. (Khaleel), meaning higher level of friendship. But I am the Khaleel of Allah. Abu Bakar is my brother and friend.

HADITH ; May Allah curse Christians and Jews who are building mosques (churches) on the graves of their prophets.)

No two religions should co – exist in Arabia. This is purely Islamic zone, free of Kufuor. Advice for salah, take care of slaves. Do not take advantage of weak, for example, women. Also when people leave Jihad they will be humiliated.

Prophet pbuh ordered that Army of Osama should go, send out the Army of Osama. Prophet pbuh was still going around the Houses of other wives, but it was difficult. He was carried into the house of Ayesha, all his wives were invited into the house of Ayesha when they were all together, prophet pbuh sought their permission to allow him to stay in the house of Ayesha, they all agreed. Ayesha said, this is the first time, I attended a sick person. Prophet pbuh stayed with Ayesha for the rest of his life.

Ayesha said, when the Messenger of Allah becoming ill, He would read Quran and blow on his hands and then rub his body. When he could' t do that, then Ayesha would recite these Surahs and blow on the hands of the prophet pbuh then use his hands to wipe his body for him. Because hands of the prophet pbuh are blessed hands.

One day her brother Abdul Rehman came in and he had a muswak (freshly cut tree branch people use for cleaning teeth). Prophet pbuh was looking at him. Ayesha understood that prophet pbuh wants muswak, she asked, prophet pbuh made gesture, in agreement. Ayesha took it from Abdul Rehman and softened the other end and gave it to the prophet pbuh.

Osama bin Zaid came to see the Messenger of Allah, Prophet pbuh unable to speak but raised his hand pointed at Osama, that blessings for him.

When Prophet pbuh unable to lead salah, he ordered Abu Bakar to lead salah. Ayesha did' t want her father to lead salah. She said O' Messenger of Allah, Abu Bakar is a soft-hearted man, If he stands in your place, He wouldn't be able to complete salah. Prophet pbuh said, you, women are companions of the women of Yousaf, they showed something but were hiding something. The wife of Al Aziz invited women as it was just a gathering but in reality, she wanted them to see Yousaf. Ayesha, her reason in public was different but her real reason was that people would' t like anybody standing in the place of the prophet pbuh. On Monday, people lined up for salah Prophet pbuh removed the curtains and was standing up. Anice bin Malik said, his face lit up, beautiful like moon and prophet pbuh smiled. It was going to be a fittana for us, we nearly walked out of salah. Abu Bakar came back but prophet pbuh told him to lead salah. However, prophet pbuh did come out and sat down. Some people say that prophet pbuh was leading but Abu Bakar was standing.

That was the last time prophet pbuh was happy to see people in salah, that was the fulfillment of the mission Prophet pbuh was happy because salah is most important after second Kalma (I bare witness that there is nothing worthy of worship other than Allah and I bare witness that Muhammad pbuh is the Messenger of Allah and slave of Allah.) When people stand for prayer together in lines, the prophet pbuh is happy.

Prophet pbuh was standing up people thought he is better. Abu Bakar got permission to go to sunnay, where his other wife lived, out of Medina, he went there. Al abas met Ali bin Abu Talib after he came out from the house of the prophet pbuh. This is in Bukhari : He asked, how is the prophet pbuh doing this Morning ? Ali bin Abu Talib said, with praise to Allah, he looks better. Al Abas said, after three days you will be a slave, ruled by a stick, meaning, you will be with out authority. Al Abas said, I can read death in the faces of sons of Abdul Mutlab. I can see death in the face of the prophet pbuh. He thought Prophet pbuh will die soon. (Al Abas does ' t know the unseen, only Allah knows). Al Abas, asked Ali bin Abu Talib to go and ask the prophet pbuh, would we be in authority ? Ali bin Abu Talib refused, because if the prophet pbuh rejects, then the Ummah will not give it to us until the end of time.

Prophet pbuh has been ill for Thirteen (13)days. Prophet pbuh has started to go through (scrat ul mout) ' The final moments, agony of death, when the sole is coming out. Ayesha brought some water, she would soak a piece of cloth in it and wipe the face of the prophet pbuh and say there is agony in death, there is agony in death.

The Messenger of Allah, best of the creation had to go through this. He was in the lap of Ayesha. Ayesha said, Prophet pbuh looked up in the roof with his eyes and I heard him say, The highest companion, the highest companion.

Ayesha says, as I understood, the Angel was asking, whether you want to stay in this world or with the highest ? The answer, with the highest companion. Then Ayesha says, the head of the prophet pbuh turned towards me, and she screamed, because of my foolishness, I yelled and screamed. Now the news was spreading. Umar bin Khattab and Al Mugharia came in, Umar bin Khattab said, prophet pbuh is unconscious. When going out Mughira said prophet pbuh is dead. This was very hard on Sohaba. Umar bin Khattab said, you are a fittana, prophet pbuh didn't die, He will not die until he terminates Munafiqeen (hypocrites). Then Umar bin Khattab went into the Mosque. People were crowding and weeping. Umar bin Khattab pulled out his sword and said, there are some Munafiqeen (hypocrites) who are claiming prophet pbuh died. Prophet pbuh is unconscious like Mosses pbuh, (he became unconscious) and he will come back. But if anybody says he is dead, I shall cut his head off with my sword.

Abu Bakar heard the news and came back from sunnay on his horse. He did not

Speak to anyone when he came to the room of Ayesha. Prophet PBUH was covered with cloth, Abu Bakar uncovered the face of the Prophet PBUH when he saw he cried and kissed the Prophet PBUH and said that " You are pure when alive and pure when you are dead".

In the name of Allah, Allah will not make you die twice, and death which is ordained on you. Then Abu Bakar came out from the room of Ayesha and went to mosque. Umar Bin Khattab was speaking Abu Bakar said, sit down Umar, but Umar ignored Abu Bakar told him to sit down second time, but Umar carried on, then Abu Bakar started to speak. People left Umar came to Abu Bakar to listen his speech. Abu Bakar said, whoever used to worship Muhammad pbuh should know Muhammad is dead and who ever worships Allah, should know that Allah is alive and will never die, then recited the Ayaa, Muhammad is not but a Messenger, other

381

Messengers have passed on before him. Now if he was to die or killed, would you turn back on your heals to unbelief and he who turns back on his heals, will never harm Allah, but Allah will reward the grateful. Umar bin Khattab asked, Is this Ayaa in the book of Allah ? Umar bin Khattab knows the Ayaa, Allah be praised, it was as he heard it first time. Umar bin Khattab says, he realized that Muhammad was dead. Umar bin Khattab collapsed and said, my feet cannot carry me anymore. Everyone was reciting this Ayaa, as they heard it first time. The family of the prophet pbuh took care of washing the body of the prophet pbuh. Abbas bin Abdul Mutlab, Ali bin Abu Talib and Fazal bin Abbas and Osama bin Zaid and servant of the prophet pbuh. Then one Ansar knocked on the door and asked, in the name of Allah, allow me in, he was allowed in but he did not participate in actual washing. Ali ABPWH had the body of the prophet pbuh on his chest. There was a debate, whether to wash with clothes or without the clothes ? The Sunna is to wash without the clothes. Then they heard a voice to wash the prophet pbuh with his clothes. So the body of the prophet pbuh was not uncovered. Ali bin Abu Talib said, we washed over garments. Al Abbas says Fazal and servant turned the body around. Ali, Osama and servant would pour the water. Ali bin Abu Talib would rub the body of the prophet pbuh, then they put him in three pieces of cloth (Shroud) Salah of Janaza was not one congregation but people would come and pray. Men would come in as many as they would fit in the room. That was funeral prayers. The body of the prophet pbuh was in the Room of Ayesha, Umma Salma says, all, the wives were together, crying and had little comfort that they had seen the body although he was not alive. Late at Wednesday night we heard the digging of the grave, we all broke down in the Masjid and all over in Madinah, now people knew that the body was going to grave. Bilal made Adhan for Fajr prayers, he said Allah o Akbar (God is great four times and I bare witness, there is no one worthy of worship other than Allah twice), when he came to (I bare witness Muhammad is the Messenger of Allah), he could not go any further. He started crying and did not finish Adhan. They dug the grave in the room of Ayesha, Prophets of Allah are buried, where they die.

Ayesha saw a dream ; she saw three moons fell in her lap. Abu Bakar said, this is the best and first of those moons.

Family lowered the body down in the grave. Mughira dropped his ring in the grave and got a reason to go in the grave and he was the last person to touch the body of the prophet pbuh.

FATIMA THE DAUGHTER OF THE
PROPHET PBUH. QUESTIONED'

Did your heart allow you to through dirt on the body of the prophet pbuh ? The washing, burying of the prophet pbuh was difficult. That is the reason, the prophet pbuh said, whenever a calamity falls on you remember the calamity of my death. The greatest calamity what can fall on a Muslim has already happened, the death of the prophet pbuh, everything else is very small as compared to the loss of the prophet pbuh.

There was fittana (trouble) many of the Tribes, apostate, left Islam. these were Munafiqeen and Jews. Muslims were like a last sheep in a cold rainy night, until Muslims were brought together under Abu Bakar. Annice bin Malik says, I saw two days, when the prophet pbuh came to Madinah, the happy day and then sad and black day when prophet pbuh passed away. By the time we were dusting our hands after the death of the prophet pbuh, the hearts were different.

One day, ABU Bakar and Umar bin Khattab visited Ummah Amin, she started to cry, asked her why was she crying ? She said, there is no more revelation. They were missing so much.

What did prophet pbuh, left behind, no inheritance. The prophet pbuh lived for Ummah, passed away clean, left behind a white mule, his weapons and Sadaka (charity) for travelers, that was all. The prophet pbuh passed on 12th of Rabia, the same day he made Hijra to Madinah. He lived exactly for ten years in Madinah, died at the age of sixty-three years.

Abu Bakar died at the age of 63, and Umar bin Khattab died at the age of 63 years.

Dear readers, this the end of the Seerah of the prophet pbuh. We say Praise be to Allah, who allowed us to go through the Seerah of the best of his creation Muhammad pbuh. This has been wonderful time, with the story of our beloved Messenger of Allah.

We ask Allah, to make us of those who truly love the prophet pbuh and to make us those who fallow his sunnah, his ways, and to make us those who will rise with him on THE DAY OF JUDGMENT, and who will drink from his hand at AL KOSER.

We ask Allah to admit us with him into Paradise.

Dear readers, be concerned about Ummah like the prophet pbuh. Remember, the prophet pbuh lived and died for his ummah. The prophet pbuh left, all the enjoyment of this world for the sake of having Islam come to us, we are grateful to Allah. Be grateful to people and to Allah. Who do we owe more as humans than the prophet pbuh. Everything we understand about Islam came to us through the prophet pbuh. How much we owe to the prophet pbuh, least we can do in recognition for what prophet pbuh did for us is that we fallow him, make salah and send Salam on the prophet pbuh.

Recite Darood Sharif. Thankyou.

BIOGRAPHY

MUHAMMAD (S. A. W)

- Name : Muhammad (SAW)
- Father : Abdullah
- Mother : Aminah
- Date of Birth :12th Rabi Al - Awwal
- Date of Death :08 Jun 632 11 after Hijra
- Age : 63 yrs
- Place of Birth : Makkahh
- Place of Death : Madinah
- Residence :Makkahh then moved to Madina
- Profession : Businessman, then a Prophet
- Age : 63 years
- Lived in Makkahh : 50 years
- Nabowat Age : 40 years
- Lived in Madinah ; 13 years
- Yrs of Preaching : 23 years
- Merchant : 26 years 583–609 CE
- Preacher : 23 years 609–632 CE

End of Worldly Life: 08 June 632. (11th after Hijra)

ACTIONS

- Virtue
- Preaching
- Jihad in Islam B E H A V I O U R
- Peace and Justice
- Loving every body
- Liking of Muslims
- Philanthropic
- Respectful of any organisms and animals

WIVES & MARRIED PERIOD

- Khadija bint Khuwaylid 595–619
- Sawda bint Zam'a 619–632
- Aisha bint Abi Bakr 619–632
- Hafsa bint Umar 624–632
- Zaynab bint Khuzayma 625–627
- Zaynab bint Jahsh 627–632
- Juwayriyya bint al-Harith 628–632
- Ramla bint Abi Sufyan 628–632
- Rayhana bint Zayd 629–631
- Safiyya bint Huyayy 629–632
- Maymunah bint al-Harith 630–632
- Maria al-Qibtiyya 630–632

CHILDREN

Boys :
- Al-Qassem
- Abdullah
- Ibrahim

Girls :
- Zaynab
- Ruqayyah
- Ummu Kalthoom
- Fatima

10 Miracles Everyone Must Know About Prophet MUHAMMAD (S.A.W)

- Do you know that > "Flies, insects, ants and mosquitoes" never landed on his body, or bit him? (S.A.W)
- Do you know that > He did not "yawn" in his life time? (S.A.W)
- Do you know that > Both "Domestic and wild Animals" were never for a second angry with him? (S.A.W)
- Do you know that > During his "sleep" he heard all "conversations? (S.A.W)
- Do you know that > He could see everything both in
- *"front" and at the "back" at the same time without turning? (S.A.W)
- Do you know that >He was always "one foot taller" than anybody that came "near" him? (S.A.W)
- Do you know that > He was "circumcised, washed and cleaned in his Mother's womb before he has been born to this world? (S.A.W)
- Do you know that >He had no "shadow" even in the "Sun", "Moon" or "Light"? (S.A.W).

9 781665 586832